SHAMAN WOMAN, MAINLINE LADY

SHAMAN WOMAN, MAINLINE LADY

Women's Writings on the Drug Experience

Edited by Cynthia Palmer and Michael Horowitz

Quill • New York • 1982

Library of Congress Cataloging in Publication Data
Main entry under title:

Shaman woman, mainline lady.

1. Women—Drug use—History—Addresses, essays,
lectures.   I. Palmer, Cynthia.   II. Horowitz, Michael.
[HV5824.W6S5   1982b]   362.2′93′088042   82-10203
ISBN 0-688-01387-2
ISBN 0-688-01385-6 (pbk.)

A FITZ HUGH LUDLOW MEMORIAL LIBRARY EDITION

Printed in the United States of America

First Quill Edition

1 2 3 4 5 6 7 8 9 10

BOOK DESIGN BY LINEY LI

Grateful acknowledgment is made to the following for permission to reproduce photographs and illustrations:

Gillian Baverstock: Enid Blyton, p. 187.

Bibliothèque Nationale, Paris: *L'Odyssée*, engraving by Flaxman, p. 25.

Bodleian Library, Oxford: "A garden like Paradise," miniature from *Les Livres du Gaunt*, p. 34.

Garnet Brennan: Garnet Brennan, p. 232.

Chicago Circle Library: Jane Addams, p. 80.

Concord Free Public Library: Margaret Fuller, p. 60.

Marlene Dobkin de Rios: Marlene Dobkin de Rios, p. 263.

Diane di Prima: Diane di Prima by Sheppard Powell, p. 224.

Doubleday & Company, New York: Florrie Fisher by New York *Daily News*, p. 149; Sara Davidson by Aliza Auerbach, p. 268.

The Ecco Press, New York: Caresse Crosby, reprinted from *The Passionate Years* by Caresse Crosby, p. 127. By permission of The Ecco Press.

Barbara Ffoulkes Edwards: "Advice From a Caterpillar" by Arthur Rackham, p. 45.

James W. Fernandez photograph, p. 41.

Harriette Frances: "LSD: Journals of an Artist's Trip," p. 196.

Bonnie Frazer: Bonnie Frazer photograph by Bob Ellison, p. 215.

Rasa Gustaitis: Rasa Gustaitis by Michelle Vignes, p. 248.

Emily Hahn: Emily Hahn, p. 135.

Henriette Harris: Mabel Dodge Luhan, p. 113.

Anita Hoffman: Anita Hoffman by Lorey Sebastian, p. 211.

Houghton Library, Cambridge, Mass.: Maria White Lowell, crayon portrait by Samuel W. Rowse, p. 60. By permission of the Houghton Library, Harvard University.

Laura Huxley: Laura Huxley by John Engstead, p. 194.

Lenore Kandel: Lenore Kandel by Kelly Hart, p. 230.

Kayo: "Harvesting Marijuana," p. 257. Used by permission.

Jill Krementz: Anaïs Nin in New York, p. 189. Copyright © 1982 by Jill Krementz.

Lick Observatory, Mt. Hamilton, Calif.: The Pleiades star cluster, p. 26. Lick Observatory photograph.

Serge Lido: Edith Piaf and Jean Cocteau, p. 169.

Little, Brown, Boston: Louisa May Alcott, from a daguerrotype, p. 71.

Louvre, Paris: *Les Femmes d'Alger* by Eugène Delacroix, p. 79. Photo Réunion des Musées Nationaux.

Fitz Hugh Ludlow Memorial Library, San Francisco: "Morphina, the Poppy Girl," engraved by N. Cleaveland (1854), p. 38; "Scheherazade," wood engraving by Steele Savage (1932), p. 34; "Mama Coca," etching by A. Robida (1902), p. 39; "Anaesthesia Aet. 17," painting by an unknown artist (c. 1863), p. 50; advertising card for a medicine containing belladonna, p. 51; engraving by B. Martin Justice, p. 47, in Maria Weed's *The Voice in the Wilderness* (1895); Elizabeth Barrett Browning, after the portrait by Field Talfourd, p. 54; "Hashish Hell on Fifth Avenue," p. 78, in *Illustrated Police News* (1876); engravings from Vin Mariani albums (1896–1900) of Sarah Bernhardt, Maud Gonne, Loïe Fuller, and one vignette by Edouard Sain, pp. 81, 96, 97, and 96; "Opium Den in Pell Street," engraved by J.B., p. 87, for *Frank Leslie's Illustrated Newspaper* (1883); "Morphine," engraving by A. Matignon, p. 86; engraved title to *Lalla Rookh* by Henry Sandham (1884), p. 89; advertising poster for *Absinthe Robette*, lithograph by Privat Livemont, p. 95; Annie Meyers, p. 97; "Belladonna," engraving by Erich Brunkal, p. 94; "Has It Come To This . . . ?, lithograph from the *San Francisco Examiner Supplement*, February 23, 1908, p. 100; *King of the Opium Ring* (1908) by Charles E. Blaney, p. 101; Hebrew edition (1911) of *Haschisch* by Fritz Lemermeier, p. 103; postcard of two women in a harem, p. 106; Chicago May (May Churchill Sharpe), p. 107; two plates by André Compte de Tokacs, pp. 111–12, in Edith Blinn's *The Ashes of My Heart* (1916); two drawings by Alexander King, p. 121, in Claude Farrere's *Black Opium* (1929); Pitigrilli's *Cocaina* (1921), p. 123; drawing by Mahlon Blaine, p. 125, in Verlaine's *Incense and Hashish* (1929); *No Bed of Roses: The Diary of a Lost Soul* (1930) by O.W., p. 129; photo by Lother and Young, p. 130, in *The Hop-Heads* (1920) by Fred Williams; Sara Graham-Mulhall, p. 132, photograph by Underwood and Underwood; photograph, p. 99, in *Battling the Wolves of Society* (1929) by Earle Albert Rowell; photograph, p. 132, in *The Last Plague of Egypt* (1936) by Baron Harry d'Erlanger; movie posters for *The Dope Traffic* and *Marijuana, Assassin of Youth*, pp. 144 and 145; Alice B. Toklas, p. 186, photograph by Samuel Steward; psychedelic line drawing by an unknown artist, p. 202; Grace Slick, p. 214, photograph by Roger Lubin; "Cocaine Lil" drawing by John Powys, p. 122.

TO LUNA WILSON

Love—Light—Life

PREFACE

This is the first collection of women's writings on their experiences with psychoactive drugs. Our intention is to present a history of mind-altering and addictive drugs in the lives of women from the early nineteenth century, when the first memoirs and poems of opium users were published, to the present, post-psychedelic era. Today, scientific exploration into the nature of consciousness and the biochemical basis of experience goes on amid stormy social, legal, and medical controversy over increased drug use and abuse. It is illuminating to learn, directly from the literature of personal accounts, how this point has been reached.

Since 1960, eight anthologies of imaginative, speculative, and self-experimental drug literature have been published in English. Almost everything in these collections was written by men. The existence of female authors who could rival the power of Thomas De Quincey, Fitz Hugh Ludlow, Charles Baudelaire, Jean Cocteau, Aldous Huxley, William Burroughs, or Carlos Castenada has been unsuspected. We suggest that among these experimental reports, stories, essays, poems, and extracts are some that invite comparison with the acknowledged masterpieces of drug literature.

Published feminine views of the drug experience generally have been limited to sociological studies and tabloid sensationalism. Media controlled by men have given us an enduring stereotype of a female drug abuser: a passive, exploited, degraded victim who becomes sexually promiscuous, ready to sell her body for the price of her next dose. Another common theme is the Hollywood actress, nightclub singer, or rock star who, unable to cope with the pressures of fame, overdoses on heroin or barbiturates—not unlike her Victorian sisters who met the same fate with laudanum and chloral hydrate.

The selections appearing in this book demonstrate that women's real experiences with drugs are far more varied and complex than the stereotypes suggest. The writers have a great variety of backgrounds and professions: housewife, schoolteacher, socialite, physician, parapsychologist, prostitute, professional writer, actress, social reformer, nutritionist, anthropologist, artist's model, shaman. The settings of their experiences, ecstasies, ordeals, or imaginary accounts include opium dens in Shanghai, San Francisco, New York, and Paris; a Fifth Avenue pharmacy; a Greenwich Village salon; a North African café; a hippie crash pad; an English theater; a French château; a Oaxacan village hut;

a Los Angeles psychiatrist's office; the Manhattan subway; the federal rehabilitation center in Kentucky; the Esalen Institute; prisons, parks, and bedrooms of every description.

The authors consume almost the entire array of popularly used and presently illegal drugs: opium, morphine, and heroin; cocaine and other stimulants; the psychedelic substances LSD, peyote, psilocybin mushrooms; marijuana and laughing gas. The external parameters of a drug experience are: purity of the substance ingested, dosage per body weight, method of consumption (eaten, smoked, sniffed, injected), individual tolerance based upon extent of previous use, psychological set, physical setting, and other factors, some unknown. The internal parameters can be expressed and understood only through personal communications, like those in this anthology.

In general, psychoactive drugs temporarily, but often quite dramatically, alter the manner in which reality is experienced by the human nervous system. Psychedelic drugs, including high-quality marijuana, heighten the senses and propel the user through inner space. Psychedelics speed up the reception of information, accelerating, fragmenting, and reintegrating consciousness. Opiates tend to carry the user to the womb-center of existence: a floating dream of peace and contentment. Cocaine and amphetamines free the intellect from consuming emotional moods and general fatigue. Their use sometimes quickens, intensifies, and sexualizes perception. Despite the many differences in the characteristic effects of these three classes of drugs, each can produce euphoria, enlarge realms of awareness, eroticize the nervous system, trigger internal visions, and mess up people who use them carelessly, immoderately, and without respect for their immense power.

In certain primitive tribes it is the shaman's role as sorcerer and healer to personally experiment with sacred mind-altering plants and become adept in their effects and uses. The shaman's knowledge of botanical medicine, courage in consuming toxic substances, and ability to control and ritualize psychoactive states of consciousness are greatly valued by other members of the tribe. Aboriginal shamanism is probably the oldest known form of religion. The shaman is the connection to the god residing in the sacred plant—the tribe's inner astronaut. And in many cultures, the shamans were shamanesses.

The power of substances to produce altered states of consciousness is understood by Western scientists in biochemical rather than supernatural terms. Apart from the peyote ceremony permitted (after a long suppression) to Native American Church members, the shaman's drug experiences have been illegal here for generations. Nevertheless, to varying degrees the writers of this book are shaman women, communicating the revelations of drug-induced visions and rituals.

Mainliners inject drugs intravenously for immediate effect. For them, personal involvement with the drug becomes overwhelming. The experience is compulsively repeated for the pleasure it provides, or to escape from pain or anxiety. Heroin, morphine, cocaine, and amphetamines are the drugs most frequently injected. Whether using it for medical or nonmedical reasons, the mainliner becomes physically dependent on the drug. Psychological dependence is another aspect of addiction.

The term "mainline lady" is here extended to include laudanum drinkers and opium smokers (in whom physical addiction develops less rapidly), as well as cocaine sniffers and excessive users of marijuana and psychedelics, as far as psychological dependence is apparent. The mainline lady, like the shaman woman, travels internal, "other-worldly" realms, sometimes experiencing increased powers of imagination and sensual enhancement, but she is often more controlled by her drug than in control of it. The shaman seeks to control the drug's effects both in recreational and ceremonial use.

Thanks to the extensive holdings of the Fitz Hugh Ludlow Memorial Library in San Francisco and the energetic awareness of some book-scouts (notably David Sachs of Oakland, California, and Dorothy Sloan of Austin, Texas), the editors have had the opportunity to examine nearly two hundred drug-related writings by women in the United States, England, and France during the last two centuries. Much of the literature was discovered in long out-of-print books and obscure periodicals. Due to space limitations, a number of valuable texts have been omitted, but these are mentioned for interested readers. We have included images from ancient and primitive cultures because they suggest a long tradition linking the nature of femininity with special states of consciousness. Male artists' works also appear in order to provide a wider visual context.

ACKNOWLEDGMENTS

This book was compiled and written at the Fitz Hugh Ludlow Memorial Library in San Francisco and at Russian Ridge Ranch in Mendocino County, California. We thank our valued friends there for all their support and assistance.

We owe special thanks for their research assistance to Dr. Michael R. Aldrich, Gary G. Gach, Amy LaPôtre, and Mariana Rexroth.

Thanks also go to the following for their input: Michelle Aldrich, Joanna Becker, Jeremy Bigwood, Suzette Burrous, Victoria and William Dailey, Elizabeth Davis, P. W. Edwards, Elinor Hayes, Kay Hayward, Nancy Kosenka, Ginger Kossow, John Kramer, Sandy LaPôtre, Barbara and Timothy Leary, Martha McKay, Patricia Morningstar, Barbara Morrissette, Jonathan Ott, Thea Rampley, Ella Russell, Jonathan Scheuer, William Smith, Peter Stafford, Julia Summermatter, David Wallechinsky, Karen Walls, David Wirshup, and Sayre Van Young.

For their professional guidance we are very grateful to Alison Brown and John Brockman. Thanks to John Benson, Ken Touchet, and Gary Howard for their photographic services.

Finally, for enduring our preparation of this book with high spirits and humor, we thank our children: Sunyata, Jubal, Winona, and Yuri.

—CYNTHIA PALMER AND MICHAEL HOROWITZ

Guerneville, California
August 1982

CONTENTS

ISIDIS
Magnæ Deorum Matris
APVLEIANA DESCRIPTIO.

Nomina varia Isidis.

Isis
Minerua
Venus
Iuno
Proserpina
Ceres
Diana
Rhea seu Tellus
Pessinuncia
Rhramnusia
Bellona
Hecate
Luna
Polymorphus dæmon.

Explicatio es Symbolorum Isidis.

A Diuinitatem, mundum, orbes cœlestes
BB Iter Lunæ flexuosum, & vim fœcundatiuam notat.
CC Tutulus, vim Lunæ in herbas, & plantas.
D Cereris symbolum, Isis enim spicas inuenit.
E Byssina vestis multicolor, multiformem Lunæ faciem.
F Inuentio frumenti.
G Dominium in omnia vegetabilia.
H Radios lunares.
I Genius Nili malorum auerruncus.
K Incrementa & decrementa Lunæ.
L Humectat, vis Lunæ.
M Lunæ vis victrix, & vis diuinandi.
N Dominium in humores, & mare.
O Terræ symbolū, & Medicinæ inuentrix.
P Fœcunditas, quæ sequitur terram irrigatam.
Q Astrorum Domina.
R Omnium nutrix.
S / Terræ marisque
M \ Domina.

Α κει Θεῶν Μήτηρ ταύτη πολίζιμ@ ΙΣΙΣ.

45   OPIUM & THE VICTORIAN IMAGINATION

99   EXPATRIATES & VAGABONDS

145   MAINLINE LADIES

INTRODUCTION

The relationship of women and drugs goes back before recorded history. In *When God Was a Woman*, Merlin Stone has suggested that in ancient matriarchies, small doses of snake venom may have been used as hallucinogens at oracular shrines by priestesses of the moon. The most important goddesses of many ancient cultures are closely associated with intoxicating plants and with gardens of delight in which grow the sacred fruits and herbs of what is variously termed knowledge, immortality, or paradise. In Taoist cosmology, women and drugs are *yin*, linked with nature, the earth, and the inner self: unfathomable, endlessly receptive, pleasurable. There is a Western tradition of a sexualized and mystical intuitive wisdom inherent in both women and visionary states of consciousness. Much more evident, however, is the tradition that regards women as inferior to men, and drugs as dangerous substances and artificial paradises.

When the serpent (shaman) turned on Eve (feminine principle) to the apple (sacred plant/mind-changing drug), the result was nothing less than the fall of man. Since then, women have been linked with drugs and their dangerous allure, and drugs always have been associated with the mystical, intuitive dimension—the forbidden, the mystery of woman.

Eve's was not an isolated turn-on. In forests and herb gardens, in temples, palaces, and kitchen laboratories, a succession of mythological goddesses, historical queens, anonymous seers and shamans, witches, and alchemical mates exemplified or sought the psychoactive connection. In "The God in the Flowerpot," Mary Barnard wrote, "Half a dozen important mythological themes—the shaman's journey, the food of immortal life, the food of occult knowledge, the fate of the disembodied soul, the communication with the dead, plant-deities—all converge . . . on some actual food (usually a drug plant) ritually consumed, *not* symbolically but for the experience it confers."

In the late Middle Ages and the Renaissance, the European church-state launched a savage persecution of women midwives and herbalists who made personal ritual use of the deadly nightshade plants—hallucinogenic plants (like henbane and belladonna) that produced, among other things, dreams of flying and sexual experiences. (Native women in colonial empires were similarly treated as witches and whores.) While the shaman pursuit of the healing knowledge of drug plants was the province of European witches, men were the official physicians, the writers of the herbals and pharmacopoeias. Women's reputations as poisoners, extending from mythical Circe and Medea to Locusta, Agrippina, Lucretia Borgia, and Catherine de Médicis, were predicated on their knowledge of dangerous plants and their proficiency in the kitchen arts. Understandably, the preparation of love potions was the province of women familiar with nature's aphrodisiac plants.

For several centuries after their introductions in Europe, today's legal social drugs—alcohol, coffee, tobacco—were much more socially taboo for women than for men. During the early nineteenth century, the concept of drug use as either a vice or a medical requirement became entrenched in the popular mind. This democratized medical and, ultimately, social drug use. While a few avant-garde women later dared to smoke and drink in public and visit opium dens, patent medicines were used in mass quantities by their sisters for psychological as well as physiological problems. Women became addicted to the pleasurable effects of the opiates, which were medically overprescribed and cheaply available, just as female "complaints" today are overtreated with mood-alterants and tranquilizers.

The twentieth century has witnessed an explosion of recreational drug use despite official anti-drug policies and generally severe laws, enforced by a narcotics police network. These restrictions have led to the development of underground societies of drug devotees, complete with etiquettes and specialized vocabularies. In the earlier decades of the present century, women who pursued a drug-related life-style compromised their reputations far more than did the men who indulged and experimented. Following World War II, there was a major trend toward middle-class involvement with illegal, recreational drugs which paralleled a steady acceleration of female participation in drug subcultures. The 1940's and 1950's were the period of the mainline lady, the reefer-smoking beat chick, the pioneers of psychedelics. Hippie women of the 1960's turned on with marijuana and LSD as routinely as men. During the extension and branching out of the drug scene in the 1970's, mind-changing substances were tried by women of nearly every age and social class.

The literature of women's drug experiences is roughly divided between accounts of repeated use with commitment to a drug-related life-style, and instances of isolated, private experiences, either intentional or accidental but almost always profound. The voices of this book often emanate from actual underworlds, or from the interior realms of consciousness. *Shaman Woman, Mainline Lady* demonstrates that for a long time women have consciously sought the experience of getting high, and that they have experimented courageously, lived dangerously, and written about it eloquently.

SHAMAN
WOMAN,
MAINLINE
LADY

IMAGES OF
WOMEN & DRUGS
IN MYTH & HISTORY

GREECE AND CRETE

The Pleiades

The Pleiades, a star cluster five hundred light-years away in Taurus, is known as "the seven stars" or "the seven sisters." The six brightest stars in the group can be seen with the naked eye; a seventh, the "lost Pleiade," disappears and reappears. The ancient Greeks named them after Atlas's daughters, who were also known as the Hesperides: guardians of the golden apple tree of immortality and fertility, the gift of earth goddess Gaia. For some ancient cultures the Pleiades symbolized the realm of higher consciousness. In the second millennium B.C., Vedic astrologers of northern India, worshipers of the sacred drug brew Soma, placed this star cluster at the center of the universe. The nineteenth-century British mushroom authority M. C. Cooke titled his book on the seven major drug plants of the world *The Seven Sisters of Sleep.*

Poppy goddess of Crete

Mycenaean Poppy Goddess

Idols of Mycenaean goddesses and priestesses were decorated with vegetative motifs, sometimes accompanied by a serpent consort or crowned with a diadem of opium capsules. On this fourteenth-century B.C. statue found in a sanctuary at Gaza near Heraklion, Crete, the poppy heads are cut to extract the opium before the pods ripen in the same way as they are in modern times. It may be deduced that some women of Crete understood the effect of opium, tended it as a mystery of their goddess, and dispensed it in cases of suffering or despair.

The Pleiades star cluster

Helen of Troy

The value of opium as a pain-killer and anti-depressent was known to the ancient Greeks. The women of Thebes used nepenthe to dispel their anxiety. Greek cameos depict Nyx, the goddess of night, distributing poppy capsules. Nepenthe was probably a mixture of opium and hypnotic drug plants like mandrake, henbane, and belladonna. A description of nepenthe as "a mirth-inspiring bowl" in a nineteenth-century translation has inspired the idea that some Indian hemp or hashish may also have been added to the drug.

According to Homer's *Odyssey*, written about 700 B.C., or five centuries after the Trojan War was supposed to have taken place, Zeus's beautiful daughter Helen obtained nepenthe from Polydamna, wife of Thoth and queen of Egypt. When Telemachus, emotionally distraught over the fate of his missing father, Odysseus, visited Helen in Sparta with his companions, "she poured into the wine they were drinking a drug, nepenthe, which lulled all pain and gave forgetfulness of grief."

Circe

Circe and her niece, Medea, archetypal sorceresses of Greek mythology, were devotees of Hecate, goddess of magic and sorcery. They arose out of matriarchal times, when they were associated with goddesses of the earth and of the powers that give and take life. In Homer's

Helen of Troy offering opium to Telemachus

"The Wine of Circe" by Edward Burne-Jones

Odyssey, the hero encounters Circe on his wanderings after the Trojan War. She prepares an enchanted brew by infusing drugs with the wine she serves to Odysseus and his crew. All turn into pigs—except their leader, whom Hermes has provided with an antidote, the moly plant. Circe's brew was possibly a form of nepenthe, containing a large percentage of the strongly hallucinogenic *Atropa* alkaloids such as henbane and belladonna, or the psychoactive plant datura, which could account for the men's psychological transformation to an animal state.

Pythia, the Delphic Oracle

The Delphic oracle, not unlike the tribal shamans of the Americas, was consulted on all matters of personal or national importance. The ceremony took place in the temple of Apollo on Mount Olympus, which was the legendary abode of Gaia, goddess of earth. Snakes sacred to the goddess religion may have been kept and fed at Delphi. Mary Barnard suggests in *The Mythmakers* that the drug used by Pythia, the priestess of Apollo, to release her power of prophecy may have been laurel leaves containing cyanide (hallucinogenic in very small doses) which were ritually chewed. The fumes of burning bay leaves, henbane, or cannabis may conceivably have been the method by which Pythia altered her consciousness.

Hymn to Demeter" and drug experiments with formulas known to the ancient Greeks, R. G. Wasson, Albert Hofmann, and Carl Ruck, in *The Road to Eleusis*, make a strong case that *kykeon* was a psychedelic potion made from an infusion of ergot-infested barley. For centuries

Pythia, the Delphic oracle

The Greek goddess Demeter with her attributes of barley, opium, and snakes

Demeter and Persephone

One of the central events of the Eleusinian Mysteries was the ingestion by participants, pledged to secrecy, of a potion called *kykeon*. The brew was taken just before a performance of the earth regeneration myth: the abduction and return of Persephone to her grain goddess mother Demeter by Hades, lord of the underworld.

On the basis of a new translation by Danny Staples of the seventh-century B.C. "Homeric

the grain fungus ergot has been used by midwives and doctors to facilitate childbirth; since 1943 it has been the source of LSD (lysergic acid diethylamide). Demeter was often called "Erysibe," the Greek word for ergot, and her special color purple is the color of the fruiting bodies of ergot. According to a Homeric hymn, following the loss of her daughter, the grief-stricken goddess of grain ordered the construction of the temple at Eleusis near Athens and the blending of *kykeon*. If the authors of *The Road to Eleusis* are correct, the return of Persephone in spring was identified not only with the beginning of the growing season but with the rebirth of participants in the Mysteries.

Sappho

Only about one hundred short poems and fragmentary lyrics survive of the writings of the greatest female poet of antiquity. Sappho lived on the island of Lesbos in the Aegean Sea around 500 B.C. Her works were destroyed by official edict of the Roman Empire in the first century A.D. One of her surviving poems, translated here by Mary Barnard, refers to the mythical drug plant ambrosia.

> Peace reigned in heaven
>
> Ambrosia stood
> already mixed
> in the wine bowl
>
> It was Hermes
> who took up the
> wine jug and poured
> wine for the gods.

"Like the wine of most primitive peoples," write the authors of *The Road to Eleusis*, "Greek wine did not contain alcohol as its sole ingredient but was ordinarily a mixture of various inebriants. . . . Inebriating herbs were indeed added to the wine." Ambrosia was "food of the gods" and bestowed immortality. Sappho imagines the gods themselves getting high; and this is associated with peace in heaven and presumably on earth.

Sappho of Lesbos

EGYPT

Hathor

Egypt was preeminent in the ancient world for its medical knowledge of drug plants. The goddess Hathor was worshiped as far back as 3000 B.C. Her temple was the home of intoxication. To appease Hathor, the sun god Ra ordered the fertile soil of the Nile Valley to be created from fermented barley. It was stained red to resemble blood, perhaps by the addition of mandrake or opium poppies, according to one interpretation

of a myth inscribed on a tomb dated 1300 B.C. The practice of getting drunk on New Year's Eve is for Egyptians a tribute to Hathor as goddess of intoxication and joy.

Isis

Isis, Egyptian goddess of immortality, was also goddess of fertility, motherhood, and herbal drug cures. She healed her slain brother, Osiris—literally put him back together—with sacred herbs, spices, and enchantments. Isis worship spread to Greece and Rome by the fourth century B.C., due in part to her resemblance to Demeter. The medieval version of Isis was *anima mundi* (world soul or witch-goddess); her headdress was decorated with magic herbs, grains, and snakes.

Nefertiti

A fourteenth-century B.C. Egyptian wall relief depicting a royal couple was the subject of a recent paper by anthropologist Judee Davidson. Davidson conjectures that the woman, who has

Hathor, Egyptian goddess of intoxication and joy

Isis, Egyptian goddess of immortality and healing

Queen Nefertiti of Egypt

been identified by some as Queen Nefertiti, is offering the man, who appears to be ill, two psychoactive plants: mandrake root and blue water lily.

Cleopatra

> Ha, ha!
> Give me to drink mandragora
> That I might sleep out this great gap of time
> My Antony is away.

Her speech in Shakespeare's *Antony and Cleopatra* reflects the traditional view of the Egyptian queen as a drug adept. Cleopatra would have been aware that the correct dose of mandrake root acted as a sedative. Like other rulers, she dabbled in the black art of poisoning; presumably she tested asp venom on her servants to determine the fatal dosage of the poison she eventually used to commit suicide. But mandragora was her Valium.

*Queen Cleopatra
of Egypt*

ASIA MINOR AND INDIA

Eve

The symbolic fruit of the tree of knowledge which grew in the Garden of Eden—and which Eve tasted upon the advice of the serpent and to which she turned Adam on—reverberates in the myths of many cultures and in the literature of sacred drug plants. Jehovah's admonition regarding the tree ("for in the day that thou eatest thereof thou shalt surely die") corresponds to the ego-death experienced under the effects of a strong psychedelic. Eating the fruit made Eve and Adam "as gods, knowing good and evil," approximating the effects of a sacred drug plant that temporarily produces feelings of cosmic perspective.

Regardless of which sacred drug plant may have been symbolized by the apple, it was a controlled substance and eating it resulted in "the first drug bust of pre-history" (according to drug historian M. R. Aldrich), for which Eve has borne the responsibility and the blame. Some view the Eden myth as a patriarchal cover-up of the suppression of the goddess religion that preceded it.

The serpent of Eden (formerly the consort of the high priestess in the matriarchal period) senses and exploits woman's apparently greater predilection for seeking the intuitive plane. The book of Genesis also implies that Eve trusted nature more than Adam, fearing less the consequences of eating a possibly toxic substance. The shaman women and mainlining ladies of this book are the descendants of a drug-choosing (or abusing), law-defying Eve.

Apsarasas

In Vedic mythology, apsarasas were female sex adepts of the angelic realm who participated in the brewing of soma, the sacred drink described in the four-thousand-year-old hymns known as the *Rig Veda*. A stone relief from a temple in northern India (of about A.D. 1000) depicts the soma-brewing ceremony of one of the later tantric cults. According to Asian scholar Philip Rawson, a priest had ritual sex with an apsarasa while she pounded in a mortar the psychoactive ingredients (notably the *Amanita muscaria* mushroom) that caused the drinker to feel immortal.

"Eve" by Lucas Cranach, c. 1520

Soma-brewing ceremony

Scheherazade by Steele Savage

Scheherazade

Scheherazade, who recited the thousand and one tales of the *Arabian Nights*, personifies the seduction of the mind by the genie of hashish. While her younger sister Dunyazad acts as her prompter and keeps the sultan's hookah filled with hashish, Scheherazade keeps him entertained with a labyrinth of stories within stories. She knows how hashish affects the mind, excites the imagination, and slows down the passage of time. She succeeds not only in avoiding her own death, but in saving the life of every virgin in the kingdom.

Houris

The legend of the Old Man of the Mountain (Hasan-i-Sabbah), with its curious blend of sex, drugs, and political intrigue, was reported by Marco Polo, who learned of the Ismaili cult leader while traveling in Persia in 1273. At his mountain fortress at Alamut, Hasan-i-Sabbah supposedly drugged young men with a certain potion (probably a mixture of opium and hashish), and arranged for them to awaken in a fabulous garden where they would be entertained "by the most beautiful damsels in the world, who could play on all manner of instruments, and sing most sweetly, and dance in a manner that it was charming to behold." Hasan's garden of delights was fashioned after Muhammad's image of paradise in the *Koran*, in which "wide-eyed Houris" would satisfy every desire. The young men would later risk death to perform assassinations for Hasan, convinced that his garden foretold the paradise they would dwell in forever.

Houris entertaining a drugged warrior in Hasan-i-Sabbah's "garden like Paradise"

Performing the alchemical work

EUROPE

Luna, the female principle in alchemy

Alchemists

Alchemy—whether it involved the transformation of base metals into gold, the preparation of mind-altering drugs and healing elixirs, or the process of spiritual regeneration—was ideally un-

dertaken by a man and a woman together. The image of the moon priestess, Luna, in a seventeenth-century manuscript represents the female principle in the alchemical working. The relationship reflects the harmony of heaven and earth; the experimental fusion is reflected in soul

and substance. In the series of pictures from the seventeenth-century book *Liber Mutus*, the alchemists' success in creating gold or the so-called universal remedy ("panacea," after the daughter of the Greek god of medicine) is symbolized by the creation of a child.

Witches

In early medieval representations, witches were often idealized as beautiful women; later they were more often portrayed as naked, sensual creatures or as crones.

The practice of witchcraft in Europe during the late Middle Ages and the Renaissance included the use of herbs and mind-altering plants, particularly the Solanaceous species containing the potent alkaloid atropine (belladonna, mandragora, henbane, hemlock, and datura). Small, precise doses of their leaves, berries, and roots were useful for a wide variety of medical and physical problems. Particular combinations and dosages resulted in deep sedation with vivid hallucinations, time-and-space distortion, sensations of flying and falling, bizarre visions, and feelings of sexual abandon.

The fly agaric (*Amanita muscaria*) or toadstool mushroom and the skin of toads (containing the hallucinogen bufotenine) were also important ingredients in witches' recipes. These preparations were sometimes rubbed into the skin or possibly (this suggested by the broomstick motif) inserted directly into the vagina. The subconscious experiences deriving from these poly-drug brews included astral travel to a "sabbat" (communal gathering) and psychic release from religious and sexual repression.

The narrow and restrictive doctrines of the established Christian church, which limited women's participation, may have been indirectly responsible for the flourishing of witchcraft. As many as one million women were tortured or killed during the witch craze of the sixteenth and seventeenth centuries.

"Compounding the Witches' Unguent" by Hans Baldung, 1514

NON-WESTERN CULTURES

Seven Sisters of Sleep

In 1860 British mycologist Mordecai C. Cooke presented his fanciful myth of the origin of drugs in *The Seven Sisters of Sleep: A Popular History of the Seven Prevailing Narcotics of the World*. The goddess Sleep ruled one-third of man's life. When her jealous sisters attempted to usurp her domain, she appeased them by offering powers equal to hers over humanity's waking hours: "My minister of dreams shall aid you by his skill, and visions more gorgeous, and illusions more splendid, than ever visited a mortal beneath my sway, shall attend the ecstasies of your subjects."

Thereafter, each of Sleep's sisters personified a major mind-altering plant drug: Morphina (opium), Virginia (tobacco), Gunja (cannabis, hashish), Sitaboa (betel), Erythroxylina (coca), Datura (datura, jimson weed), and Amanita (*Amanita muscaria*, the toadstool mushroom). They were destined for use on a global scale:

> Thousands and millions of Tartar tribes and Mongolian hordes welcomed Morphina, and blessed her for her soothing charms and . . . marvels of dreams. . . . Four-fifths of the race of mortals burned incense upon [Virginia's] altars. . . . The dark impetuous Gunja . . . established her throne in millions of ardent and affectionate hearts. . . . Honored by the Incas, and flattered by priests—persecuted by Spanish conquerors, but victorious, Erythroxylina . . . received the homage of a kingdom of enthusiastic devotees.

Sleep's other sister-drugs (to which Cooke might have added yagé, kava, peyote, and psilocybin mushrooms, had he known about them) were also widely used during the mid-Victorian period, just as they are in the present era.

According to Mary Barnard, writing one hundred years after Cooke, in "The God in the Flowerpot":

All are drug plants: they inebriate, soothe pain or function as mind-changers. Some of them are open doors to the otherworld, and as such they have religious uses. They are sacred plants, magic herbs or shrubs, magic carpets on which the spirit of the shaman can travel through time and space.

Morphina, the poppy girl

Mama Coca

Coca, the world's strongest organic stimulant, was long regarded as a sacred plant by the Inca civilization of Peru. The plant was deified as Mama Coca and associated with the constellation of the Virgin. As a symbol of divinity, coca was initially used only by Inca royalty; in the thirteenth and fourteenth centuries Mama Coca was the designation of several Inca queens, and some princesses adopted Coca as a middle name. Eventually many chewed and worshiped the leaves of the coca bush.

At the height of the European and North American craze for coca wines and tonic drinks in the late nineteenth century, the French artist Robida portrayed Mama Coca as an Inca queen introducing the sacred plant to the Spanish conquistadores, whose priests denounced coca worship as demonic. The feminine associations of the drug have continued into the modern era: cocaine, the prohibited active agent of the plant first isolated in 1860, was popularly known as "girl" during the 1930's and 1940's, and more recently as "lady" or "white lady."

Harvesting Opium

The opium poppy is one of the oldest cultivated drug plants. Its characteristic effects—euphoria, relief from pain and anxiety—were known to people of ancient cultures throughout the Mediterranean region, Asia Minor, and the Orient. The Golden Triangle of Southeast Asia has in recent years supplied much of the world's opium. The Thai harvester shown will later use the dried cap of the poppy for her baby's rattle.

Kavakava Ceremony

Young female virgins prepared kavakava, a Polynesian ceremonial drink, by first chewing the roots of a shrub (*Piper methysticum*). The drug, which is used socially as well as in religious ceremonies, has both hypnotic and euphoriant qualities.

Iboga Initiation

Young women of the Bwiti cult undergo an initiation rite under the influence of eboka, the psychoactive root of a forest shrub (*Tabernanthe iboga*) found in the Congo and parts of West Africa. In Bwiti mythology, a Pygmy woman, searching the jungle for her husband, finds he

Mama Coca introducing the divine plant of the Incas to the Spanish Conquistadores, by A. Robida, 1902

Harvesting opium

Iboga initiation

Kavakava ceremony

has been slain by the god of creation. She discovers the iboga plant growing out of his body. After eating the root she can communicate with the spirit of her dead husband.

Yagé Session

Yagé (or ayahuasca), the psychoactive drug ritually used by the Indians of Colombia, is a beverage made from a visionary vine (*Bannisteriopsis caapi*) and other plants. In the creation myth of the Desana Indians, the first woman was the yagé woman. She appeared before a group of men who wanted to become intoxicated, and gave birth to a child who was dismembered and eaten like the root of the psychoactive vine. The experience for the men was also sexual; their hallucinations expressive of orgasm. The origin of sex for the Desana occurs with the discovery of yagé.

Yagé vision
by Yando Rios, 1971

Peyote Woman

The bitter-tasting peyote cactus, famous for its visionary and medicinal powers, has long been the sacred drug of many North American Indian tribes. Mescaline is its active agent. In Alice Marriot and Carol K. Rachlin's modern retelling *Peyote* (1971), a pregnant Aztec woman is the protagonist of the cosmic drama.

The Tarahumare, the Yaqui, and the Otomí of the northern Sonoran desert and mountains are the peoples whose names are most familiar to citizens of the United States. From which group the story originally came it would be hard to say, for they all tell it to this day. It must have reached them from the south, for it is, and has long been, told by the Aztecan peoples of Mexico's central Great Valley.

The revelation came through a woman's dream. She was lost from her band, they say. She had fallen back from the wandering group of hunting men and root-gathering women, and had given birth to a child. In some versions of the legend the child was a boy; in others, a girl.

Had the band been in its home village there would have been other women to tend the mother and child—to sprinkle ashes on the cut navel cord, to bring the mother lukewarm unsalted corn gruel. Here she was alone. She cut the navel cord with a stone knife from the pouch at her waist and then lay helpless under a low, leafy bush, watching the buzzards gather overhead, watching them swooping and soaring lower with each downward beat of their great black wings.

Out of this desolation and terror, the woman heard a voice speak to her. "Eat the plant that is growing beside you," it said. "That is life and blessing for you and all your people."

Weakly, the woman turned her head against the earth. The only plant in sight, besides the bush that sheltered her, was a small cactus. It was without thorns, and its head was divided into lobes. She reached for the plant, and it seemed to grow outward to meet her fingers. The woman pulled up the

Encountering the divine spirit in peyote, by Nan Cuz

cactus, root and all, and ate the head.

Strength returned to the woman immediately. She sat and looked around her. It was dawn; the sun was just about to rise. She raised her child to her filling breasts and fed it. Then, gathering as many cactus plants as she could find and carry, she rose and walked forward. Something wonderful must have been leading her, for by evening she had reached the main group of her people again.

The woman took the plants to her uncle, her mother's brother. He was a man of great wisdom and was much respected by his people. "This is truly a blessing," the uncle said when he heard the woman's story. "We must give it to all the people."

OPIUM & THE VICTORIAN IMAGINATION

For social and medical reasons, opium in its various forms was the dominant drug in Western society during the nineteenth century. Approximately two-thirds of opium users were women.

Opium's therapeutic uses for a wide variety of illnesses and discomforts are described in the earliest printed pharmacopoeias. The sixteenth-century physician and mystic Paracelsus first prepared laudanum, opium in alcohol tincture. Thomas Sydenham popularized laudanum for medical use in England during the late seventeenth century. By 1700, two dozen varieties of laudanum were available commercially, prescribed according to the sex and constitution of the sufferer. Opium's euphoric effect and addictive nature did not go unnoticed, although these were considered secondary characteristics to the drug's medical benefits.

In her important treatise *Opium and the Romantic Imagination*, Alethea Hayter writes: "By the 18th century the opium addict would be met in most walks of life in England. . . . Lively Lady Stafford, whom Horace Walpole remembered having seen when he was a child . . . used to say when she arrived to see her sister, 'Well, child, I have come without my wit today,' meaning that she had not taken her opium which, said Walpole, 'she was forced to do if she had any appointment, to be in particular spirits.'" Despite her addiction, opium enabled actress "Perdita" Robinson, literary precursor of Samuel Coleridge and Thomas De Quincey, to sustain a prolific writing career after a crippling and painful nervous disease forced her off the stage and into a wheelchair.

Disease and infection were much more rampant during the Victorian period than in the West today. The death of loved ones at an early age was a common experience in most families. Tuberculosis wasted the lungs of several generations and established invalidism as a way of life. Opium's medical benefits and ready availability easily overshadowed concern about its addictive nature. Opium was called "God's own medicine"; besides relieving pain and stress it was believed to remedy an astonishing array of ailments—coughs, fevers, diarrhea, rheumatism, neuralgia, and insomnia, among others. Opium was also cheap. "Happiness might now be bought for a penny," wrote De Quincey, "and carried in the waist-coat pocket; portable ecstasies might be had corked up in a pint bottle."

Although some warnings of addiction were sounded, and a moral crusade against opium was launched in the wake of the mid-nineteenth-century opium wars between England and China, the narcotic found its way into scores of patent medicines in Europe, England, and the United States. Opium products were widely advertised in newspapers, magazines, and even on billboards. A typical one, Godfrey's Cordial, sold at the rate of ten gallons per week (enough for twelve thousand doses) in a medium-sized British city in the 1850's. In sparsely populated Iowa in the 1880's, opium preparations were available in three thousand grocery and general stores.

After German pharmacologist F. W. Sertürner and others isolated and extracted opium's most active alkaloid, morphine, in the early 1800's, a more concentrated form of the drug gradually became available. Poet Elizabeth Barrett Browning wrote of taking morphine draughts during a long illness beginning in the 1830's. The invention of the hypodermic syringe by Alexander Wood in 1854 brought about morphine injection, which increased the drug's effects and also hastened the onset of addiction. Wood's wife was the first recorded morphine needle addict. This method was particularly favored by the upper classes during the late nineteenth century.

Jeweled cases for gold and silver hypodermics were purchased by society ladies in the best shops.

Opium addiction was not limited to the wealthy. Members of the working class drank laudanum as a cheap substitute for ale, and opium smokers of all classes frequented dens in the Chinatowns of large metropolises. Infants and young children became habituated to opiated tonics given to soothe them while their mothers were away working in factories. Among medical users the largest proportion were women—from 60 percent to 70 percent in most surveys. Women in the twenty-five to fifty-five age group were the most frequent users, as the opiates were universally prescribed for menstrual and menopausal discomforts. Multiple, often unwanted pregnancies presented a major health hazard and wore down the strongest.

The social and psychological oppression of Victorian women also made them vulnerable to opium dependence. A male-dominant social order viewed women as intellectually simpler. Marriage, maternity, and the domestic arts were thought to be her natural duties. Higher education and the professions were the province of men. A woman served her family, first under her father, then later her husband. There were few options, and women usually participated in their own subordination by internalizing the code and values.

Nineteenth-century women were further burdened by their culture's veneration of flawless virtue and grace. An unrealistic standard of etiquette and behavior was demanded of them, and few avenues of even temporary escape were permissible. The drinking of alcohol was considered a male vice, not proper for women. The same held true for tobacco smoking; George Sand created a mild scandal when she dared to smoke in public in the 1850's. Opiated medicines, so readily prescribed by women's doctors for a range of physical and psychosomatic complaints, became their "silent friends." Rural and urban homes shrouded the intoxications of lady laudanum-drinkers.

Many of the writers in this section had been prescribed laudanum or morphine by their family

A fictional morphine addict. The heroine of Maria Weed's novel, A Voice in the Wilderness (1895), *is a wealthy young widow. On the table lie her hypodermic syringe and bottle of morphine solution; above is a portrait of her late husband. Her doctor, who is attempting to cure her through psychological techniques and dose reduction, is secretly observing her.*

doctors during periods of confinement due to chronic ill-health. Addiction went unnoticed until the victims were motivated to stop using opiates, as was Elizabeth Barrett by her fiancé, Robert Browning. His success in guiding her through dose reduction is depicted in their love letters. The anonymous "young lady laudanum-drinker," in an 1889 letter to the physician attempting a cure, rails against the practice of prescribing opium without warning of its addictive nature. Sarah Bernhardt, striken by illness, defied her personal physician by making her London stage debut after taking a large dose of opium to mask fatigue and illness.

Maria White Lowell wrote about physical and emotional transformations after taking opium draughts. Caroline Riddell claims she would never undertake a journey without her bottle of laudanum, to alleviate her undiagnosed pain. Like Perdita Robinson and Elizabeth Barrett Browning, Louisa May Alcott used opium medicinally.

The deadliness of opium is exemplified by the fate of the great Pre-Raphaelite beauty Elizabeth Siddal, model, mistress, and wife of painter Dante Gabriel Rossetti, who committed suicide with laudanum in 1862. The state of oblivion produced by opium, and later chloral hydrate, heroin, and the barbiturates, lured others into fatally increasing their dosages.

The effects of laudanum, opium mixed with alcohol, are quite different from opium taken straight in a pill or paste, or opium smoked—a practice that did not begin until the influx of Chinese to America in mid-century. To the euphoric, tranquilizing, and sedative qualities of opium, the alcohol adds an excitation and intensification of the senses and the imagination. This is dramatized in the narration of Lucy Snowe, the heroine of Charlotte Brontë's *Villette*. The

effect of this combination of drugs on literary composition is one of the more discussed subjects of nineteenth-century literature.

Many eminent writers of the Romantic and Victorian periods used opium in some form, and a number became seriously addicted. Critics—most recently and thoroughly Alethea Hayter—have discussed the influence of opium on the imagery and content of celebrated works by De Quincey, Coleridge, John Keats, Edgar Allan Poe, Charles Dickens, Wilkie Collins, and Francis Thompson. De Quincey's *Confessions of an English Opium-Eater* (1822), romanticizing opium's visionary powers even as it warned against the drug, has inspired generations of drug confession writers. Charlotte Brontë wrote De Quincey a letter of praise on behalf of her sisters, even though their own brother had been a tragic victim of opium addiction. After reading De Quincey, social reformer Jane Addams experimented with opium with her college roommates. Santa Louise Anderson, a young California writer, expects "De Quincean dreams of paradise" after borrowing her Chinese servant's pipe for an experimental bout of opium smoking, and is not disappointed. Elizabeth Browning found her own De Quincean inspiration in her "hourly succession of poetical paragraphs and morphine draughts," producing one poem, "A True Dream," directly under the drug's influence. Perdita Robinson was similarly intoxicated with laudanum when she dreamed and managed to relate upon waking the full-length narrative poem "The Maniac"; more than twenty years later Coleridge published his celebrated "Kubla Khan," conceived in the same state.

Opium as a literary device is found not only in Brontë's *Villette*. In George Sand's second novel, *Valentine*, the drug makes the heroine vulnerable to seduction. In George Eliot's

Middlemarch, not excerpted here, one of the major characters is murdered with an overdose of opium. Eaten in the form of confections, the drug hashish generates unexpected character interactions and plot twists in Alcott's "Perilous Play."

Cannabis (marijuana) and hashish were first used recreationally in the West by the French cultural avant-garde ("Club des Haschischins") in the early 1840's. By mid-century cannabis was available as a medicinal tincture as well as "Arabian candy." Since it was taken orally, the drug was sometimes a hallucinogen of psychedelic intensity, much stronger than marijuana smoked today. When Mary Hungerford, an American children's writer, exceeds her "three small daily doses of Indian hemp," she experiences a phantasmagorical mind trip. Like opium, cannabis was both legal and cheap. Alcott's characters buy their hashish bonbons for a quarter apiece. Cannabis tinctures were widely prescribed for a variety of medical problems, from diphtheria to impotence. Recreational use of this substance increased in the late nineteenth century; there were soon "hashish houses" as well as opium dens.

Although Lewis Carroll's Alice is a product of Victorian times, her adventures look back to ancient Celtic use of hallucinogenic mushrooms (*Amanita muscaria*) in shamanic ceremonies, and look forward to our present poly-drug society. During the course of her adventures underground Alice twice eats psychoactive cake akin to imported hashish confections available in England at that time, twice drinks from a bottle similar to contemporary ones that contained opiate medicines, and five times eats a piece of hallucinogenic, two-sided mushroom. She experiences a classic array of drug effects: time distortion, ego-loss, difficulty in thinking logically, the occasional intrusion of paranoia, and the subjective experience of transformation in physical size. Alice meets a host of seemingly stoned creatures masquerading as animals who engage her in nonsensical games and situations; she endures persecution in an outrageous trial. Finally the effects of the various drugs wear off and she returns to her normal state, not sure if it wasn't all a dream.

The hookah-smoking caterpillar is a nineteenth-century version of the Eden serpent—equally authoritative but more laid-back from constantly toking up hashish. He is an old trickster and con artist pushing a new drug (the mushroom) on Alice; but he is also a tribal shaman or modern trip guide who dispenses advice on flowing with the changes of psychedelic transformation.

Among other mind-altering drugs of the nineteenth century were nitrous oxide (laughing gas) and ether, both widely used for recreational purposes before and after they were introduced as anesthetics for surgery. The inhalation of the gas at the proper dosage levels induces brief, quasi-psychedelic trips characterized by bizarre, laughter-provoking mental associations and cosmic perspectives. In the first half of the nineteenth century, nitrous oxide sideshows and parties and ether "frolics" were the rage in England and America. In Bristol, England, in 1800, women participated in one of the earliest systematic drug experiments, conducted by Humphry Davy, who had just discovered the mental effects of nitrous oxide. His subjects inhaled the vapors from a silk bag. Following is an eyewitness account:

To witness the effect this potent gas might produce on the softer sex, Dr. Thomas Beddoes, Davy's associate, prevailed on a courageous young lady (Miss ————) to breathe out of his pretty green bag this delightful nitrous oxide. After a few inspirations, to the astonishment of everybody, the young lady dashed out of the room and the house, when, racing down Hope Square, she leaped over a great dog in her way, but being hotly pursued by the fleetest of her friends, the fair fugitive, or rather the temporary maniac, was at length overtaken and secured, without further damage.

About half the female subjects displayed languor, fainted, or developed headache, attributed to their delicate constitution. Many had positive, exhilarating experiences. It is said that Davy developed a small cult of female admirers, and that he assessed the marriageable qualities of one woman by conversing with her while she was under the effects of the gas. The dreamy languor and semiconsciousness sometimes produced by nitrous oxide (not unlike opium, as the selection from Sand's *Valentine* shows) resulted in some women accusing dentists of real and imagined seductions. The case of Stephen T. Beale, a Phila-

delphia dentist accused of having sex with his anesthetized patient, Narcissa Mudge, was a major scandal in 1855. Such events resulted in the practice of dentists always having female assistants present when they were giving gas to a woman. Other women, like writer Margaret Fuller, had an archetypal mystical experience while in the dentist's chair—the gas-induced "anesthetic revelation" discussed by philosophers Benjamin Blood and William James.

During the 1880's and 1890's, two mind-altering beverages were introduced in Western countries. Coca wine and absinthe were consumed with equal gusto in both high society and in neighborhood saloons and cafés. Maria Corelli's novel *Wormwood* (1890), the first popular anti-drug book, roused public opinion against the "French vice" of absinthe drinking. "The Fairy with the Green Eyes" is a potent liquor made from oil of wormwood, angelica, and sweet flag root; star anise; and other herbs and aromatics. Long illegal, absinthe acts as both a stimulant and narcotic, and has also been used as an aphrodisiac. Corelli warned her readers of its dangers: "Who can predict that French drug-drinking shall not also become *à la mode* in Britain?—particularly at a period when our medical men are bound to admit that the love of Morphia is fast becoming almost a mania with hundreds of English women!"

Coca wines were far less dangerous. One product, Vin Mariani, received a worldwide advertising campaign, with the endorsements of hundreds of celebrities, including Pope Leo XIII, Queen Victoria, President McKinley, and prominent artists, writers, and entertainers, many of them women. But cocainism—a wasted condition resulting from hypodermic injection of coca's active agent—was rising. Initially cocaine, used successfully as a local anesthetic, was re-

"Anesthesia at Seventeen." Anesthesia personified as a young Victorian woman in a painting done in 1863 by an unknown British artist.

cure all aches and pains!
(OVER.)

Advertisement for a patent medicine. During the last quarter of the nineteenth century, patent medicines were advertised on colored lithographed trade cards. The ingredients usually included one or more psychoactive substances and were listed on the back. The dreamy eyes of the young girl on the card shown display the effects of belladonna, a drug so-named because of its cosmetic use for eye allure by women during the Italian Renaissance.

garded as a wonder drug; none other than Sigmund Freud believed it would cure morphine addiction. The same claim was made for heroin, introduced by a German pharmacist in 1898, although it proved to be three times more addictive than morphine.

These were also the peak years for patent medicines. Hundreds of opiate-based brands were available, as well as many containing cannabis, cocaine, and the traditional hypnotic sedatives such as mandrake, belladonna, and henbane. Annie Meyers, an upper-middle-class midwestern woman, developed cocaine addiction after first using it in a cold remedy prescribed by her doctor. Once the holder of a congressional appointment, Meyers became a derelict and petty criminal before seeking a cure at one of the many sanitariums that were being set up in those years to handle mounting numbers of cases of drug addiction. A self-described "typical woman of society," Meyers was the author of the first book-length drug confession written by a woman (*Eight Years in Cocaine Hell*, 1902).

Nineteenth-century England and America have been described as a dope fiend's paradise. But, largely in reaction to the excesses of the late nineteenth century, an abrupt switch to drug control was about to take place. And with it, the popular view of drug users and their place in society would have to change.

MARY "PERDITA" ROBINSON
1758–1800

The Romantic tradition of drug-induced literature, exemplified in the writings of De Quincey, Coleridge, Poe, Baudelaire, Ludlow, and other "master addicts" of the nineteenth century, may have originated with the British actress Mary Robinson. Robinson was famous for her performances at Garrick's Drury Lane Theatre, as well as for her love affairs with such celebrities as the Prince of Wales (later George IV). A rheumatic invalid in her middle years, Perdita (as she was called after her most famous role in Shakespeare's *Winter's Tale*) turned to two things for solace: opium and poetry.

One night in 1791, after taking "near eighty drops of laudanum" at bedtime on her doctor's order, Robinson had a vivid and terrifying dream about a madman she previously had seen in the street. She summoned her daughter and dictated a poem of 120 lines ("The Maniac"), "much faster than it could be committed to paper," all the time lying with "her eyes closed, apparently in the stupor which opium frequently produces, repeating like a person talking in her sleep." The next morning Perdita had no recollection of the experience nor the lines she had recited.

Alethea Hayter cites a stanza from this poem for "the ideas of watching eyes, of cold, of petrifaction, so often found in opium dreams."

> Fix not thy steadfast gaze on me,
>   Shrunk atom of mortality!
> Nor freeze my blood with thy distracted groan;
>   Ah! quickly turn those eyes away,
>   They fill my soul with dire dismay,
> For dead and dark they seem, and almost chill'd
>   to stone!

The themes of the outcast, of the addict's sense of isolation and her feelings of alternating shame and pride are also apparent in "The Maniac."

In "Stanzas Written After Successive Nights of Melancholy Dreams," Robinson describes the fitful, nightmare-plagued sleep of one deprived of her narcotic.

> O'erwhelm'd with agonizing dreams,
>   And bound in spells of fancied Night,
> I start, convulsive, wild, distraught!
>   By some pale Murd'rer's poinard press'd,
> Or by the grinning Phantom caught.

The phantom is opium, with its alternating cycles of euphoria and desolation:

> The Form in silence I adore
> His magic smile, his murd'rous eye!

Coleridge knew and deeply admired the "English Sappho," as Robinson was then called.

Mary "Perdita" Robinson, after a painting by Sir Joshua Reynolds

ELIZABETH BARRETT BROWNING
1806–61

Like that of her contemporaries Margaret Fuller and George Sand, Elizabeth Barrett's education far exceeded existing standards for women. She studied the classics, admired the Romantic poets, and showed talent at an early age. Her delicate constitution, which made her a chronic invalid and an opium user, did not prevent her from becoming one of the century's finest poets and one of its legendary lovers.

Barrett was a fairly typical nineteenth-century medical junkie. Opiated medicines, laudanum and morphine, were routinely prescribed by her doctors during several long illnesses. She began using opium at the age of fifteen after suffering a spinal injury complicated by nervous hysteria. A poem from this period, "The Development of Genius," displays in one passage the heightened sensitivity to sound that is one of opium's characteristic effects.

"A True Dream" (1833) purports to be based on an actual dream. According to Alethea Hayter, "It is almost a case-book list of opium-inspired imagery, with its slimy, glittering snakes, its stony face, its poisonous kisses, its rainbow smoke, its breaths of icy cold." Elements of alchemy, magic, and astral travel add drama.

The poet's second major illness began in 1837 and lasted for almost a decade. It affected her lungs and heart and necessitated more of the standard medication. She was taking forty drops of laudanum daily, an advanced addict's dosage, at the time she met the poet Robert Browning and fell in love with him. She defended her use of the drug to him in a letter: "My opium comes in to keep the pulse from fluttering and fainting

Both he and De Quincey were familiar with the circumstances surrounding the composition of "The Maniac." One of Coleridge's biographers conjectures that he may even have contrived from this anecdote the quite similar circumstances under which he claimed to have written "Kubla Khan," the most famous opium-inspired poem. (The earliest printed reference to "Kubla Khan" occurs in a poem Robinson sent to Coleridge in the year of her death.) More likely he was acknowledging, or even exploiting as a sales gimmick for his book, a method of literary creation that his friend Perdita Robinson had brought into vogue.

*Elizabeth Barrett Browning. "I am writing such poems— allegorical—
philosophical—poetical—ethical—synthetically arranged! I am in a fit of writing
—could write all day & night—& long to live by myself for 3 months
in a forest of chestnuts & cedars, in an hourly succession of poetical paragraphs
& morphine draughts" (from a letter to her brother, 1843).*

. . . to give the right composure and point of balance to the nervous system. I don't take it for 'my spirits' in the usual sense; you must not think such a thing." Obviously his concern over her addiction became more acute, for she wrote to him again a few months later with even more intensity, but also promising to give up her habit.

And that you should care so much about the opium! Then *I* must care, and get to do with less—at least. On the other side of your goodness and indulgence (a very little way on the other side) it might strike you as strange that I who have had no pain—no acute suffering to keep down from its angles—should need opium in any shape. But I have had restlessness till it made me almost mad: at one time I lost the power of sleeping quite—and even in the day, the continual aching sense of weakness has been intolerable—besides palpitation—as if one's life, instead of giving movement to the body, were imprisoned undiminished within it, and beating and fluttering impotently to get out, at all the doors and windows. So the medical people gave me opium—a preparation of it, called morphine, and ether—and ever since I have been calling it my amreeta draught, my elixir—because the tranquillizing power has been wonderful. Such a nervous system I have—so irritable naturally, and so shattered by various causes, that the need has continued in a degree until now, and it would be dangerous to leave off the calming remedy, Mr. Jago says, except very slowly and gradually. But slowly and gradually something may be done—and you are to understand that I never *increased* upon the prescribed quantity. . . . prescribed in the first instance—no! Now think of my writing all this to you!—

Robert, whose chief work up to that time was the poem "Paracelsus," became identified in Elizabeth's mind with the great sixteenth-century alchemist and physician who introduced laudanum into European medicine. It was Paracelsus's reputation as a healer of the incurable that probably provoked Elizabeth's imagination, for Robert was serving her in a similar manner, helping her through her dose-reduction withdrawal and inspiring some of her greatest lyric flights.

Although Mrs. Browning's opium addiction was not well known to her contemporaries—or perhaps was not considered remarkable enough to warrant their attention—it was central to the publicized literary skirmish the Brownings had with the American writer Julia Ward Howe in 1857. Robert was furious at Howe's assertion that Elizabeth's poetic imagination was dependent upon her use of opium. Mrs. Browning did not consider this attack worthy of defense. Her integrity as a poet was unquestionable.

The Development of Genius

PART III

A dream was on my soul. It seemed to be
That silence fled me as mine enemy:
That all sounds, in a conclave wild and drear,
Were gathered in the chambers of mine ear
To agonize its sense—that I could hear
The grasses sprouting up,—the leaves down-
    falling—
The floating of the clouds—the sunlight
    palling—
The dropping dews—the multitudinous wings
Of birds and insects—the deep rush of springs
Fathoms beneath the sea—the blind mole
    creeping
Thro' earth with sooty hide—the gumtree
    weeping
Sweet smells: the cracking of worn cerement
In distant graves whose dust with dust is blent:
Mine own hair's growth—mine own blood
    pulsing free—
Yea! and their thousand echoes—sensibly
As you may hear my speaking voice. Their
    sound

Concentered not in one crash; nor was drowned
The less tone in the greater: but, around,
Each, with its separate curious torture broke,
Till Discord cracked mine ear—Whereat I
    woke.

A True Dream

(DREAMED AT SIDMOUTH, 1833)

I had not an evil end in view,
    Tho' I trod the evil way;
And why I practised the magic art,
    My dream it did not say.

I unsealed the vial mystical,
    I outpoured the liquid thing,
And while the smoke came wreathing out,
    I stood unshuddering.

The smoke came wreathing, wreathing out,
    All mute, and dark, and slow,
Till its cloud was stained with a fleshly hue,
    And a fleshly form 'gan show.

Then paused the smoke—the fleshly form
    Looked steadfast in mine eye,
His beard was black as a thundercloud,
    But I trembled not to see.

I unsealed the vial mystical,
    I outpoured the liquid thing,
And while the smoke came wreathing out,
    I stood unshuddering.

The smoke came wreathing, wreathing out,
    All mute, and dark and slow,
Till its cloud was stained with a fleshly hue,
    And a fleshly form 'gan show.

Then paused the smoke—but the mortal form
    A garment swart did veil,
I looked on it with fixed heart,
    Yea—not a pulse did fail!

I unsealed the vial mystical,

I outpoured the liquid thing,
And while the smoke came wreathing out,
    I stood unshuddering.

The smoke came wreathing, wreathing out,
    And now it was faster and lighter,
And it bore on its folds the rainbow's hues,
    Heaven could not show them brighter.

Then paused the smoke, the rainbow's hues
    Did a childish face express—
The rose in the cheek, the blue in the eyne,
    The yellow in the tress.

The fair young child shook back her hair,
    And round me her arms did wreathe,
Her lips were hard and cold as stone,
    They sucked away my breath.

I cast her off as she clung to me,
    With hate and shuddering;
I brake the vials, and foresware
    The cursed, cursed thing.

Anon outspake a brother of mine—
    'Upon the pavement, see
Besprent with noisome poison slime,
    Those twining serpents three.'

Anon outspake my wildered heart
    As I saw the serpent train—
'I have called up three existences
    I cannot quench again.

'Alas! with unholy company,
    My lifetime they will scathe;
They will hiss in the storm, and on sunny days
    Will gleam and thwart my path.'

Outspake that pitying brother of mine—
    'Now nay, my sister, nay,
I will pour on them oil of vitriol,
    And burn their lives away.'

'Now nay, my brother, torture not,
    Now hold thine hand, and spare.'
He poured on them oil of vitriol,
    And did not heed my prayer.

I saw the drops of torture fall;
 I heard the shriekings rise,
While the serpents writhed in agony
 Beneath my dreaming eyes.

And while they shrieked, and while they
  writhed,
 And inward and outward wound,
They waxed larger, and their wail
 Assumed a human sound.

And glared their eyes, and their slimy scales
 Were roundly and redly bright,
Most like the lidless sun, what time
 Thro' the mist he meets your sight.

And larger and larger they waxed still,
 And longer still and longer;
And they shrieked in their pain, 'Come, come
  to us,
 We are stronger, we are stronger.'

Upon the ground I laid mine head,
 And heard the wailing sound;
I did not wail, I did not writhe—
 I laid me on the ground.

And larger and larger they waxed still
 And longer still and longer;
And they shrieked in their pangs, 'Come, come
  to us,
 We are stronger, we are stronger.'

Then up I raised my burning brow,
 My quiv'ring arms on high;
I spake in prayer, and I named aloud
 The name of sanctity.

And as in my anguish I prayed and named
 Aloud the holy name,
The impious mocking serpent voice
 Did echo back the same.

And larger and larger they waxed still,
 And stronger still and longer!
And they shrieked in their pangs, 'Come, come
  to us,
 We are stronger, we are stronger.'

Then out from among them arose a form
 In shroud of death indued—
I fled from him with wings of wind,
 With whirlwinds he pursued.

I stood by a chamber door, and thought
 Within its gloom to hide;
I locked the door, and the while forgot
 That I stood on the outer side.

And the knell of mine heart was wildly tolled
 While I grasped still the key;
For I felt beside me the icy breath,
 And knew that *that* was *he*.

I heard these words, 'Who'er doth *taste*,
 Will *drink* the magic bowl;
So her body may do my mission here
 Companioned by her soul.'

Mine hand was cold as the key it held,
 Mine heart had an iron weight;
I saw a gleam, I heard a sound—
 The clock was striking eight.

GEORGE SAND
1804–76

George Sand, born Aurore Lucie Dupin, possessed a brilliant, revolutionary intelligence. Traditional convent training was followed by an apprenticeship to the village chemist and doctor. Her experience dressing wounds, bloodletting, and compounding drugs at the age of sixteen strongly influenced her; what was later called her immodest frankness about the human body was more the professional detachment of a doctor. Her medical knowledge caused her to be critical of the overuse of patent medicines. Of the repulsive tonics and physics thrust upon her for various childhood illnesses, she later said, "I was perpetually drugged, and my generation must have been tough indeed to survive the cures of those who were trying to preserve it."

George Sand gave birth to two children before her nine-year marriage ended, after which she established a lifelong pattern of alternating the tranquility of her inherited country estate, Nohant, with the excitement of Paris. Joining the staff of *Le Figaro*, she entered the bohemian literary scene during the flourishing of the French Romantic movement. She assumed her *nom de plume*, wore men's tailored suits, and smoked in public—perhaps the first European woman to do so. (She smoked cigarettes as well as Egyptian tobacco in her favorite pipe.) She wrote more than seventy books and had passionate love affairs with, among others, Alfred de Musset, Frederic Chopin, and the actress Marie Dorval.

George Sand's second novel, *Valentine* (1832), deals with a love affair doomed by social forces. On her wedding night the heroine feigns illness and takes an especially strong dose of opium medication to avoid her detested husband. The novelist, familiar with the action of the opiates, creates a scene of erotic tension by contrasting the sexual vulnerability that opium elicits from Valentine, with the barely controlled passion of her true love, Bénédict, who is observing her while hiding in her bedchamber.

From Valentine

Bénédict heard all the doors of the house closed and locked one after another. Little by little the footsteps of the servants receded from the ground floor; the reflection cast on the foliage by a few stray lamps disappeared; only the sound of the instruments in the distance, and an occasional pistol shot, which is customary in Berri to fire at weddings and baptisms as a sign of enjoyment, broke the silence at rare intervals. Bénédict was in a most extraordinary situation, of which he would never have dared to dream. That night—that ghastly night which he had expected to pass in the agony of impotent rage—had brought him and Valentine together! Monsieur de Lansac returned to his quarters alone, and Bénédict, the forsaken, who proposed to blow out his brains in a ditch, was locked into that room alone with Valentine! He felt a sting of remorse for having denied his God, for having cursed the day of his birth. This unforeseen joy, coming so close upon the heels of thoughts of murder and suicide, took possession of him with such irresistible violence, that it did not occur to him to contemplate its terrible sequel. He did not admit to himself that, if he should be discovered in that place, Valentine was ruined; he did not ask himself whether that unhoped-for conquest of an instant of joy would not

George Sand, by Alfred de Musset. "Once in Nohant, George plunged into work on a new novel. To Boucoiran in Paris there came urgent requests for her hookah, for volumes of Greek drama, Shakespeare, Plato, the Koran" (Renee Winegarten, The Double Life of George Sand*).*

render the necessity of dying even more hateful. He abandoned himself to the delirious excitement which such a triumph over destiny aroused in him. He pressed both hands against his breast to check its frantic palpitations. But just as he was on the point of betraying himself by his agitation, he paused, mastered by the dread of offending Valentine, by that respectful and chaste shyness which is the principal characteristic of true love.

He stood irresolute, his heart overflowing with agonizing joy and impatience, and was about to take some decisive step, when she rang, and in a moment Catherine appeared.

"Dear nurse," said Valentine, "you didn't give me my potion."

"Ah! your *potion!*" said the good woman. "I thought that you would not need to take it to-day. I will go to prepare it."

"No, that would take too long. Just dissolve a little opium in some orange-flower water."

"But that may do you harm."

"No; opium can never injure me in the state I am in now."

"I don't know anything about it. You are no doctor; would you like me to go and ask madame la marquise?"

"Oh! for heaven's sake, don't do that. Don't you be afraid. Here, give me the bottle; I know the dose."

"Oh! you put in twice too much."

"No, I tell you; since I am free to sleep at last, I propose to make the most of it. While I am asleep, I shall not have to think."

Catherine sadly shook her head as she diluted a strong dose of opium, which Valentine took in several swallows while she undressed; and, when she was wrapped in her *peignoir,* she dismissed her nurse once more and went to bed.

Bénédict, crouching in his hiding-place, had not dared to move hand or foot. But the fear of being discovered by the nurse was much less painful than that which he felt when he was alone with Valentine. After a terrible battle with himself, he ventured to raise the curtain gently. The rustling of the silk did not wake Valentine; the opium was doing its work already. However, Bénédict fancied

that she partly opened her eyes. He was frightened and dropped the curtain, the fringe of which caught on a bronze candlestick which stood on the light stand, and dragged it noisily to the floor. Valentine started, but did not come out of her lethargy. Thereupon, Bénédict stood beside her, with even greater liberty to gaze at her than on the day when he adored her reflection in the water. Alone at her feet in the solemn silence of the night, protected by that artificial slumber which it was not in his power to interrupt, he fancied that he was fulfilling a supernatural destiny. He had naught to fear from her anger. He could drink his fill of the happiness of gazing at her, without being disturbed in his enjoyment; he could speak to her unheard, tell her of his great love, of his agony, without putting to flight that faint, mysterious smile which played about her half-parted lips. He could put his lips to hers with no fear of being repelled by her. But the certainty of impunity did not embolden him to that point. For Valentine was the object of an almost divine adoration in his heart, and she needed no exterior protection against him. He was her safeguard and defender against himself. He knelt beside her, and contented himself with taking her hand as it hung over the edge of the bed, holding it in his, examining with admiration its whiteness and the fineness of the skin, and putting his trembling lips to it. That hand bore the wedding ring, the first link of a burdensome and indissoluble chain. Bénédict might have taken it off and destroyed it, but his heart had recurred to gentler sentiments. He determined to respect everything about Valentine, even the emblem of her duty.

For in that ecstasy of rapture he speedily forgot everything. He deemed himself as fortunate and as sure of the future as in the happy days at the farm; he imagined that the night would never end, that Valentine would never wake, and that he would live out his eternity of happiness in that room.

For a long time that blissful contemplation was without danger; the very angels are less pure than the heart of a man of twenty when he loves passionately; but he trembled when Valentine, excited by one of those happy dreams to which opium gives birth, leaned gently toward him and feebly pressed his hand, murmuring indistinct words. Bénédict trembled and moved away from the bed, afraid of himself.

"Oh! Bénédict!" said Valentine slowly, in a faint voice, "Bénédict, was it you who married me to-day? I thought that it was somebody else. Tell me that it was really you!"

"Yes, it was I, it was I!" said Bénédict, beside himself with excitement, as he pressed to his wildly beating heart that soft hand which sought his.

Valentine, half awake, sat up in bed, with eyelids parted, and gazed at him with expressionless eyes, wandering uncertainly in the vague land of dreams. There was an expression of something like terror in her features; then she closed her eyes, and smiled as her head fell back on the pillow.

"It was you whom I loved," she said; "but how did they ever allow it?"

She spoke so low and her articulation was so indistinct that her words fell upon Bénédict's ears like the angelic murmur one hears in dreams.

"O my beloved!" he cried, leaning over, "tell me that again, tell me again, and let me die of joy at your feet!"

But Valentine pushed him away.

"Leave me!" she said.

And her words became unintelligible.

Bénédict thought that he could understand that she took him for Monsieur de Lansac. He called himself by name again and again, and Valentine, hovering between reality and illusion, now waking, now falling asleep, innocently revealed all her secrets to him.

MARGARET FULLER
1810–50

Margaret Fuller, born and raised in New England, is generally considered to have been the most intellectually influential woman of the nineteenth century. A teacher, critic, and essayist, she was closely linked to the transcendentalist movement of Ralph Waldo Emerson and Henry David Thoreau, and edited and wrote for the *Dial* during the early 1840's. The Conversations for Boston women were a unique Fuller creation: five winters of meetings led by Margaret, who interpreted feminine history through mythology, philosophy, and the arts. Her serious interest in spiritualism and psychic healing was too eccentric for most of her peers.

Fuller's book *Women of the Nineteenth Century* (1845) was a testament to personal freedom and basic human rights. In 1846 she went to Europe and met the aging opium-eater De Quincey, Sand, and the Brownings, among others. She wrote travel sketches and eventually settled in Italy. There she married a young count, Angelo Ossoli, bore him a son at age thirty-eight,

Margaret Fuller. "I quitted the body instantly."

and surrendered her energies to the Roman Revolution of 1848.

When the uprising failed, all foreign supporters of the revolutionary cause, including the Ossolis, were forced to leave the country. With the dramatic events of Rome's struggle for independence documented in a manuscript, Margaret sailed for the United States with her husband and son in 1850. After two months at sea their ship sank in a storm only a few hundred yards from Fire Island, New York. The Atlantic Ocean claimed the Ossoli family as well as Margaret Fuller's last writings.

In the earliest days of ether anesthesia, which was formally introduced in 1846, Fuller had a tooth extracted under its influence while staying in Paris in 1847. She eloquently describes time distortion and out-of-body experience; her dentist becomes Dr. Faust speaking French. The aftereffects of the ether were not too pleasant, however, probably because early doses were more concentrated than was necessary. A performance of Mozart's *Don Giovanni* served to dispel these effects some days later.

From At Home and Abroad

Don Giovanni conferred on me a benefit, of which certainly its great author never dreamed. I shall relate it, first begging pardon of Mozart, and assuring him I had no thought of turning his music to the account of a "vulgar utility." It was quite by accident. After suffering several days very much with the toothache, I resolved to get rid of the cause of sorrow by the aid of ether; not sorry either, to try its efficacy, after all the marvelous stories I had heard. The first time I inhaled it, I did not for several seconds feel the effect, and was just thinking, "Alas! this has not power to soothe nerves so irritable as mine," when suddenly I wandered off, I don't know where, but it was a sensation like wandering in long

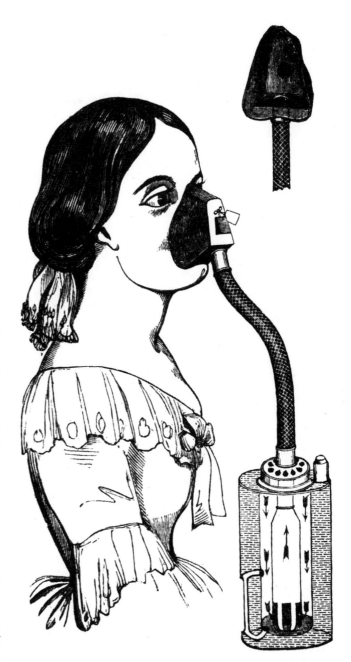

Dr. Snow's chloroform inhaler. Dr. John Snow invented the first chloroform inhaler in 1847. Six years later he delivered Queen Victoria's fifth child while she was anesthetized by the vapor. In her private journal the queen wrote, "Dr. Snow gave that blessed chloroform and the effect was soothing, quieting and delightful beyond measure."

garden-walks, and through many alleys of trees—many impressions, but all pleasant and serene. The moment the tube was removed, I started into consciousness, and put my hand to my cheek; but, sad! the throbbing tooth was still there. The dentist said I had not seemed to him insensible. He then gave me the ether in a stronger dose, and this time I quitted the body instantly, and cannot remember any detail of what I saw and did; but the impression was as in the Oriental tale, where the man has his head in the water an instant only, but in his vision a thousand years seem to have passed. I experienced that same sense of an immense length of time and succession of impressions; even now, the moment my mind was in that state seems to me a far longer period in time than my life on earth does as I look back upon it. Suddenly I seemed to see the old dentist, as I had for the moment before I inhaled the gas, amid his plants, in his nightcap and dressing gown; in the twilight the figure had somewhat of a Faust-like, magical air, and he seemed to say, *"C'est inutile."* Again I started up, fancying that once more he had not dared to extract the tooth, but it was gone. What is worth noticing is the mental translation I made of his words, which my ear must have caught, for my companion tells me he said, *"C'est le moment,"* a phrase of just as many syllables, but conveying just the opposite sense.

Ah! how I wished then that you had settled, there in the United States, who really brought this means of evading a portion of the misery of life into use. But as it was, I remained at a loss whom to apostrophize with my benedictions, whether Dr. Jackson, Morton, or Wells, and somebody thus was robbed of his due;—neither does Europe know to whom to address her medals [a reference to the great controversy over the credit for the discovery of anesthesia].

However, there is no evading the heavier part of these miseries. You avoid the moment of suffering and escape the effort of screwing up your courage for one of these moments, but not the jar to the whole system. I found the effect of having taken the ether bad for me. I seemed to taste it all the time, and neuralgic pain continued; this lasted three days. For the evening of the third, I had taken a ticket to *Don Giovanni*, and could not bear to give up this opera, which I had always been longing to hear; still I was in much suffering, and as it was the sixth day I had been so, much weakened. However, I went, expecting to be obliged to come out; but the music soothed the nerves at once. I hardly suffered at all during the opera; however, I supposed the pain would return as soon as I came out; but no! it left me from that time. Ah! if physicians only understood the influence of the mind over the body, instead of treating as they so often do, their patients like machines, and according to precedent!

MARIA WHITE LOWELL
1821–53

Maria White Lowell. "Soft hangs the opiate in the brain."

Transcendentalist Maria White Lowell, a gifted poet of exquisite beauty, was one of the blue-stockings who attended Margaret Fuller's Conversations in Boston in the early 1840's. An ardent abolitionist, Maria met and married James Russell Lowell and is credited with instilling in him a political conscience as well as poetic inspiration. During eight years of marriage the Lowells had four children, but only one survived infancy. Maria, whose pale fragility had always hinted at consumption (tuberculosis), died at thirty-two, when her husband's fame as an American man of letters was becoming firmly established.

Mrs. Lowell's poems were collected and privately published after her death. "An Opium Fantasy" stands out among them. The poem elicited from Maria's descendant, imagist poet Amy Lowell, the following remark: "That is poetry! It is better than anything her husband ever wrote, and he always said that she was a better poet than he."

An Opium Fantasy

Soft hangs the opiate in the brain,
  And lulling soothes the edge of pain,
Till harshest sound, far off or near,
  Sings floating in its mellow sphere.

What wakes me from my heavy dream?
  Or am I still asleep?
Those long and soft vibrations seem
  A slumberous charm to keep.

The graceful play, a moment stopped,
  Distance again unrolls
Like silver balls, that, softly dropped,
  Ring into golden bowls.

I question of the poppies red,

The fairy flaunting band,
While I a weed, with drooping head,
  Within their phalanx stand.

"Some airy one, with scarlet cap,
  The name unfold to me
Of this new minstrel, who can lap
  Sleep in his melody?"

Bright grew their scarlet-kerchiefed heads,
  As freshening winds had blown,
And from their gently swaying beds
  They sang in undertone,

"Oh, he is but a little owl,
  The smallest of his kin,
Who sits beneath the midnight's cowl
  And makes this airy din."

"Deceitful tongues, of fiery tints,
  Far more than this you know,—
That he is your enchanted prince,
  Doomed as an owl to go;

"Nor his fond play for years hath stopped,
  But nightly he unrolls
His silver balls, that, softly dropped,
  Ring into golden bowls."

CHARLOTTE BRONTË
1816–55

Charlotte Brontë was one of six children of Maria and Patrick Brontë, a Protestant clergyman of the Yorkshire Hills. The life of the Brontës expresses the pathos of the Victorian life. Disease was common yet uncomprehended, and almost every family witnessed sudden invalidism and death. By age nine, Charlotte had three times experienced the upstairs sick room claiming a loved one, her mother and two older sisters each dying of consumption.

Later in life Charlotte watched the quicksilver mind of her only brother, Branwell, decline into obsessive melancholy. Weakened with chronic illness and excesses of gin and laudanum, he experienced opiated poetic reveries as well as too-frequent stupefaction. Between September 1848 and June 1849, Branwell, Emily, and Anne Brontë all died of consumption, tended by Charlotte during their last months. The last year of her life, at thirty-eight, she married and experienced an unexpected happiness. But, like each member of her family, she too was stricken with consumption and died, five months pregnant, after only nine months of married life.

Villette, Brontë's last novel, was published in 1853, six years after *Jane Eyre* had captivated readers. Lucy Snowe, the heroine, is modeled upon Jane. Both women have inner resources that enable them to transcend the prevailing repressive behavioral codes of Victorian society. Rejecting the prosaic subservience of the Victorian woman's role, they strive for equality between the sexes, partnership in marriage, and the right to work.

In the denouement of *Villette*, the heroine is given an accidental misdosage of an opiated sleeping potion: a fraction too much alcohol in the laudanum solution causes excitability instead of sedation. Lucy Snowe, intended for a deep sleep, is overstimulated. She steals from her bed into the streets and a park, where a night festival is in progress. A refined elation escorts her opiated midnight stroll through an enchanted world. With heightened sensibilities, she observes several scenes that answer anxious questions.

In a meeting with Elizabeth Gaskell, who subsequently wrote the definitive Brontë biography, Charlotte said she had never, "to her knowledge," taken opium, that she had finally reached an understanding of its effects through a concentrated dream state. It is certain, however, that Charlotte witnessed both excitability and sedation in Branwell, her opium-addicted brother.

From Villette

Madame Beck did not herself summon me to bed that night—she did not come near me: she sent Ginevra Fanshawe—a more efficient agent for the purpose she could not have employed. Ginevra's first words—"Is your headache very bad tonight?" (for Ginevra, like the rest, thought I had a headache—an intolerable headache which made me frightfully white in the face, and insanely restless in the foot)—her first words, I say, inspired the impulse to flee anywhere, so that it were only out of reach. And soon, what followed—plaints about her own headaches—completed the business.

I went upstairs. Presently I was in my bed—my miserable bed—haunted with quick scorpions. I had not been laid down five minutes, when another emissary arrived: Goton came, bringing me something to drink. I was consumed with thirst—I drank eagerly; the beverage was sweet, but I tasted a drug.

"Madame says it will make you sleep chou chou," said Goton, as she received back the emptied cup.

Ah! the sedative had been administered. In fact, they had given me a strong opiate. I was to be held quiet for one night.

The household came to bed, the night light was lit, the dormitory hushed. Sleep soon reigned: over those pillows, sleep won an easy supremacy: contented sovereign over heads and hearts which did not ache—he passed by the unquiet.

The drug wrought. I know not whether Madame had over-charged or under-charged the dose; its result was not that she intended. Instead of stupor came excitement. I became alive to new thought—to reverie peculiar in colouring. A gathering call ran among the faculties, their bugles sang, their trumpets rang an untimely summons. Imag-

Charlotte Brontë. "In a land of enchantment, a garden most gorgeous, a plain sprinkled with coloured meteors, a forest with sparks of purple and ruby and golden fire gemming the foliage."

ination was roused from her rest, and she came forth impetuous and venturous. With scorn she looked on Matter, her mate—

"Rise!" she said; "Sluggard! this night I will have *my* will: nor shalt thou prevail."

"Look forth and view the night!" was her cry; and when I lifted the heavy blind from the casement close at hand—with her own royal gesture, she showed me a moon supreme, in an element deep and splendid.

To my gasping senses she made the glimmering gloom, the narrow limits, the oppressive heat of the dormitory, intolerable. She lured me to leave this den, and follow her forth into dew, coolness, and glory.

She brought upon me a strange vision of Villette at midnight. Especially she showed me the park, the summer-park, with its long alleys all silent, lone and safe; among these lay a huge stone basin—that basin I knew, and beside which I had often stood—deep-set in the tree-shadows, brimming with cool water, clear, with a green, leafy, rushy bed. What of all this? the park-gates were shut up, locked, sentinelled: the place could not be entered.

Could it not? A point worth considering; and while revolving it, I mechanically dressed. Utterly incapable of sleeping or lying still—excited from head to foot—what could I do better than dress?

The gates were locked, soldiers set before them: was there, then, no admission to the park?

The other day, in walking past, I had seen, without then attending to the circumstance, a gap in the paling—one stake broken down: I now saw this gap again in recollection—saw it very plainly— the narrow, irregular aperture visible between the stems of the lindens, planted orderly as a colonnade. A man could not have made his way through that aperture, nor could a stout woman, perhaps not Madame Beck; but I thought I might: I fancied I should like to try, and once within, at this hour the whole park would be mine—the moonlight, midnight park!

How soundly the dormitory slept! What deep slumbers! What quiet breathing! How very still the whole large house! What was the time? I felt restless to know. There stood a clock in the classe below: what hindered me from venturing down to consult it? By such a moon, its large white face and jet black figures must be vividly distinct.

As for hindrance to this step, there offered not so much as a creaking hinge or a clicking latch. On these hot July nights, close air could not be tolerated, and the chamber-door stood wide open. Will the dormitory planks sustain my tread untraitorous? Yes. I know wherever a board is loose, and will avoid it. The oak staircase creaks somewhat as I descend, but not much:—I am in the carré.

The great classe-doors are closed shut: they are bolted. On the other hand, the entrance to the corridor stands open. The classes seem, to my thought, great dreary jails, buried far back beyond thoroughfares, and for me, filled with spectral and intolerable Memories, laid miserable amongst their straw and their manacles. The corridor offers a cheerful vista, leading to the high vestibule which opens direct upon the street.

Hush!—the clock strikes. Ghostly deep as is the stillness of this convent, it is only eleven. While my ear follows to silence the hum of the last stroke, I catch faintly from the built-out capital, a sound like bells or like a band—a sound where sweetness, where victory, where mourning blend. Oh, to approach this music nearer, to listen to it alone by the rushy basin! Let me go—oh, let me go! What hinders, what does not aid freedom?

There, in the corridor, hangs my garden-costume, my large hat, my shawl. There is no lock on the huge, heavy, porte-cochère; there is no key to seek: it fastens with a sort of spring-bolt, not to be opened from the outside, but which, from within, may be noiselessly withdrawn. Can I manage it? It yields to my hand, yields with propitious facility. I wonder as that portal seems almost spontaneously to unclose—I wonder as I cross the theshold and step on the paved street, wonder at the strange ease with which this prison has been forced. It seems as if I had been pioneered invisibly, as if some dissolving force had gone before me: for myself, I have scarce made an effort.

Quiet Rue Fossette! I find on this pavement that wanderer-wooing summer night of which I mused; I see its moon over me; I feel its dew in the air. But here I cannot stay; I am still too near old haunts: so close under the dungeon, I can hear the prisoners moan. This solemn peace is not what I seek, it is not what I can bear: to me the face of that sky bears the aspect of a world's death. The park also will be calm—I know, a mortal serenity prevails everywhere—yet let me seek the park.

I took a route well known, and went up towards the palatial and royal Haute-Ville; thence the music I had heard certainly floated; it was hushed now, but it might re-waken. I went on: neither band nor bell-music came to meet me; another sound replaced it, a sound like a strong tide, a great flow, deepening as I proceeded. Light broke, movement gathered, chimes pealed—to what was I coming? Entering on the level of a Grande Place, I found myself, with the suddenness of magic, plunged amidst a gay, living, joyous crowd.

Villette is one blaze, one broad illumination; the whole world seems abroad; moonlight and heaven are banished: the town, by her own flambeaux, beholds her own splendour—gay dresses, grand equipages, fine horses and gallant riders throng the bright streets. I see even scores of masks. It is a strange scene, stranger than dreams. But where is the park?—I ought to be near it. In the midst of this glare the park must be shadowy and calm—*there*, at least, are neither torches, lamps, nor crowd?

I was asking this question when an open carriage passed me filled with known faces. Through the deep throng it could pass but slowly; the spirited horses fretted in their curbed ardour. I saw the occupants of that carriage well: me they could not see.

*   *   *

It gave me strange pleasure to follow these friends viewlessly, and I *did* follow them, as I thought, to the park. I watched them alight (carriages were inadmissible) admist new and unanticipated splendours. Lo! the iron gateway, between the stone columns, was spanned by a flaming arch built of massed stars: and, following them cautiously beneath that arch, where were they, and where was I?

In a land of enchantment, a garden most gorgeous, a plain sprinkled with coloured meteors, a forest with sparks of purple and ruby and golden fire gemming the foliage; a region, not of trees and shadow, but of strangest architectural wealth—of altar and of temple, of pyramid, obelisk, and sphinx; incredible to say, the wonders and the symbols of Egypt teemed throughout the park of Villette.

No matter that in five minutes the secret was mine—the key of the mystery picked up, and its illusion unveiled—no matter that I quickly recognized the material of these solemn fragments—the timber, the paint, and the pasteboard—these inevitable discoveries failed to quite destroy the charm, or undermine the marvel of that night. No matter that I now seized the explanation of the whole great fête—a fête of which the conventual Rue Fossette had not tasted, though it had opened at dawn that morning, and was still in full vigour near midnight.

*   *   *

While looking up at the image of a white ibis, fixed on a column—while fathoming the deep, torch-lit perspective of an avenue, at the close of which was couched a sphinx—I lost sight of the party which, from the middle of the great square, I had followed—or, rather, they vanished like a group of apparitions. On this whole scene was impressed a dream-like character; every shape was wavering, every movement floating, every voice echo-like—half-mocking, half-uncertain. Paulina and her friends being gone, I scare could avouch that I had really seen them; nor did I miss them as guides through the chaos, far less regret them as protectors amidst the night.

That festal night would have been safe for a very child. Half the peasantry had come in from the environs of Villette, and the decent burghers were all abroad and around, dressed in their best. My straw-hat passed amidst cap and jacket, short petticoat, and long calico mantle, without, perhaps, attracting a glance; I only took the precaution to bind down the broad leaf gipsy-wise, with a supplementary ribbon—and then I felt safe as if masked.

Safe I passed down the avenues—safe I mixed with the crowd where it was deepest. To be still was not in my power, nor quietly to observe. I took a revel of the scene; I drank the elastic night-air—the swell of sound, the dubious light, now flashing, now fading. As to Happiness or Hope, they and I had shaken hands, but just now,—I scorned Despair.

My vague aim, as I went, was to find the stone-basin, with its clear depth and green lining; of that coolness and verdure I thought, with the passionate thirst of unconscious fever. Amidst the glare, and hurry, and throng, and noise, I still secretly and chiefly longed to come on that circular mirror of crystal, and surprise the moon glassing therein her pearly front.

I knew my route, yet it seemed as if I was hindered from pursuing it direct: now a sight and now a sound, called me aside, luring me down this alley and down that. Already I saw the thick-planted trees which framed this tremulous and rippled glass, when, choiring out of a glade to the right, broke such a sound as I thought might be heard if heaven were to open—such a sound, perhaps, as was heard above the plain of Bethlehem, on the night of glad tidings.

The song, the sweet music, rose afar, but rushing swiftly on fast-strengthening pinions—there swept through these shades so full a storm of harmonies that, had no tree been near against which to lean, I think I must have dropped. Voices were there, it seemed to me, unnumbered; instruments varied and countless—bugle, horn, and trumpet, I knew. The effect was as a sea breaking into song with all its waves. The swaying tide swept this way, and then it fell back, and I followed its retreat. It led me towards a Byzantine building—a sort of kiosk near the park's centre. Round about stood crowded thousands, gathered to a grand concert in the open air. What I had heard was, I think, a wild Jäger chorus; the night, the space, the scene and my own mood, had but enhanced the sounds and their impression.

ELIZABETH SIDDAL
1834–62

Lizzie Siddal, whose sensual, spiritual look and flowing, flaming red-gold hair are immortalized in the paintings of her husband, Dante Gabriel Rossetti, was one of the most famous artist's models in history. Her physical appearance epitomized the medieval standard of beauty then in vogue. Between 1850, when Rossetti met her working as a milliner's assistant, and 1862, when he found her dead in their bedroom, she posed for a remarkable series of oil paintings, most memorably as the Madonna and as Dante's Beatrice.

Although Lizzie was an accomplished artist

Elizabeth Siddal.
"Do we clasp dead hands, and quiver
With an endless joy for ever?"

"Beata Beatrix" by Dante Gabriel Rossetti. Rossetti painted his wife, Lizzie Siddal, as Dante's beloved Beatrice. The bird, death's messenger, drops an opium poppy between her hands. The painting was begun before the model's death from a laudanum overdose in 1862, and completed afterward as a memorial to her.

and poet, she was overshadowed by the ambitious genius of her husband and other men of the Pre-Raphaelite brotherhood. Her lack of social refinement made her feel insecure, her health was poor, she and Dante were not sexually compatible, and his infidelities caused her great pain and depression. Their private life together gradually became a living hell. She turned more and more to laudanum to keep up the social pretense required of their relationship. After their first child was stillborn, she descended into invalidism and opium addiction.

Some of the facts surrounding her death were covered up for scores of years to protect reputations. At twenty-eight she succumbed to an overdose of laudanum she had taken before bedtime, following dinner with her husband and the poet Algernon Swinburne. After an inquest, the death was officially ruled accidental. It wasn't until after her husband's death, from a chloral hydrate overdose ten years later, that it became known to friends that he had found a suicide note pinned to her nightgown.

The poem included here, reputedly written under the effects of laudanum a few days before her death, was ultimately made public by her brother-in-law, the distinguished critic William Michael Rossetti.

███

Untitled

Life and night are falling from me,
Death and day are opening on me.
Wherever my footsteps come and go
Life is a stony road of woe.
    Lord, have I long to go?
Hollow hearts are ever near me,
Soulless eyes have ceased to cheer me:
    Lord, may I come to Thee?
Life and youth and summer weather

To my heart no joy can gather:
Lord, lift me from life's stony way.
Loved eyes, long closed in death, watch o'er
    me—
Holy Death is waiting for me—
    Lord, may I come to-day?
My outward life feels sad and still,
Like lilies in a frozen rill.

I am gazing upwards to the sun,
Lord, Lord, remembering my lost one.
    O Lord, remember me!
How is it in the unknown land?
Do the dead wander hand in hand?
Do we clasp dead hands, and quiver
With an endless joy for ever?
Is the air filled with the sound
Of spirits circling round and round?
Are there lakes, of endless song,
To rest our tired eyes upon?
Do tall white angels gaze and wend
Along the banks where lilies bend?
Lord we know not how this may be;
Good Lord, we put our faith in Thee—
    O God, remember me.

LOUISA MAY ALCOTT
1832–88

Louisa May Alcott grew up in a household permeated with the domestic energies of her mother and three sisters and the transcendental idealism of her father. At an early age she began teaching and writing to support her family, a role that she never relinquished.

In 1862, the thirty-year-old future author of the world-famous *Little Women* series went to Washington to nurse the wounded Union Army soldiers and victims of disease. After three weeks' service she became extremely ill with typhoid pneumonia and was treated with "heroic" doses of calomel, a mercury compound that proved poisonous and was soon banned. Alcott lost a yard of hair and for months wore lace hats over her bald head. Long-term side effects—trembling, chills, sleeplessness, and delirium—dogged her remaining years, during which she used opium and morphine intermittently to ease her pain and help her sleep.

Between 1863 and 1869, writing under several different pen names, Alcott produced thrillers exploring themes of evil, violence, thwarted love, mind control, and drug experimentation. One, "The Marble Woman; or, The Mysterious Model" deals with a beautiful young woman who becomes an opium addict in response to a loveless marriage. The story that follows, "Perilous Play," appeared in 1869 in *Frank Leslie's Chimney Corner*, which was billed as the "great family paper of America." It was rediscovered by Madeleine Stern and reprinted in *Plots and Counterplots*.

Here, Alcott relates how the effects of eating hashish bonbons breaks down the social restraints of a group of young, upper-class picnickers.

"Perilous Play"

"If someone does not propose a new and interesting amusement, I shall die of ennui!" said pretty Belle Daventry, in a tone of despair. "I have read all my books, used up all my Berlin wools, and it's too warm to go to town for more. No one can go sailing yet, as the tide is out; we are all nearly tired to death of cards, croquet, and gossip, so what shall we do to while away this endless afternoon? Dr. Meredith, I command you to invent and propose a new game in five minutes."

"To hear is to obey," replied the young man, who lay in the grass at her feet, as he submissively slapped his forehead, and fell a-thinking with all his might.

Holding up her finger to preserve silence, Belle pulled out her watch and waited with an expectant smile. The rest of the young party, who were indolently scattered about under the elms, drew nearer, and brightened visibly, for Dr. Meredith's inventive powers were well-known, and something refreshingly novel might be expected from him. One gentleman did not stir, but then he lay within earshot, and merely turned his fine eyes from the sea to the group before him. His glance rested a moment on Belle's piquant figure, for she looked very pretty with her bright hair blowing in the wind, one plump white arm extended to keep order, and one little foot, in a distracting slipper, just visible below the voluminous folds of her dress. Then the glance passed to another figure, sitting somewhat apart in a cloud of white muslin, for an airy burnoose floated from head and shoulders, showing only a singularly charming face. Pale and yet brilliant, for the Southern eyes were magnificent, the clear olive cheeks

Louisa May Alcott at twenty.
"Ladies go off sooner, and don't need so many."

contrasted well with darkest hair; lips like a pomegranate flower, and delicate, straight brows, as mobile as the lips. A cluster of crimson flowers, half falling from the loose black braids, and a golden bracelet of Arabian coins on the slender wrist were the only ornaments she wore, and became her better than the fashionable frippery of her companions. A book lay on her lap, but her eyes, full of a passionate melancholy, were fixed on the sea, which glittered around an island green and flowery as a summer paradise. Rose St. Just was as beautiful as her Spanish mother, but had inherited the pride and reserve of her English father; and this pride was the thorn which repelled lovers from the human flower. Mark Done sighed as he looked, and as if the sigh, low as it was, roused her from her reverie, Rose flashed a quick glance at him, took up her book, and went on reading the legend of "The Lotus Eaters."

"Time is up now, Doctor," cried Belle, pocketing her watch with a flourish.

"Ready to report," answered Meredith, sitting up and producing a little box of tortoiseshell and gold.

"How mysterious! What is it? Let me see, first!" And Belle removed the cover, looking like an inquisitive child. "Only bonbons; how stupid! That won't do, sir. We don't want to be fed with sugarplums. We demand to be amused."

"Eat six of these despised bonbons, and you *will* be amused in a new, delicious, and wonderful manner," said the young doctor, laying half a dozen on a green leaf and offering them to her.

"Why, what are they?" she asked, looking at him askance.

"Hashish; did you never hear of it?"

"Oh, yes; it's that Indian stuff which brings one fantastic visions, isn't it? I've always wanted to see and taste it, and now I will," cried Belle, nibbling at one of the bean-shaped comfits with its green heart.

"I advise you not to try it. People do all sorts of queer things when they take it. I wouldn't for the world," said a prudent young lady warningly, as all examined the box and its contents.

"Six can do no harm, I give you my word. I take twenty before I can enjoy myself, and some people even more. I've tried many experiments, both on the sick and the well, and nothing ever happened amiss, though the demonstrations were immensely interesting," said Meredith, eating his sugarplums with a tranquil air, which was very convincing to others.

"How shall I feel?" asked Belle, beginning on her second comfit.

"A heavenly dreaminess comes over one, in which they move as if on air. Everything is calm and lovely to them: no pain, no care, no fear of anything, and while it lasts one feels like an angel half asleep."

"But if one takes too much, how then?" said a deep voice behind the doctor.

"Hum! Well, that's not so pleasant, unless one likes phantoms, frenzies, and a touch of nightmare, which seems to last a thousand years. Ever try it, Done?" replied Meredith, turning toward the speaker, who was now leaning on his arm and looking interested.

"Never. I'm not a good subject for experiments. Too nervous a temperament to play pranks with."

"I should say ten would be about your number. Less than that seldom affects men. Ladies go off sooner, and don't need so many. Miss St. Just, may I offer you a taste of Elysium? I owe my success to you," said the doctor, approaching her deferentially.

"To me! And how?" she asked, lifting her large eyes with a slight smile.

"I was in the depths of despair when my eye caught the title of your book, and I was saved. For I remembered that I had hashish in my pocket."

"Are you a lotus-eater?" she said, permitting him to lay the six charmed bonbons on the page.

"My faith, no! I use it for my patients. It is very efficacious in nervous disorders, and is getting to be quite a pet remedy with us."

"I do not want to forget the past, but to read the future. Will hashish help me to do that?" asked Rose with an eager look, which made the young man flush, wondering if he bore any part in her hopes of that veiled future.

"Alas, no. I wish it could, for I, too, long to

know my fate," he answered, very low, as he looked into the lovely face before him.

The soft glance changed to one of cool indifference and Rose gently brushed the hashish off her book, saying, with a little gesture of dismissal, "Then I have no desire to taste Elysium."

The white morsels dropped into the grass at her feet; but Dr. Meredith let them lie, and turning sharply, went back to sun himself in Belle's smiles.

"I've eaten all mine, and so has Evelyn. Mr. Norton will see goblins, I know, for he has taken quantities. I'm glad of it, for he does not believe in it, and I want to have him convinced by making a spectacle of himself for our amusement," said Belle, in great spirits at the new plan.

"When does the trance come on?" asked Evelyn, a shy girl, already rather alarmed at what she had done.

"About three hours after you take your dose, though the time varies with different people. Your pulse will rise, heart beat quickly, eyes darken and dilate, and an uplifted sensation will pervade you generally. Then these symptoms change, and the bliss begins. I've seen people sit or lie in one position for hours, rapt in a delicious dream, and wake from it as tranquil as if they had not a nerve in their bodies."

"How charming! I'll take some every time I'm worried. Let me see. It's now four, so our trances will come about seven, and we will devote the evening to manifestations," said Belle.

"Come, Done, try it. We are all going in for the fun. Here's your dose," and Meredith tossed him a dozen bonbons, twisted up in a bit of paper.

"No, thank you; I know myself too well to risk it. If you are all going to turn hashish-eaters, you'll need someone to take care of you, so I'll keep sober," tossing the little parcel back.

It fell short, and the doctor, too lazy to pick it up, let it lie, merely saying, with a laugh, "Well, I advise any bashful man to take hashish when he wants to offer his heart to any fair lady, for it will give him the courage of a hero, the eloquence of a poet, and the ardor of an Italian. Remember that, gentlemen, and come to me when the crisis approaches."

"Does it conquer the pride, rouse the pity, and soften the hard hearts of the fair sex?" asked Done.

"I dare say now is your time to settle the fact, for here are two ladies who have imbibed, and in three hours will be in such a seraphic state of mind that 'No' will be an impossibility to them."

"Oh, mercy on us; what *have* we done? If that's the case, I shall shut myself up till my foolish fit is over. Rose, you haven't taken any; I beg you to mount guard over me, and see that I don't disgrace myself by any nonsense. Promise me you will," cried Belle, in half-real, half-feigned alarm at the consequences of her prank.

"I promise," said Rose, and floated down the green path as noiselessly as a white cloud, with a curious smile on her lips.

"Don't tell any of the rest what we have done, but after tea let us go into the grove and compare notes," said Norton, as Done strolled away to the beach, and the voices of approaching friends broke the summer quiet.

At tea, the initiated glanced covertly at one another, and saw, or fancied they saw, the effects of the hashish, in a certain suppressed excitement of manner, and unusually brilliant eyes. Belle laughed often, a silvery ringing laugh, pleasant to hear; but when complimented on her good spirits, she looked distressed and said she could not help her merriment; Meredith was quite calm, but rather dreamy; Evelyn was pale, and her next neighbor heard her heart beat; Norton talked incessantly, but as he talked uncommonly well, no one suspected anything. Done and Miss St. Just watched the others with interest, and were very quiet, especially Rose, who scarcely spoke, but smiled her sweetest, and looked very lovely.

The moon rose early, and the experimenters slipped away to the grove, leaving the outsiders on the lawn as usual. Some bold spirit asked Rose to sing, and she at once complied, pouring out Spanish airs in a voice that melted the hearts of her audience, so full of fiery sweetness or tragic pathos was it. Done seemed quite carried away, and lay with his face in the grass, to hide the tears that would come; till, afraid of openly disgracing himself, he started up and hurried down to the little wharf, where he sat alone, listening to the music with a countenance which plainly revealed to the stars the passion which possessed him. The sound of loud laughter from the grove, followed by entire silence, caused him to wonder what demonstrations were taking place, and half resolve to go and see. But that enchanting voice held him captive, even when a boat put off mysteriously from a point nearby, and sailed away like a phantom through the twilight.

Half an hour afterward, a white figure came down the path, and Rose's voice broke in on his midsummer night's dream. The moon shone clearly now, and showed him the anxiety in her face as she said hurriedly, "Where is Belle?"

"Gone sailing, I believe."

"How could you let her go? She was not fit to take care of herself!"

"I forgot that."

"So did I, but I promised to watch over her, and I must. Which way did they go?" demanded Rose, wrapping the white mantle about her, and running her eye over the little boats moored below.

"You will follow her?"

"Yes."

"I'll be your guide then. They went toward the lighthouse; it is too far to row; I am at your service. Oh, say yes," cried Done, leaping into his own skiff and offering his hand persuasively.

She hesitated an instant and looked at him. He was always pale, and the moonlight seemed to increase this pallor, but his hat brim hid his eyes, and his voice was very quiet. A loud peal of laughter floated over the water, and as if the sound decided her, she gave him her hand and entered the boat. Done smiled triumphantly as he shook out the sail, which caught the freshening wind, and sent the boat dancing along a path of light.

How lovely it was! All the indescribable allurements of a perfect summer night surrounded them: balmy airs, enchanting moonlight, distant music, and, close at hand, the delicious atmosphere of love, which made itself felt in the eloquent silences that fell between them. Rose seemed to yield to the subtle charm, and leaned back on the cushioned seat with her beautiful head uncovered, her face full of dreamy softness, and her hands lying loosely clasped before her. She seldom spoke, showed no

further anxiety for Belle, and soon seemed to forget the object of her search, so absorbed was she in some delicious thought which wrapped her in its peace.

Done sat opposite, flushed now, restless, and excited, for his eyes glittered; the hand on the rudder shook, and his voice sounded intense and passionate, even in the utterance of the simplest words. He talked continually and with unusual brilliancy, for, though a man of many accomplishments, he was too indolent or too fastidious to exert himself, except among his peers. Rose seemed to look without seeing, to listen without hearing, and though she smiled blissfully, the smiles were evidently not for him.

On they sailed, scarcely heeding the bank of black cloud piled up in the horizon, the rising wind, or the silence which proved their solitude. Rose moved once or twice, and lifted her hand as if to speak, but sank back mutely, and the hand fell again as if it had not energy enough to enforce her wish. A cloud sweeping over the moon, a distant growl of thunder, and the slight gust that struck the sail seemed to rouse her. Done was singing now like one inspired, his hat at his feet, hair in disorder, and a strangely rapturous expression in his eyes, which were fixed on her. She started, shivered, and seemed to recover herself with an effort.

"Where are they?" she asked, looking vainly for the island heights and the other boat.

"They have gone to the beach, I fancy, but we will follow." As Done leaned forward to speak, she saw his face and shrank back with a sudden flush, for in it she read clearly what she had felt, yet doubted until now. He saw the telltale blush and gesture, and said impetuously, "You know it now; you cannot deceive me longer, or daunt me with your pride! Rose, I love you, and dare tell you so tonight!"

"Not now—not here—I will not listen. Turn back, and be silent, I entreat you, Mr. Done," she said hurriedly.

He laughed a defiant laugh and took her hand in his, which was burning and throbbing with the rapid heat of his pulse.

"No, I *will* have my answer here, and now, and never turn back till you give it; you have been a thorny Rose, and given me many wounds. I'll be paid for my heartache with sweet words, tender looks, and frank confessions of love, for proud as you are, you do love me, and dare not deny it."

Something in his tone terrified her; she snatched her hand away and drew beyond his reach, trying to speak calmly, and to meet coldly the ardent glances of the eyes which were strangely darkened and dilated with uncontrollable emotion.

"You forget yourself. I shall give no answer to an avowal made in such terms. Take me home instantly," she said in a tone of command.

"Confess you love me, Rose."

"Never!"

"Ah! I'll have a kinder answer, or—" Done half rose and put out his hand to grasp and draw her to him, but the cry she uttered seemed to arrest him with a sort of shock. He dropped into his seat, passed his hand over his eyes, and shivered nervously as he muttered in an altered tone, "I meant nothing; it's the moonlight; sit down, I'll control myself—upon my soul I will!"

"If you do not, I shall go overboard. Are you mad, sir?" cried Rose, trembling with indignation.

"Then I shall follow you, for I *am* mad, Rose, with love—hashish!"

His voice sank to a whisper, but the last word thrilled along her nerves, as no sound of fear had ever done before. An instant she regarded him with a look which took in every sign of unnatural excitement, then she clasped her hands with an imploring gesture, saying, in a tone of despair, "Why did I come? How will it end? Oh, Mark, take me home before it is too late!"

"Hush! Be calm; don't thwart me, or I may get wild again. My thoughts are not clear, but I understand you. There, take my knife, and if I forget myself, kill me. Don't go overboard; you are too beautiful to die, my Rose!"

He threw her the slender hunting knife he wore, looked at her a moment with a far-off look, and trimmed the sail like one moving in a dream. Rose took the weapon, wrapped her cloak closely about her, and crouching as far away as possible, kept her eye on him, with a face in which watchful terror contended with some secret trouble and bewilderment more powerful than her fear.

The boat moved round and began to beat up against wind and tide; spray flew from her bow; the sail bent and strained in the gusts that struck it with perilous fitfulness. The moon was nearly hidden by scudding clouds, and one-half the sky was black with the gathering storm. Rose looked from threatening heavens to treacherous sea, and tried to be ready for any danger, but her calm had been sadly broken, and she could not recover it. Done sat motionless, uttering no word of encouragement, though the frequent flaws almost tore the rope from his hand, and the water often dashed over him.

"Are we in any danger?" asked Rose at last, unable to bear the silence, for he looked like a ghostly helmsman seen by the fitful light, pale now, wild-eyed, and speechless.

"Yes, great danger."

"I thought you were a skillful boatman."

"I am when I am myself; now I am rapidly losing the control of my will, and the strange quiet is coming over me. If I had been alone I should have given up sooner, but for your sake I've kept on."

"Can't you work the boat?" asked Rose, terror-struck by the changed tone of his voice, the slow, uncertain movements of his hands.

"No. I see everything through a thick cloud; your voice sounds far away, and my one desire is to lay my head down and sleep."

"Let me steer—I can, I must!" she cried, springing toward him and laying her hand on the rudder.

He smiled and kissed the little hand, saying dreamily, "You could not hold it a minute; sit by me, love; let us turn the boat again, and drift away together—anywhere, anywhere out of the world."

"Oh, heaven, what will become of us!" and Rose wrung her hands in real despair. "Mr. Done—Mark—dear Mark, rouse yourself and listen to me. Turn, as you say, for it is certain death to go on. Turn, and let us drift down to the lighthouse; they will hear and help us. Quick, take down the sail, get out the oars, and let us try to reach there before the storm breaks."

As Rose spoke, he obeyed her like a dumb animal; love for her was stronger even than the instinct of self-preservation, and for her sake he fought against the treacherous lethargy which was swiftly overpowering him. The sail was lowered, the boat brought round, and with little help from the ill-pulled oars it drifted rapidly out to sea with the ebbing tide.

As she caught her breath after this dangerous maneuver was accomplished, Rose asked, in a quiet tone she vainly tried to render natural, "How much hashish did you take?"

"All that Meredith threw me. Too much; but I was possessed to do it, so I hid the roll and tried it," he answered, peering at her with a weird laugh.

"Let us talk; our safety lies in keeping awake, and I dare not let you sleep," continued Rose, dashing water on her own hot forehead with a sort of desperation.

"Say you love me; that would wake me from my lost sleep, I think. I have hoped and feared, waited and suffered so long. Be pitiful, and answer, Rose."

"I do; but I should not own it now."

So low was the soft reply he scarcely heard it, but he felt it and made a strong effort to break from the hateful spell that bound him. Leaning forward, he tried to read her face in a ray of moonlight breaking through the clouds; he saw a new and tender warmth in it, for all the pride was gone, and no fear marred the eloquence of those soft, Southern eyes.

"Kiss me, Rose, then I shall believe it. I feel lost in a dream, and you, so changed, so kind, may be only a fair phantom. Kiss me, love, and make it real."

As if swayed by a power more potent than her will, Rose bent to meet his lips. But the ardent pressure seemed to startle her from a momentary oblivion of everything but love. She covered up her face and sank down, as if overwhelmed with shame, sobbing through passionate tears, "Oh, what am I doing? I am mad, for I, too, have taken hashish."

What he answered she never heard, for a rattling peal of thunder drowned his voice, and then the storm broke loose. Rain fell in torrents, the wind blew fiercely, sky and sea were black as ink, and the boat tossed from wave to wave almost at their mercy. Giving herself up for lost, Rose crept to her lover's side and clung there, conscious only that they would bide together through the perils their own folly brought them. Done's excitement

was quite gone now; he sat like a statue, shielding the frail creature whom he loved with a smile on his face, which looked awfully emotionless when the lightning gave her glimpses of its white immobility. Drenched, exhausted, and half senseless with danger, fear, and exposure, Rose saw at last a welcome glimmer through the gloom, and roused herself to cry for help.

"Mark, wake and help me! Shout, for God's sake—shout and call them, for we are lost if we drift by!" she cried, lifting his head from his breast, and forcing him to see the brilliant beacons streaming far across the troubled water.

He understood her, and springing up, uttered shout after shout like one demented. Fortunately, the storm had lulled a little; the lighthouse keeper heard and answered. Rose seized the helm, Done the oars, and with one frantic effort guided the boat into quieter waters, where it was met by the keeper, who towed it to the rocky nook which served as harbor.

The moment a strong, steady face met her eyes, and a gruff, cheery voice hailed her, Rose gave way, and was carried up to the house, looking more like a beautiful drowned Ophelia than a living woman.

"Here, Sally, see to the poor thing; she's had a rough time on't. I'll take care of her sweetheart—and a nice job I'll have, I reckon, for if he ain't mad or drunk, he's had a stroke of lightnin', and looks as if he wouldn't get his hearin' in a hurry," said the old man as he housed his unexpected guests and stood staring at Done, who looked about him like one dazed. "You jest turn in yonder and sleep it off, mate. We'll see to the lady, and right up your boat in the morning," the old man added.

"Be kind to Rose. I frightened her. I'll not forget you. Yes, let me sleep and get over this cursed folly as soon as possible," muttered this strange visitor.

Done threw himself down on the rough couch and tried to sleep, but every nerve was overstrained, every pulse beating like a trip-hammer, and everything about him was intensified and exaggerated with awful power. The thundershower seemed a wild hurricane, the quaint room a wilderness peopled with tormenting phantoms, and all the events of his life passed before him in an endless procession, which nearly maddened him. The old man looked weird and gigantic, his own voice sounded shrill and discordant, and the ceaseless murmur of Rose's incoherent wanderings haunted him like parts of a grotesque but dreadful dream.

All night he lay motionless, with staring eyes, feverish lips, and a mind on the rack, for the delicate machinery which had been tampered with revenged the wrong by torturing the foolish experimenter. All night Rose wept and sang, talked and cried for help in a piteous state of nervous excitement, for with her the trance came first, and the after-agitation was increased by the events of the evening. She slept at last, lulled by the old woman's motherly care, and Done was spared one tormenting fear, for he dreaded the consequences of this folly on her, more than upon himself.

As day dawned he rose, haggard and faint, and staggered out. At the door he met the keeper, who stopped him to report that the boat was in order, and a fair day coming. Seeing doubt and perplexity in the old man's eye, Done told him the truth, and added that he was going to the beach for a plunge, hoping by that simple tonic to restore his unstrung nerves.

He came back feeling like himself again, except for a dull headache, and a heavy sense of remorse weighing on his spirits, for he distinctly recollected all the events of the night. The old woman made him eat and drink, and in an hour he felt ready for the homeward trip.

Rose slept late, and when she woke soon recovered herself, for her dose had been a small one. When she had breakfasted and made a hasty toilet, she professed herself anxious to return at once. She dreaded yet longed to see Done, and when the time came armed herself with pride, feeling all a woman's shame at what had passed, and resolving to feign forgetfulness of the incidents of the previous night. Pale and cold as a statue she met him, but the moment he began to say humbly, "Forgive me, Rose," she silenced him with an imperious gesture and the command, "Don't speak of it; I only remember that it was very horrible, and wish to forget it all as soon as possible."

"All, Rose?" he asked, significantly.

"Yes, *all*. No one would care to recall the follies of a hashish dream," she answered, turning hastily to hide the scarlet flush that would rise, and the eyes that would fall before his own.

"I never can forget, but I will be silent if you bid me."

"I do. Let us go. What will they think at the island? Mr. Done, give me your promise to tell no one, now or ever, that I tried that dangerous experiment. I will guard your secret also." She spoke eagerly and looked up imploringly.

"I promise," and he gave her his hand, holding her own with a wistful glance, till she drew it away and begged him to take her home.

Leaving hearty thanks and a generous token of their gratitude, they sailed away with a fair wind, finding in the freshness of the morning a speedy cure for tired bodies and excited minds. They said little, but it was impossible for Rose to preserve her coldness. The memory of the past night broke down her pride, and Done's tender glances touched her heart. She half hid her face behind her hand, and tried to compose herself for the scene to come, for as she approached the island, she saw Belle and her party waiting for them on the shore.

"Oh, Mr. Done, screen me from their eyes and questions as much as you can! I'm so worn out and nervous, I shall betray myself. You will help me?" And she turned to him with a confiding look, strangely at variance with her usual calm self-possession.

"I'll shield you with my life, if you will tell me why you took the hashish," he said, bent on knowing his fate.

"I hoped it would make me soft and lovable, like other women. I'm tired of being a lonely statue," she faltered, as if the truth was wrung from her by a power stronger than her will.

"And I took it to gain courage to tell my love. Rose, we have been near death together; let us share life together, and neither of us be any more lonely or afraid?"

He stretched his hand to her with his heart in his face, and she gave him hers with a look of tender submission, as he said ardently, "Heaven bless hashish, if its dreams end like this!"

THE HOOKAH, 1770–1910

"Secret Dissipation of New York Belles: Interior of a Hasheesh Hell on Fifth Avenue," from Illustrated Police News, *New York, 1876.*

"'There are several small rooms there, shut off from this room by the curtains you see move. Each is magnificently fitted up, I am told. They are reserved for persons, chiefly ladies, who wish to avoid every possibility of detection, and at the same time enjoy the hashish and watch the inmates of this room.'

'Are there many ladies of good social standing who come here?'

'Very many. Not the cream of the demi-monde, *understand me, but* ladies. *Why, there must be at least six hundred in this city alone who are* habitués. *Smokers from different cities, Boston, Philadelphia, Chicago, and especially New Orleans, tell me that each city has its hemp retreat, but none so elegant as this.' And my companion swallowed another lozenge and relapsed into dreamy silence"* (H. H. Kane, "A Hashish House in New York," 1884).

"Joy of Music." An eighteenth-century Indian princess listens to music while she smokes a hookah.

"Les Femmes d'Alger" by Eugene Delacroix, 1834

JANE ADDAMS
1860–1935

Jane Addams was a leading social reformer, president of the International Congress of Women, and winner of a Nobel Peace Prize. In her autobiography, *Twenty Years at Hull-House* (1910), she recalls the time that she and four classmates at an exclusive women's seminary in Illinois got into trouble for being overly influenced by Thomas De Quincey's wicked book.

From Twenty Years at Hull-House

The school at Rockford in 1877 had not changed its name from seminary to college, although it numbered, on its faculty and among its alumnae, college women who were most eager that this should be done, and who really accomplished it during the next five years. The school was one of the earliest efforts for women's higher education in the Mississippi Valley, and from the beginning was called "The Mount Holyoke of the West." It reflected much of the missionary spirit of that pioneer institution, and the proportion of missionaries among its early graduates was almost as large as Mount Holyoke's own. In addition there had been thrown about the founders of the early western school the glamour of frontier privations, and the first students, conscious of the heroic self-sacrifice made in their behalf, felt that each minute of the time thus dearly bought must be conscientiously used. This inevitably fostered an atmosphere of intensity, a fever of preparation which continued long after the direct making of it had ceased, and which the later girls accepted, as they did the campus and the buildings, without knowing that it could have been otherwise.

As I attempt to reconstruct the spirit of my contemporary group by looking over many documents, I find nothing more amusing than a plaint registered against life's indistinctness, which I imagine more or less reflected the sentiments of all of us. At

any rate here it is for the entertainment of the reader if not for his edification: "So much of our time is spent in preparation, so much in routine, and so much in sleep, we find it difficult to have any experience at all." We did not, however, tamely accept such a state of affairs, for we made various and restless attempts to break through this dull obtuseness.

At one time five of us tried to understand De Quincey's marvelous "Dreams" more sympathetically, by drugging ourselves with opium. We solemnly consumed small white powders at intervals during an entire long holiday, but no mental reorientation took place, and the suspense and excitement did not even permit us to grow sleepy. About four o'clock on the weird afternoon, the young teacher whom we had been obliged to take into our confidence, grew alarmed over the whole performance, took away our De Quincey and all the remaining powders, administered an emetic to each of the five aspirants for sympathetic understanding of all human experience, and sent us to our separate rooms with a stern command to appear at family worship after supper "whether we were able to or not."

Jane Addams at sixteen. "We solemnly consumed small white powders at intervals during an entire long holiday."

SARAH BERNHARDT
1844–1923

Called "the Divine Sarah" on both sides of the Atlantic, Sarah Bernhardt was the ultimate classical actress, unrivaled in scope, depth, and innovation. Born in France as Rosine Bernard, she spent her childhood in surrogate homes, boarding school, and later a convent. Her family forcibly enrolled her in the Paris Conservatory—against her impulse to become a nun—and she eventually became the charismatic idol of the Comédie Française. With brilliant virtuosity she played Hamlet (not Ophelia), *Phèdre*, Cleopatra, and the Lady of the Camelias. She was daring and independent both onstage and off.

In 1879, on her first London tour, Sarah with her unmanageable blond curls was a rising star. Her opening performance of *Phèdre* had stunned the English audience. Though she was eager to amplify this impression with her second performance, her health was suffering and cancellation seemed imminent. To avoid this, the aspiring actress took opium. In her memoirs, she recounts the performance of Dumas's *L'Etrangère* she gave under its influence.

From Memoirs of
Sarah Bernhardt

My intense desire to win over the English public had caused me to overtax my strength. I had done my utmost at the first performance and had not spared myself in the least. The consequence was that in the night I coughed up blood in such an alarming way that a messenger was dispatched to the French embassy in search of a physician. Dr. Vintras, who was at the head of the French Hospital in London, found me lying on my bed exhausted, and looking more dead than alive. He was afraid that I should not recover, and requested that my family be sent for. I made a gesture with my hand to the effect that it was not necessary. As I could not speak, I wrote down with a pencil, "Send for Dr. Parrot."

Dr. Vintras remained with me part of the night, putting crushed ice between my lips every five minutes. At length, towards five in the morning, the bleeding ceased and, thanks to a potion that the doctor gave me, I fell asleep.

We were to play "L'Etrangère" that night at the Gaiety, and, as my *rôle* was not a very fatiguing one, I wanted to perform my part *quand-même*.

Dr. Parrot arrived by the four o'clock boat and refused categorically to give his consent. He had attended me from my childhood. I really felt much better, and the feverishness had left me. I wanted to get up, but to this Dr. Parrot objected.

Presently Dr. Vintras and Mr. Mayer, the impresario of the Comédie Française, were announced. Mr. Hollingshead, director of the Gaiety Theatre, was waiting in a carriage at the door to know whether I was going to play in "L'Etrangère," the piece announced on the bills. I asked Dr. Parrot to rejoin Dr. Vintras in the drawing-room, and I gave instructions for Mr. Mayer to be introduced into my room.

"I feel much better," I told him, quickly. "I'm very weak still, but I will play. H'sh! Don't say a word here. Tell Mr. Hollingshead, and wait for me

Sarah Bernhardt as she appears in the Vin Mariani coca wine testimonial book (1896). "I was in that delicious stupor that one experiences after chloroform, morphine, opium, or hasheesh."

in the smoking-room; but don't let anyone else know."

I then got up and dressed very quickly. My maid helped me, and, as she had guessed what my plan was, she was highly amused.

Wrapped in my cloak, with a lace fichu over my head, I joined Mayer in the smoking-room, and then we both got into his hansom.

"Come to me in an hour's time," I said, in a low voice, to my maid.

"Where are you going?" asked Mayer, perfectly stupefied.

"To the theatre; quick, quick!" I answered.

The cab started, and I then explained to him that if I had stayed at home neither Dr. Parrot nor Dr. Vintras would have let me act upon any account.

"The die is cast now," I added, "and we shall see what happens."

When once I was at the theatre I took refuge in the manager's private office, in order to avoid Dr. Parrot's anger. I was very fond of him and I knew how wrongly I was acting with regard to him considering the inconvenience to which he had put himself in making the journey especially for me, in response to my summons. I knew, however, how impossible it would have been to have made him understand that I felt really better, and that in risking my life I was really only risking what was my own, to dispose of as I pleased.

Half an hour later my maid joined me. She brought with her a letter from Dr. Parrot, full of gentle reproaches and furious advice, finishing with a prescription in case of a relapse. He was leaving an hour later, and would not even come and shake hands with me. I felt quite sure, however, that we should make it all up again on my return. I then began to prepare for my *rôle* in "L'Etrangère." While dressing I fainted three times, but I was determined to play *quand-même*.

The opium I had taken in my potion made my head rather heavy. I arrived on the stage in a semi-conscious state, yet delighted with the applause I received. I walked as though I were in a dream, and could scarcely distinguish my surroundings. The house itself I only saw through a luminous mist. My feet glided without effort over the carpet, and my voice sounded to me far away—very far away. I

was in that delicious stupor that one experiences after chloroform, morphine, opium, or hasheesh.

The first act went off very well, but in the third act, just when I was to tell the Duchesse de Septmonts (Croizette) all the troubles that I, Mrs. Clarkson, had gone through during my life, just as I should have commenced my interminable story, I could not remember anything. Croizette murmured my first phrase for me, but I could only see her lips move without hearing a word. I then said, quite calmly:—

"The reason I sent for you here, madame, is because I wanted to tell you my reasons for acting as I have done, but I have thought it over and have decided not to tell you them today."

Sophie Croizette gazed at me with a terrified look in her eyes; she then rose and left the stage, her lips trembling and her eyes fixed upon me all the time.

"What's the matter?" everyone asked, when she sank almost breathless into an arm-chair.

"Sarah has gone mad!" she exclaimed. "I assure you she has gone stark mad. She has cut out the whole of her scene with me."

"But how?" everyone asked.

"She has cut out two hundred lines," said Croizette.

"But what for?" was the eager question.

"I don't know. She looks quite calm."

The whole of this conversation, which was repeated to me later on, took much less time than it does now to write it down. Coquelin had been told, and he now came on to the stage to finish the act. The curtain fell. I was stupefied and desperate afterwards on hearing all that people told me. I had not noticed that anything was wrong, and it seemed to me that I had played the whole of my part as usual, but I was really under the influence of opium. There was very little for me to say in the fifth act, and I went through that perfectly well. The following day the accounts in the papers sounded the praises of our company, but the piece itself was criticised. I was afraid at first that my involuntary omission of the important part in the third act was one of the causes of the severity of the Press. This was not so, however, as all the critics had read and re-read the piece. They discussed the play itself, and did not mention my slip of memory. . . . Among the spectators who saw the first performance of "L'Etrangère" in London—and there were quite as many French as English present—not one remarked that there was something wanting, and not one of them said that he had not understood the character.

I talked about it to a very learned Frenchman.

"Did you notice the gap in the third act?" I asked him.

"No," he replied.

"In my big scene with Croizette?"

"No."

"Well, then, read what I left out," I insisted.

When he had read this he exclaimed:—

"So much the better. It's very dull, all that story, and quite useless. I understand the character without all that rigmarole and that romantic history."

Later on, when I apologized to Dumas fils for the way in which I had cut down his play, he answered, "Oh, my dear child, when I write a play I think it is good; when I see it played I think it is stupid; and when anyone tells it to me I think it is perfect, as the person always forgets half of it."

SANTA LOUISE ANDERSON
(d. 1886)

The practice of opium smoking was introduced to the United States by the Chinese who entered the port of San Francisco to work as laborers on the first transcontinental railroad. Within a decade or two San Francisco's Chinatown district was famous throughout America and Europe as a place to observe this exotic vice: it drew the world-famous pharmacologist Louis Lewin, as well as members of northern California's post–Gold Rush upper class like Santa Louise Anderson, an author from Sacramento.

Her friends compiled and published a collection of Miss Anderson's stories shortly after her tragic drowning in the Sacramento River. The following story was written in 1879.

An Opium Dream

My Chinese cook saw a ghost. His name (the Chinaman's) was Hang Gong Wah, and this may have had something to do with his visions of the night when deep sleep had fallen upon men. However, I tried to persuade him that he had been dreaming, for he was too valuable a servant to lose without a demur.

"No dleam," he answered sadly, "goost come; I no like." My logic was of no avail. He went, and I drowned my sorrow in the excitement of training another Celestial to do my bidding.

Yee Hop did not "sabe" so much as Hang Gong Wah, but he was anxious to learn "Melican ways," and expressed his entire approval of the room I assigned him by an exhaustive grin. Ten days passed uneventfully, and I felt that the ghost had indeed been a figment of the heathen brain. But one day Yee Hop came to me with his hat and a bundle containing his "little all," and some other things, as I afterwards discovered, that had struck his fancy, such as odd spoons and a napkin ring or two.

"I go," was his laconic exordium.

"What is the matter, Hop?" I asked, a little crestfallen, for I had done everything in reason to make him contented with his work.

"I no sleep. Debbla come."

"Devil come?" I repeated, interested in this new phase of the story. "What does he do?"

"Oh, debbla come down stairs weely early morning; set table; go way; no one see."

"Well," I said, taking a pleasant view of the situation, "why not let him help you if he likes to?"

Hop seemed amused at this companionable aspect of the great unknown power, but evidently could not bring himself to enter into partnership, for even useful purposes with the "debbla." So Yee Hop, too, went his way.

I fell to wondering if the creatures did not really see or hear something strange. I resolved to test it for myself in the haunted apartment. When the room had been thoroughly scrubbed and aired, I had a bed-lounge carried there, and the rest of the family being well out of the way, I slipped in and locked the door, prepared to experiment with the powers of darkness.

Looking around, before extinguishing my light, I spied an opium pipe.

The mystery was explained. No wonder the "debbla" had been a nocturnal visitor in the apartment.

Beside the lamp was a small thick bottle almost full of the divine papaver juice.

Here was a rare opportunity to try the dream-giving power of the wonderful drug, and no one would be the wiser. Having watched the *modus manipulandi* during visits to San Francisco Chinatown, I was at no loss in the preparation.

I moved a little table close to the lounge, and lay down in my long white wrapper, preferring a pillow to the block of wood usually made to serve that purpose by connoisseurs in their symposia. I rolled up a little ball of the waxy narcotic, melting it in the lamp, and working it on the rim of the pipe until it was of the proper consistency. The odor emitted was not unlike that of fresh chocolate caramels. Then I held my pipe in the flame, puffed three or four whiffs of whitish smoke, and the bowl was empty.

Six or eight pipes are required to produce much effect on even a novice. After each one I stopped to take cognizance of my sensations. There was nothing peculiar until I had finished the seventh pipe, when a kind of languor began to creep over my limbs, the striking of the clock above stairs seemed far off, and the noises of the street came as from a partial vacuum.

Then followed a delicious sense of lightness. I seemed made of air, and though my eyes were shut I saw everything with remarkable clearness. Now for De Quincean dreams of paradise, I thought, as I still rolled and smoked the rapture-giving pellets.

I do not know how long a time passed before the pipe fell from my grasp. I arose slowly from the lounge, up, up, up, with the light, easy motions of a swimmer. The roof offered no resistance. I passed through it out into the moonlight. A eucalyptus tree was in bloom by the front gate, and I paused on my upward way to look at the blossoms, circling round and round the tree as I did so, rejoicing in my new freedom of motion and admiring the curves I made and my flowing drapery of white.

A light south wind was blowing as I floated

San Francisco opium den, 1873. "Having watched the modus manipulandi *during visits to the San Francisco Chinatown, I was at no loss in the preparation" (Santa Louise Anderson).*

easily toward the north. The aurora shot lines of greenish red almost to the zenith, and towards this I directed my course.

"Now," I thought exultingly, "is the time to clear up the mystery of the North Pole."

Here was the chance to win immortal glory, to demonstrate beyond a doubt the existence of the classic landmark—a woman, too, to achieve it! The sex should be vindicated. Dim visions of the establishment of a female seminary on the very summit of the Pole began to shape themselves in my brain as I sped on at an increasing rate. I recognized the ice fields where Dr. Kane had reaped immortality; where Sir John Franklin suffered and died; then I floated over regions upon which, I felt certain, no human eye had ever gazed.

In the center of a vast sea of ice stood a slender column which a huge polar bear was making abortive efforts to climb. The column was topped by a globe of ice, reflecting, in dazzling rays, the retreating sun of an arctic winter and the efforts of the undiscouraged bear.

I knew I beheld the Pole, and my emotions overcame me. Like the lachrymose hero of Mace-

donia, I wept, while my heart beat fast as does a pendulum when the bob is taken off.

My sensations, up to this time, had been exquisitely delightful. The Aurora Borealis seemed a great drop curtain which might at any moment rise to reveal new wonders. To survey the situation better I seated myself upon the ice ball. For the first time I appeared to have weight, for the Pole vibrated up and down like an old-fashioned churndasher. I slid off the glassy surface of the ball and began a headlong descent. The bear made a frantic clutch for me as I passed him, whether to lend a helping hand or with an eye to dinner I had not time to determine.

For a breathless time I went down, down. Suddenly I felt myself hurried toward the torrid zone by some malignant power whose delight it seemed to hold me suspended over craters of howling volcanoes, letting me fall slowly till I almost touched the boiling cauldron, then whirling me off to fresh tortures.

I neared the steaming jungles of the Amazon, on the sides of whose mighty current lay boundless forests, silent except for the hissing of reptiles or the cry of some solitary bird. Along the vast swamps on the margins lay huge alligators waiting for their prey. I shuddered with terror. Fear seemed to make me subject to gravitation. I fell headlong, grasping at ropes that dangled before me, which, when I had almost touched them, broke like ropes of sand and vanished. With a heavy thud I struck the ground, where I remained motionless for fear the alligators would hear me.

Now and then there was a sluggish movement in the water as of some heavy body turning on its side.

I could not move hand or foot without coming in contact with the slimy writhings of reptiles. They began to creep over me. They wound about legs and body and twined in my hair, "hissing but stingless." One tightened his folds around my neck and strangled me.

Then I found myself pacing the burning sand of the Sahara Desert. The Day of Judgment had come and gone, and my doom was to wander there forever alone.

Waves of heat rose from the sand till it seemed an ocean ready to burst into flame. Not even a lion roared to break this silence of eternity.

A strange feeling commenced in my head. Putting up my hand I discovered that I could not reach my ears, although I stood on tiptoe. My cheeks were tremendous and knocked against my shoulders. I staggered, for my head threatened to pull me over. Finally I fell forward, my feet in the air, not unlike a huge potato with a fork stuck in it handlewise. And still it grew.

It was like a world itself, for it soon filled the desert. The moon looked disturbed, and moved unsteadily in her orbit. The planets, as one by one they rose, seemed troubled and uncertain; then the sun himself reeled, for my head had grown out beyond the orbits of Venus and Mars, and the Earth clinging to it was no larger than a barnacle on a ship's keel.

Suddenly there was a terrific crash. I found myself lying on the sofa with my head hanging over the side and my neck nearly broken.

I felt dizzy, but I managed to crawl up-stairs to my room. It was almost midnight.

It might be said that I had seen the "debbla," also.

"Morphine" by Albert Matignon. "Women who might be frightened off by the bad taste and deadly nausea of the drug taken in the usual way allow themselves to fall under its spell, because it is only the prick of a needle in the arm, and almost instantly the languid delights of the morphine are flowing through their veins" (from a Montreal newspaper, 1888).

"La Morphiniste" by Eugène Grasset, 1893

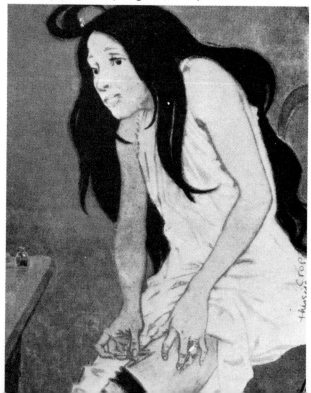

FRANK LESLIE'S
ILLUSTRATED
NEWSPAPER

Entered according to Act of Congress, in the year 1883, by Mrs. Frank Leslie, in the Office of the Librarian of Congress at Washington.—Entered at the Post Office, New York, N. Y., as Second-class Matter.

No. 1,442.—Vol. LVI.] NEW YORK—FOR THE WEEK ENDING MAY 12, 1883. [Price, 10 Cents. $4.00 Year 13 Weeks.

"A growing metropolitan evil—scene in an opium den, in Pell Street, frequented by working-girls," Frank Leslie's Illustrated Newspaper, *New York, 1883*

MARY C. HUNGERFORD

Little is known of this author of two novels for juveniles, who appears to have been the first woman to publish a description of the effects of a psychedelic experience. The effects of eating a very substantial amount of cannabis extract or hashish cannot be duplicated by smoking the substance. "An Overdose of Hasheesh" (1884) holds its own with the classic accounts of cannabis overdoses written thirty to forty years earlier by Théophile Gautier, Bayard Taylor, and Fitz Hugh Ludlow (the hashish eater).

Hungerford's account is remarkably similar to some of Ludlow's. They had the same religious orientation: nineteenth-century American Christian consciousness suddenly placed upon a Middle Eastern magic carpet. The hashish shattered their nervous systems, sending them on a seemingly endless fall from grace while they hoped in vain for their savior to bear them up and resurrect their souls. Despite her despair as she lay unable to communicate and virtually paralyzed in her bed, surrounded by doctor and relatives, Hungerford realizes that "in place of my lost senses I had a marvelously keen sixth sense or power, which I can only describe as an intense superhuman consciousness that in some way embraced all the five and went immeasurably beyond them."

An Overdose of Hasheesh

Being one of the grand army of sufferers from headache, I took, last summer, by order of my physician, three small daily doses of Indian hemp (hasheesh), in the hope of holding my intimate enemy in check. Not discovering any of the stimulative effects of the drug, even after continual increase of the dose, I grew to regard it as a very harmless and inactive medicine, and one day, when I was assured by some familiar symptoms that my perpetual dull headache was about to assume an aggravated and acute form, such as usually sent me to bed for a number of days, I took, in the desperate hope of forestalling the attack, a much larger quantity of hasheesh than had ever been prescribed. Twenty minutes later I was seized with a strange sinking or faintness, which gave my family so much alarm that they telephoned at once for the doctor, who came in thirty minutes after the summons, bringing, as he had been requested, another practitioner with him.

I had just rallied from the third faint, as I call the sinking turns, for want of a more descriptive name, and was rapidly relapsing into another, when the doctors came. One of them asked at once if I had been taking anything unusual, and a friend who had been sent for remembered that I had been experimenting with hasheesh. The physicians asked then the size and time of the last dose, but I could not answer. I heard them distinctly, but my lips were sealed. Undoubtedly my looks conveyed a desire to speak, for Dr. G—, bending over me, asked if I had taken a much larger quantity than he had ordered. I was half sitting up on the bed when he asked me that question, and, with all my energies bent upon giving him to understand that I had taken an overdose, I bowed my head, and at once became unconscious of everything except that bowing, which I kept up with ever-increasing force for seven or eight hours, according to my computation of time. I felt the veins of my throat swell nearly to bursting, and the cords tighten painfully, as, impelled by an irresistible force, I nodded like a wooden mandarin in a tea-store.

In the midst of it all I left my body, and quietly from the foot of the bed watched my unhappy self nodding with frightful velocity. I glanced indignantly at the shamefully indifferent group that did not even appear to notice the frantic motions, and resumed my place in my living temple of flesh in time to recover sufficiently to observe one doctor lift his finger from my wrist, where he had laid it to count the pulsations just as I lapsed into unconsciousness, and say to the other: "I think she moved her head. She means us to understand that she has taken largely of the cannabis indica." So, in the long, interminable hours I had been nodding my head off, only time enough had elapsed to count my pulse, and the violent motions of my head had in fact been barely noticeable. This exaggerated appreciation of sight, motion, and sound is, I am told, a well-known effect of hasheesh, but I was ignorant of that fact then, and, even if I had not been, probably the mental torture I underwent during the time it enchained my faculties would not have been lessened, as I seemed to have no power to reason with myself, even in the semi-conscious intervals which came between the spells.

These intervals grew shorter, and in them I had no power to speak. My lips and face seemed to myself to be rigid and stony. I thought that I was dying, and, instead of the peace which I had always hoped would wait on my last moments, I was filled with a bitter, dark despair. It was not only death that I feared with a wild, unreasoning terror, but there was a fearful expectation of judgment, which must, I think, be like the torture of lost souls. I felt half sundered from the flesh, and my spiritual sufferings seemed to have begun, although I was conscious of living still.

One terrible reality—I can hardly term it a fancy even now—that came to me again and again, was so painful that it must, I fear, always be a vividly remembered agony. Like dreams, its vagaries can be accounted for by association of ideas past and passing, but the suffering was so intense and the memory of it so haunting that I have acquired a horror of death unknown to me before. I died, as I believed, although by a strange double consciousness I knew that I should again reanimate the body I had left. In leaving it I did not soar away, as one delights to think of the freed spirits soaring. Neither did I linger around dear, familiar scenes. I sank, an intangible, impalpable shape, through the bed, the floors, the cellar, the earth, down, down, down! As if I had been a fragment of glass dropping through the ocean, I dropped uninterruptedly through the earth and its atmosphere, and then fell on and on forever. I was perfectly composed, and speculated curiously upon the strange circumstances that even in going through the solid earth there was no displacement of material, and in my descent I gathered no momentum. I discovered that I was transparent and deprived of all power of volition, as well as bereft of the faculties belonging to humanity. But in place of my lost senses I had a marvelously keen sixth sense or power, which I can only describe as an intense superhuman consciousness that in some way embraced all the five and went immeasurably beyond them. As time went on, and my dropping through space continued, I became filled with the most profound loneliness, and a desperate fear took hold of me that I should be thus alone for evermore, and fall and fall eternally without finding rest.

* * *

For five hours I remained in the same condition—short intervals of half-consciousness, and then long lapses into the agonizing experience I have described. Six times the door of time seemed to close on me, and I was thrust shuddering into a hopeless eternity, each time falling, as at first, into that terrible abyss wrapped in the fearful dread of

Lalla Rookh and her hookah. "I died, as I believed, although by a strange double consciousness I knew that I should again reanimate the body I had left" (Mary Hungerford).

the unknown. Always there were the same utter helplessness and the same harrowing desire to rest upon something, to stop, if but for an instant, to feel some support beneath; and through all the horrors of my sinking the same solemn and remorseful certainty penetrated my consciousness that, had I not in life questioned the power of Christ to save, I should have felt under me the "everlasting arms" bearing me safely to an immortality of bliss. There was no variation in my trances; always the same horror came, and each time when sensibility partially returned I fought against my fate and struggled to avert it. But I never could compel my lips to speak, and the violent paroxysms my agonizing dread threw me into were all unseen by my friends, for in reality, as I was afterward told, I made no motion except a slight muscular twitching of the fingers.

Later on, when the effect of the drug was lessening, although the spells or trances recurred, the intervals were long, and in them I seemed to regain clearer reasoning power and was able to account for some of my hallucinations. Even when my returns to consciousness were very partial, Dr. G—— had made me inhale small quantities of nitrite of amyl to maintain the action of the heart, which it was the tendency of the excess of hasheesh to diminish. Coming out of the last trance, I discovered that the measured rending report like the discharge of a cannon which attended my upward way was the throbbing of my own heart. As I sank I was probably too unconscious to notice it, but always, as it made itself heard, my falling ceased and the pain of my ascending began. The immense time between the throbs gives me as I remember it an idea of infinite duration that was impossible to me before.

For several days I had slight relapses into the trance-like state I have tried to describe, each being preceded by a feeling of profound dejection. I felt myself going as before, but by a desperate effort of will saved myself from falling far into the shadowy horrors which I saw before me. I dragged myself back from my fate, faint and exhausted and with a melancholy belief that I was cut off from human sympathy, and my wretched destiny must always be unsuspected by my friends, for I could not bring myself to speak to any one of the dreadful foretaste of the hereafter I firmly believed I had experienced. On one of these occasions, when I felt myself falling from life, I saw a great black ocean like a rocky wall bounding the formless chaos into which I sank. As I watched in descending the long line of towering, tumultuous waves break against some invisible barrier, a sighing whisper by my side told me each tiny drop of spray was a human existence which in that passing instant had its birth, life, and death.

"How short a life!" was my unspoken thought.

"Not short in time," was the answer. "A lifetime there is shorter than the breaking of a bubble here. Each wave is a world, a piece of here, that serves its purpose in the universal system, then returns again to be reabsorbed into infinity."

"How pitifully sad is life!" were the words I formed in my mind as I felt myself going back to the frame I had quitted.

"How pitifully sadder to have had no life, for only through life can the gate of this bliss be entered!" was the whispered answer. "I never lived—I never shall."

"What are you, then?"

I had taken my place again among the living when the answer came, a sighing whisper still, but so vividly distinct that I looked about me suddenly to see if others besides myself could hear the strange words:

"Woe, woe! I am an unreal actual, a formless atom, and of such as I am is chaos made."

CHARLOTTE RIDDELL
1832–1906

Charlotte Riddell was a British traveler and satirist. She is the author of thirty volumes of novels and tales. *A Mad Tour* was published in 1891.

From A Mad Tour, Or a Journey Undertaken in an Insane Moment Through Central Europe on Foot

Laudanum is not generally considered a toilet luxury, but except some cold cream, vaseline, and camphorated spirits, I carried none other. Bobby had implored, adjured me to leave the laudanum behind. He has, even now, something of the same horror of it that many people have of a pistol. To this day he seems to imagine it may go off by itself, and kill somebody without any evil intention.

He said, with urgent pathos, when we were packing our things:

"But you don't take laudanum, do you?"

No, I don't take it in his, or a coroner's, sense; yet it certainly does not seem well to me to be without it.

The fact is, I am occasionally the possessor of a pain which, so far as I know, is scarcely common property. I never heard but of one other person who owned it, and he has long passed to a world where, we may hope, physical pain is unknown. I have taken the best advice on the matter, and the advice has left me where I was. The mysterious pain proceeds in some wonderful way from the "nerves," about which doctors seem to know as little now as they used to do concerning that unsentimental and greatly neglected organ, the liver.

Whenever, without any apparent reason, I am going to be very ill, or whenever, with reason, I have been overworking that which, for want of a more modest word, must be called my brain, the abominable THING seizes and rends me. It is no pain for which pity can be asked or help obtained. A silver penny-piece would cover the seat of my ache, but it sometimes seems as if the whole world were far too small to contain the aching!

Laudanum does not assuage, but laudanum enables me to bear it, therefore I am never without the anodyne if I can get it. Sometimes a druggist refuses to supply it; sometimes he professes his willingness to supply me by the pint. Fortunately, though that grim pain never seized me tooth and nail while abroad, I was able to obtain a satisfactory supply before leaving home. Otherwise, probably, these pages had never been written.

An illustration by John Tenniel for Alice's Adventures in Wonderland, *1865. "It got me into such a state of indifference that I no longer took the least interest in anything and did nothing all day but loll on the sofa reading novels, falling asleep every now and then, and drinking tea" (Young Lady Laudanum-Drinker).*

ANONYMOUS

Anonymously published and long buried in a British medical journal, *The Journal of Mental Sciences* (January 1889), this young lady's confession documents the life of an upper-class opium addict. The narrator is very musical and enjoys going to concerts high. She becomes addicted from using laudanum as a sleeping aid after intense bouts of piano practice. Her family's social standing and their concern somewhat protect her, but also heighten her moral dilemma. Her mother and doctor serve as authority figures. Upon recognizing her addiction, the narrator becomes a self-analyst, graphically depicting her withdrawal and recovery. She broke a taboo by writing openly in 1889 about her drug use, and by condemning the medical profession for ignoring the harmful side effects of the drugs they prescribed. The following is addressed to the family physician.

Confessions of a Young Lady Laudanum-Drinker

Dear Sir,

Perhaps you may remember a lady calling on you with her daughter about the middle of August, to ask you if there was any way of curing the habit of taking opium, which the girl had contracted. I, who write, am that same girl, and think you may perhaps be interested to hear how I got on. It is hateful to me to think of that horrible time, and one of my chief reasons for writing to you is to beg you to try and make known by every means in your power, what a terrible thing opium-eating is. If people only knew of the consequences sure to follow on such a habit, of its insidiousness, and the difficulty of leaving it off, surely they would never touch it.

Perhaps it is rather soon for me to imagine myself cured, but I do not think I can ever feel more horrified about it than I do now. There was no excuse for me taking it, brought up by such a mother, and with such a constant example of unselfishness before me in the rest of the family. All my tastes and fancies were gratified; as mother says, when I take a whim into my head, the whole house is turned upside down. When I came home from school I insisted on practising seven hours a day, and the family put up with it, though it was a great infliction to them. It would have been better for me had they not done so, for I was naturally so tired-out at night that I could not sleep, and knowing that sleep would come easily with a little laudanum, it was difficult to resist taking it.

Of course, it didn't become habitual all at once; the first time I got it was at school, after a concert, when its effects were so soothing, that it became quite usual for me to get it, mixed up with quinine, which I was forced to take, though there was not the slightest necessity for it, as nobody could be stronger than I am. Thank goodness, we have all inherited splendid constitutions, and would almost think it a disgrace to the family to have anything the matter with us. I am quite sure I would never have had neuralgia, if it had not been for stewing up for exams. Mother was always writing to tell me not to do them, but I did not feel it my duty to obey her on that point, as what does one go to school for if not to learn; and to own one's self beaten by a headache would surely show a very weak mind.

I'm just mad at myself for having given in to such a fearful habit as opium-eating. None but those who have as completely succumbed to it as I did, could guess the mischief it would do. Even you, with an experience which must be extremely varied, being as you are, in such a good place for studying people's brains (or rather their want of them), cannot know the amount of harm it did to me morally, though I must say you did seem to have a pretty fair idea of it. It got me into such a state of indifference that I no longer took the least interest in anything, and did nothing all day but loll on the sofa reading novels, falling asleep every now and then, and drinking tea. Occasionally I would take a walk or drive, but not often. Even my music I no longer took much interest in, and would play only when the mood seized me, but felt it too much of a bother to practice. I would get up about ten in the morning, and make a pretence of sewing; a pretty pretence, it took me four months to knit a stocking!

Worse than all, I got so deceitful, that no one could tell when I was speaking the truth. It was only this last year it was discovered; those living in the house with you are not so apt to notice things, and it was my married sisters who first began to wonder what had come over me. They said I always seemed to be in a half-dazed state, and not to know what I was doing. However they all put it down to music. Mother had let me go to all the Orchestral Concerts in the winter, and they thought it had been too much for me. By that time it was a matter of supreme indifference to me what they thought, and even when it was found out, I had become so callous that I didn't feel the least shame. Even mother's grief did not affect me, I only felt irritated at her; this is an awful confession to have to make, but it is better to tell the whole truth when you once begin, and it might be some guide to you in dealing with others. If you know of anyone indulging in such a habit, especially girls, just tell them what they will come to.

Of course its effects differ according to one's nature, and it's to be hoped few get so morally degraded as I did. This much is certain, few would have the constitution to stand it as I did, and even I was beginning to be the worse for it. For one thing, my memory was getting dreadful; often, in talking to people I knew intimately, I would forget their names and make other absurd mistakes of a similar kind. As my elder sister was away from home, I took a turn at being housekeeper. Mother thinks every girl should know how to manage a house, and she lets each of us do it in our own way, without interfering. Her patience was sorely tried with my way of doing it, as you may imagine; I was constantly losing the keys, or forgetting where I had left them. I forgot to put sugar in puddings, left things to burn, and a hundred other things of the same kind.

*   *   *

One thing I would like to know, and that is—whether you could tell that I had not left off laudanum that day we called. Surely you must know the state one gets into when suddenly deprived of it; they could no more sit up and speak as I did than fly. By that time I had brought myself down to a quarter of an ounce a day, and as you had put mother on her guard, I had no means of getting any more (I hate having to own that I tried to do so) so the day after we saw you was the last I had any. Then began a time I shudder to look back upon. I don't like owning to bodily suffering, but will not deny that I suffered them. I wonder if leaving off opium has the same effect on everyone! My principal feeling was one of awful weariness and numbness at the end of my back; it kept me tossing about all day and night long. It was impossible to lie in one position for more than a minute, and of course sleep was out of the question. I was so irritable that no one cared to come near me; mother slept on the sofa in my room, and I nearly kicked her once for suggesting that I should say hymns over to myself, to try and make me go to sleep. Hymns of a very different sort were in my mind, I was once or twice very nearly strangling myself, and I am ashamed to say that the only thing that kept me from doing so was the thought that I would be able to get laudanum somehow. I was conscious of feeling nothing but the mere sense of being alive, and if the house had been burning, would have thought it too much of an effort to rise. . . .

However, I gradually got over that, and now am perfectly well, with the exception of my back, which has that nasty aching feeling now and then. Our medical man, who is a bright specimen of the country doctor, said "it might be anything," and when asked to explain what that meant said "per-

haps her corsets are too tight." This was indeed a bright idea as I don't happen to wear corsets at all. Those country doctors are fit for nothing but measles and teething. What I think so very queer when I was taking laudanum is that though my memory was going for other things, it was as good as ever for music; I could pick up by ear and play off even better than before. I often think had that faculty gone it would have alarmed me so much that perhaps I would have been able to stop my evil habits, but it's unlikely.

Oh, why do you doctors not try prevention as well as cure? You have it in your power to warn those who take laudanum now and then for toothache or headache, what an insidious thing it is, and how easily they may become the victims of it. I began that way, and see what it came to. Even now I often wonder if I've quite got over its effects. Does anyone who has gone up to three or four ounces a day, and is suddenly deprived of it, live to tell the tale? I can hardly believe it. My own sufferings were bad enough, and I had got down to a quarter of an ounce. I'll end this by alluding again to the object of my writing, namely, the prevention of people getting into such a state as I was: if they were to know the state of moral idiocy to which they would in the end be brought, would they ever allow themselves to once begin the habit? They need not say to themselves "Oh, we can stop it when we like"; opium takes away their power to do that. There can't be a more determined person than I am naturally, and what good did that do me! I determined a hundred times to stop it, but never succeeded, and at last I got that I didn't care a rap what became of me, all the reasoning and affection expended on me, being a mere waste of time and love. You doctors know all the harm those drugs do, as well as the "victims" of them, and yet you do precious little to prevent it. If that subject were to be taken up instead of some so often spoken of in the health-lectures which are now given, it might do some practical good. Well, I wonder at myself being able to write such a long letter on a subject which is so repugnant to me that I try never even to think of it. I can hardly finish up in my usual style which is "hoping to see you soon again"; because I certainly don't hope so, and if I ever do have the pleasure of seeing you again, let us hope it will be under very different circumstances.

PATENT MEDICINES

"Belladonna" by Erich Brunkal, c. 1885. "The subject is helplessly laid back, anaesthetized by the poisonous essence of Belladonna, which has called forth a seductively beautiful woman. It appears to be all over for him" (original text for the engraving).

Advertising poster for Absinthe Robette. "I thought of that white half-naked witch who had been my chief companion in the flying phantasmagoria of the past wild night. . . . Oh, she was a blithe brave phantom, that Absinthe-witch of mine. . . . We had flown through the dark, she and I, on green outspread wings. . . . A wondrous wedlock was consummated—an indissoluble union with the fair wild Absinthe-witch of my dreams!" (Marie Corelli, Wormwood, 1890).

COCA WINE AND COCAINE, 1880–1900

Advertisement for Vin Mariani

Martha Bernays and Sigmund Freud in 1885. Freud kept his fiancée in Vienna informed of his experiments with cocaine in Berlin. He also "kept sending Martha cocaine . . . although he warned her against acquiring the habit" (Ernest Jones, Life of Freud).

Maud Gonne

Loïe Fuller. Among the hundreds of celebrities who gave their public endorsement to Vin Mariani, a Parisian tonic wine made by the infusion of coca leaves in alcohol, were Maud Gonne, Irish actress and revolutionary leader, Sarah Bernhardt, and dancer Loïe Fuller, who wrote: "'My kingdom' for a Shakespeare head—a Moliere tongue—a Dumas pen to praise our Mariani! It is not wine, it is the sustenance of the home of the soul! Let us then all learn—not its abuse—but its use."

MRS. MEYERS AFTER USING COCAINE THREE MONTHS

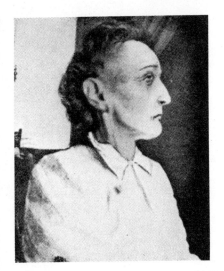

MRS. MEYERS ON HER RELEASE FROM THE BRIDEWELL

Annie Meyers, author of Eight Years in Cocaine Hell, *1902. "I invented what is known as the 'Cocaine Dance,' and would go to the sporting houses and dance and a collection would be taken up and given to me. I would run without a hat to the drug store immediately to get my idol." Cocaine was still legal; it was the expense of her habit that forced Meyers to become a derelict and shoplifter. After being arrested she told police, "Gentlemen, excuse me while I take a blow of my cocaine."*

An American opium den of the 1920's. This image, either
posed by professional models or a still from a Hollywood
film, was reproduced in a popular anti-drug book, Battling
the Wolves of Society, 1929.

EXPATRIATES
& VAGABONDS

"Has It Come To This?" William Randolph Hearst's San Francisco Examiner *for February 23, 1908, relates that "during the Christmas shopping season some persons were amazed and shocked to discover among the gifts offered for sale in the best jewelry houses of New York gold jewelled morphine sets. Apparently they were intended for women, and certainly for persons of great wealth."*

Anti-drug sentiment that began building during the mid-nineteenth century developed into a crusade in the early twentieth. Like the temperance movement against saloons and the sale of liquor, public reaction to drugs was generated partly by prevailing ethical and moral standards and partly by increasingly visible evidence of addiction problems, particularly among mainliners of morphine, heroin, and cocaine; chloral hydrate users and absinthe drinkers; and to a more subtle but no less real extent among the "grand army of sufferers" (in Mary Hungerford's phrase) who freely and somewhat unknowingly used the habit-forming, opium-based patent medicines. The tremendously popular coca-based wines, tonics, and soft drinks were considered, if not physically degenerating, at least insidious. Lurid newspaper accounts of drug abuse and related crimes, often grossly exaggerated and with a racist slant, advanced the belief that Western society would eventually crumble if those pathetic victims continued to be supplied with their "dope."

The term dope began to be used at this time not only by the establishment and media but, with a tone of irony and defiance, by drug users. Dope meant not only narcotics like opium, morphine, heroin, and chloral hydrate, but cocaine, cannabis, and peyote, the sacred drug of Native Americans. It implied the use of drugs for pleasure and recreation, rather than as a "soothing elixir for baby's cough" or a woman's "monthly distress." In the public mind, opium changed from "God's own medicine" to a seductive and deadly weapon in the Devil's arsenal.

A social and political climate was created for the federal government's regulation and control of the preparation and distribution of drugs, beginning with the Pure Food and Drug Act of 1906. Manufacturers of patent medicines were forced to list ingredients and warn of addiction;

soft-drink makers were ordered to take the coca out of their colas. Vin Mariani and other coca wines and tonics disappeared from the market. Scare stories in the press about American women held in the bondage of white slavery by Chinese opium purveyors and about sex crimes committed by cocaine-crazed southern blacks made ideal propaganda for the anti-drug forces. The Harrison Narcotics Act in 1914 strictly controlled all narcotic drugs, limiting their use to medical purposes.

The idea that women were more easily led astray and victimized by drugs carried over from the nineteenth century. This view was expressed

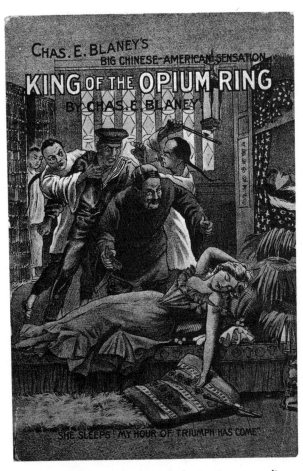

Cover of a 1908 paperback novel about opium smuggling

by journalists, writers, and dramatists, as well as in underground drug ballads like "Cocaine Lil" and "The Girl in the Blue Velvet Band," which became popular folk songs. During Prohibition in the twenties, newspaper and magazine readers were treated to lurid accounts of dope orgies in European sin capitals and drug scandals in the Hollywood film colony, involving Juanita Hansen, the original Mack Sennett girl; Olive Thomas, star of *The Flapper*; and celluloid goddesses Barbara LaMarr, Mabel Normand, and Alma Rubens. Similar stories of the degradation of the wives and daughters of leading families in American small towns and cities intrigued a national audience. This emphasis on the tragic plight of drug-using socialites and entertainers who had beauty, fame, and money established a lasting media tradition.

The anti-drug crusade resulted in legislation that made criminals out of several million drug users, driving many underground. Undoubtedly many were deterred from using drugs, but others preferred a state of intoxication and some became addicted. To meet the needs of a new criminal class (which derived, as our writers show, from all social classes), an international black market controlled by organized crime developed along the same lines as the bootleg liquor industry. The price of illicit drugs increased enormously. A user could stay high on morphine for about five cents a day in the 1880's, but it cost several dollars to buy the same amount between the wars. (In another thirty years the cost escalated to several hundred dollars a day.)

American diplomats helped organize an international convention in Geneva from 1923 to 1925 to launch a world war on drugs. Heroin, the most powerful narcotic and the one preferred by mainliners, was totally banned in the United States in 1924. Influential anti-drug crusaders of the time included Hearst columnist Winifred Black, who wrote under the pseudonym Annie Laurie, and Sara Graham-Mulhall, who did everything from banning De Quincey's *Confessions* in public schools and running raids in New York City to mapping international strategies against the demon poppy. During the Depression, when jazz music was being transmitted upriver from New Orleans and pot-smoking Mexican wetbacks were supplying cheap labor in the Southwest, the newly formed Federal Bureau of Narcotics planted stories of reefer madness in the press. The Marijuana Tax Act of 1937 prohibited the giggly and medically useful weed.

The typical drug-using female depicted in early-twentieth-century women's literature had made a conscious break—or had been set adrift by circumstances—from her family and her traditional role of daughter, wife, and mother. She was usually a member of the middle or upper class, well educated, and possessed of the social graces. Quite a few may be regarded as embodying, if not "flaming youth," at least the new, independent, self-willed "modern woman." For those drawn toward bohemia and the arts, to travel and exploration, drug experience represented a stage in their social and psychological evolution. For others drugs became an obsession, drawing them into a criminal underworld.

Lily Bart, the tragic heroine of Edith Wharton's *The House of Mirth* (1905), feels anxiety much deeper than her Victorian sisters would have endured when she presents a falsified prescription for chloral hydrate at a swank Fifth Avenue pharmacy: "The dread lest the pharmacist should question her, or keep the bottle back, choked the murmur of acquiescence in her throat; and when at length she emerged safely from the shop she was almost dizzy with the intensity of her relief." Lily Bart became a cult figure; thousands of readers wept over her fate.

"Chicago May" described a 1904 "dope party" in Edwardian England where aristocratic ladies and well-known actresses enjoyed morphine, heroin, and cocaine in company with denizens of London's underworld. On the eve of World War I, American heiress and writer Mabel Dodge Luhan hosted a peyote party with her intellectual friends in her fashionable Greenwich Village townhouse, using the psychedelic cactus

Cover of the 1908 Hebrew translation of the German novel Hashish by Fritz Lemermeier

known to S. Weir Mitchell, William James, Havelock Ellis, Aleister Crowley but few others at that time outside of American Indian reservations. Peyote had just been declared illegal in 1914.

A few notable nineteenth-century travel writers recounted taking opium or hashish while traveling in exotic lands, but they did not immerse themselves in alien cultures with the commitment of some early-twentieth-century authors. Isabelle Eberhardt renounced her European heritage, living the last seven years of her short life in Algeria and smoking kif (a form of marijuana) as one of her adopted culture's pastimes. "The Oblivion Seekers" is a richly detailed study of a turn-of-the-century kif café and its habitués. The heroine of Edith Blinn's *The Ashes of My Heart* (1916) is a gambling woman who breaks through a deep prejudice by forming an emotional bond with a Chinese man through the ritual of opium smoking. In "The Big Smoke," Emily Hahn's memoir set in 1934, a Chinese literary man with a penchant for Jean Cocteau attracts the author, who is passing through Shanghai. She finds the euphoria and stylized oblivion of opium so pleasing that it is a long time before she notices her addiction.

The vast consumption of alcohol in Ernest Hemingway and F. Scott Fitzgerald novels does not express the full range of psychoactive substances available in Paris during the twenties. Other expatriated writers like Mina Loy, Caresse Crosby, and Baroness Loringhoven were attracted to the drug hedonism evident there. In Loy's poem "Lunar Baedeker," "cocaine in cornucopia" is served in the "hallucinatory citadels" of the Paris evening. Crosby accompanied her husband to an elegant opium den, "the one place in Paris where the sumptuous rapture of the East was evoked by the ease and luxury of the surroundings." The baroness favored hashish; she smoked it openly in her "big china German pipe" and wrote poems about her stoned perceptions.

No Bed of Roses, the diary of an anonymous twenties' heroin and cocaine mainliner who turned to prostitution to support her habit, was the first best-selling drug confession written by a woman. It was praised by social reformers and literary critics. Along with two sequels, one written by the author's daughter, who followed in her footsteps, it was in print until the late 1940's, when female addict literature was becoming established as a genre. The harrowing dope and sex adventures of "O.W." were presented as social realism.

A more liberal view of the drug addict as a victim of circumstances emerged during the Depression. Box-Car Bertha Thompson's autobiography, *Sister of the Road* (1937), emphasized the sociology of narcotics addiction. A self-described hobo, radical, prostitute, thief, reformer, social worker, and revolutionist, Bertha spent fifteen years on the road, claiming that "it was all worthwhile . . . there were no tragedies in my life." She observed a great deal of opium and marijuana smoking, occasionally participating.

Women's drug writings from the turn of the twentieth century to the eve of World War II reflect change both in their social status and in the situation of drug users in general. While millions of women continued to doctor themselves and soothe their nervous systems in the nineteenth-century tradition with an herbal alcoholic patent medicine known as Lydia Pinkham's Vegetable Compound, a small but significant number lived their newfound freedom to its outlaw limits, exercising a prerogative of men in Victorian times—using drugs for recreation. Brave, fool-hardy, curious, sometimes suicidal, they are prototypes of the female junkies, psychedelic explorers, beats, and hippies of the postwar period.

ISABELLE EBERHARDT
1877–1904

Isabelle Eberhardt was the illegitimate daughter of an Armenian scholar, who was formerly pope of the Russian Orthodox Church, and a German noblewoman. Raised in Geneva, she was educated by her father, who demanded an austere life committed to studies, physical labor, and horsemanship. At the age of twenty, Isabelle moved to Tunisia where she fell in love with the desert and began a nomadic infusion into Islamic culture. She adopted the male attire of a full-length hooded robe and turban, rode and caroused freely with the Arabs, smoked kif (cannabis resin sometimes mixed with tobacco), drank, and took lovers. Her carefully constructed, sparing, bittersweet tales of Islamic life are written in a modernist style.

The chronicle of her seven years in North Africa portrays a series of flights from political dangers. In 1900 she adopted the identity of a Tunisian student and man of letters; she also met a young Algerian soldier, whom she later married. In the next four years she survived an assassination attempt, long bouts with malaria, and the poverty of her vagabond life.

After surviving a bout of malaria at Kenadsa, where she wrote the following story, twenty-seven-year-old Isabelle was reunited with her husband for one last night together, smoking kif

Isabelle Eberhardt at nineteen. "The seekers of oblivion sing and clap their hands lazily; their dream-voices ring out late into the night."

in their newly rented hut. The following day a flash flood drowned her and washed away most of her manuscripts. Some were rescued and published in France years later.

Isabelle Eberhardt saw kif as a gift of her adopted culture, part of the way of life. "The Oblivion Seekers" evokes the exotic texture of a kif den where altered consciousness is an acceptable social pastime.

The Oblivion Seekers

In this ksar, where the people have no place to meet but the public square or the earthen benches along the foot of the ramparts on the road to Bechar, here where there is not even a café, I have discovered a kif den.

It is in a partially ruined house behind the Mellah, a long hall lighted by a single eye in the ceiling of twisted and smoke-blackened beams. The walls are black, ribbed with lighter-colored cracks that look like open wounds. The floor has been made by pounding the earth, but it is soft and dusty. Seldom swept, it is covered with pomegranate rinds and assorted refuse.

The place serves as a shelter for Moroccan vagabonds, for nomads, and for every sort of person of dubious intent and questionable appearance. The house seems to belong to no one; as at a disreputable hotel, you spend a few badly-advised nights there and go on. It is a natural setting for picturesque and theatrical events, like the antechamber of the room where the crime was committed.

In one corner lies a clean red mat, with some cushions from Fez in embroidered leather. On the mat, a large decorated chest which serves as a table. A rosebush with little pale pink blooms, surrounded by a bouquet of garden herbs, all standing in water inside one of those wide earthen jars from the Tell. Further on, a copper kettle on a tripod, two or three teapots, a large basket of dried Indian hemp. The little group of kif-smokers requires no other decoration, no other mise-en-scène. They are people who like their pleasure.

On a rude perch of palm branches, a captive falcon, tied by one leg.

The strangers, the wanderers who haunt this retreat sometimes mix with the kif-smokers, notwithstanding the fact that the latter are a very closed little community into which entry is made difficult. But the smokers themselves are travellers who carry their dreams with them across the countries of Islam, worshippers of the hallucinating smoke. The men who happen to meet here at Kenadsa are among the most highly educated in the land.

Hadj Idriss, a tall thin Filali, deeply sunburned, with a sweet face that lights up from within, is one of these rootless ones without family or specific trade, so common in the Moslem world. For twenty-five years he has been wandering from city to city, working or begging, depending on the situation. He plays the guinbri, with its carved wooden neck and its two thick strings fastened to the shell of a tortoise. Hadj Idriss has a deep clear voice, ideal for singing the old Andaluz ballads, so full of tender melancholy.

Si Mohammed Behaouri, a Moroccan from Meknès, pale-complexioned and with caressing

"In the Harem," a North African postcard, c. 1910

eyes, is a young poet wandering across Morocco and southern Algeria in search of native legends and literature. To keep alive, he composes and recites verse on the delights and horrors of love.

Another is from the Djebel Zerhoun, a doctor and witch-doctor, small, dry, muscular, his skin tanned by the Sudanese sun under which he has journeyed for many years following caravans to and fro, from the coast of Senegal to Timbuctoo. All day long he keeps busy, slowly pouring out medicine and thumbing through old Moghrebi books of magic.

Chance brought them here to Kenadsa. Soon they will set out again, in different directions and on different trails, moving unconcernedly toward the fulfillment of their separate destinies. But it was community of taste that gathered them together in this smoky refuge, where they pass the slow hours of a life without cares.

At the end of the afternoon a slanting pink ray of light falls from the eye in the ceiling into the darkness of the room. The kif-smokers move in and form groups. Each wears a sprig of sweet basil in his turban. Squatting along the wall on the mat, they smoke their little pipes of baked red earth, filled with Indian hemp and powdered Moroccan tobacco.

Hadj Idriss stuffs the bowls and distributes them, after having carefully wiped the mouthpiece on his cheek as a gesture of politeness. When his own pipe is empty, he picks out the little red ball of ash and puts it into his mouth—he does not feel it burning him—then, once his pipe is refilled, he uses the still red-hot cinder to relight the little fire. For hours at a time he does not once let it go out. He has a keen and penetrating intelligence, softened by being constantly in a state of semi-exaltation; his dreams are nourished on the narcotic smoke.

The seekers of oblivion sing and clap their hands lazily; their dream-voices ring out late into the night, in the dim light of the mica-paned lantern. Then little by little the voices fall, grow muffled, the words are slower. Finally the smokers are quiet, and merely stare at the flowers in ecstasy. They are epicureans, voluptuaries; perhaps they are sages. Even in the darkest purlieu of Morocco's underworld such men can reach the magic horizon where they are free to build their dream-palaces of delight.

CHICAGO MAY
1876–?

The autobiography of Chicago May (May Churchill Sharpe) is the bawdy confession of an Irish-American con artist whose exploits were known internationally. May considered herself a freethinker and voiced pride in her own brand of outlaw morality. She consorted with criminals of every class; with audacity and wit she breezed

Chicago May (May Churchill Sharpe). "The orgy was held . . . sometime in 1904 . . . opposite the British Museum."

through many an outrageous caper. Not all came off, however; fifteen years of her life were spent in prison.

From Chicago May: Her Story

After I had recovered from the shock of my French experience of prisons, and had gotten together considerable dough, my friends said I owed them a swell banquet, out of gratitude for my deliverance, and the backing-up I had received from the gang. I thought so myself, and had had it in my mind, before they mentioned it. A committee was formed; and I thought it would be the regular eating and drinking kind of an affair. But the committee was unanimously in favor of a dope party. I was in the hands of my friends, though I disapproved of it.

Accordingly, the orgy was held. I am not sure about dates; but I think this feast of wit, wisdom, and dreams was pulled off some time in 1904. I had a house, at the time, in Montague Place. The party was held opposite the British Museum.

I went down to Limehouse Causeway, and engaged the services of a high-class chef to cook the pills. Then I ordered plenty of morphine, heroin, and cocaine. You may be sure I did not neglect getting another kind of chef, with plenty of good things to eat and drink. I, at least, was going to have a good time in my own way. The list was made up of all the crooks, dopes, or otherwise, that the committee and myself could think of.

And maybe we didn't have a crowd! There must have been more than a hundred there. No bums! Just a crowd of men and women who would compare favorably with any function in polite society, either as to dress, looks or manners. There was Polly Carr, the swan-neck beauty; Bromogan Liz; Jennie, the Pick; Dopey Sallie; Pretty Bessie, the American beauty, operating then, in London; my old friend, Annie Gleason; the beautiful Ada Bernard, who was playing in London at the time; many of the stage girls; and others too numerous or too dangerous to set forth here.

There is no doubt we began by having plenty of fun. Then things got to be hilarious, what with speeches, toasts, and boisterous conversation. When I had had my fill of eating and drinking, and the rest were getting to the drowsy, or fighting, stage, Baby Thompson, my admirer, asked me to leave with him for a drive. We did so, very fortunately.

On my return home, I learned that my party had been raided by the police. They arrested my housekeeper, Skinner, and she took the fall. The law in England, at that time, allowed one to smoke for pleasure, as long as one did not sell.

EDITH WHARTON
1862–1937

Born into a socially prominent New York family, Edith Wharton was educated in America and Europe. She began writing to relieve the stress of caring for her mentally deteriorating husband. *The House of Mirth* (1905), Wharton's first literary success, describes the career of a beautiful but doomed aspirant to wealth and social standing. Lily Bart, the heroine, becomes increasingly dependent upon the hypnotic-sedative chloral hydrate, which she purchases with little difficulty in the best Fifth Avenue pharmacies. One night, overwhelmed by the complexities of her situation, she raises the dosage of her sleeping potion for the last time. It is an act reminiscent of Elizabeth Siddal's death, and one that darkly forecasts the barbiturate overdose syndrome of the mid-twentieth century.

From The House of Mirth

It was growing late, and an immense weariness once more possessed her. It was not the stealing sense of sleep, but a vivid wakeful fatigue, a wan lucidity of mind against which all the possibilities of

Edith Wharton in 1905. "The little bottle was at her bedside, waiting to lay its spell on her."

the future were shadowed forth gigantically. She was appalled by the intense clearness of the vision; she seemed to have broken through the merciful veil which intervenes between intention and action, and to see exactly what she would do in all the long days to come. There was the cheque in her desk, for instance—she meant to use it in paying her debt to Trenor; but she foresaw that when the morning came she would put off doing so, would slip into gradual tolerance of the debt. The thought terrified her—she dreaded to fall from the height of her last moment with Lawrence Selden. But how could she trust herself to keep her footing? She knew the strength of the opposing impulses—she could feel the countless hands of habit dragging her back into some fresh compromise with fate. She felt an intense longing to prolong, to perpetuate, the momentary exaltation of her spirit. If only life could end now—end on this tragic yet sweet vision of lost possibilities, which gave her a sense of kinship with all the loving and foregoing in the world!

She reached out suddenly and, drawing the cheque from her writing-desk, enclosed it in an envelope which she addressed to her bank. She then wrote out a cheque for Trenor, and placing it, without an accompanying word, in an envelope inscribed with his name, laid the two letters side by side on her desk. After that she continued to sit at the table, sorting her papers and writing, till the intense silence of the house reminded her of the lateness of the hour. In the street the noise of wheels had ceased, and the rumble of the "elevated" came only at long intervals through the deep unnatural hush. In the mysterious nocturnal separation from all outward signs of life, she felt herself more strangely confronted with her fate. The sensation made her brain reel, and she tried to shut out consciousness by pressing her hands against her eyes. But the terrible silence and emptiness seemed to symbolize her future—she felt as though the house, the street, the world were all empty, and she alone left sentient in a lifeless universe.

But this was the verge of delirium . . . she had never hung so near the dizzy brink of the unreal. Sleep was what she wanted—she remembered that she had not closed her eyes for two nights. The little bottle was at her bedside, waiting to lay its spell upon her. She rose and undressed hastily, hungering now for the touch of her pillow. She felt so profoundly tired that she thought she must fall asleep at once; but as soon as she had lain down every nerve started once more into separate wakefulness. It was as though a great blaze of electric light had been turned on in her head, and her poor little anguished self shrank and cowered in it, without knowing where to take refuge.

She had not imagined that such a multiplication of wakefulness was possible: her whole past was reënacting itself at a hundred different points of consciousness. Where was the drug that could still this legion of insurgent nerves? The sense of exhaustion would have been sweet compared to this shrill beat of activities; but weariness had dropped from her as though some cruel stimulant had been forced into her veins.

She could bear it—yes, she could bear it; but what strength would be left her the next day? Perspective had disappeared—the next day pressed close upon her, and on its heels came the days that were to follow—they swarmed about her like a shrieking mob. She must shut them out for a few hours; she must take a brief bath of oblivion. She put out her hand, and measured the soothing drops into a glass; but as she did so, she knew they would be powerless against the supernatural lucidity of her brain. She had long since raised the dose to its highest limit, but tonight she felt she must increase it. She knew she took a slight risk in doing so—she remembered the chemist's warning. If sleep came at all, it might be a sleep without waking. But after all that was but one chance in a hundred: the action of the drug was incalculable, and the addition of a few drops to the regular dose would probably do no more than procure for her the rest she so desperately needed. . . .

She did not, in truth, consider the question very closely—the physical craving for sleep was her only sustained sensation. Her mind shrank from the glare of thought as instinctively as eyes contract in a blaze of light—darkness, darkness was what she must have at any cost. She raised herself in bed and swallowed the contents of the glass; then she blew out her candle and lay down.

She lay very still, waiting with a sensuous pleasure for the first effects of the soporific. She knew in advance what form they would take—the gradual cessation of the inner throb, the soft approach of passiveness, as though an invisible hand made magic passes over her in the darkness. The very slowness and hesitancy of the effect increased its fascination: it was delicious to lean over and look down into the dim abysses of unconsciousness. Tonight the drug seemed to work more slowly than usual: each passionate pulse had to be stilled in turn, and it was long before she felt them dropping into abeyance, like sentinels falling asleep at their posts. But gradually the sense of complete subjugation came over her, and she wondered languidly what had made her feel so uneasy and excited. She saw now that there was nothing to be excited about—she had returned to her normal view of life. Tomorrow would not be so difficult after all: she felt sure that she would have the strength to meet it. She did not quite remember what it was that she had been afraid to meet, but the uncertainty no longer troubled her. She had been unhappy, and now she was happy—she had felt herself alone, and now the sense of loneliness had vanished.

She stirred once, and turned on her side, and as she did so, she suddenly understood why she did not feel herself alone. It was odd—but Nettie Struther's child was lying on her arm: she felt the pressure of its little head against her shoulder. She did not know how it had come there, but she felt no great surprise at the fact, only a gentle penetrating thrill of warmth and pleasure. She settled herself into an easier position, hollowing her arm to pillow the round downy head, and holding her breath lest a sound should disturb the sleeping child.

As she lay there she said to herself that there was something she must tell Selden, some word she had found that should make life clear between them. She tried to repeat the word, which lingered vague and luminous on the far edge of thought—she was afraid of not remembering it when she woke; and if she could only remember it and say it to him, she felt that everything would be well.

Slowly the thought of the word faded, and sleep began to enfold her. She struggled faintly against it, feeling that she ought to keep awake on account of the baby; but even this feeling was gradually lost in

an indistinct sense of drowsy peace, through which, of a sudden, a dark flash of loneliness and terror tore its way.

She started up again, cold and trembling with the shock: for a moment she seemed to have lost her hold of the child. But no—she was mistaken—the tender pressure of its body was still close to hers: the recovered warmth flowed through her once more, she yielded to it, sank into it, and slept.

EDITH BLINN'S *THE ASHES OF MY HEART*

"*She held up with admiration a large poppy. 'Its substance is so sweet. I always smoke it in my cigarettes. Here, try one. It will do you no harm. And here,' crossing the room and opening the writing desk, 'I shall put the box. At your pleasure, my dear. Come to my apartment when you have recovered, and I shall show you marvellous results from the flowers you Americans trample beneath your feet.'*"

*"She quietly disrobed and donned a weblike silk gown of the faintest hues,
then stretched out upon a couch of pillows and inhaled the yellow smoke of the opium pipe
which Chong had carefully prepared for her."*

MABEL DODGE LUHAN
1879–1962

Mabel Dodge Luhan in 1930. "I visualized the scene I had left, the darkened room, the 'fire,' the Peyote Path, and the Mountain of the Moon. I saw, in my mind's eye, the three people sitting there absorbed, unheeding, lost."

Mabel Dodge Luhan, strong-willed heiress, literary patron, and indefatigable avant-gardist, was the first person to record a peyote ceremony in white America—in New York's Greenwich Village on the eve of World War I. The peyote religion, which had spread among the beleaguered Plains Indian tribes in the late nineteenth century, was considered diabolic and was forcibly suppressed by the government. The Harrison Narcotics Act, outlawing the nonmedical use of drugs, was passed by Congress the same year (1914) as Mabel's peyote party. This contributed to the paranoia of the host and several guests.

In *Movers and Shakers*, each participant in this "experiment with consciousness" is beautifully delineated, and his or her reactions, ranging from the ludicrous to the profound, are representative of any random group taking a psychedelic substance for the first time. Mabel attempts to maintain her self-control by refusing to eat the second peyote button offered, but freaks out when reminded she is hosting a dope party of which the press might hear. An anthropologist, anarchist, and society doctor who calms the hysteria are among the Bohemians who make this peyote meeting memorable in American social history.

The second peyote button Mabel did not eat that night turned up in her life five or six years later. Ironically, it was the destiny of this woman for whom peyote was a frightening, uncontrollable force to marry Tony Luhan, a Pueblo Indian whose "God was in peyote." For Mabel, their different viewpoints "seemed to be a terribly important issue between us, perhaps actually the most important adjustment we had to make." She describes their life in *Edge of Taos Desert*.

Lying ill in an abandoned hotel near Taos, Mabel passively accepted a cup of peyote tea prepared by Luhan and his friend. Ingesting peyote in this form made it more familiar, more palatable; the transition to altered consciousness was smoother. The author's nervous system "shifted like particles in a kaleidoscope"; soon her inner conflicts were resolved and "the whole universe fell into place." Mantric peyote songs guided her through the night. A second cup of tea at dawn returned her full health. Luhan's trip description is very fifties in character and style. She used the term "expansion of consciousness" twenty years before the psychedelic movement.

From Movers and Shakers

During the Spring of 1914 in one of the intervals when Reed was away, I had a strange experience with my friends. Bobby Jones had returned from Germany and was staying in one of the rooms in the back end of the apartment on Ninth Street, Andrew was in and out all the time, and Genevieve Onslow was staying for a few days in the other end of the apartment, too. Genevieve had returned from China and was on her way home to Chicago. She was in a highly stimulated mood—full of a mystical elation, and scraps of Chinese philosophy fell from her occasionally.

"If you *want* to do a thing, Mabel, don't do it, but if you *feel* to do it, do it," she would exclaim. But I didn't know what she meant.

The Hapgoods had a cousin staying with them, Raymond Harrington. He had been living among the Indians in Oklahoma doing ethnological research. He looked rather strange and had sunken eyes and an intense expression. I had never seen any Indians, but I told the Hapgoods that I thought he looked like one and they agreed.

Now Raymond told us about a peculiar ceremony among the Indians he lived with that enabled them to pass beyond ordinary consciousness and see things as they are in Reality. He said they used an Indian medicine called *peyote* in the ceremony, and sang all night long. He told us that the Indians that belonged to the Peyote Cult were the most sober and industrious of all, that they made better beadwork and seemed to be able to recover old designs through their use of the stuff and to become imbued with a nobility and a religious fervor greater than those who didn't use it.

We were all most curious about it and begged him to tell us more. When I pressed him, I found he actually had some *peyote* with him; then of course I said we must all try it. But he was grave and said it was not a thing to play with, that if we would go through with it seriously he would try to reconstruct the ceremony for us and give us an opportunity of experiencing the magnificent enhancement and enlargement of consciousness possible only through its power. It was not like hashish or any other drug, he said. In fact, it was not a drug at all, but a marvelous vehicle of the Indian life enabling one to be more deeply and wholly and concisely what one inherently was when not inhibited and overlaid by the limitations of the senses we used every day.

We were all thrilled.

Certain things were necessary to the ceremony, Raymond said. We must have a green arrow, some eagle feathers, a fire, the Mountain of the Moon, and the Peyote Path. All these he must procure or simulate to compose the structure of the experience. Then there would have to be singing. The singing must never cease all through the ritual. One or another of us must always be singing, taking up the song as another left off. And we must enter the event after fasting, and continue all night until the morning star arose, when we could break our fast with fruit juice and then eat.

Raymond himself was very serious as he told us about it, almost somber, seeming wholly a convert to the practice. We grew serious, too, and tried to carry it all out as he desired. We decided to ask Max Eastman and Ida to come because Ida was a friend of Genevieve's; and we were to have Andrew, Bobby, the Hapgoods, and Terry.

Terry was a grand anarchist, possessing a beautiful skeleton, a splendid head with noble features, a great quantity of iron gray hair and Irish blue eyes. He was a literal I.W.W. and a true anarchist. When he was a young man he passed up the capitalistic system and swore he would never take a job or do a day's work under it, and he had carried out his vow. He was incredibly poor, thin to starvation, for he was nearly always hungry, but he never did an hour's work for anyone or "earned" a dollar. He was a splendid talker, a dreamer, a poet, a man. Wonderful Terry! Mukerji has written of him in *Caste and Outcast*. In that book he was Jerry, one of Mukerji's two companions in San Francisco; but Mukerji had not the depth to reach, himself, to Terry's deep levels.

Raymond went out and found a green branch to make the arrow, and he found the eagle feathers. For a "fire" he laid a lighted electric bulb on the floor with my Chinese red shawl over it, and for the Mountain of the Moon—I forget what he did about that—but the Peyote Path was a white sheet folded into a narrow strip, running towards the east along the floor.

The evening we were to engage ourselves to experiment with consciousness, none of us ate any dinner. We, at Raymond's order, had dressed in our best, and the room had been thoroughly cleaned beforehand. Everything had to be tuned up a little for this, evidently—all of the accessories and surroundings must be of the finest and cleanest, the most shining. Like Church, I thought to myself.

At nine o'clock we extinguished the lights and sat on the floor in a crescent shape with the Peyote Path running eastward out of our midst. Raymond, who constituted himself the Chief, sat at the foot of the path behind the fire, an arrow in one hand, and a few lovely eagle feathers in the other. The *peyote* lay in a little heap in the center of the space before him. It looked like small, dried-up buttons with shriveled edges, and it had a kind of fur on the upper side.

Raymond told us to just take it and chew it, as many as we liked—but, once we began the Ceremony, to beware of stopping before it was over, when the Morning Star should rise. He looked so somber sitting there cross-legged that I was filled to bursting with sudden laughter. I was thrilled and excited and amused.

Suddenly Raymond seized a piece of the *peyote* and popped it into his mouth and began to sing. At last he raised his chin and began to howl like a dog, as it seemed to me. I looked covertly at the others.

The mere presence of that *peyote* seemed already to have emphasized the real nature in us all. I was laughing, but Neith looked down at the fire, distantly grave and withdrawn, beautiful and strange. Hutch appeared rather boyish, like a boy in church who lowers his head and peeps over his prayer book at another boy. Bobby's face was stimulating a respectful attention, while it hid his thoughts. Ida looked more like a superior lioness than ever, cynical and intolerant; Max grinned amiably, complacent and friendly to anything, and Terry seemed more remote than the others—as he

contemplated the end of his cigarette (for cigarettes were *de rigueur* and, in fact, compulsory, I believe).

Genevieve Onslow's frog-like eyes were brilliant and intense. Her thin face looked like parchment. Andrew's brows twitched as he gave and yet did not give himself to the occasion; a half smile played over his sulky lips, but it was an irritated smile. Only I seemed to myself to be just exactly as usual, unaffected by anything and observant of it all.

Raymond chewed on his *peyote* and sang his song that was like the howl of a dog. He swung the tempo faster and motioned to us to begin.

Then we all, in our different fashions, reached out and took the *peyote* and put it into our mouths, and began to chew upon it. But it was bitter! Oh, how it was bitter! I chewed for a little while and watched the others. They all seemed to be chewing away, too. Everybody chewed.

But after a while, as I swallowed the bitter saliva, I felt a certain numbness coming over me in my mouth and limbs. But it was only over my body. My brain was clearly filled with laughter! Laughter, laughter, laughter at all the others there. Laughter, and at the same time a canny, almost smug discretion took possession of me.

When Raymond had chewed up his first *peyote*, and the others had all chewed theirs, he, still singing, handed his green arrow to the one who sat on his right hand, and motioned him to sing, and motioned to us all to take another *peyote* with him.

Raymond's unfortunate neighbor didn't know how to sing Indian songs. Raymond, with an urgently anxious look on his face, continued to sing himself, as he beckoned the other to sing. Evidently he *must* sing—it was frightfully important.

Raymond impressed this need so acutely that Hutch (it was Hutch!) actually lifted up his voice—and popping a *peyote* into his mouth, sat with the green arrow in a hieratical pose, and howled in a disjointed and unrhythmical way that, however, did not seem unpleasant to Raymond. It was evidently not so much the *way* you did a thing, it was that you *did* it, that counted.

Presently, I raised a *peyote* to my mouth, made a movement with my lips, and, prudently, I secreted it deeper into the palm of my hand. Shaking with ghoulish laughter, I held it until my first move to take it was forgotten, and then I thrust it behind me on the floor. But the others chewed and chewed on their second *peyote*, and each of them had sunk just a little deeper into themselves—had become a trifle *more* themselves. . . .

Useless to describe the slow inward progress of the *peyote*. On the surface everything remained the same. Forgetting self-consciousness in a deepened being, each one sang in his turn. Some time after the second *peyote*, Max and Ida got up and left almost unnoticed. My one and only taste had started me laughing and the laughter endured. Everyone seemed ridiculous to me—utterly ridiculous and immeasurably far away from me. Far away from me, several little foolish human beings sat staring at a mock fire and made silly little gestures. Above them I leaned, filled with an unlimited contempt for the facile enthrallments of humanity, weak and petty in its activities, bound so easily by a dried herb, bound by its notions of everything—anarchy, poetry, systems, sex and society.

Bobby! Look at Bobby's beard! Like a Persian miniature of a late period, not well drawn, inexpressive, he rolled subjugated eyes, increasingly solemn as he viewed the changing colors unrolling before him. And Hutch! Good heavens! Hutch looked like a Lutheran monk! Genevieve stared continually at a spot on the rug before her, her eyes enormous now, the whites showing all round them in an appalled revelation of something.

But Terry! Almost I stopped laughing when I looked at Terry, for he had increased in stature. His head was huge, and clear cut, every bone in his face, as he looked with a terrible intensity of Seeing at the lighted end of his cigarette. No, I could not laugh at Terry. He frightened me a little.

Another thing that was noticeable was the eerie effect upon everyone's expression from the dim light of the "fire," that electric globe smoldering under the red shawl. It reminded me of the ghastly results we used to procure as children by having two of us stare fixedly at each other, while another turned the gas jet up and then lowered it; continuing thus, we were able to induce the most devilish expressions, with deathly shades of color that fluctuated with the varying light. So now, although the light was fixed, though dim, it seemed that various and strange changes came over the faces before me.

The night wore on, and a more and more peculiar atmosphere enclosed us. The songs kept up—monotonous and outlandish, and gradually my laughter wore itself out and I grew weary and longed to leave. For me to long to leave was but a signal for my departure, for I was an impatient soul—undisciplined. I began to whisper and make signs, nodding my head towards my bedroom, and most of the others, I discovered, were as ready as I to go. As inconspicuously as possible, then, the Hapgoods, Bobby and Andrew and I rose—and stood—looking at the others.

But the others were oblivious. Harrington, Terry and Genevieve continued their fixedness of attention upon other worlds than ours. They were lost to us. They did not see us or take any notice of us at all. We crept off to bed, I to my white room at the far end of the suite, the Hapgoods, Andrew and Bobby out through the kitchen to the little bedrooms beyond in the Ninth Street part of the apartment.

After I was in bed I lay still and listened. The weird song from the front room came only in a faraway, muffled fashion through my closed door. I visualized the scene I had left, the darkened room, the "fire," the Peyote Path, and the Mountain of the Moon. I saw, in my mind's eye, the three people sitting there absorbed, unheeding, lost.

And my mind grew angry all of a sudden. Very angry! To think that that was going on there in my house and *I could not stop it* if I wanted to! Until this thought came to me, I had not particularly wanted to stop it, but as soon as I did think of it, it frightened me by its intensity. It was not so much that something was going on, but that something was going on *in my house* that I could not stop even if I wanted to. And instantly, because this was the case, I wanted terribly to stop it. I *must* stop it! But how?

Nothing could reach those entranced people. They were gone! Gone into the *peyote* world and I did not know how to follow them and bring them back. I grew more and more angry and more in a panic than ever before in my life, except, perhaps, that time at Aunt Clarissa's on Staten Island.

How could I stop that thing?

I began to throw all my attention into praying, with the fullest concentration and passion of which I was capable—praying to It—to that Force in which I believed and which I thought I knew how to contact.

"Oh, Great Force, hear me! Stop that thing in there! *Stop it!* STOP IT!" I breathed my whole being into my prayer.

And as I prayed I heard in the distance—further away than the muffled chant—a sound of steps, of hobbling, hasty steps, and the tap of a cane, coming nearer and nearer through the silent house. I held my breath. The hurried steps came nearer and nearer—they were coming from the other end of the house. I recognized them. Only Andrew sounded like that. I had summoned him. Let anyone, who doubts these possibilities, try once with power and passion to invoke the Force that lies about us.

I lay scarcely breathing now and waited for him to carry out my prayer, and I heard him stamp as though in a fury, past my door, through the dining room and the next room, to where I knew the three others sat cross-legged and oblivious on the floor, enwrapped in another consciousness than his.

I listened to him "stop" that thing. I heard him trampling heavily about, uttering short, angry words; I heard the windows thrown up, and I heard—what was that?—something like a dreadful cry of anguish. An instant's silence, and then a tapping at my door.

I turned on the electric light and I jumped out of bed and rushed to open it a crack. Genevieve stood there. Her face gleamed almost phosphorescent, her large eyes, showing the whites all round them, glared at me.

"Mabel!" she gasped. "Oh, Mabel! It is *terrible*," and she was gone.

I flung on a dressing gown and ran out. Andrew was lurching around the room with a furious face—looking like an avenging angel, striking his cane into the red shawl that lay in a heap, at the white sheet that had been the "path," and at the few

peyotes that were scattered, now, about the floor.

Terry sat gazing fixedly at the end of his cigarette—but Harrington looked about him dazed and horrified.

"Stop, man! That is terribly dangerous!" he said over and over as I came in.

When Andrew saw me, he cried:

"After I got to bed I suddenly felt I couldn't stand having this thing going on any more! I *had* to break it up."

"Where is Genevieve?" I cried.

But she was gone.

While I went to call Hutch and Neith and tell them what had happened, Harrington sat like a haunted, helpless creature in a corner of a sofa and Terry, moved now to the little room off the drawing room, sat serene and attentive, always gazing at the end of his cigarette.

Genevieve was gone. There was no doubt about that. We hunted the rooms for her, but she had fled like a phantom out of the apartment, down the stairs and out—out—

Where?

And now we entered upon the second phase of that crazy night.

The thought of Genevieve out in the windy streets of the city was unthinkable, the condition she was in—unaccountable for herself—unable to explain anything—not even knowing where she was—it frightened us all. We didn't know where to look for her—where to go first should one of us start out after her.

I saw Hutch fumbling on his hands and knees behind a chair and went to look closer and ask what on earth he was doing. He gave me a queer look. He was gathering up bits of *peyote*—whole ones and the broken ones I had thrust behind me.

"If the *Police* should come in here and find this . . ."

Police! Heavens, I *was* scared!

Harrington, muttering to himself in a corner, seemed not to be with us at all—no more did Terry, sitting alone and smiling down at his cigarette. Hutch and Neith and I and Andrew—we were the only ones to deal with the situation and we hadn't the remotest idea where to begin.

A sharp ring at the telephone startled us all. I ran to answer it and it was Max.

"Genevieve is here," he said. "We heard her crying under the window."

"How *is* she?" I cried.

"Well, I don't know. We will put her to bed and see you in the morning."

The sickening light of dawn began to creep into the rooms and show up the strange disorder about us. Furniture displaced, the red shawl and the white sheet lying on the floor. And two men with white faces with us, but not of us.

The fear about Genevieve somewhat allayed, we turned back to the *peyote*—that most mysterious of all the growing things that I had ever encountered.

Hutch, lowering his voice, came up and spoke to me. I noticed he had altered. He appeared diminished and shrunken as though he had lost fifty pounds of flesh. He was pale and he looked awed.

"Mabel," he said, "I have learned tonight something wonderful. I cannot put it into words exactly, but I have found the short cut to the Soul."

"What is it?" I asked.

"The death of the flesh," he almost whispered, and I saw from his eyes that the *peyote* in him lent a far deeper significance to the words for him than for me.

"I *saw* it," he went on. "I saw the death of the flesh occur in my body and I saw the Soul emerge from that death."

"I saw no such thing," said Neith, smiling with a beautiful strangeness. "As I sat there, I saw the walls of this house fall away and I was following a lovely river for miles and miles through the most wonderful virginal forest I have ever known." She was elated and enhanced.

"I saw what Sex is," Andrew broke in. "And it is a square crystal cube, transparent and colorless; and at the same time I saw that I was looking at my Soul."

Then Harrington sprang up. In the early cold light of the morning his face was greenish and his eyes stared horrified.

"I can't breathe," he gasped. "My heart— Get

me something. Some fruit . . ."

Scared, I ran into the kitchen looking for some oranges. When I came back Hutch was bending over him.

"It is like a palpitation," he said.

And Terry sat on—smiling, not hearing or seeing us—just gazing down at his cigarette.

"If only the *day* would come," I exclaimed. "And the cook and breakfast and everything!"

From Edge of Taos Desert

All day as we slowly wound our way up the Hondo road, back and forth, over nine bridges, crossing the cold, rough stream again and again, I felt weak, and I could hardly hold myself upright on my horse, but Tony was solicitous and tried to make me forget myself by calling my attention to the red-winged birds that flitted into the shadows, or the brightly singing invisible birds in the higher branches. Once he dismounted and gathered a few huge mauve columbines and brought them to me and they were like large butterflies.

When we finally reached Twining at four o'clock, it was raining again and all I wanted on earth was to lie down.

The old white abandoned hotel was there, empty, and Tony and Juan Concha helped me into it while the others unpacked. They spread blankets on the floor and I lay down gratefully. Tony went out to look for Jack Bidwell but he was away that day.

I don't know how long I lay there. The others came in to see me once in a while, but I told them I was really all right, only very tired, and they left me to myself. There were fires to be made and cabins to choose for themselves, empty and windowless but dry, and then supper had to be cooked. The quiet, persistent rain made a soft, soothing whisper on the roof and I was comfortable enough.

Finally Tony and Juan Concha appeared, carrying a lighted lantern. Juan Concha knelt down beside me and offered me a tin cup, saying, "Here. Drink this. Help you."

"What is it?" I asked them, raising up on my elbow.

"Medicine Juan fix for you. Better drink," Tony told me.

I would do anything he told me to do, and I obediently took the cup from the gentle, solicitous figure bending over me and drained it. It was very hot and bitter. "What *is* it?" I sputtered.

"The medicine," Tony said gravely.

Peyote! Well!!

Tony arranged the blanket so it covered me up and then they, too, left me to myself. Immediately the Indian singing commenced out beside the fire.

The medicine ran through me, penetratingly. It acted like an organizing medium co-ordinating one part with another, so all the elements that were combined in me shifted like the particles in a kaleidoscope and fell into an orderly pattern. Beginning with the inmost central point in my own organism, the whole universe fell into place; I in the room and the room I was in, the old building containing the room, the cool wet night space where the building stood, and all the mountains standing out like sentries in their everlasting attitudes. So on and on into wider spaces farther than I could divine, where all the heavenly bodies were contented with the order of the plan, and system within system interlocked in grace. I was not separate and isolated any more. The magical drink had revealed the irresistible delight of spiritual composition; the regulated relationship of one to all and all to one.

Was it this, I wondered, something like this, that *artists* are perpetually trying to find and project upon their canvases? Was this what musicians imagine and try to formulate? Significant Form!

I laughed there alone in the dark, remembering the favorite phrase that had seemed so hackneyed for a long time and that I had never really understood. Significant form, I whispered; why, that means that all things are *really* related to each other.

These words had an enormous vitality and importance when I said them, more than they ever had afterwards when from time to time I approximately understood and realized their secret meaning after I relapsed into the usual dream-like state of everyday life.

The singing filled the night and I perceived its design which was written upon the darkness in color that made an intricate pictured pattern, not static like one that is painted but organic and moving like blood currents, and composed of a myriad of bright living cells. These cells were like minute flowers or crystals and they vibrated constantly in their rank and circumstance, no one of them falling out of place, for the order of the whole was held together by the interdependence of each infinitesimal spark. And I learned that there is no single equilibrium anywhere in existence, and that the meaning and essence of balance is that it depends upon neighboring organisms, one leaning upon the other, one touching another, holding together, reinforcing the whole, creating form and defeating chaos which is the hellish realm of unattached and unassimilated atoms.

A full realization of all this broke upon me in a new way not just apprehended as an idea but experienced in my body, so that oddly I felt that the singing and the pattern that it was composed of was also the description of my own organism and all other people's, and it was my blood that sang and my tissues that vibrated upon the ether, making a picture and a design. There was such a consolation in this discovery that I was strengthened and raised up, and I got to my feet and went out to the others.

The abandoned little village was all lighted and rosy, the flames of the big campfire ran high and showed up the farthest cabins with dim trees standing behind them, and there was a circle of people lying and sitting in the firelight.

The Indians sat upright, shoulder to shoulder, and their voices were perfectly in unison. They sang a phrase repeatedly, over and over until the waves of it spread rapidly out from them one after another and the surrounding night became filled with it. When it was packed and complete, they changed the phrase.

The waves of their living power ran out from them upon the vehicle of sound. They penetrated and passed through each listener, altering him a little, shaking old dead compactnesses of matter apart, awakening the paralyzed tissues. This kind of singing is mantric and has a magical influence. No one can lay himself open to it and not be imperceptibly altered by it. Few know and realize this, however; people constantly play in dangerously magnetic neighborhoods and never know what is happening to them.

I wrapped myself in my shawl and sat upon a log. Tony's eyes fell upon me across the blaze but they did not linger and he made no sign. I felt a vast peace all through me and a sense of secret knowledge.

Though I had just had a lesson in the invisible coherence of all human beings, it did not seem illogical that I felt entirely separated from the others out here. There was a new faculty of detachment from them dawning upon me, a different kind from the solitary, unbalanced attitude which was the only one I had ever known. It is difficult to define. There was the beginning of objectivity in it, a realization of our oneness and dependence upon all others, with, at the same time, the realization of the need for withdrawal, for independence, for non-identification with the mass. In a new dimension one might, nay must, realize that one is related to and identified with this universe and all its aspects, and yet that one must become more than that, more than a bright neighborly cell in the great organism. One must know that one is that cell, seeing it flash, and sensing the quiver and vibration of being, one must observe and keep the order of creation, always understanding one is a part of that scheme, but the step beyond is to know that one is also more than that, and in the strict detachment from organic life that characterizes the new-born observer, he watches himself functioning as a material cell, and by this detachment he draws the material to nourish the infant soul up out of the observed activity of the organism. How this flash of revelation worked out into fact and substance took twenty years of living to be proved a reality.

The Indians sang for many hours until one by one our party slipped away, but I sat sleepless all night and I felt fresh and made over when morning came.

That long, wakeful night was the most clarifying I had ever had, and the momentary glimpse of life I was given by an expansion of consciousness always remained with me, though it was often forgotten.

HOPHEADS, SNOWBIRDS, AND VIPERS IN SONG

The folk traditions of drug undergrounds have been expressed in ballads. "The Girl in the Blue Velvet Band" and "Cocaine Lil" probably date to the period from 1900 to 1920. By the thirties songs about reefer, hop, and snow were in the repertoires of most jazz bands. Writer Maya Angelou remembers that her mother often sang a popular song, Rosetta Howard's "If You're a Viper," "that at its worst didn't condemn grass, and at its best extolled it."

The Girl in the Blue Velvet Band
(Opening Stanzas)

In that city of wealth, beauty and fashion,
　　Dear old 'Frisco, where I first saw the light,
And the many frolics that I had there
　　Are still in my memory to-night.

One evening while out for a ramble,
　　Here or there, without thought or design,
I chanced on a girl tall and slender,
　　At the corner of Kearney and Pine.

To a house where they ruined you gently
　　She invited me with a sweet smile;
She seemed so refined, gay, and charming
　　That I thought I would tarry awhile.

After lunch, to a well-kept apartment
　　We repaired, to the third floor above;
And I thought myself truly in heaven
　　With a wonderful Goddess of Love.

My lady's taste was resplendent,
　　From the graceful arrangement of things,
From the pictures that stood on the bureau
　　To the little bronze Cupid with wings.

But what struck me most were some objects
    Designed by an artistic hand;
'Twas the costly lay-out of a hop fiend,
    And that fiend was my Blue Velvet Band.

On a pile of soft cushions and pillows
    She reclined, and I lay on the floor;
Then we both smoked the pipe and I dreamed
       there,
    And I dreamed again, over and o'er.

It is months since the craven arm grasped me,
    And in bliss did my life glide away,
From doping and drugs, then to thieving,
    She artfully led me astray.

Cocaine Lil

Did you ever hear about Cocaine Lil?
She lived in Cocaine Town up on Cocaine
    Hill.
She had a heroin dog and a morphine cat
Which fought all night with an opium rat.

She had cocaine hair on her heroin head;
She had a crimson dress that was poppy red;
She wore a snow-white hat and sleigh-riding
    clothes,
And on her coat she wore a morphine rose.

She had big gold chariots on the Milky Way,
With snakes and elephants blue and grey.
Oh, the cocaine blues made her feel sad,
And the cocaine blues they drove her mad.

She went to a snow party one cold night,
And the way she sniffs—she was soon alight.
There was Hop-head Mag with Dopy Slim
And Kanakee Liz and Yen-shi Jim.

There was Morphine Sue and the Peach-Faced
    Kid,
Climbing up snow ladders, which down they
    slid.
There was lofty Sadie, tall, a good six feet,
And a sleigh-riding sister who was hard to beat.

Two opium drawings by Alexander King, 1929

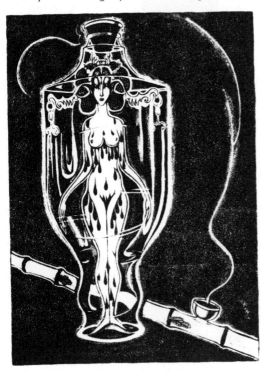

Cocaine Lil

Along in the morning at half-past three
They were all lit up like a Christmas tree;
And so Lil got home and went into bed:
She took another sniff and it knocked her dead.

They laid her out in her cocaine clothes.
She wore a snowbird hat with a crimson rose;
On her tombstone you'll find this refrain:
"She died as she lived—sniffing cocaine."

If You're a Viper

ROSETTA HOWARD

Dreamed about a reefer five feet long
Mighty immense but not too strong

You'll be high but not for long
If you're a viper

I'm the king of everything
I gotta be high before I can swing
Light a tea and let it be
If you're a viper

When your throat gets dry and you know you're
   high
Everything is dandy
Truck on down to the candy store
Blow your top on peppermint candy

Then you know your body is sent
You don't care if you don't pay the rent
The sky is high and so am I
If you're a viper

WHITE LADY

Best-selling drug novel of the twenties.
This 1921 Italian novel was
translated into French, Spanish,
German, and English.

Characters from Pitigrilli's Cocaine, by Jim Osborne.
The notorious Madam Katlantan Ter-Gregorianz,
"an Armenian who lives at the Porte Maillot and is
very famous for her white orgies."

MINA LOY
1882–1966

British Mina Loy was a leading imagist poet of the twenties. The title poem of her first and best-known collection, *Lunar Baedeker* (1923), is one of the most perfect poems of drug-heightened perception ever written. "The essence of her style is its directness," wrote William Carlos Williams. No drug is more characterized by its directness than cocaine, the qualities of which give surrealistic perspective to the glittering images of the poem.

Loy had two daughters, one by the Dadaist poet and prizefighter Arthur Cravan. She lived into the 1960's, long enough to see a strong revival of her work.

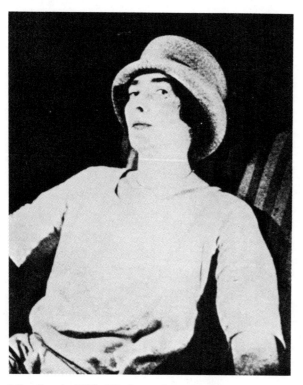

Mina Loy in 1920. "Cyclones of ecstatic dust"

Lunar Baedeker

A silver Lucifer
serves
cocaine in cornucopia

To some somnambulists
of adolescent thighs
draped
in satirical draperies

Peris in livery
prepare
Lethe
for posthumous parvenues

Delirious Avenues
lit
with the chandelier souls
of infusoria
from Pharaoh's tombstones

lead
to mercurial doomsdays
Odious oasis
in furrowed phosphorous

the eye-white sky-light
white-light district
of lunar lusts

            Stellectric signs
"Wing shows on Starway"
"Zodiac carrousel"

Cyclones
of ecstatic dust
and ashes whirl
crusaders
from hallucinatory citadels
of shattered glass
into evacuate craters

A flock of dreams
browse on Necropolis

*Drawing by Mahlon Blaine, 1929.
"Illumined strangely—/appalling sister!"
(Baroness Freytag-Loringhoven).*

From the shores
of oval oceans
in the oxidized Orient

Onyx-eyed Odalisques
and ornithologists
observe
the flight
of Eros obsolete

And "Immortality"
mildews . . .
in the museums of the moon

"Nocturnal cyclops"
"Crystal concubine"

Pocked with personification
the fossil virgin of the skies
waxes and wanes

BARONESS ELSE VON FREYTAG-LORINGHOVEN
1874–1927

"If there was ever a one-man or one-woman happening, it was the Baroness," wrote poet Kenneth Rexroth. "She smoked marijuana in a big china German pipe that must have held half an ounce or more."

German poet Else von Freytag-Loringhoven published in English literary magazines during the mid-1920's. Her poems sometimes sound like utterances of a modern Delphic oracle. "Appalling Heart" shows how marijuana opened up all her senses.

Baroness Loringhoven nearly starved to death while selling newspapers on Berlin street corners before going to Paris, where she died by her own hand. "She is not a Futurist," said her friend Marcel Duchamp. "She is the future." This was as true of her style of dress as it was of her visionary poems. She attended balls with postage stamps decorating her face and wearing a girdle of kitchen utensils—a New Wave fashion leader fifty years ahead of her time.

Appalling Heart

City stir—wind on eardrum—
dancewind: herbstained—
flowerstained—silken—rustling—
tripping—swishing—frolicking—
courtesing—careening—brushing—
flowing—lying down—bending—
teasing—kissing: treearms—grass—
limbs—lips.
City stir on eardrum—.
In night lonely
peers—:
moon—riding!
pale—with beauty aghast—
too exalted to share!
in space blue—rides she away from mine chest—
illumined strangely—
appalling sister!

Herbstained—flowerstained—
shellscented—seafaring—
foresthunting—junglewise—
desert gazing—
rides heart from chest—
lashing with beauty—
afleet—
across chimney—
tinfoil river
to meet
another's dark heart!

Bless mine feet!

CARESSE CROSBY
1892–1970

Caresse and Harry Crosby played key roles in the expatriate literary scene that flourished in Paris after World War I. Their Black Sun Press published important works by James Joyce and D. H. Lawrence, among others. The Crosbys were equally renowned for their lavish parties and their trend-setting hedonic lives.

"The Poppy Merchant" by Georges Barbier, 1921. "Another deep breath and the soft clouds wooed one's body, winding and unwinding its spell, holding one in a web of lustless rapture" (Caresse Crosby).

Caresse Crosby in 1927. "We stepped in upon a scene from the Arabian Nights."

Harry's recently published diaries show that, prior to his suicide in 1930, he experimented with every drug available. The memoirs of Caresse show her to have been curious about drugs but more restrained. Two episodes are recounted in her book *The Passionate Years*: a bout of hashish smoking with Kurd shepherds in Istanbul, and a visit, reprinted here, to an exclusive Parisian opium den exhibiting the decadent glamour of a Barbier print. The author deftly describes the *Arabian Nights* decor, the other smokers, the ritual of the pipe, and the effects of the poppy, "holding one in a web of lustless rapture."

From The Passionate Years

One night that winter the Lady of the Golden Horse, as Harry called her, because she wore one on her wrist, appeared at our doorway in the rue de Lille just as we were about to turn out the lights. She was wrapped in a mysteriously dark cloak and her eyes had a look of childish fear and anticipation that enticed one to follow her even against one's better sense. "You must come with me," she said, looking furtively over her shoulder. "Everything is arranged—Pierre will meet us there."

"Where?" we asked.

"At Drosso's," she almost hissed. Harry and I, who were already undressed, leapt for our clothes. In one minute we were ready. I had put on a loose silver-grey dress, nothing under it and my big squirrel coat over it. Colours and fabrics and comfort would be important. We let ourselves out without waking the household and scurried across the murky courtyard.

The chauffeur tucked the monkey rug around our knees and we turned northward toward the Bois. "We will get out around the corner," Constance whispered. "The place is sometimes watched." Harry held my hand in his. We had smoked once before, but not at Drosso's. This was the one place in all Paris where the sumptuous rapture of the East was evoked by the ease and luxury of the surroundings. Only a few habitués and an occasional new friend (we had met D at the races) were admitted. The ritual of the pipe was observed in its most sybaritic manner. No dissenting note ever ruffled the trance-like surface of one's "Kief."

We left the car around the corner and Harry made sure that no watcher lurked in the shadows of the chestnut trees. We pushed the iron grille of No. 30 and entered the vestibule like thieves. After we had tapped on the glass as instructed, the door swung open and we followed the tiny Chinese servant down a blacked-out passage. There was a tinkle of temple bells and through the folds of a heavy curtain, we stepped in upon a scene from the Arabian Nights. The apartment was a series of small fantastic rooms, large satin divans heaped with pillows, walls covered with gold-embroidered arras, in the centre of each room a low round stand on which was ranged all the paraphernalia of the pipe. By the side of each table, in coolie dress, squatted a little servant of the lamp. The air was sweet with the smell of opium.

We were shown first into an undressing room where one could choose one's own kimono and slip one's toes into soft glove-like sandals. Our host always wore one with a huge red and gold butterfly across the back; we called him "Monsieur Papillon." He looked like an insect with gaudy wings that were attached to a dry little body.

Pierre was waiting at ease, stretched out on a big black divan, one arm around a tiny French woman whose poppy-filled head drowsed against his heart. He did not stir but drew Constance down to snuggle at his other side. Harry and I found a place among the pillows near them. Drosso came to crouch at our feet, followed by a servant carrying a tray holding candied rose petals and tiny bubble-like cups of tea.

"We will prepare the next pipe for you," he promised. I settled back in Harry's arms to wait and watch. The pellet of black magic is rolled deftly between the ends of the long spatula-like needle; it is roasted in the flame of the tiny lamp until it glows red-hot; then it is wheedled into position on the flat porcelain or metal bowl of the pipe; ours was of jade and bamboo.

*   *   *

My pipe was ready now. It was handed to me and I crouched above the tray. I drew the sweet smoke deeply into my lungs, then very slowly exhaled and breathed again. With each indrawn breath, the little pellet glowed; cooled by the long jade stem, the smoke seeped into the crannies of one's heart. Another deep breath and the soft clouds wooed one's body, winding and unwinding its spell, holding one in a web of lustless rapture. Smiling, one relaxed and drowsed, another's arms about one, it mattered little whose.

Two pipes sufficed me, although the others smoked several. The night passed in confidence. When the first rays of light pierced the iron shutters, we rose to go. It was like dragging chains to

leave that couch. Once out in the dawn-lit street, I felt sick and dizzy; so sick I had to lean against the outer wall while Harry went to find a taxi. It seemed as if I stayed there for days, clinging to those topless heights—then into the swaying cab, held tight, and home to a hot bath and to bed for a little sleep and a huge breakfast. I awoke with the appetite of a lioness and sang all that day.

For eighteen years I kept a blob of the sticky substance in a little silver *bonbonnière* on my dressing table, and when I wished to evoke visions of long past joys, I would take it out, heat it ever so slightly under the hot water tap, and sniff the poppy dream. At last, my zealous maid went on a silver-cleaning jag while I was out of town. When I returned home, everything shone dazzlingly clean, including the inside of my *bonbonnière!* Now I must close my eyes to see again, *fermer les yeux pour voir.* I have never craved the drug but I am glad that visions remain.

O.W.

The anonymous O.W.'s *No Bed of Roses* (1930) was the first best-selling book of drug memoirs written by a woman. It married the drug confession genre to the emerging modern sociological viewpoint. The timing couldn't have been better: the Depression had begun, Prohibition was about to end, and the drug abuser was the new epitome of the failed American.

No literary masterpiece, but unmistakably authentic, *No Bed of Roses* remained in print for twenty years and spawned two successful sequels, one written by O.W.'s daughter. The author describes her descent into drug addiction with the swagger of a latter-day Moll Flanders. Excerpted here is her solo cocaine "bat" in a Manhattan hotel room ending in paranoid hallucinations;

1930 drug confession best seller

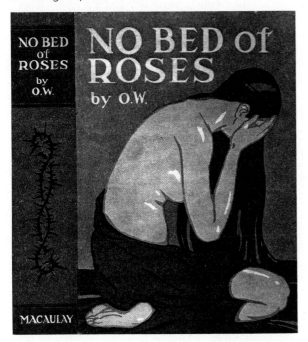

her subsequent stay in Bellevue Hospital's psychopathic ward; and her commitment to "a very exclusive sanitarium" in Connecticut.

From No Bed of Roses:
The Diary of a Lost Soul

I hunted up Dante Biano, and bummed ten decks of cocaine out of him. I told him it was for Stella and her sweetheart, who were going on a bat. The order was a large one, and I knew he wouldn't give it to me, if he thought I wanted to use it myself. I said that I would pay him when I got the money from them. I got away with this lie because Dante was going out of town for a vacation, and he wouldn't find out. He knew I was absolutely honest and would pay him, if I had to hock my hat. But I wasn't sure of having the money this time. I might be dead, even, when he returned, who knows?

I came back to my hotel, and started using it in large quantities . . . staggering quantities, but I must have been on the verge of insanity. Somewhere back in my head I knew that it would be

disastrous, but I didn't care. Deep down in my heart, I guess, I hoped it would be fatal. For about three nights, I used the stuff regardless. All sorts of queer things happened to me.

Finally, I locked myself in my room, and phoned the clerk I was not to be disturbed under any circumstances. I tried to sleep, but that was impossible. I thought if I took a hot bath, I would grow weary, and drop off to sleep. I drew a tub of scalding water and got into it.

Then my mind seemed to crack completely. I thought I could hear Marian and her sister in the other room, and they were both supposed to be in Philadelphia. I called to the maid, who was outside in the hall, and asked her who was in my room. She swore that nobody was there, and I denounced her terribly. I said she was lying to me, as I could hear them, and she ran out of the room screaming. My appearance must have frightened her.

After she had gone, the voices continued. I could plainly hear many people singing and laughing. I listened closer to make sure. Then great searchlights were thrown upon my window, sweeping through the glass and flooding the room with light. I was conscious of being naked, and I was afraid to go to the window. The lights played back and forth across the room until I thought I would go mad.

I crouched deeper into the hot water. My body turned to ice. I screamed in terror. I beat my fists against the sides of the tub, and tried to hide myself from the powerful rays. Everywhere I turned they followed me. Everywhere I looked jeering men and women stared into my very soul, and pointed scornful fingers at me. They grouped about, demanding money, and threatening me when I swore I had none. Jackson yelled for the furniture money, and I said I had nothing, not even clothes to cover me.

Cold chills ran up and down my spine. I screamed for Morton to come and take me from these people, but he laughed at me. I screamed for Guardie to take me home, away from those awful lights, but he wouldn't come to me. I called to God, to Jesus, to the saints, but no one heard me.

Suddenly the lights stopped moving through the room, but I could hear Marian's sister in the hall, telling a bunch of detectives about me. Angelina and her gang were there, too, putting in the worst words for me. Every one said that I was a bad woman, and should be stoned to death. The detectives said I would be thrown in jail. I ran into the closet and hid under some old newspapers.

I heard them all getting out onto the fire escapes, and come breaking into my room. I ran from the closet, and sat on the bath stool, crying my eyes out. I thought they stood in front of me laughing and joking about my appearance.

I told them they would have to wait until I got dressed and then I would go with them quietly. I looked around for my clothes and couldn't find them. I wrapped myself in a large bath towel. I quickly remembered that I had all my dope in my hand and frantically put it down the toilet and pulled the chain.

On a Cocaine "Bat." "I came back to my hotel, and started using it in . . . staggering quantities" (O.W.).

Then I began stalling and said I was ill. They seemed to laugh at me, and reach to grab me by the throat. I struggled, and kicked and screamed. I asked if I might phone to the doctor, which I did. Then, I left the phone off the hook. Of course, this had all been an hallucination.

However, when the doctor really did come to my room they had to break the door down. I was afraid to open the door. I still thought the place was surrounded by police, and that the detectives were standing in my room. I moaned and carried on. I had phoned to Dr. Stanley, because I knew that he knew I took dope. I wasn't sure whether he would remember me but I took a chance, and thought if he saw me surrounded by policemen, he would do something for me.

He came in, and I learned that everything was in my imagination, and I had been alone all the time. He saw that I was really ill, and he sent for an ambulance. They brought me to the Flower Hospital.

I could hear the people laughing at me as I went down the hall, and all the way to the hospital. I was examined, and was found to be suffering from an overdose of cocaine. All through the night the voices followed me, but I never could see the people. It was a terrifying experience.

* * *

The night nurse was Miss Gray, a talkative creature with a face like a battle-ax. I took one look at her and knew immediately what she was. One nostril was almost entirely eaten away by cocaine. She made no bones about being a doper, so I could talk to her without being afraid. In the office was a big bottle marked "Gray, Morphine Solution." That was hers, and she took shots at certain times. Of course, she was limited, but they gave her enough to keep her comfortable. She could also steal it from the patients, because some of the violently insane were given morphine nightly. Otherwise, they would have kept the whole place awake with their screaming.

Gray was always hopped up to the ears, but she wasn't a bad gal, and I was glad she was on my reception committee.

* * *

The last week I was there they let me go out with Nurse Gray. As she worked nights, the poor thing had to sleep days, but she would get up about three in the afternoon, and we would walk to the general store at Brown's Farms. It was a typical country general store, but had everything in it from a post office to hardware and ice cream. I enjoyed going there.

The first day we went over I thought I would drop dead before I got there. I was still terribly weak, and never could get enough strength to walk long distances. When we did reach the store, I was so exhausted that I dropped into the porch hammock, and simply couldn't move for fifteen minutes.

While I was dozing, my friend Gray, charged to the ears with morphine, was regaling the village youths. There was a gang of them who hung about the store, and wanted everyone to know that they were regular devils. I lay in the hammock, half asleep. She was telling them weird stories of the sanitarium, and one of the tales was how I ran away in the dead of night. I heard her tell them that I was there for "junk" and that I vamped every man within eyeshot of the place.

I couldn't help but laugh because they all stood there like clods, with eyes staring and mouths gaping. I decided to join in the fun, and kid the hicks along a little more. I knew that they were the kind that you could take over for every cent they had, especially if you told them that they were more devilish and daring than most New York men.

I never had any money to spend, and neither did Nurse Gray. When I was allowed to go to the store, they gave me a quarter for some candy. You couldn't get much for a quarter anywhere, even in Brown's Farms. Of course, they were afraid to give me more, as they figured that I would fly to New York for dope. If I didn't leave the sanitarium, they suspected that I might send for some. I was forever hungry, too.

This day I was particularly hungry, and saw a chance to get a square meal out of the hicks. I told Gray this, and we went to work on them. I praised them, and said they were too speedy for this small town, and that they ought to be in New York, where brains and looks got a man something.

After much talking, I got them into the store, and they took the fish hooks out of their pockets. How I ate. Gray didn't eat much as she was always loaded, but when anyone is getting off dope, as I was, they are hungry all the time. I ate four sandwiches, dishes of ice cream, rice pudding, cake and coffee. The men looked awfully funny at me, but didn't say a word. They acted like heroes who had just saved the life of a starving woman.

Two of the dumbbells walked all the way back with us. Gray talked the arm off her man, and he looked rather startled. I knew that she was telling him some dizzy tale about the place. She even got quite kittenish, and held his arm. It was a funny sight—Gray, the old battle-ax, and the kid with his ears glued to her every word. It was probably the first time in years a man had looked at her, and she was getting a kick out of being the center of attention. You could just picture him standing the next night in front of the general store telling all the other hicks about his "wild women."

My friend asked me if it was true that I used dope. He said I looked well, but he had an idea I was a doper. He said he had once been on it, but was off. He said that he would put some cocaine and heroin in the bottom of a box of candy and bring it out to the sanitarium for me. I didn't believe him, of course. They left us at the state road, and no one saw us.

Sure enough, though, two days later the fellow came out to the sanitarium, and asked Dr. Farley to present him to Nurse Gray. He handed her the box of candy for me. Gray told Dr. Farley that I had picked the man up on the road.

When the candy came to me it had been opened and the box thoroughly gone through. She had probably suspected it a hiding place for dope. She said later that there was nothing in it, but I am inclined to doubt her word. If that kid came all the way out here, he certainly would have kept his promise.

Next day Gray showed every symptom of a cocaine bat. She was having the grandest pipe dreams. I can spot a cocaine bat anywhere and easily so when a morphine addict changes to cocaine. Anyway, she and I had some good times together—so what the deuce?

THE WAR ON DRUGS

Sara Graham-Mulhall in 1926. The internationally known anti-drug crusader served as the First Deputy Commissioner of the New York State Department of Narcotic Drug Control in the early 1920's. Graham-Mulhall had a central role in the "demon-drug" and "dope-in-the-school-yard" mythologies, and personally conducted raids in the city. She represented the United States at the various European drug-control conferences, helped Congress pass laws to wipe out heroin traffic, and penned the influential book, Opium: The Demon Flower, *1926.*

Smuggling heroin in special garters. A 1930's dope ring included two young women nicknamed "Fanny," who passed themselves off as students of an Egyptian dancing school. They visited ships in port and received heroin and cocaine from personnel on board. "They had been thoughtfully provided with special garters," reported a Cairo narcotics official, "which allowed each of them to carry as much as ten packets of 250 grams strapped to their thighs. A reasonably ample and fairly stiff skirt sufficed to hide the burden from the most appraising and admiring of male glances" (Baron Harry d'Erlanger, The Last Plague of Egypt, *1936).*

BOX-CAR BERTHA
1905–?

"Box-car Bertha" Thompson was the daughter of a freethinking Kansas woman and a railroad foreman. Her parents were arrested for refusing to marry, and Bertha spent her first six months in jail, where "Father caught up on his reading and Mother did the jail cooking and sewing, nursed me, and studied Esperanto and socialism." Before she was fifteen Bertha had traveled with her mother through a series of midwestern towns, living in railroad yards and socialist camps with a colorful variety of transients and hoboes. Then she hit the road by herself. Her autobiography, *Sister of the Road* (1937), chronicles her experiences into the Depression years.

In the tough and tawdry interiors of Chicago whorehouses and cheap hotels, Bertha went from being a shoplifter to a prostitute, from a petty thief to a clever con artist. Like Chicago May, she preferred to drink, but she met many drug users while riding the rails. This excerpt gives her assessment of opium, heroin, and morphine, as well as an account of her first toke of "muggles," a marijuana cigarette not illegal until 1937.

From Sister of the Road

Anna and Jake and other habitual users smoked the pipe in recumbent position, lying either on the bed or on a mattress on the floor. Before this stage of the procedure they were careful to stuff all keyholes, and to paste adhesive tape over the cracks around the door and to hang wet sheets over the doors and windows.

The actual smoking process was very compli-cated, and very quick, only about ten seconds to smoke a pill. Anna, whom I watched many times, placed the stem against her lips and inhaled quickly. She took six or eight short deep breaths, and, then, as her lungs filled, one final, prolonged draw to get all of the smoke possible from the pill into her lungs.

For the habitual smoker the desire is to produce a state of self-satisfaction that he must have. Really he smokes not so much for pleasure as to avoid pain and mental anguish which he suffers if free from opium. Anna was a habitual smoker and had a hunger only opium could satisfy. She put it this way:

"I smoke my habit off before going to bed and I smoke my habit off when I wake up in the morning."

To smoke her habit off meant to take enough opium to protect her from pain and anxiety.

With the pleasure smoker who takes the pipe only occasionally, the reaction is quite different. I watched a number of women just learning to smoke. After the first pill they began to experience buoyancy and a sense of well-being. They got talkative. These emotions increased until the fourth pill, and then they became drowsy and quickly fell asleep. Even after eight hours' sleep they retained some of the same buoyant feeling. As far as I could learn, neither the habitual nor the pleasure smoker had any fantastic dreams or illusions of grandeur, nor did they become bold or courageous.

The sex life of a pipe smoker is lessened. Desire is suspended and capacities are extremely weakened. Anna admitted to me that what sex she had meant little to her or to any of them on the regular habit. On the other hand, the pleasure smoker has his desires greatly stimulated by the pipe, although it retards considerably the culmination of the sex act.

Lucille and Jimmie used "white stuff," heroin and morphine, which are the alkaloids of opium. "White stuff" comes in small tablets, cubes, or in powder. It is sold in New York for twenty dollars an ounce, and was shipped out to our group by mail in ten ounce lots. They never kept more than an ounce in their possession at one time. They kept the balance in a safety deposit box in a Chicago bank, and when they were out of town they arranged for a friend to send it to them. Lucille and Jimmie always carried a small heroin "plant," or supply, sewed in their clothing, to be ready in case of emergency, such as an arrest. Heroin was more easily used than morphine, as it could be inhaled.

Lucille told me that her "junk" habit cost her at least thirty-five dollars a month. If anything interfered with their source of supply in New York, they had to pay thirty-five dollars an ounce instead of twenty from a different dealer in Chicago.

I did not know then, but I do now, that very few women hoboes use drugs in any form. The number I have known is not even one percent. In the first place, women of the road are invariably broke, and junk costs money. The same is true of the women who spend much of their time in shelter homes. The only sisters of the road who indulge in it are those whose hoboing is secondary to their racket. Crooks or prostitutes who occasionally hobo their way about sometimes go in for dope. In the south this is much more common than in the north. The specialty there is marijuana cigarettes.

Marijuana is called among the users, "muggles." It is really a form of hasheesh, slightly changed when grown on American soil. It came to this country first from Mexico. New Orleans and all the southern cities are full of it. In New Orleans it is grown commonly in the back yards of the Old Town. It is available also in every northern city. In south Chicago there is a whole field growing wild, which is harvested by Mexicans and various small wholesale dealers.

Marijuana is popular because it is prepared without trouble and because it gives tremendous effect at very low cost. The leaves and blossoms are gathered, dried, and rolled into cigarettes slightly thinner than the ordinary package cigarettes, and twisted together on the ends so that none of the substance may be spilled. In almost every city they may be had as low as twenty-five cents each. In New Orleans they are two for a quarter. One cigarette, if smoked by those who know the way, will give a thorough "muggles jag" to at least three persons for an entire night.

Otto was the only one of the grifters I was with who had ever used marijuana. He stopped, he said, because he didn't intend to get into the dope habit. Just twice while I was with him did he make a buy, once in Philadelphia, where he just walked into a poolroom and secured one cigarette at the cigar counter, and the other time on a party down on Dumaine Street in New Orleans.

We had driven down to New Orleans from Savannah on one of the road trips and the gang had put in three days grifting [shoplifting], making good hauls. Otto had had a narrow escape, being pinched the last day and having to pay two hundred dollars to a fix to get him out. It was summer and terribly hot. The night was stifling as we walked down in the little streets of the French quarter. Suddenly he declared he wanted "a weed" and after asking a few questions of some of the loafers around Tony Vaccaro's saloon, we made a purchase of a half dozen cigarettes in a little charcoal store on Saint Ann Street. Otto didn't even wait to get back to the hotel. He lit one right there and walked out with it. After a few short drags he handed it to me.

"Try it, kid," he said, already cheering up, "it will kill the blues. Now don't waste it. Draw the smoke inward in short drags and hold it in your lungs for a minute and then let it out very slowly. There . . . there's enough for a beginning. Did it put on the rose-colored glasses?"

I didn't get much effect at first. The cigarette was sweetish in flavor. The flat dead smell almost nauseated me. But after the second drag I began to feel very happy and light-hearted. Otto promptly snubbed out the cigarette carefully in the palm of his hand and put it in his pocket.

"Here's once we save butts, kid," he told me jovially, "that's good to the last shred. Here, smoke a regular cigarette now. That will keep the effect of the other longer."

As we went on down toward the old French market, all the objects in the street suddenly became very vivid. Colors were stronger. Objects and people larger. The lights shone more brightly, and the edges of their flares diffused into reds and greens. We found ourselves very gay and joking. Everything Otto said seemed exceedingly important. People were amusing to us.

EMILY HAHN
1905–

American travel writer and biographer Emily
Hahn lived in Shanghai, where she taught English in the years preceding World War II. As a
foreigner, she approached opium smoking in the
romantic tradition, remembering a girlhood wish
to do unusual things when she grew up. Her entrée to a circle of smokers resulted from a warm
friendship with a literary Chinese man.

In her memoir, "The Big Smoke," first
printed in *The New Yorker* in 1950, Hahn deftly
portrays the subtle, constantly rationalized drift
into addiction; the timelessness of the opium
high; the camaraderie of the smokers as they read
Jean Cocteau's *Opium* while ignoring the artil-
lery shelling from the Japanese Navy; the slow
physical breakdown following habituation; and
her revolutionary cure through hypnosis.

For most of the characters in "The Big
Smoke," opium smoking is viewed as one of the
few remaining *fin-de-siècle* indulgences. Ahead
lay a quite different perspective: the mean streets
of the modern urban junkie.

From "The Big Smoke"

Though I had always wanted to be an opium addict, I can't claim that as the reason I went to
China. The opium ambition dates back to that
obscure period of childhood when I wanted to be a
lot of other things, too—the greatest expert on
ghosts, the world's best ice skater, the champion
lion tamer, you know the kind of thing. But by the
time I went to China I was grown up, and all those
dreams were forgotten.

Helen kept saying that she would go home to

California, where her husband was waiting, as soon
as she'd seen Japan, but as the time for her departure drew near she grew reluctant and looked
around for a good excuse to prolong the tour. As
she pointed out to me, China was awfully close by
and we knew that an old friend was living in Shanghai. It would be such a waste to let the chance slip.
Why shouldn't we go over and take just one look,
for a weekend? I was quite amenable, especially as,
for my part, I didn't have to go back to America.
My intention was to move on south in leisurely
fashion, after Helen had gone home, and land
someday in the Belgian Congo, where I planned to
find a job. All this wasn't going to have to be done
with speed, because I still had enough money to
live on for a while. My sister accepted these plans as
natural, for she knew that a man had thrown me
over. Officially, as it were, I was going to the

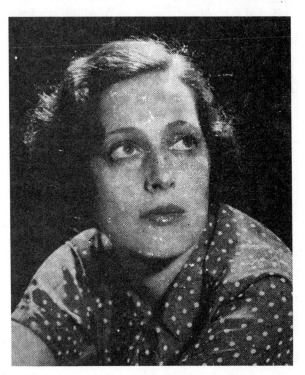

*Emily Hahn in 1934. "I would think of the lamp in the
shaded room, the coziness, the peace and comfort with
great longing. Then my nose would start to run and I was
afraid somebody from outside would have the sense to
understand what was the matter with me."*

Congo to forget that my heart was broken; it was the proper thing to do in the circumstances. My attitude toward her was equally easygoing. If she didn't want to go home just yet, I felt, it was none of my business. So when she suggested China I said, "Sure, why not?"

We went. We loved Shanghai. Helen shut up her conscience for another two months, staying on and cramming in a tremendous variety of activities—parties, temples, curio shops, having dresses made to order overnight, a trip to Peiping, embassy receptions, races. I didn't try to keep up with her. It had become clear to me from the first day in China that I was going to stay forever, so I had plenty of time. Without a struggle, I shelved the Congo and hired a language teacher, and before Helen left I had found a job teaching English at a Chinese college. It was quite a while before I recollected that old ambition to be an opium smoker.

As a newcomer, I couldn't have known that a lot of the drug was being used here, there, and everywhere in town. I had no way of recognizing the smell, though it pervaded the poorer districts. I assumed that the odor, something like burning caramel or those herbal cigarettes smoked by asthmatics, was just part of the mysterious effluvia produced in Chinese cookhouses. Walking happily through side streets and alleys, pausing here and there to let a rickshaw or a cart trundle by, I would sniff and move on, unaware that someone close at hand was indulging in what the books called that vile, accursed drug. Naturally I never saw a culprit, since even in permissive Shanghai opium smoking was supposed to be illegal.

It was through a Chinese friend, Pan Heh-ven, that I learned at last what the smell denoted. I had been at a dinner party in a restaurant with him, and had met a number of his friends who were poets and teachers. Parties at restaurants in China used to end when the last dish and the rice were cold and the guests had drunk their farewell cup of tea at a clean table. That night, though, the group still had a lot to say after that—they always did—and we stood around on the pavement outside carrying on a discussion of modern literature that had started at table. We were in that part of town called the Chi-

nese city, across Soochow Creek, outside the boundaries of the foreign concessions. It was hot. A crumpled old paper made a scraping little sound like autumn leaves along the gutter, and the skirts of the men's long gowns stirred in the same wind. During dinner, they had spoken English out of courtesy, but now, in their excitement, they had long since switched to the Chinese language, and I stood there waiting for somebody to remember me and help me find a taxi, until Heh-ven said, "Oh, excuse us for forgetting our foreign guest. We are all going now to my house. Will you come?"

Of course I would. I'd been curious about his domestic life, which he seldom mentioned. So we all moved off and walked to the house—an old one of Victorian style, with more grounds than I was used to seeing around city houses in America. I say Victorian, but that was only from the outside, where gables and a roughcast front made it look like the kind of building I knew. Indoors was very different. It was bare, as one could see at a glance because the doors stood open between rooms—no carpets, no wallpaper, very little furniture. Such chairs and sofas and tables as stood around the bare floor seemed as impersonal as lost articles in a vacant shop. Yet the house wasn't deserted. A few people were there in the rooms—a man who lounged, as if defiantly, on the unyielding curve of a sofa, four or five children scampering and giggling in whispers, an old woman in the blue blouse and trousers of a servant, and a young woman in a plain dark dress.

This last, it appeared, was Heh-ven's wife, and at least some of the children were theirs. I was embarrassed because the whole household gawked at me; one small boy who looked like a miniature Heh-ven said something that made the others giggle louder. Heh-ven spoke briefly to his family and told us to follow him upstairs, where we emerged on a cozier scene. Here the rooms were papered, and though everything still seemed stark to my Western eyes, there was more furniture around. We trooped into a bedroom where two hard, flat couches had been pushed together, heads against a wall and a heap of small pillows on each. In the center of the square expanse of white sheet that covered them was a tray that held several unfamiliar objects—a little silver oil lamp with a shade like an inverted glass tumbler, small boxes, and a number of other small things I didn't recognize. I sat on a stiff, spindly chair, and the men disposed themselves here and there in the room, very much at home as they chattered away, picked up books and riffled through them, and paid no attention to what was going on on the double couch. I found the proceedings there very odd, however, and stared in fascination.

Heh-ven had lain down on his left side, alongside the tray and facing it. He hit the lamp. One of his friends, a plump little man named Hua-ching, lay on his right side on the other side of the tray, facing Heh-ven, each with head and shoulders propped on the pillows. Heh-ven never stopped conversing, but his hands were busy and his eyes were fixed on what he was doing—knitting, I thought at first, wondering why nobody had ever mentioned that this craft was practiced by Chinese men. Then I saw that what I had taken for yarn before the two needles he manipulated was actually a kind of gummy stuff, dark and thick. As he rotated the needle ends about each other, the stuff behaved like taffy in the act of setting; it changed color, too, slowly evolving from its earlier dark brown to tan. At a certain moment, just as it seemed about to stiffen, he wrapped the whole wad around one needle and picked up a pottery object about as big around as a teacup. It looked rather like a cup, except that it was closed across the top, with a rimmed hole in the middle of this fixed lid. Heh-ven plunged the wadded needle into this hole, withdrew it, leaving the wad sticking up from the hole, and modelled the rapidly hardening stuff so that it sat on the cup like a tiny volcano. He then picked up a piece of polished bamboo that had a large hole near one end, edged with a band of chased sliver. Into this he fixed the cup, put the opposite end of the bamboo into his mouth, held the cup with the tiny cone suspended above the lamp flame, and inhaled deeply. The stuff bubbled and evaporated as he did so, until nothing of it was left. A blue smoke rose from his mouth, and the air was suddenly full of that smell I had encountered in the streets of Shanghai. Truth lit up my mind.

"You're smoking opium!" I cried. Everybody jumped, for they had forgotten I was there.

Heh-ven said, "Yes, of course I am. Haven't you ever seen it done before?"

"No. I'm *so* interested."

"Would you like to try it?"

"Oh, yes."

Nobody protested, or acted shocked or anything. In fact, nobody but Hua-ching paid any attention. At Heh-ven's request, he smoked a pipe to demonstrate how it was done, then relaxed against the pillows for a few minutes. "If you get up immediately, you are dizzy," explained Heh-ven. I observed his technique carefully and, by the time I took my place on the couch, had a reasonable notion of how it was done. You sucked in as deeply as possible, and held the smoke there as long as you could before exhaling. Remembering that I'd never been able to inhale cigarette smoke, I was worried that the world of the opium addict might be closed to me. In daydreams, as in night dreams, one doesn't take into account the real self and the failings of the flesh. The romantic is always being confronted by this dilemma, but that night I was spared it. When I breathed in I felt *almost* sick, but my throat didn't close, and after a moment I was fine. I couldn't dispose of the tiny volcano all in one mighty pull, as the others had done, but for a beginner I didn't do badly—not at all. Absorbed in the triumph of not coughing, I failed to take notice of the first effects, and even started to stand up, but Heh-ven told me not to. "Just stay quiet and let's talk," he suggested.

We all talked—about books, and books, and Chinese politics. That I knew nothing about politics didn't put me off in the least. I listened with keen interest to everything the others had to say in English, and when they branched off into Chinese I didn't mind. It left me to my thoughts. I wouldn't have minded anything. The world was fascinating and benevolent as I lay there against the cushions, watching Heh-ven rolling pipes for himself. Pipes—that's what they called the little cones as well as the tube, I suppose because it is easier to say than pipe-fuls. Anyway, the word "pipeful" is not really accurate, either. Only once, when Hua-ching asked me how I was, did I recollect the full significance of the situation. Good heavens, I was smoking opium! It was hard to believe, especially as I didn't seem to be any different.

"I don't feel a thing," I told him. "I mean, I'm enjoying myself with all of you, of course, but I don't feel any different. Perhaps opium has no effect on me?"

Heh-ven pulled at the tiny beard he wore and smiled slightly. He said, "Look at your watch." I cried out in surprise; it was three o'clock in the morning.

"Well, there it is," Heh-ven said. "And you have stayed in one position for several hours, you know—you haven't moved your arms or your head. That's opium. We call it Ta Yen, the Big Smoke."

"But it was only one pipe I had. And look at you, you've smoked four or five, but you're still all right."

"That's opium, too," said Heh-ven cryptically.

Later that morning, in my own bed, I tried to remember if I'd had drug-sodden dreams, but as far as I could recall there hadn't been dreams at all, which was disappointing. I didn't feel any craving, either. I simply wasn't an addict. I almost decided that the whole thing was just a carefully nurtured myth. Still, I gave it another chance a few days later, and again a third time, and so on. To make a surprisingly long story short, a year of earnest endeavor went by. It's impossible now to pinpoint the moment in time when I could honestly claim to be an addict, but I do remember the evening when Heh-ven's wife, Pei-yu, said I was. I had arrived in their house about six in the evening, when most of the family was in the smoking room. It was a nice domestic scene, the children playing on the floor, Pei-yu sitting on the edge of the couch really knitting, with wool, and Heh-ven lying on his side in the familiar position, idly stocking up opium pellets to save time later, now and then rolling a wad on his second finger to test the texture. A good pellet should be of just the right color, and not too dry, but not too sticky, either. These refinements added a lot to one's pleasure. I suppose people who are fussy about their tea have the same impulse.

I was feeling awful that evening. I had a cold

and I'd been up too late the night before. I was also in a tearing rage with Heh-ven. By this time, I was publishing a Chinese-English magazine at a press he owned in the Chinese city—or, rather, I was trying to publish it, and Heh-ven was maddeningly unbusinesslike about the printing. That day, I'd waited at home in vain for hours because he had faithfully promised that some proofs would be delivered before three o'clock. When I marched in on the peaceful scene in the smoking room, only a fit of sneezing prevented my delivering him a stinging scolding. At the sound of the sneezes, Pei-yu looked at me sharply. Then *she* started scolding Heh-ven. I hadn't learned any of the Shanghai dialect—it was Mandarin I was studying—but the spirit of her speech was clear enough.

"Pei-yu says you are an addict and it's my fault," interpreted Heh-ven cheerfully.

I felt rather flattered, but my feelings about Heh-ven's lack of performance on the press made me sound surly as I replied, "Why should she say that?" I lay down in the accustomed place as I spoke, and reached for the pipe.

"Because your eyes and nose are running."

"So? Is that a symptom?" I looked at Pei-yu, who nodded hard. I inhaled a pipe and continued, "But that isn't why my nose is running. I've got the most awful cold."

"Oh yes, opium smokers always have colds." Heh-ven prepared another pipe. "When you don't get the Big Smoke, you weep. Still, in your case, I think my wife is mistaken. You are not yet an addict. Even *I* am not an addict, really—not very much addicted, though I smoke more than you. People like us, who have so much to do, are not the type to become addicted."

No, I reflected, Pei-yu was certainly exaggerating to a ridiculous degree. Of course I could do without it. I liked it, of course—I liked it. I had learned what was so pleasant about opium. Gone were the old romantic notions of wild drug orgies and heavily flavored dreams, but I didn't regret them, because the truth was much better. To lie in a quiet room talking and smoking—or, to put things in their proper order, smoking and talking—was delightfully restful and pleasant. I wasn't addicted, I told myself, but you had to have a bit of a habit to appreciate the thing. One used a good deal of time smoking, but, after all, one had a good deal of time. The night clubs, the cocktail and dinner parties beloved of foreign residents in Shanghai would have palled on me even if I'd kept up drink for drink with my companions. Now I hardly ever bothered to go to these gatherings. Opium put me off drinking, and people who didn't smoke seemed more and more remote, whereas smokers always seemed to have tastes and ideas compatible with mine. We would read aloud to each other a good deal—poetry, mostly. Reading and music and painting were enough to keep us happy. We didn't care for eating or drinking or voluptuous pleasures. . . . I seem to fall into a kind of *fin-de-siècle* language when I talk about opium, probably because it was rather a *fin-de-siècle* life I led when I was smoking it, and in a social as well as a literary sense. The modern, Westernized China of Shanghai frowned on smoking—not on moral grounds but because it was considered so lamentably old-fashioned. My friends, in their traditional long gowns, were deliberately, self-consciously reactionary, and opium was a part of this attitude, whereas modern people preferred to stun themselves with whiskey or brandy. Opium was decadent. Opium was for grandfathers.

We used to read Cocteau's book on opium and discuss it. Hua-ching loved the drawings that represent the feelings of a man under cure, in which the pipe grows progressively larger and the man smaller. Then the pipe proliferates—his limbs turn into pipes—until at last he is built up completely of pipes. During such talks, Heh-ven sometimes spoke of himself frankly as an addict but at other times he still said he wasn't. I never knew what sort of statement he was going to make on the subject. "My asthma caused it, you know," he said once. "My father is asthmatic, so he smokes. I, too, am asthmatic, and so is Pei-yu. Now and then, when hers is very bad, she will take a pipe, because it is a good medicine for that disease."

One day, after he had been even more contradictory than was his custom, I drew up a table of the smoker's creed:

1. I will never be an addict.
2. I can't become addicted. I am one of those people who take it or let it alone.
3. I'm not badly addicted.
4. It's a matter of will power, and I can stop any time.

Any time. Time. That was something that had lost its grip on me. It was amazing how watches varied their rate of running, sometimes galloping, at other times standing still. To keep up with my job, I had to look at my watch often; it had a trick of running away when I didn't notice, causing me to forget dates or arrive at appointments incredibly late. I appeared sleepy. I know this from what outsiders told me about myself—"You need sleep," they would say—but I never *felt* sleepy, exactly; inside, my mind was unusually clear, and I could spend a whole night talking without feeling the need of rest. This was because I was an addict. I admitted it now, and was pleased that I could feel detached. We opium smokers, I reflected, *are* detached, and that is one of our advantages. We aren't troubled with unpleasant emotions. The alcoholic indulges in great bouts of weeping sentiment, but the smoker doesn't. You never find a smoker blubbering and blabbing his secrets to the opium seller. We are proud and reserved. Other people might think us drowsy and dull; we know better. The first reaction to a good long pull at the pipe is a stimulating one. I would be full of ideas, and as I lay there I would make plans for all sorts of activity. Drowsiness of a sort came on later, but even then, inside my head, behind my drooping eyes, my mind seethed with exciting thoughts.

Still, I couldn't ignore the disadvantages. If I had, I would have been unworthy of the adjective "detached." Being an addict was awfully inconvenient. I couldn't stay away from my opium tray, or Heh-ven's, without beginning to feel homesick. I would think of the lamp in the shaded room, the coziness, the peace and comfort with great longing. Then my nose would start to run and I was afraid somebody from the outside would have the sense to understand what was the matter with me. When I say afraid, that is what I mean—for some reason, there was dread in the idea of being spotted. This was strange. True, smoking was against the law in Shanghai, but only mild penalties were likely to have been visited on me. Still, I was afraid. I think

"One used a good deal of time smoking, but, after all, one had a good deal of time" (Emily Hahn).

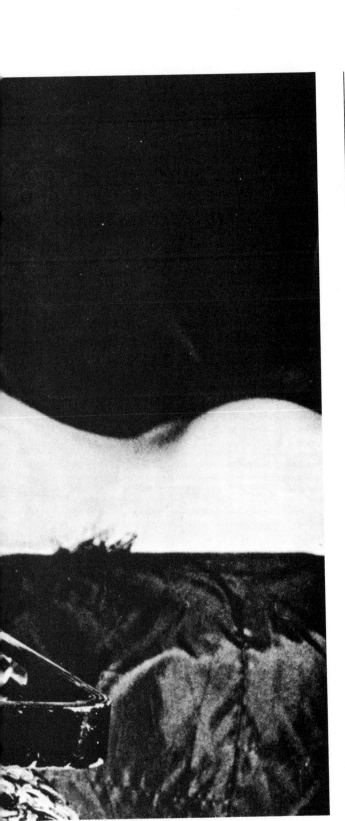

it may have been a physical symptom, like the running nose.

All of these little points we discussed at great length, lying around the tray. Hua-ching had a theory that addiction lay not so much in the smoking itself as in the time pattern one got used to. "If you vary your smoking every day, you have far less strong a habit," he assured us earnestly. "The great mistake is to do it at the same hour day after day. I'm careful to vary my smoking times. You see, it's all in the head."

Jan, a Polish friend who sometimes joined us, disputed this. "It's the drug itself," he said. "If it's all in the head, why do I feel it in my body?" The argument tailed off in a welter of definitions. A smoker loves semantics. However, I resolved one day to test myself and see who was the master, opium or me, and I accepted an invitation to spend the weekend on a houseboat upriver with an English group. In the country, among foreigners, it would be impossible to get opium.

Well, it wasn't as bad as I'd expected. I was bored, and I couldn't keep my mind on the bridge they insisted that I play, but then I never can. I had an awful cold, and didn't sleep much. My stomach was upset and my legs hurt. Still, it wasn't so bad. I didn't want to lie down and scream—it could be borne. On the way home, my cold got rapidly worse—but why not? People do catch cold. The only really bad thing was the terror I felt of being lost, astray, naked, shivering in a world that seemed imminently brutal. . . . Half an hour after I got back, I was at Heh-ven's, the cronies listening to my blow-by-blow report, expressing, according to their characters, admiration, skepticism, or envy. I was glad that none of them failed to understand my impulse to flee the habit. Every one of them, it seemed, had had such moments, but not everyone was as stubborn as I.

"You could have given her pills," said Hua-ching reproachfully to Heh-ven. I asked what he meant, and he said that addicts who had to leave the orbit of the lamp for a while usually took along little pellets of opium to swallow when things got bad. A pellet wasn't the same thing as smoking, but it alleviated some of the discomfort.

Heh-ven said, "I didn't give them on purpose.

She wanted to see what it was like, and the pills would have spoiled the full effect. Besides, they are somewhat poisonous. Still, if she wants them, next time she can have them."

Snuggling luxuriously on a pillow, I said, "There won't be a next time."

Some weeks later, I got sick. I must have smoked too much. In a relatively mild case of over-indulgence, one merely gets nightmares, but this wasn't mild. I vomited on the way home from Heh-ven's, and went on doing it when I got in, until the houseboy called the doctor. This doctor was an American who had worked for years in the community, but I didn't know him well. Of course, I had no intention of telling him what might be wrong, and I was silent as he felt my pulse and looked at my tongue and took my temperature. Finally, he delivered judgment. "Jaundice. Haven't you noticed that you're yellow?"

"No."

"Well, you are—yellow as an orange," he said. "How many pipes do you smoke in a day?"

I was startled, but if he could play it calm, so could I. "Oh, ten, eleven, something like that," I said airily, and he nodded and wrote out a prescription, and left. No lecture, no phone call to the police, nothing. I ought to have appreciated his forbearance, but I was angry, and said to Heh-ven next day, "He doesn't know as much as he thinks he does. People don't count pipes—one man's pipe might make two of another's." The truth was that I resented the doctor's having stuck his foot in the door of my exclusive domain.

All in all, if I'd been asked how I was faring I would have said I was getting on fine. I had no desire to change the way I was living. Except for the doctor, foreign outsiders didn't seem to guess about me; they must have thought I looked sallow, and certainly they would have put me down as absent-minded, but nobody guessed. The Chinese, of course, were different, because they'd seen it all before. I annoyed one or two people, but I managed to pass, especially when the war between China and Japan flared up just outside the foreign-occupied part of the city. Shells fell all around our little is-land of safety, and sometimes missed their mark and bounced inside it. It is no wonder that the American doctor didn't take any steps about me—he had a lot of other things to occupy his mind. The war didn't bother me too much. I soon got used to the idea of it. Opium went up in price—that was all that mattered.

But the war cut me off definitely from the old world, and so, little by little, I stopped caring who knew or didn't know. People who came calling, even when they weren't smokers, were shown straight into the room where I smoked. I now behaved very much like Heh-ven; there was even an oily smudge on my left forefinger, like the one on his, that wouldn't easily wash off. It came from testing opium pellets as they cooked. Heh-ven, amused by the smudge, used to call the attention of friends to it. "Look," he would say, "have you ever before seen a white girl with that mark on her finger?"

I wasn't the only foreign opium smoker in Shanghai. Apart from Jan, there were several others I knew. One was connected with the French diplomatic service. He and his wife had picked up their habit in Indo-China. It was through them that I met Bobby—a German refugee, a doctor who had built up enough of a practice in Shanghai to live on it. He wasn't an addict—I don't think I ever saw him touch a pipe—but he seemed to spend a lot of time with addicts. Sometimes I wondered why he dropped in at Heh-ven's so often. I rather wished he wouldn't, because he was dull. Still, it didn't matter much whether outsiders were dull or bright, and as he happened to call on me one afternoon when I had received a shattering letter, I confided in him.

"It's about this silly magazine I've been publishing," I said. "They want to expand its circulation—the people who own it, that is—and they say I've got to go to Chungking to talk to them."

"And you can't go, of course," said Bobby.

"I can, too," I lifted myself up on my elbow and spoke indignantly. "Certainly I can go. What do you mean, I can't? Only, it's a bother." I lay down and started rolling a pellet fast. My mind buzzed with all the things that would have to be done—arranging about my house, getting a permit to travel. And I'd have to go through Hong Kong, taking a boat down there and then flying inland. It was tiring just to think about it, and here was Bobby talking again.

"Listen to me. Listen carefully. You can't do it—*you* can't."

This time he managed to worry me. "Why not?"

"Because of the opium. Your habit," said Bobby.

I laughed. "Oh, that's what it is, is it? No, that'll be all right." The pellet was ready, shaped into a cone, and I smoked it, then said, "I can stop whenever I want to. You don't know me well, but I assure you I can stop any time."

"How recently have you tried?" he demanded, and paused. I didn't reply because I was trying to reckon it. He went on, "It's been some time, I'm sure. I've known you myself for a year, and you've never stopped during that period. I think you'll find you can't do it, young lady."

"You're wrong," I said violently. "I tell you, you're all wrong—you don't know me."

"And in the interior it's not so funny if you're caught using it, you know. If you're caught, you know what happens." He sliced a stiff hand across his throat. He meant that the Kuomintang had put a new law into effect; people they caught smoking were to be decapitated. But surely that couldn't happen to *me*.

I looked at him with new uncertainty and said, "What will I do?"

"You'll be all right, because I can help you," said Bobby, all of a sudden brisk and cheerful. "You can be cured quite easily. Have you heard of hypnosis?"

I said that of course I'd heard of it, and even witnessed it. "There was a medical student at school who put people to sleep—just made them stare at a light bulb and told them they were sleepy."

Bobby made a call on my telephone, talking in German. He hung up and said, "We start tomorrow morning. I have a bed for you at my little hospital—a private ward, no less. Get up early if you can and do what you usually do in the morning—smoke if you like, I have no objections—but be there at nine o'clock. I'll write down the directions for the taxi-driver." He did so. Then, at the door, he added, "Heh-ven will try to talk you out of it, you know. Don't let him."

I said, "Oh, no, Bobby, he wouldn't do that. This is my own affair, and he'd never interfere."

"Just don't let him, that's all. Don't forget a suitcase with your night things. You'll probably bring some opium pills, but if you do I'll find them, so save yourself the trouble."

Before I became an addict, I used to think that a confirmed smoker would be frantically afraid of the idea of breaking off. Actually, it isn't like that—or wasn't with me. At a certain stage, a smoker is cheerfully ready to accept almost any suggestion, including the one of breaking off. Stop smoking? Why, of course, he will say—what a good idea! Let's start tomorrow. After a couple of pipes, I was very pleased about it, and rang up Heh-ven to tell him. He, too, was pleased, but couldn't see why I was in such a hurry.

"Oh, wonderful!" he said. "But why tomorrow? If you wait, we can do it together. It's always easier with somebody else. Wait, and I'll ask Bobby to fix me up, too."

"I'd like to, Heh-ven, but he's got everything arranged for me at the hospital, and I can hardly change things around now. And, as he said, I haven't got much time—only a couple of weeks before I have to go to Chungking. It'll be easier when your turn comes."

The high sweetness in his voice when he replied was significant, I knew, of anger. "Of course, since you are so happy to take the advice of a man you hardly know . . ."

It was a struggle, but I hadn't given in by the time I hung up. Full of opium or not, I knew all too well what would happen if I consented to wait for Heh-ven, for anything at all—a tea party or a cure. He'd put it off and put it off until it was forgotten. I shrugged, and had another pipe, and next morning I almost overslept, but didn't. The old man who took care of the house carried my bag out to the taxi, talking to himself, and stood there as I climbed in, a worried look on his face. He didn't trust anything about the project. "I come see you soon," he promised.

Movie poster for The Dope Traffic, *c. 1935*

MAINLINE
LADIES

Not long after heroin was introduced in 1898 as the latest pharmaceutical wonder—a safe form of opium and a cure for morphine addiction—it became the most despised drug of the twentieth century. It has not relinquished that position, even during periods of public condemnation of cocaine, marijuana, LSD, and PCP ("angel dust"). During the 1940's and 1950's, America's estimated one million heroin users were regarded as socially useless addicts and criminals. They may have been victims of circumstance or environment, but they were nevertheless outcasts.

Terms like "junkie," "horse," "fix," "mainline," "pusher," "connection," and "monkey on my back" crept into the vocabulary. Paperback novels about schoolyard pushers and teenage users were widely read. The "cold turkey" drug withdrawal scene was obligatory in every book, play, and film on the subject. The rampage of Sinatra's Frankie Machine trying to kick his habit in a locked room in the film of *The Man with the Golden Arm* shocked and fascinated audiences. People unaware of their own material addictions felt superior to the junkie "against the bathroom grimy sink/ pumping her arms full of life" ("Blues for Sister Sally"). To the Beat Generation, the drug addict was a doomed nirvana-seeker, an outlaw rather than a criminal.

Mainlining heroin is a much more intense experience than smoking opium or drinking laudanum. The isolation of morphine, approximately ten times stronger than the poppy's resinous juice, and the invention of the hypodermic syringe in the nineteenth century had initiated an escalation of the powers of opium. The formulation of heroin, Dilaudid, Demerol, and methadone, which are two or three times stronger than morphine, brought about a further intensification.

Typically, the heroin addict started out by sniffing the white or brown powder before going on to skin-popping and finally mainlining. Tolerance builds fast, dosage levels are raised, and the user develops the infamous habit.

Heroin's tremendous addiction potential makes it "the ideal product . . . the ultimate merchandise. The client will crawl through a sewer and beg to buy," wrote William Burroughs. Addict crime, primarily petty theft and prostitution, resulted from the relatively high expense of black-market heroin. In the 1950's, a daily habit could cost over a hundred dollars, a high price for someone whose life-style precluded regular work. In England, where addiction is treated as a medical problem, heroin was supplied by clinics at approximately fifteen cents per dose. The overlooked British writer Anna Kavan led a productive life despite her addiction to heroin. In her short story "Julia and the Bazooka," Julia's doctor helps her maintain her habit, feeling it is "quite right for her to use the syringe . . . without it she could not lead a normal existence, her life would be a shambles."

The women whose writings appear here tell far more about the opiates and the circumstances of their use than can be found in dry official or lurid journalistic reports. Ever since Thomas De Quincey's *Confessions of an English Opium-Eater* (1822), addict writers have presented their drug confessions with loving detail and stark candor. After their experiences as addicts, they could not care less what readers might think of them. The act of writing their memoirs contributes to their rehabilitation. Feeling guilty and defiant by turns, they apologize for their weakness while extolling the kicks of drugs. Not a nuance of their pleasure or pain is left out.

Heroin can produce a state of euphoria and well-being that makes a squalid environment seem splendid and the user's problems blissfully irrelevant. "There is a tremendous physical joy in the sensation of moving your arm," writes Janet Clark after her first shot. The initial rush, which lasts several minutes but seems endless, is compared to sexual orgasm. Barbara Quinn enjoys the "sharp prick" of the needle "as a promise of the good sensations that always followed." Her lesbian lover "boots" the drug into her arm, giving her "an unbelievably exciting feeling of warmth and composure . . . increasing the pleasure of the first rush and spreading it out for what seems like ages but is usually less than a minute." Lenore Kandel's Sister Sally "masturbates with needles." Florrie Fisher describes the rush of a mainline fix as "being seized by the hand of a giant, lifting you higher, higher up to his mouth. But the giant doesn't eat you. He kisses you and it feels wonderful."

After the rush comes the nod, an afterglow of soothing tranquility lasting up to six hours. It seems to recreate early childhood or perhaps fetal security. For Clark, it is "like having warm milk flow through your veins instead of blood." After shooting heroin the junkie floats in a dream, experiencing stunning perceptions and rich visions. Drug historian Richard Ashley has compared this activation of the "internal theater" to an LSD high, with the opiate user a more passive participant in her fantasies than the acidhead.

The tribal quality of junkie society is implied in the accounts of Fisher, Clark, and Quinn. Each is initiated by her lover; they are love junkies before they're heroin junkies. They each long to get near that part of their lover that is separate from them. Along with the euphoria of the first highs comes entrée into an underground society similar to groups of opium smokers of past eras. "When you're introduced to someone, the first thing you find out is whether he's a junkie or not," writes Clark. "It's like be-

longing to some fantastic lodge, you know, but the initiation ceremony is a lot rougher."

Junkie society has its own vocabulary and etiquette, developed around the daily routine of scoring, shooting up, and nodding out. It is relatively free of sexism, for dope is the common denominator. Although shooting up together usually substitutes for lovemaking, several women have written explicitly of intense erotic encounters with lovers of both sexes immediately after getting high. But attachments to loved ones are nearly impossible to maintain through time spent in prison or hospitals. Janet Clark supplies a graphic picture of the controversial narcotics "farm" in Lexington, Kentucky. She and Fisher describe women sharing their drug experiences in jail, exchanging information on connections in different cities, and plotting to score drugs while incarcerated. The loss of friends to overdoses is taken in stride. Survival is gratuitous; but wherever they are, junkies form new relationships based on being outcast drug addicts.

Drug rehabilitation programs have generally failed. The standard withdrawal treatments of dose reduction or drug substitution do not cure the addict of her craving; seeking a shot when she hits the street is not uncommon. Private clinics such as Synanon and Odyssey, described in the books by Quinn and Fisher, have been somewhat more successful at curing heroin addiction with brutally honest encounter-therapy techniques and by providing jobs in drug rehabilitation for ex-addicts. The reactivation of the religious impulse occasionally worked, as it had in the nineteenth century. When self-motivation is lacking, a mission in life reforms some drug addicts.

Edith Piaf and Françoise Sagan were medical junkies who became hooked on the morphine prescribed for injuries from near-fatal auto accidents. The singer remained addicted despite four attempts to kick the habit in detoxication clinics. The writer managed a cure in nine days ("Artificial paradise of nonsuffering, I shall know you no more"), keeping a diary that imaginatively conveys the inner drama of withdrawal by dose reduction.

Certain drugs' availability and wide use in the entertainment world have given them more than a tinge of glamour. Marijuana, cocaine, and heroin don't produce creativity, but can affect it. In the entourage of performers in the jazz and nightclub world of the 1940's and 1950's there was always someone with the connections to score. The autobiographies and biographies of Billie Holiday and Edith Piaf reveal a self-destructive reliance on hard drugs. These women drove themselves in their art as well as their lives, refusing to accept limits.

Holiday's harassment by narcotics agents and the courts encouraged her to speak out on drug addiction as a medical problem. "We end up with the government chasing sick people like they were criminals, telling doctors they can't help them, prosecuting them because they had some stuff without paying the tax, and sending them to jail." It was a dangerous statement for a black singer in 1956, the year Wilhelm Reich's books were burned, all existing stocks of heroin in the United States were ordered destroyed, and capital punishment was legislated for certain narcotics offenses for the first time in American history.

The works that follow confirm that the modern junkie is one of the most vulnerable pleasure-seekers. Although many more people were actually addicted to the opiates in the nineteenth century, the mid-twentieth-century heroin user took more risks because her drug was illegal. The craving for a state of consciousness that can be satisfied only by an Asian poppy has led to the rapid growth of a trio of billion-dollar international industries: drug trafficking, narcotics law enforcement, and drug rehabilitation.

In addition, the heroin problem of the 1940's and 1950's was a convenient diversion for pharmaceutical corporations that pushed on an eager public a vast array of antidepressants, barbiturates, tranquilizers, and analgesics—many with an addictive and suicide potential as great as heroin's. Jacqueline Susann's novel *Valley of the Dolls* (1966) (not reprinted here) described barbiturate use in Hollywood, drawing on the highly publicized fatal overdoses of actresses Judy Garland and Marilyn Monroe. The pep pills that helped the housewife through her day were called "mother's little helpers" after a Rolling Stones hit song of the sixties. With the proliferation of mood-altering pharmaceuticals for the age of anxiety, the addiction syndrome became as evident in affluent households as in the "shooting galleries" of the urban ghetto.

FLORRIE FISHER
1920–

Florrie Fisher's memoir of her life as a junkie is unflinchingly realistic. Images of her scooping up toilet water to prepare a fix in the ladies' room of a Manhattan cafeteria, or eating the Benzedrine-soaked cotton inside plastic inhalers smuggled to her in prison, portray her absolute addiction.

The Brooklyn-born author began smoking marijuana at a Catskill Mountains resort. Her initiator was a fast-talking hotel musician. Fisher's middle-class background remained with her in the junkie underworld of New York City during

Florrie Fisher. "Dope seizes you like the hand of a giant."

the 1940's and 1950's: She used only her own hypodermic needle, felt guilty about her addict's diet of doughnuts, and preferred to tell her mother, who discovered a morphine bottle in her daughter's bathroom, that she had cancer rather than admit she was a junkie. But Fisher loved to get high.

Like most female heroin addicts, Fisher turned to prostitution as the cost of her habit mounted to nearly two hundred dollars per day. Arrested seventy-five times, she spent a large part of two decades behind bars. She was a tough sur-vivor of the streets and the prison system, eventually kicking her habit at Synanon, becoming an anti-drug advocate, and publishing this memoir in 1971.

From The Lonely Trip Back

Junkies get abscesses from using dirty needles, usually one that has been used by someone else and not carefully cleaned. Like I said, when you want a shot, you don't want anything else but a shot, and it has to be right now.

I would never use anyone else's works unless I had absolutely no other way of shooting dope. Right after I started using heroin, I couldn't wait to have somebody score for a set of works for me. I didn't loan it out and I didn't borrow anybody's, unless I was in prison and had no other choice.

I was particularly careful, I guess, because when I was still new on dope, one of my girl friends came to me to help her out. She wanted a place to stay because she was sick.

She had an abscess on her arm, a big, ugly, running sore. She was lying there, resting on my bed, when she started groaning and writhing. I felt her and she was burning up with fever. Her arm was swollen around the abscess like a shiny, pink watermelon. She didn't know me, she didn't know anything, and I was afraid she was going to die on my hands. We took her to Bellevue and dropped her off in the emergency entrance. I heard later that she almost died there, from that sore, the result of a dirty needle.

I never forgot that and I was careful. Well, as careful as a junkie could be. I remember going into old Hector's Cafeteria on Forty-second Street lots of times. The first thing I wanted to do was take off in the bathroom.

You can't take your shot out where the other women will see you, of course; you've got to get into one of the toilet stalls and lock the door. I would get into one and take everything out, the junk, spoon, eyedropper, matches, and the needle: the works.

When this little smorgasbord was laid out in front of me on the back of the toilet, I'd want to go out to the sink and draw some water, but some woman would be bound to come in and see, so I couldn't risk it.

But you couldn't wait, not for a minute. So instead of waiting for the woman to finish and wash her hands and get out, I'd flush the toilet, reach in, pull the swirling water up from the commode into my syringe and put it into the spoon. Then I'd rationalize, "I'm heating the spoon. That must be killing the germs," and I'd jam that needle, stool water and all, into my vein.

Sometimes, when I had more time than one

flush of the toilet, I'd flash it, shoot about a tenth of the stuff, draw a little blood back into the needle, shoot another tenth, and draw up a little blood again. I'd do this until the stuff was gone, the needle empty. Each time I'd shoot that little bit there would be this great feeling, like an orgasm in the belly, then finally the great high set in. Some junkies can draw it out into even more flashes, drawing it up and shooting it back until that final high sweeps them up. I'd get so anxious for the final jolt I couldn't wait out more than five or six flashes.

Like other junkies, I'd also flash, or boot it, when I wasn't sure of my connection. If the stuff is dirty, contaminated, or weak, you test it by shooting just a small amount first, waiting for your body's reaction, until you shoot the full load.

When I was in jail, I'd try to clean the needle to make sure nobody's blood was stuck on it. Not so much for cleanliness, but because the blood would clog up the needle and you couldn't get the junk into your arm. When you're in the House, everything good you've learned outside, even Jewish housekeeping, goes out those barred windows.

Mamma always used to nag at me, "Eat, Florrie, eat. You're as thin as a bird," she used to say as she shoved more food at me.

Like all junkies, I never had an appetite. Sometimes I weighed, like, seventy-five pounds. No more. I'd keep eating the same things, chocolate-covered doughnuts with chocolate milk, or strawberry shortcake. I'd get on kicks, but even with these special cravings, I'd try to pamper my stomach; I wouldn't eat in dirty places. When I did get hungry, I'd try to pack in something substantial and healthy. I was lucky Mamma always fed us properly.

On those rare occasions when I did sit down to a steak-and-potatoes meal, I could almost imagine her, standing over me, wiping her hands on her apron, counting every mouthful I took and every time I swallowed. She would be telling me to eat like she used to when I was little, but in my mind's eye, she was also always crooning, "My daughter's a junkie, but she eats well." That's probably what my mother would have said, too, if she'd known.

Those big meals were rare. Most of the time,

when I'd think I was starving, I'd eat a doughnut, and bam, I'd feel full, satisfied.

Why should I have worried about my stomach, though? I was murdering my body. There were tracks all over me, where the veins finally gave up the fight against the needle, and died, collapsed, withered to tiny, blue trickles of blood, covered by mushy membrane that had more holes in it than a sponge.

I have only one good vein left. It's in my neck, and even that vein can't be used for anything but a blood test. If I need a transfusion, an incision down to an artery must be made, then stitched back up. I carry in my wallet at all times a card reading:

IN CASE OF EMERGENCY FOR INTRAVENOUS
DO cut-down immediately Re: all veins collapsed
Herbert S. Kaufman, M.D.   San Francisco

But you don't think of this stuff when you're on junk, about collapsing your veins and getting track marks.

You think about one thing, getting high. That's why you don't wait until you get into your apartment to shoot, why you have to go into a cafeteria and use water from the toilet bowl, because you can't wait, you just can't wait.

How do you explain that feeling? It's nothing like getting tight on liquor. There's no comparison. I don't like liquor much, but I'd been high on it in college, and it's different. Liquor has nothing that grabbed me enough to make me want to get that kind of high.

Grabs you. That's what it does. You don't slide into a high like you do on booze. Dope seizes you like the hand of a giant, lifting you higher, higher up to his mouth. But the giant doesn't eat you. He kisses you and it feels wonderful.

After you shoot, there's this rush. It lasts about four minutes. You are all pins and needles.

And then, boing, a skyrocket explodes. A lobster couldn't be that hot. It levels off and you feel good. The giant's just kissed you and you feel as though the insides have been kicked out of all your problems and everybody else's. You have a tremendous feeling of climbing up, out of the hole you've been in. You're nodding, out of it. Zonked.

That lasts about four hours. Then the euphoria wears off and you're normal. You're fine. But after another two or four hours you begin to feel sick.

The gentle giant isn't kissing you any longer. He's about to attack you.

It starts with yawning. You keep yawning and your eyes begin to tear. Your nose starts dripping. Then you feel sweaty, an odd kind of sweat, not the kind you get if you've been exercising or working hard. It's a damp, clammy feeling. You start itching all over.

Your head starts thumping, thumping, thumping like you're inside a bass drum when it's struck. If you don't take a fix soon, you're vomiting. You throw up and throw up, and when there's nothing left, your guts are still convulsing with the dry heaves.

The giant is squeezing the last drop out of you.

It's nothing like the way you feel when you're coming down with the flu. You can always tell when it's dope sickness.

I never waited for the yawns to start. I'd think, "I'd better take a shot, I was so sick the last time." And before I'd have a chance to stay normal, I'd be zonked again.

Most junkies come off the nod, they come to, and that's their normal. But they won't accept that. They think that as soon as they come off the nod, they've got to get high again.

That's why it costs so much, feeding that giant, keeping that big bastard happy and mellow. Most of us got three times the amount we really need physically. You'd think you'd need more and more all the time.

Maybe one bag got it for you this month. Well, next month you're going to need two bags. You start with half a three-dollar bag. Then you go to two three-dollar bags. Then you're using two five-dollar bags for a shot. Then you start buying a twenty-dollar bag, quarter-ounce. You go up and up.

I used to think I wasn't in the same class as the other junkies. Most addicts, if they have a fifty-dollar-a-day habit to support, figure, "I've got to get at least forty-five dollars, I'll owe the connection five."

I always prided myself on being a money-maker.

If I had a fifty-dollar-a-day habit, then I'd have to make a hundred a day, because I liked to live in a decent place. I wanted good clothes. I liked having money for a beauty parlor, for cabs, for living like a big shot. Those kinds of things keep you thinking you're not like the old whores and bums you'd see on the street. Sure, you're a junkie like they are, but you're never going to wind up like that.

*   *   *

I had a bachelor's degree from college, but I got my master's in the House of Detention. My doctorate was earned at Bedford, New York, and Raiford, Florida.

This was how I got the education I needed for the life of a junkie. How to "make" doctors for prescriptions, all about moll-buzzing, tick-tacking. I learned about shoplifting, how to boost, carrying anything between my thighs from a chicken to a bottle. This was valuable, for a good booster is a good shoplifter.

My best schemes were hatched while I was in jail while I was being "rehabilitated."

I began Judge Pearlman's sentence on December 8, 1944, for possession of a needle, violation of public health law No. 422.

I had been in the House of Detention before, but only until I could get out on bail or was released with a suspended sentence. I'd never served real time.

But I'd been a good student, I knew there were tricks to pull to make the time easy. I intended to use them all.

For instance, in those days they had a fifty-six hour reduction cure. The nurse would wheel in this cart with ten to twenty hypos on it, with a mixture planned to ease you off the stuff gradually.

We'd stick out an arm and get a shot.

There were alcoholics mixed up with the junkies, and for a dollar an alky would "sell up" her arm, let you take her place. I'd start at the front of the row in the tank and get my first shot. Then, when the nurse was looking down at the tray, change places with an alky and put my arm out again. I was tiny, and could slide behind the other girls without being seen to get in still another spot at the end of the row for the final shot.

This way, instead of getting a mild shot to ease me up, I was getting a powerful kick each time the nurse came in.

After fifty-six hours I paid for it. Everybody else had reduced gradually, but I was still on a peak and had to kick it cold turkey. I vomited, sweated, and went through the whole thing while the screws, the women guards, ignored me.

But I never really got off it, anyway. There was so much turnover at the House, so many women leaving and entering, that it was easier than most places to get stuff. And we were getting it.

One of the best ways was to make a deal with a girl who was being released. She'd pick up stuff for us outside, and then she'd come down to the House about 4 A.M., after the trucks had picked up all the garbage from the pails outside.

Our contact would have an empty pack of cigarettes with her with the dope inside. She'd crush the pack, throw it into an empty pail, and would quickly take off. There was always something left in the bottom of those garbage pails and anybody who was checking wouldn't suspect a thing, just a crumpled empty cigarette pack left in the bottom of a garbage can.

There was heroin in the pack, or maybe goofballs.

In those days the men in the Tombs had jobs around the House, and we would work a deal with one who went to scrub the emptied cans. He would just reach in, get the empty pack, take it with him on the freight elevator to the tenth floor where the empty cans were being returned to the kitchen.

We used to stay on the point, be on the lookout. There was a guard in the hall, another in the kitchen, but just at the corner we could get the pack if our timing was perfect.

We almost always managed. The few times we missed, if one of the guards was watching, the man would stash it somewhere—in the pickle barrel, in the bread—and he'd always let us know where to find it by getting a kite to us.

Once we had the stuff we didn't have trouble getting a needle or spoon. If one of us couldn't steal a needle, we'd get one of the squares who worked in the hospital to get us a needle, then pass it around.

At one time when we couldn't get dope we were using benzedrine inhalers. We could always find a guard to bring them in for us. They'd sell for $2.50 apiece.

Actually, we were *eating* the inhalers. We all smelled like menthol. In those days the inhalers contained saturated cardboard inside, folded up into little accordion pleats. There would be eight pleats, with the two end strips slightly smaller because the ends were turned in. We'd fight to get the bigger pieces, nobody wanted the end strips just because of the small difference.

I started out eating the one strip, but ended up eating the whole eight. They tasted horrid, awful. We'd roll them up as small as we could, like spitballs, then stick them way back in our throats and wash them down with coffee.

It acted like an exhilarant, like cocaine. It hopped us up. I worked with the dishwasher, and had a small space I had to mop, but with the benzedrine inside me I would start mopping up all over the place and the girls would pass the word, "Get Florrie. Put an anchor on her. She's drawing heat."

The benzedrine and the way we were chewing it up had bad effects on some of the girls. They began having hallucinations. They got hives and abscesses. But nothing happened to me from the inhalers. Not then, anyway.

* * *

I had only been away from the House of Detention two years, not long enough for much to change.

The junkies and whores, the girls of the streets with whom I had lost contact while I was in Miami and serving time in Raiford, were coming and going in there, as usual.

They filled me in on the street gossip: who the connections were, who had died, who was pimping, and who was running what.

Among the girls there were a few who had been on the bennie kick with me, who had eaten the insides of the benzedrine inhalers.

I told them how lucky they had been to have only gotten hives and sores from the bennies, how I had almost died in Miami from what I had eaten.

Yes, if we couldn't have gotten any dope in the House, and the only thing available were the benzedrine inhalers, we'd have been eating them anyway, even knowing what might happen. That is just how irresponsible junkies are when they think they must have dope.

I hadn't had much chance to do any boosting at Raiford; there wasn't anything worth bothering with in that kitchen. However, I did practice up on my technique at the House of Detention, figuring it would be good for shoplifting when I got out. And my busy little mind worked out lots of schemes to use on the outside.

But I didn't get much of a chance to work any of those schemes right away.

On October 14, 1949, I was released from the House, and the next month, the day before Thanksgiving, I was picked up on a narcotics charge and held without bail.

Waiting for trial, I spent Thanksgiving, Christmas and New Year's in the House. On January 3, 1950, I was acquitted and went back on the street to continue a pattern of living which wouldn't change for thirteen more years.

It was thirteen years of hustling, shoplifting, conning for money, thirteen years in and out of jail, the House of Detention for thirty-, sixty- or ninety-day sentences, Bedford for two years, Raiford for four years, Lexington several times.

During those thirteen years I also made thousands of dollars, when my "work" wasn't interrupted by the law. I wasn't lazy. I had a habit to support, a habit more expensive and more demanding as time went by.

It was only natural that I would run into Davy Bohm during these years. We were in the same life. I knew many of his girls. Any love we might have had for each other had died long before, but we weren't mad; we stayed friends. The one big thing we still had in common was the junk. If he got some really good stuff he'd call me. If I got lucky, I'd let him know.

In fact, one time he even saved my life!

One night two other girls and I were in the Whelan's drugstore on Forty-fourth Street about 2 A.M. hustling, when three good-looking young Italian boys walked in.

Even Pat, the newest of us, recognized that these weren't "sucker" tricks. They sat down next to us, bought the coffee and we soon were laughing it up.

The tallest, sitting next to me, finally copped out to me in a whisper, "We were just on a score, broke into a drugstore a few blocks over. The money didn't amount to a hell of a lot, so we broke into the narcotics cabinet and snatched a bunch of bottles. Do you know anything about any of this?"

He reached into his pocket and pulled out a handful of bottles of morphine, Dilaudid, pills.

But what caught my eye right away, mixed up with the rest, was a one-ounce bottle of hydrochloride cocaine, the pure stuff, with the government narcotics seal still unbroken.

My God, this was Hanukkah, Succoth, Christmas and my birthday, all rolled into one big beautiful package with a bow on top!

The other girls were junkies, too. They'd know what that cocaine was worth if they saw it. And if the guys found out just how rich a haul they actually made, they would be long gone.

Casually I reached down and slid my fingers around the bottle.

"Hey, this looks good. I might try some of it some day. Let's make a deal!"

The others were talking and laughing while I drew him aside.

"Look, you're real cute guys. For fifty bucks each, you three can stay at my place until daylight. Anything goes, but no more than twice each." I tried hard to sound calm, disinterested, when I added, "I'll even take the junk off your hands so you don't get into trouble."

I knew they weren't users, couldn't know just what goodies their score had netted, especially the value of the "coke." I knew I had to set a good price or they'd be suspicious.

They took the bait, whispered among themselves, and left the other girls gap-mouthed as they trooped off with me.

I can't remember four hours dragging out so long in my entire life. I felt I just couldn't live so long, long enough to be lucky enough to get to that coke, to do what I wanted . . . wham!

After what must have been a hundred years it started to get light outside.

"Look, it's been fun, but you guys are hot after that break-in, I know the cops watch my place and I wouldn't want them to pick you up . . ." I hurried their exit, worrying over their safety, until they thought I was a real Florence Nightingale.

As soon as the door closed, I was on the phone to Davy.

"Davy, I've got some 'coke.' You bring the horse and we'll have a speed ball."

Davy started to hedge. He wanted to know just how much I had so he wouldn't be kicking in more than I did.

"Look, no matter how much you bring, I got enough to cover it," I screamed, banging down the phone.

It was an hour and ten minutes from his place to mine. He made it in half that time. When I was in a hurry to make a connection I'd pull on a blouse inside out and throw a scarf over my head rather than comb my hair. Davy always took time to look just right, so I knew he had really hurried when that doorbell rang a half hour later, and he hadn't bothered with his usual snap-brimmed hat.

I was living in a fifth-floor apartment in a brownstone at 103rd and Central Park West. We spread the stuff out there on the bed and started shooting up in turns. Soon we had a rhythm worked up as I dropped the horse into the cooker by dropper so we could measure it, and Davy kept the cocaine measured off in squares on a mirror.

We mixed them together, booting it as long as we could to draw out the effect, passing the needle to the other.

Back and forth, back and forth, cook, mix, shoot, cook, mix, shoot: God, it was beautiful, beautiful. When you boot, the needle gets clogged, so Davy'd clean it for me, I'd clean it for him.

All of a sudden I heard a knock at the door.

Who the hell is it?" I screamed.

"Open the damned door, it's me, Bill, and time is of the essence."

I knew Bill, recognized his flowery talk. Normally I'd have kidded him about his "time is of the essence," but now it terrified me.

Cocaine is an exhilarant and amplifies everything. A dripping faucet suddenly becomes cops pounding at the door; wind outside a window is a woman screaming; a chair scraped across a floor is really a truck rumbling through your room.

When Bill said, ". . . time is of the essence . . ." the horrors grabbed me, something exploded. It had to mean the cops were downstairs.

I was wrapping the stuff up and handing it to Davy, he was unwrapping it and handing it to me. I was passing it back to him in a mounting panic which must have looked like a Keystone Cops movie with each of us undoing what the other was trying to do.

After a few seconds of this, I screamed, "I know it's Kitty Barry and Johnny Cuttone coming for me, I'm not going in. They can't take me back for that kind of time, I'm going out the fire escape."

I threw open the window and crawled out, letting myself down while my feet frantically felt for the fire escape. They couldn't get me, I wouldn't let them take me.

Five floors below me was the back alley, littered with broken beer bottles and jagged cans. The fire escape wasn't on this side of the building.

Davy grabbed hold of my wrists, tried to pull me back into the room.

"My God, Florrie. I can't hold you, you're so heavy," he grunted.

"Let me drop, let me drop, I'd rather die than go back to prison," I pleaded, trying to kick free of his grasp.

"Whoever the hell you are, kick the door down and get in here," Davy shouted over his shoulder. Within seconds Bill was beside him and together they dragged me back across the windowsill.

It wasn't until many, many hours later, when I had fixed a meal for the three of us, that the reality of what had happened finally penetrated. I'd been hanging from the sill of a five-story window, hanging there and trying to pull loose.

I hadn't cared if I died.

I fainted dead away!

BILLIE HOLIDAY
1915–59

Her fame as a blues singer, her earning power as a black woman, and her visibility as a heroin addict cast Billie Holiday into a doomed struggle with the law. Her habit made her prey both to drug dealers who grossly overcharged her and to

Billie Holiday. "People on drugs are sick people. So now we end up with the government chasing sick people like they were criminals."

the narcotics police who tailed and busted her, sometimes on tips from the private clinics where she went vainly seeking a cure during the last fifteen years of her life.

For Holiday, addiction was an illness. Like Lenny Bruce, she developed an obsession with the medical and legal establishment that hunted her ("grown men getting their kicks out of this"). Toward the end of her career she sometimes performed knowing she was being observed by narcs who earlier might have planted heroin in her hotel room. The operative who headed the CIA's secret drug experiments in northern California in the 1950's set up and arrested the singer. The year Billie Holiday's autobiography was published, 1956, saw the passage of the stringent Narcotic Drug Act in response to a legislative and media outcry against junkies. Announcing her book's publication led to her arrest.

From Lady Sings the Blues

Trouble is a thing I've learned to smell.

And I smelled it for sure that night in May 1947 when we closed at the Earle Theatre in Philadelphia. It was almost a year since I left that private sanatorium in New York clean—and the law had been tailing me on and off ever since, from New York to Hollywood and back. They were around in Chicago when we worked there.

And then they picked us up the week we were booked at the Earle Theatre on the same bill with Louis Armstrong and his group. We had come down from New York in a hired car—me and Joe Guy, Bobby Tucker, my accompanist, and Jimmy Asundio, a young fellow who was then my road manager. Joe went back to New York early in the week, and the rest of us were going to drive back to New York with the car and the chauffeur. After the last show something told me not to go back to the hotel.

If they're going to bust you, they always try to wait and do it after you've closed. If somebody is pinched in the middle of the week, club owners and theatre managers have a fit; they complain the publicity gives their place a bad name and stuff like that. And the cops are usually very considerate of their feelings. But as soon as your last show is over you're on the street and all bets are off.

I begged Bobby and Jimmy not to go back to the hotel. But they wouldn't listen to me. They had left things in their room. Some of my clothes and make-up were in my room. They wanted to go back and pack up. I learned to trust my hunches. I told them to leave it. We could call the hotel later and they would send the stuff on to New York.

But they laughed at me and my hunches and went on ahead to the hotel. When I had finished taking off my make-up and getting into something comfortable I left the theatre, and the hired chauffeur drove me to the hotel to pick up the boys. My dog Mister was in the back seat.

When we pulled up in front of the hotel I knew I was right. I could see through the windows. The lobby was full of cops. Quickly I told the chauffeur to pull around the corner. From the way he acted, I could tell he wasn't going to be any help. It's awful to be in trouble with someone who doesn't have the heart for it.

We stopped around the corner, and then I saw a federal agent cross the street and come toward us. He was an Indian chap. I recognized him. I had never driven a car in my life before. But that didn't matter. I knew I had to do it that night and there wasn't two seconds to waste taking any lessons.

I hollered to the chauffeur to get out from behind the wheel and leave the motor running. As the Treasury agent came toward us, I stepped on the gas. He hollered "Halt!" and tried to stop the car by standing in the road. But I kept driving right on and he moved. I pulled away through a rain of bullets.

My boxer dog Mister was in the back seat whimpering, scared. And the chauffeur was in the front seat the same way. I didn't listen or stop for nothing. I knew I couldn't do anything to help Bobby and Jimmy unless I could make it to New York. And I couldn't make it to New York unless I kept my head and kept my nose on the road. I figured they might try to barricade the streets in Philly somewhere, so I made the chauffeur show me how to go over the river and come up through Camden, New Jersey. I'll never know how I made it, but I made it.

This was Friday. I was scheduled to open at the Onyx Club on 52nd Street the next night. First I had to get a lawyer. Bobby was as innocent as a babe; he never used nothing; he didn't even drink. He'd go to parties and have a glass of pop and have a ball, thinking he was loaded like everybody else.

I got Bobby out of jail and he joined me. He told me that a couple of federal agents had come to their room in the hotel, walked in without a warrant or anything, and searched the place. They said they found the "evidence" under the bed.

I opened at the Onyx and nothing happened. They didn't even come around until the third night. They hung around from then on. And they let me work the full week. It's always that way. While they were trying to get a case against me they were also doing the management a favor by not busting me on the premises.

But I knew they would try and get me again when the week was over. I was sick. I had been tailed for a year and I couldn't face having it go on like that forever. I knew I could never kick again, and stay kicked, as long as they were after me. I could try. But that would take money. It had cost two thousand dollars before. It would probably cost as much now. And I couldn't get it together without Joe Glaser's help.

With my salary from the Philly week, plus the Onyx week, I could afford to get admitted to the best hospital in the country. Without it, they could hunt me down like a dog and send me to jail. Joe Glaser told me this was the best thing that could happen to me. And I had nowhere else to turn.

When I finished the week at the Onyx, I took a cab to the Hotel Grampion. Two agents were waiting for me in the lobby with a warrant for my arrest. They walked me to my room. Joe Guy was waiting there. The door was locked when we got there. While the Treasury agents knocked, I hollered "Joe, it's the fuzz, clean up."

They arrested both of us and took us off, him to New York and me to Philadelphia. Most of my belongings, gowns, clothes, jewelry, were stolen from the hotel before Bobby Tucker could come back and claim them.

Most federal agents are nice people. They've got a dirty job to do and they have to do it. Some of the nicer ones have feeling enough to hate themselves sometime for what they have to do. But they don't have anything more to say about the laws than me. They just got to take orders. They're not like some city cops, nasty and wrong. Federal agents will get a doctor for you; they don't want you around sick and throwing up, or worse, on their hands.

Maybe they would have been kinder to me if they'd been nasty; then I wouldn't have trusted them enough to believe what they told me. While I was in their hands they gave me decent food, always kept me in someone's office while they questioned me. I was never behind bars the whole time. I've seen a federal judge bawl out one of them when they brought a sick man into court. He said to take the man to a doctor, get him out of there. That's better than they're allowed to do under the law. Under the law they have got to treat sick people like criminals. But they treat them like sick people, too, whenever they can.

It reminded me of Welfare Island. If someone's got eyes for you, it's easier for them to treat you like a human being. The matron at Welfare Island was nice to me and saved my life because she was on the make. And it was the same way at the Federal Building in Philly. I wasn't too much of a drug addict for some of these federal men not to make passes at me. They might not speak to me in the street, but they'd gladly sleep with me in the Federal Building.

*   *   *

It was called "The United States of America versus Billie Holiday." And that's just the way it felt.

They brought me into a courtroom in the U.S. District Courthouse at Ninth and Market streets in Philly—only two blocks from the Earle Theatre where it had all begun eleven days before. But those two damn blocks seemed like the Atlantic Ocean. It was Tuesday, May 27, 1947.

Somebody read off the charge: "On or about May 16, 1947, and divers dates theretofore in the Eastern District of Pennsylvania, Billie Holiday did receive, conceal, carry and facilitate the transportation and concealment of . . . drugs . . . fraudulently imported and brought into the United States contrary to law, in violation of Section 174, Title 21, U.S.C.A."

An assistant U.S. district attorney opened. "All right, Billie Holiday," he said. "You are charged with violation of the Narcotics Act and you have been shown a copy of the information and have indicated your desire to waive the presentation of an indictment by the Grand Jury. You are entitled to a lawyer."

"I have none," I said. And that was the truth. I hadn't seen one, talked to one.

"Do you want a lawyer, Miss Holiday?" the D.A. asked.

"No," I answered.

I didn't think there was anyone who would help me. And worse, I had been convinced that nobody *could* help me.

"Then this is a waiver of appointment of counsel if you will sign 'Billie Holiday' on that line."

They shoved me a pink paper to sign and I signed it.

I would have signed anything, no matter what. I hadn't eaten anything for a week. I couldn't even keep water down. Every time I tried to take a nap, some big old officer would come around and wake me up to sign something, make me dress, go to another office.

When it came time for me to appear in court I couldn't even walk. I was in no shape to go before the judge. So they agreed to give me a shot to keep me from getting sick. It turned out to be morphine.

Then the judge spoke up. "Was this woman ever represented by counsel?" he asked.

The district attorney replied, "I had a call today from a man who had been her counsel, and I explained the matter to him and then he returned a call and stated they were not interested in coming down and wanted the matter handled as it is being handled now."

I can read that sentence today and weep. "They were not interested in coming down and wanted the matter handled as it is being handled." In plain English that meant that no one in the world was interested in looking out for me at this point.

If a woman drowns her baby, about the worst thing you can do, she's still got a right to see a lawyer, and I'd help get her one if I could.

I couldn't very well expect the Legal Aid Society to come rushing in to help a chick making a couple thousand a week or more. I knew I was on my own. Glaser had told me this before. "Girl," he said, "this is the best thing that could happen to you."

I needed to go to a hospital and he was telling me the woodshed would be better.

So they handed me a white paper to sign. "This is a waiver of the presentation of an indictment to the Grand Jury, Miss Holiday." They never had it so easy. I signed the second paper. The rest was up to them. I was just a pigeon.

"How do you plead?" said the clerk.

"I would like to plead guilty and be sent to a hospital," I said.

Then the D.A. spoke up. "If Your Honor please, this is a case of a drug addict, but more serious, however, than most of our cases. Miss Holiday is a professional entertainer and among the higher rank as far as income is concerned. She has been in Philadelphia and appeared at the Earle Theatre, where she had a week's engagement; our agents in the Narcotics Bureau were advised from our Chicago office that she was a heroin addict and undoubtedly had heroin on her."

"The Chicago office advised you?" the judge asked.

"That is right," the D.A. replied. "She had previously been in Chicago on an engagement. They checked and found that when she left the Earle Theatre or prepared to leave the Earle Theatre, prior to leaving she had in her possession some capsules . . . and transferred them to a man who was supposed to be her manager, named James Asundio.

"Subsequent to that, while James Asundio and Bobby Tucker were packing the bags, the agents came and identified themselves and told them why they were there, and Asundio said it was his room. They made a search of the room with his permission and found wrapped up a package, wrapped in silk lining, containing some capsules . . .

"Subsequently, Miss Holiday was apprehended in New York," he went on. "She has given these agents a full and complete statement and came in here last week with the booking agent (Glaser) and expressed a desire to be cured of this addiction. Very unfortunately she has had following her the worst type of parasites and leeches you can think of. We have learned that in the past three years she has earned almost a quarter of a million dollars, but last year it was $56,000 or $57,000, and she doesn't have any of that money.

"These fellows who have been traveling with her," this young D.A. continued melodramatically, "would go out and get these drugs and would pay five and ten dollars and they would charge her one hundred and two hundred dollars for the same amount of drugs. It is our opinion that the best thing that can be done for her would be to put her in a hospital where she will be properly treated and perhaps cured of this addiction."

Then the judge took over. He asked my age, if I was married, how long I'd been separated from my husband, if we had any kids, where he worked, my life story, my show-business history.

He asked me if I didn't know it was "wrong" to have possession of narcotics. What did he expect me to say? I told him I couldn't help it after I started. Then he asked how much I used. When the federal agent Roder told him, the judge wanted to know if this was a large amount. Roder told him it was enough to kill either of them. They wouldn't be dead, they'd be damned high, that's all.

Then he wanted to know how many grains I had started with. Hell, I was no more of a pharmacist than he was. I was sick of grown men getting their kicks out of all this. They had told me if I pleaded guilty they'd send me to a hospital. I was sick and wanted to get there. This wasn't getting anyone anywhere.

I broke in and spoke to the judge. "I'm willing to go to the hospital, Your Honor," I said.

"I know," he said, brushing me off.

"I want the cure," I told him.

"You stand here indicted criminally as a user of narcotics," he said, looking me in the eye. Then the judge and the federal agents got into a long has-

sle which had nothing to do with me, either. The chief of the Philadelphia bureau stepped up and gave the judge a lecture on how hard they were working and said, "I am only saying very little, if any, good will be served with her indictment and conviction other than her individual interest if we do not get some lead as to the source."

The judge seemed to be saying they were doing me a favor. And he kept talking about an indictment and conviction, but there was nobody there to object.

Then the judge started on me again, asking me where I'd been on tour, who was with me, how much money I made, and where it was. This might have gone on forever except that somebody came in, went into a huddle with the judge. He must have been a probation officer or a social worker or something.

Then the judge lowered the boom.

"I want you to understand, as I intimated at the time of your plea, that you stand here as a criminal defendant, and while your plight is rather pitiful, we have no doubt but that you, having been nine years associated in the theatrical world, pretty well appreciate what is right—and your experiences have been many, I have been led to understand.

"I want you to know you are being committed as a criminal defendant; you are not being sent to a hospital alone primarily for treatment. You will get treatment, but I want you to know you stand convicted as a wrongdoer. Any other wrongdoer who has associated with you is a matter that is not for our consideration now.

"In your imprisonment you are going to find that you are going to get the very best medical treatment which can be accorded you. That is the beneficial part of the government's position in this case.

"I do not think you have told the whole truth about your addiction at all. . . . Your commitment will depend largely on yourself, that of the supervisor and the government generally, and we hope that within the time limit in which you are to serve you will rehabilitate yourself and return to society a useful individual and take your place in the particular calling which you have chosen and in which you have been successful.

"The sentence of the court is that you undergo

imprisonment for a period of one year and one day. The Attorney General will designate the prison in which the incarceration will be made."

It was all over in a matter of minutes; they gave me another shot to keep me from getting sick on the train, and at nine o'clock that night I was in an upper berth on a train headed for the Federal Woman's Reformatory at Alderson, West Virginia, with two big fat white matrons guarding me.

They acted as though they were scared to death of me. When I asked one of them to get me a bottle of beer she gasped and told me it was against regulations. Hell, I had a package of stuff to keep me from getting sick. That was against regulations too. Except nobody wanted to take a chance of letting me get deadly sick on the train. Finally one matron gave up and went and got me one little old bottle of beer.

But the Philadelphia story wasn't over yet. They started bringing me back from Alderson to Philly to question me and question me. I hated that. They brought me up so often, the girls at the place began to think I was a stool pigeon. And there's no place worse than the Philadelphia jail where they used to keep me. It's worse than Welfare Island, damp all the time, with rats in it as big as my chihuahua. There were women there with t.b. and worse, doing life terms for murder and stuff, and I had to eat with them and sleep with them.

When they weren't finding out what they thought I knew, the Treasury agent fixed it so I'd arrive at the Philly jail on Friday night and have to lay over in that hellhole until Monday before I was questioned. Talk about your brain-washings. I've had it.

What made it worse was that they brought me up when they tried Jimmy Asundio and again later when they tried Joe Guy. Both of them stood on their legal rights, had good lawyers, and both of them got off. Jimmy's conviction was reversed by a higher court because the federal agents had come into his room without a warrant. And Joe Guy was acquitted by a jury in a few minutes. They had no case; the judge told them so, and the jury agreed.

I felt like the fool of all time.

People on drugs are sick people. So now we end up with the government chasing sick people like they were criminals, telling doctors they can't help them, prosecuting them because they had some stuff without paying the tax, and sending them to jail.

Imagine if the government chased sick people with diabetes, put a tax on insulin and drove it into the black market, told doctors they couldn't treat them, and then caught them, prosecuted them for not paying their taxes, and then sent them to jail. If we did that, everyone would know we were crazy. Yet we do practically the same thing every day in the week to sick people hooked on drugs. The jails are full and the problem is getting worse every day.

JANET CLARK
1924–58

Janet Clark (her true identity has not yet been revealed) was a female counterpart of musician Mezz Mezzrow, whose classic autobiography of the jazz world, *Really the Blues* (1946), she avidly read. Her own book, *The Fantastic Lodge*, is based on tapes of her informal talks with the eminent sociologist of hipsters, Howard Becker.

The author penetrated the black society of blues and bop musicians to a degree white people seldom do. She was an aficionado of avant-garde jazz as well as the ubiquitous reefer and horse (marijuana and heroin) that fueled the scene. Her access to the jazz world was through her husband, Bob, a horn player. Their total commitment to an underground life kept their relationship solid until imprisonment separated them.

Presented here are Janet Clark's first experiences with marijuana and heroin, followed by her devastating impressions of the women's section of the controversial national drug treatment center in Lexington, Kentucky. The creation of this book was self-therapy while she was trying to kick her drug habit. Sadly, she died of a barbiturate overdose just before its publication.

From The Fantastic Lodge: The Autobiography of a Girl Drug Addict

So I must have started even before I was married—smoking pot. Yes, that's right; I started with Lil. We both had eyes and I had read *Really the Blues*, by Mezz Mezzrow, and I had eyes for everything after reading that book. He kept saying that pot was cool; it wasn't habit-forming. And then I read the *New York State Report on Narcotics* [*The Marihuana Problem in the City of New York* (1944), *aka.* the "LaGuardia Report"], whatever that was, to make sure before I was going to try. I was very cautious at this point.

One night some cats turned us on for the first time. And I got high, wham, immediately. Lil, it took her about eight to ten times. She went through some terror periods, hysteria periods. She had a hard time getting the kick, you know, but not me. It was made for me, I could see that, and from there on in, I carried a can of pot with me everywhere. I never had less than half a can on me, never, and I turned everybody on. That was my way of getting into the circle, too; I found out. Turn someone on and they're your friends; everything is solid, makes friends with everybody, you know. Pat would supply me with my pot, too, during this period. He was on bennies [Benzedrine]. What a horrible kick! I mean really that's a moron's kick if I ever heard of one. He was a real brrr cat, nervous.

I think most people tend to group narcotics all in one bunch; you know, "dope." But they're so entirely different, each one is an entirely different kick. Pot, pot is a young high, I think. It's for the time when you're in your teens and twenties and when you're operating a lot, making it to parties and bars and places like that because it's an all-inclusive high and a very social high. You learn after you start making it often that every social situation is a scream with pot, no matter what it is.

At first, when I first started smoking it, I couldn't do anything on it. I just had to sit somewhere and dig or else giggle helplessly, and that was the end of it. But it got so I'd be smoking it day and night, you know, and doing all kinds of strange things. I got on a kick, I remember, for a while. I would get high and it would just gas me to make phone calls because they always turned out completely strange, each one was an entirely new adventure, you know, without moving. And what was even better was getting a phone call, because this was an entirely different thing. Everything has worlds and worlds of meaning with pot.

*   *   *

I knew that Bob'd been using heroin and I thought at first that maybe the feelings he had for me could substitute, in part at least, for the heroin. But then I didn't know much about heroin in those days. I knew everybody was doing it and it was just a socially accepted thing. More than that, you just *had* to. It was like just the next most natural step for anyone to take, after joining that group.

So Bob didn't stop and I found out that the one time I felt apart from him was when he made it, you know. Then he was mostly snorting up. When that happened, when he'd make it, then we were apart for the first time. And at first I couldn't understand it and that, I saw, was because he was in an entirely different world, and I just wasn't there. So I gave up; I don't think I'd ever tried, anyway. And one night I told him to turn me on. Well, we both lied to one another. I told him I'd made it before. And he said "Yes," knowing that I hadn't, "So, solid! I'm not really turning you on for the first time"—that sort of thing, both absolving one another.

We were at my mother's house, that particular night. It was the first time I ever saw anything as far as ritual is concerned with any of the opping [operating or performing], you know. He got out a mirror and a razor blade—I was fascinated—and the caps and started cutting it into lines. Then he rolled the straw, the dollar bill, to snort it up with. I made it that night and it's difficult for me to remember exactly what my feelings were. Why, I don't know, when I can remember other things so well. But the first thing I noticed about it after I made it was when I got up to change a phonograph record that was playing. As I reached out to get the arm of the phonograph, I had the same feeling, almost identically, to the feeling I had when I was in the hospital and I'd gotten a shot of morphine—this tremendous physical joy in the sensation of moving your arm. But outside of that, nothing much was shaking and I used to get very sick the first couple of times.

I pulled a real foolish trick one night. I didn't know anything about horse and I made about a cap, which is pretty strong for someone who is just starting. We were going out, Brick, Bob and I, down at the Key—we were always running around. So I went in the bathroom. I was going to get all dressed up in my usual fashion and spend a couple of hours dressing and take a nice hot bath and so forth. And I started to op everything and I started getting violently ill. At least for the first six months that I was using heroin, I couldn't move after I made it or I would get violently ill. I had to be lying down, completely relaxed. So I got real sick and kept thinking I was going to faint and things like that and it was dragging me.

If it had stayed like that, maybe I would never even have stood around with it, any more. But after we got down to the Key that's when I really started digging it, what was happening. We walked into that place and everything was a hundred miles away. First kicks on horse are strange, just the strangest, just the biggest gas in life, you know. I guess that's why you keep on it. Everything was cold, but not terribly cold, just impersonally, beautifully cold and I saw all of these rows and rows of people and faces and everything and they were all just statues. They didn't mean anything to me. I sat down at the bar and Bim Connors was there too, and he kept insisting that we go out and smoke some pot; that's all I can remember of his conversation. He kept saying, "Well, I've got some pot, man. Don't you want to get high?" And I didn't realize it, but he'd been sitting there talking to me

for about three quarters of an hour, sounding me. Finally he said, "Well, do you? Or don't you?" And I couldn't talk. I just sat there and smiled, listened to everything that everybody had to say but I didn't say anything; I couldn't. It was like being paralyzed in a very pleasant manner.

And Bob was beginning to get worried and everybody was beginning to get worried. I didn't realize it at the time. Bob thought he'd given me too much. He'd never seen anybody get such a strange reaction.

So I'm sitting there on the stool and I guess what he started to do was twirl the seat, and move me to see what would happen. By this time everyone thought I was off my wig for sure, because all I did was sit there and just dig everything. So he twirled the seat and as he turned it around, I just got up off the seat and walked to the back and got real sick again in the john and came sailing back and was back to where I was and stayed there for two hours that way, not saying a word, not moving. But I was, really, I was in a completely different world: nothing could bother me. And finally after two hours they'd all given up. They were just letting me sit there, see when it was going to wear off, after they saw that I wasn't going to turn blue or anything. And I came to after the two hours. I remember I had terrible eyes for a straight [an ordinary cigarette]. I never had such eyes for a straight in my life. I had to have one and so the first words I said were "Hurry up, give me a straight!" So Brick drove Bob and I out to his place, and that ride was all just one beautiful ride.

So after that, that cinched it in every way. But still, oh, those first three or four months I was making it, just making it when I wanted to, not being hooked. Taking very small amounts, naturally. And just digging the kicks for the first time!

When you're not hooked you feel, first of all, there's a definite body sensation with horse, with the high that you get from horse, with being stoned. In fact, I can always measure whether I'm coming up or down by exactly how much of that feeling I have. This is when I'm *not* hooked. But it's difficult to define the feeling. The best way I can state it is to say that it's like having warm milk flowing through your veins, instead of blood—and *cold* blood. But really, it changes things so little and yet so much, you know, it's such a delicate thing to pin down.

After you make it, first there's a flash. That's the sudden onrush of the horse feeling. It starts usually in about the third time you jag it off. There's a term in the jargon that Bob always used a lot and this is the best, the only, word I can think of to describe a flash, and that's "getting a buzz." I never use that with pot. I always use it referring to horse because that's exactly what it is, you know, that first flash. Flash! When you use that word, most people think of something in terms of dynamite, you know, wham! And those words too, "dynamite" and "wham," are used in connection with the flash. But it's a feeling as though, all of a sudden, something good and easy and fine has happened. I think squares, when they think of somebody taking off and having flash, they expect him to all of a sudden jump up and say, "Oh, goody! goody! I felt it!" or something like that. When somebody else is making some junk for the first time and they want to know how it is before they make it, they say, "Well, how does it feel? How is it? Is it cool, man?" And if someone asked me that I would just say, as I feel the flash, you know, I'd wait and I'd say, "Yeah, yeah," like that. Nothing warmer, just "yeah." I think it's a warm feeling. But that isn't enough; that isn't a good description.

About the sixth time I made it I found out what this talking business was—how right after you snort up all you have eyes to do is just quack! Everything is possible! Everything is good! The best of all possible worlds, everything. You'd sit and just have maybe to-somebody-else-unintelligible conversations and they would just be gassing you.

And one of the biggest effects of horse is that you simply do not worry about things you worried about before. You look at them in a different way. You still think about them. I mean horse is a thinking op. You know, making all things possible and changing the entire outlook on all of your problems. Everything is always cool, everything is all right. It makes you not feel like fighting the world. It's not an aggressive high, but as though if someone were to come up and ask you to fight, you

know, you would say no, but not because you didn't want to necessarily get involved in it but because you know that you can't; so why bother. I mean it's that sort of a thing, you know, when you're *not* hooked.

* * *

They led me in there. There were a bunch of chicks and the first impression—looking at those women—it was really terrifying. That really made me want to cut and run. You never get over that first shock. After a while, they all start looking like people to you, and everything, and you get used to it. You get used to looking at the sores, at women that are so thin that it just shouldn't be. I mean, they look like those pictures from Dachau and the concentration camps, of people who have been starving for hundreds and hundreds of years or so, and all sort of hunched-over and huddled-up and sick-looking, you know. And they all stared at me, openly. So I sat there like a bump on a log, scared to death to open my mouth or do anything, and not really caring.

Then someone yelled, "Take her back to her room." Everyone yells, very informally, around there. So they took me back to the back room of the wards. There were these narrow, uncomfortable metal beds with some mattresses of sorts on them and clean linen, and beside each bed a little metal nightstand. But the bareness, and the bars at the window, the misery in everyone's face, oh God! I hate to even think about it. Gertie, the one that had come in just before me, was there, too, and several other chicks. And they were mostly just lying around in their beds and talking, mostly about junk, already.

I laid on the bed with my face away from everyone, looking out the window, and thought about Bob, and people, and, good God, where was I, what was this place like, and what could I expect?

This paralysis passed off after about three hours. By that time, it was shot time. Already some of the girls from the other rooms in the ward had come back to see the newcomers. And they put on a little act. You know, each one has a routine. I met, first, Belle, an eighteen-year-old girl who was on morphine. Black hair, talked in a broad Southern drawl. She was an end junkie, and hard as tacks. Nothing could do anything to Belle! She laughed a lot, showed us a good section of her tits, flung up her nightgown, and passed butts around.

I sat and listened mostly to them quack on, tell about the glamour of their outside lives, and outside junk histories. It's amazing! They don't become any less junkies, at all, for being in the place. All is junk, and that's all, you know; that's the way it is. This identification of yourself as a junkie. After the first six, eight months that I was making it, I never said, "Well, I'm a junkie," as an excuse or as anything. But now I say it constantly. I always refer to myself as a junkie, even when I'm not hooked or anything. And when you're introduced to somebody for the first time, the first thing you find out is whether he's a junkie or not. It's like belonging to some fantastic lodge, you know, but the initiation ceremony is a lot rougher.

While they were talking, I was getting an idea of what the withdrawal treatment actually consisted of. They said, "Wait till you get the first shot. Ha! ha! ha! It's nothing but water. It's *all* water. You won't even *feel* the first one. And by the end, ugh, it's terrible."

So I started sounding Belle: "How long do they keep you up here in the withdrawal ward?" She said, "Well, I've been up here fourteen days." I said, "Fourteen days!" She says, "Yeah, and I'm still getting two shots and three sedatives." She says, "You know, I had the goofball [barbiturate] habit, too." I found that out soon enough. She went into convulsions later on that evening. It's really terrible. I never had any real contacts with goofballs. As far as that goes, I never had any contact with any of the messes that those chicks were using in that joint. I never heard of such conglomerations: even a paraldehyde, believe it or not! Codeine, morphine, dilaudid, and demerol and pantopon! And oh, the list is fantastic! It was just a mess, just a mess!

So, at any rate, shot time came around and already the idea was turning over in my mind that I can't stay up here for fourteen days; I can't! The best thing to do now that I'm here, is to kick my own way cold and get it over with, you know. So I sounded one of the chicks about what could happen if I didn't take the shot.

"Didn't take a shot? What's wrong with you, girl? Don't you want your shot?"

I said, "Well, what would happen *if* . . . ?"

She said, "Oh, you *have* to take it."

That immediately made me furious, and determined me not to. No one was going to tell me what I had to take. They can't *force* you to take a narcotic. And I wanted to get out of the withdrawal ward, and immediately, because I found out I couldn't have any books, I couldn't read, I couldn't do anything, nothing. What can you do? You can only take so many baths a day, and you're weak. I mean, that was at least a diversion, you know. And there's nothing to do—nothing—except talk about junk. And oh, that was wigging me already.

So when my turn came—they call your name down the hall, and you run down to this little room—I said, "Would you mind awfully if I don't take my shot?" And there was a long pause, and the nurse's aide sort of did a double-take. She says, "Not take your shot?" She says, "Look, honey, we have your shots three times a day for girls who have it your size. We have it at six o'clock in the morning, two o'clock in the afternoon, and nine o'clock in the evening. We take our shots at those times and that's that. Now, c'mere. No monkey business." And I said, "No, I mean it. I don't want to take them." "Well, you *have* to take them." I said, "I don't have to do any such thing." And she says, "Well, now look, honey . . ." Then she tried cajoling. She said, "The doctor'll be around in the morning, and you tell him. Let it be on his authority," she says, "I don't want to get into any trouble and lose my job. Why not be a nice girl?" She said, "Boy, I never thought I'd have to coax anyone in this joint into letting a needle go into their arm." I said, "So okay, solid."

My arm was sore for days after needling the junk. They grab ahold of your arm and give you a skin pop, you know, just knock it in, on the top of your shoulder, somewhere, and hit eight or nine tendons and things. After she made it, I sat around and waited. Didn't feel a thing. It was just like everyone said: the first shot is the strongest and the first shot is nothing.

Well, of course, when you think about it, they certainly aren't going to give you anything that will let you feel anything, because they want you to get over that idea of getting a kick from the needle.

Then they gave me my sedative—I *loved* my sedatives. I don't think I could have made the place without sedatives. I went back to bed after sitting up for a while and talking to the girls, and fell out, and had a wonderful night's sleep, that first night. That was the only night I got a wonderful night's sleep. If I'd known that back room was directly under psycho, I certainly would have asked for another; they kept me awake night after night after night.

I was only up in the withdrawal ward for four or five days, whereas most of the inmates were there anywhere from eighteen to twenty-four. Of course, they were going through the full withdrawal treatment, breaking their shots down, and so on and so forth.

The first thing that amazed me, more than anything else, was the high number of what I call medical junkies that were there. These would be people who had something legitimately wrong with them, at one time or another, and went to a doctor for a prescription, and he prescribed morphine or dilaudid or some of the other various kinds of narcotics, pantopon or something of that sort. And then, without even knowing that they were drawn up in the drug fascination, and before they knew it, they were hooked. Then—the thing that always interested me in these cases, the pattern was almost always identical—the doctor would become aware that they were asking for too many prescriptions. And the doctor would call the patient in for a conference, man to man, or woman to woman, or what have you. He would say, "Miss So-and-So, I hate to tell you this, but I think you're an addict!" Now this doctor was the son of a bitch that turned it on in the first place, and obviously gave her too much.

Most of these medical junkies there were Southerners. And they were pretty strange people. They were junkies from their hearts, that's for sure. In fact, they had a tendency, the medical junkies in the withdrawal ward, to complain, to play the sick-woman act, and say, "There's something vitally wrong with me that this place doesn't do anything about. I really need to have something . . ."

Like Brownie. She was a little old whore,

around fifty-six, thin as a toothpick, just unbelievably so. She had death written on her face, if I've ever seen it. In fact, I think the woman must be dead by now. She did have something very wrong with her. There's no question about it. I believe it was cancer of the liver or something like that. But she had gotten so hooked and hung up that she *had* to come there. Her family couldn't support the cost of the drug, even in spite of the fact that she wasn't paying much. She said to me once in a very horrified voice, "Sometimes it added up to ten dollars a week!" I said, "Ten dollars a week! Are you kidding?" So she was hung up and came up there. And every few days, she'd say, "Now, it's been"—and she'd count—"sixteen days since I had any dilaudid and I feel like hell, I don't mind telling you. You don't realize I'm a sick woman. I *need* my dilaudid."

Well, the illicit junkies, of course, they have an entirely different attitude toward the whole thing. In the illicit junkie you don't find any of this real hypochondria that you find in the medical junkie. But also, whereas the medical junkie always thinks in terms of himself as being a sick person, the illicit junkie thinks in terms of himself or herself as a member of the underworld. It's odd. What they're actually doing is the same damn thing when it comes down to it.

At first, in Lexington, I was very shy. I needn't have been. I found out that every accidental stranger knows every other accidental stranger's choice of narcotic, first of all. No, the first is "Vol or Con," but the second question they are liable to ask is: "What kind of stuff are you using?" One time I answered, "Horse," and I happened to get a medical junkie, and she looked at me and said, "Horse! I never heard of that." I explained I meant heroin. And so, then, *that* got around.

The third thing they ask is your location, where you're from. Originally, you sort of get your friendships via location and choice of drug. "There's a girl downstairs who uses heroin and who comes from your town. She wants to meet you." And, actually, in the end, by choice of drug, because the people who use horse all look down on the people who use M and the people who use M all think they're much better than the people who use dilaudid, and everybody looks down on demerol users as notorious fools.

There were all types, of course, everything from A to Z. There were hustling bitches from the larger cities—San Francisco, Washington, Los Angeles—I found out how the heat was in every town across the United States. It's an international exchange for information concerning dope. That's all it is, really. You sit around in this dayroom (they won't let you do anything in the withdrawal ward; they won't even let you have a book) and tell one another stories about junk. And sometimes it would really be tremendous. I mean the eyes that you develop talking about it. I found it very demoralizing, I must say.

BARBARA QUINN
1942–

Barbara "Cookie" Goodman Quinn's teenage years were lived in and around New York City in the 1950's. She pursued a variety of antisocial roles available to urban adolescent rebels: gang leader, heroin addict, prostitute, and thief. Delighted to gain the acceptance of the slightly older crowd of teenage addicts by scoring Dilaudid for them in pharmacies with faked prescriptions, she liked the image of herself as a white girl going to meet her connection in Spanish Harlem. She gained a measure of security with her two junkie lovers, Harriet and Franco. As she moved up from skin-popping to mainlining heroin, she began to examine her compulsion for acquiring "a habit [that] could excuse anything." She decided to reform after seeing the Eartha Kitt movie *The Synanon Story*, in 1965. She proved to be an excellent subject for the Synanon relentless style of group encounters.

Quinn overcame her addiction to heroin and wrote a probing account of her life as a drug addict, *Cookie* (1971). (The title was changed to *Junkie* in the paperback edition.) She is a founder of New York City's Phoenix House, an addict rehabilitation center.

Barbara Quinn. "When I woke up in the morning I wanted to feel able to get through the day, so I shot up. I wanted to feel good at night, so I shot up again. And in between, I took off whenever I had the chance."

From **Cookie**

I went to school only two or three days a week; the other days I went with Harriet to cop our dope. I had my own set of works now; I'd bought the needle from Harriet's connection and the dropper from an unsuspecting drugstore. I'd learned to skin-pop for myself. I shot up at home before I went to school, nodding during the day, then took off again in the bathroom shortly before school was over. The ride home was great: It didn't matter whether I had a seat or not, the bumping and the jerking of the train only added to the great feeling, and even people bumping and rubbing up against me in the crush felt good. Standing or sitting, I could slump and nod and experience the motions of the train pulsating all the way inside me.

When I didn't go to school I went with Harriet to Lexington Avenue at 100th Street in Spanish Harlem. Our connection was a black janitor named Maurice. He let us shoot up in his apartment, and if his wife happened to be home we shot up in the boiler room. We usually bought a nickel bag between us and took off, then we went up on a rooftop to nod; though it was winter, we didn't feel the cold when we were high. We stayed up on the roof for quite a while, then we came down to hang around the block for another three or four hours and copped a few extra bags for that evening and the next day. It was a real community. Everyone knew everyone else by name. There were only a few white addicts there and most of the people were blacks or Puerto Ricans. Harriet and I were always together, just about the only white girls there. I felt at home, I was part of the community. At the time I was still rather pretty, innocent, and girlish-looking with my hair worn in two braids. The addicts treated me like the neighborhood mascot. They called me Cookie—or Baby. . . .

We met there almost every morning, made our connection, and shot up. If we didn't see Maurice we'd stand around, and soon enough someone would always come up and say, "Hey, Baby! I can cop for you." We'd give him the money for however many bags we wanted and we'd turn him on, sharing two bags between the three of us. Some-times we got beat for our money: The cat would simply disappear or he'd bring us a few bags of milk sugar—known as dummy—and be off before we discovered our mistake.

On the whole, though, I felt I was among friends. "You shouldn't be shooting up," people would tell me solicitously—even while we were sharing together. They warned me I'd start hustling one day. I laughed. "Me? Never!" But I was glad they really cared for me. I didn't know they were simply trying to edge me away from Harriet who was watching over me like a mother hen. They knew that sooner or later every addict starts hustling and they wanted to be there once I got started.

I knew about hustling, but I thought I was a special case and I had a special strength that would let me stop whenever I wanted to. Harriet probably wasn't as convinced as I was. "If I ever catch you hustling, Cookie, I'll break your arm. I swear I will, Cookie," she warned.

*   *   *

I stayed at the beauty school on Eighth Avenue for only a month, then quit. They would have kicked me out anyway because I showed up so seldom and when I did I was always stoned and nodding. Now I could spend every day with Harriet. She was my man. I wanted to do everything with her and I wanted to be as much like her as I could.

I told Harriet I wanted to mainline, injecting the dope directly into the vein as she did instead of popping it under the skin. Everyone else was mainlining, too; it was much better. I was used to the needle now and in fact I enjoyed the sharp prick itself as a promise of the good sensation that always followed.

Harriet tried to talk me out of it. "You start mainlining and before you know it you'll have a habit," she warned.

I persisted.

The first time I mainlined was at Harriet's place in the Bronx, perhaps two months after Leslie had first turned me on to skin-popping. She took the belt off her pants and fastened it around my arm just above the elbow, to make the vein stand out, then she slapped my arm to stimulate the blood and make the vein even more prominent. I watched her as she pushed in the spike; I wanted to learn from her. She loosened the belt and squeezed on the bulb. The dope went into my vein. I got an immediate rush. She tightened the belt a moment and the pressure from my heart pushed the blood and heroin through the vein again and up the eyedropper. She loosened the belt and injected the mixture again. Again she tightened the belt and when she let go of the syringe bulb the blood and heroin rose once more. She did it a few times. Each time she squeezed the dropper I got the same rush, an unbelievably exciting feeling of warmth and composure. Addicts call this trick "booting"; it increases the pleasure of the first rush and spreads it out over what seems ages but is usually less than a minute. With popping I'd had the sensation first in my stomach; with mainlining it went directly to my head. It was everything I'd expected—and more.

On 100th Street they knew I was mainlining now. They warned me again. "You'll get a habit, Baby, and then you'll be hustling just like all them other chicks." We were the only white girls in the neighborhood who weren't hustling, the only girls who still had their looks. We still looked fresh.

I laughed at them. "Me a streetwalker? You must be out of your fucking mind."

"Yeah, Baby! You'll be strung out soon enough. Just you keep mainlining all that dope."

"But I can control myself. And Harriet would never let me get a habit."

Did I mean it? In a way I did. I wanted to believe that I could always stop myself before it got too late. And yet there was a fascination in going the whole way, tasting everything, knowing there was nothing I wouldn't dare do. Did I really want control? Perhaps not. Perhaps I wanted to shuck off all responsibility. A habit was a hallmark of sorts, a license. A habit could excuse everything. With a habit I could throw off all restraints, be responsible to no one, not even to myself.

"How do you know when you have a habit?" I asked the junkies on 100th Street. I wanted to be around when it happened to me. I wanted to be the first to recognize it.

They laughed and snickered. "A habit, Baby, is a habit. And when you have it, Baby, you'll know you have it. And if you want to know if you have it

right now, try not taking it for just one day."

I knew I wasn't hooked. I could have stopped any time I wanted to. Sure I was taking off twice each day, but that was because I *wanted* to, not because I *had* to. When I woke in the morning I wanted to feel able to get through the day, so I shot up. I wanted to feel good at night, so I shot up again. And in between, I took off whenever I had the chance.

It wasn't easy finding the money for dope each day. I'd lost my Saturday job, and I could no longer tell my mother I needed the money for tuition at the hairdressing school. But occasionally I could wangle five dollars out of her for pocket money, and I could also—as I'd been doing since I was a little kid—snitch money from her pocketbook when she was asleep. One day, for some reason, I had no money and Harriet had none either. She'd stayed over with me that night in Yonkers and we had no dope to shoot up in the morning. I thought that maybe if I could wait until my mother came home at night, I could get some off her and then we could go down to the block and score. But now it was only noon and Harry and I were walking down Riverdale Avenue and the weather was chilly and windy and I felt just awful. Really terrible. There was a pain in my calves that got worse with each step. I was yawning like crazy. I shivered, the water rolling out of my eyes with each yawn.

"Harry," I said, "I feel really weird." I described my symptoms. "Is it a habit? Does it mean I have a habit?"

Harriet took it philosophically. "Yeah, baby. You got a habit. Ain't that what you wanted?"

I was thrilled. A real habit. An honest-to-goodness, high-flying, down-to-earth, real McCoy habit. Wow, man! I was a junkie. Jay-you-en-kay-eye-ee junkie. Junkie was something special, something big and important and heroic. Real wild. A name that meant something powerful and gutsy like Annie Oakley or Wild Bill Hickok. I was as excited as I'd been that other time, coming home on the bus from hairdressing school with Sally and Leslie when Leslie had promised to turn us on to the real thing. That was a lifetime ago. That was . . . could it really have been only four months earlier? It seemed impossible.

EDITH PIAF
1915–63

Edith Piaf and Jean Cocteau. These longtime friends had both been addicted to opium; they died on the same day in 1963, mourned by millions.

Like Billie Holiday, the great Parisian *chanteuse realiste* was a mainline addict for her last fifteen years. Edith Piaf began using morphine while recovering from injuries received in a 1951 auto accident, acquiring a habit she never kicked for long, despite four stays in detoxication clinics. These years nonetheless marked the peak of her international fame. Piaf was outspoken about addictive drugs; the following is from *Piaf: A Biography*, written by her sister, Simone Bertault.

From Piaf: A Biography

Drugs are a carnival in hell. They're merry-go-rounds and roller coasters. You shoot up, you rocket down; you go up again, you come down again. . . . Everything's like everything else, always the same; monotonous; gray; dirty. But you don't even notice, you go right on.

*   *   *

When I stuck the needle into my flesh, I didn't gasp with pleasure—I gasped with relief. You're in a hurry to give yourself a shot, not because it makes you feel good but because it makes you stop feeling bad. Christ, are we stupid! The more you take, the more you suffer, and the more you have to take so you won't hurt so much inside. Your mind's been gone for a long time. It's like living in a fog.

FRANÇOISE SAGAN
1935–

Like Edith Piaf six years earlier, Françoise Sagan became addicted to the morphine given to her daily for three months to allay the pain of injuries suffered in an auto accident. The diary kept by the novelist, whose *Bonjour Tristesse* (1954) brought her international recognition at age eigh-

teen, describes her agonizing nine-day cure in a detoxication clinic. Bernard Buffet illustrated her diary with stark line drawings, and the resulting publication, in large quarto format, is a unique masterpiece of drug literature, bearing comparison in style and appearance to Jean Cocteau's celebrated *Opium: Journal d'une Désintoxication* (1930).

After drifting on waves of pain and remorse to a state of utter cynicism and despair, Sagan slowly returned, object by object, perception by perception, to a sense of hope.

Françoise Sagan.
"Artificial paradise of nonsuffering,
I shall know you no more."

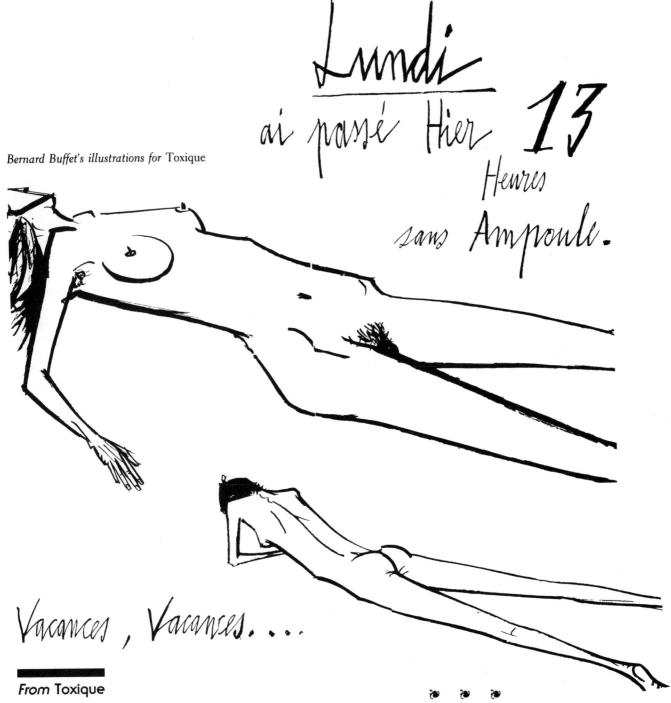

Bernard Buffet's illustrations for Toxique

Lundi
ai passé Hier **13**
Heures
sans Ampoule.

Vacances, Vacances. . . .

From Toxique

Monday
Yesterday I went 13 hours without a shot.

🐦 🐦 🐦

I think that's quite an accomplishment.

Morrel is very kind. I like him a lot. Yesterday he suggested I take an Orchar test. I said "yes," but I was worried. The weather is beautiful, the grass is green, mosquitoes are swarming over the pond. And a small something is stirring inside me.

🐦 🐦 🐦

Artificial paradise of nonsuffering, I shall know you no more. I'll no longer see Fifi or Felix deftly decapitating those little ampoules with the blue-inked labels, those little ampoules that look so innocent and aren't innocent at all. As treacherous as X—— is, perhaps, as reassuring as Annibal is in a very real way, etc. Annibal has brought me a black shetland-wool sweater. If I hadn't decided not to talk about anyone in this diary I'd sing a hymn to the glory of Annibal, and to a black shetland-wool sweater on a tanned skin. Vacation, vacation . . .

ANNA KAVAN
1901–1968

Anna Kavan's character Julia is like a nineteenth-century laudanum addict—Elizabeth Barrett Browning and the Young Lady Laudanum-Drinker come to mind. She is not forced to become a thief or a prostitute for a fix, because prevailing British practice permitted doctors to dispense maintenance doses of heroin to addicts. But her total reliance on her "bazooka," as she calls her hypodermic needle, isolates her from society as completely as any street junkie.

The autobiographical nature of the story "Julia and the Bazooka" is well known. Anna Kavan was a heroin addict for the last three decades of her life. Her health was poor, and she had an increasingly difficult time getting her legal heroin when British drug laws stiffened in the 1960's. She was found dead at age sixty-seven with a loaded syringe in her hand.

Kavan traveled widely, living for a time in California, and broke new ground in literature by bringing Kafkaesque techniques to science fiction. Like William Burroughs, Kavan effectively used a cinematic style to portray the dissociated mind of a drug addict.

Julia and the Bazooka

Julia is a little girl with long straight hair and big eyes. Julia loved flowers. In the cornfield she has picked an enormous untidy bunch of red poppies which she is holding up so that most of her face is hidden except the eyes. Her eyes look sad because she has just been told to throw the poppies away, not to bring them inside to make a mess dropping their petals all over the house. Some of them have shed their petals already, the front of her dress is quite red. Julia is also a quiet schoolgirl who does not make many friends. Then she is a tall student standing with other students who have passed their final examinations, whose faces are gay and excited, eager to start life in the world. Only Julia's eyes are sad. Although she smiles with the others, she does not share their enthusiasm for living. She feels cut off from people. She is afraid of the world.

Julia is also a young bride in a white dress, holding a sheaf of roses in one hand and in the other a very small flat white satin bag containing a lace-edged handkerchief scented with Arpège and a plastic syringe. Now Julia's eyes are not sad at all. She has one foot on the step of a car, its door held open by a young man with kinky brown hair and a rose in his buttonhole. She is laughing because of something he's said or because he has just squeezed her arm or because she no longer feels frightened or cut off now that she has the syringe. A group of indistinct people in the background look on approvingly as if they are glad to transfer responsibility for Julia to the young man. Julia who loves flowers waves to them with her roses as she drives off with him.

Julia is also dead without any flowers. The doctor sighs when he looks at her lying there. No one else comes to look except the official people. The ashes of the tall girl Julia barely fill the silver cup she won in the tennis tournament. To improve her game the tennis professional gives her the syringe. He is a joking kind of man and calls the syringe a bazooka. Julia calls it that too, the name sounds funny, it makes her laugh. Of course she knows all the sensational stories about drug addiction, but the word bazooka makes nonsense of them, makes the whole drug business seem not serious. Without the bazooka she might not have won the cup, which as a container will at last serve a useful purpose. It is Julia's serve that wins the decisive game. Holding two tennis balls in her left hand, she throws one high in the air while her right hand flies up over her head, brings the racket down, wham, and sends the ball skimming over the opposite court hardly bouncing at all, a service almost impossible to return. Holding two balls in her hand Julia also lies in bed beside the young man with kinky hair. Julia is also lying in wreckage under an army blanket, and eventually Julia's ashes go into the silver cup.

The undertaker or somebody closes the lid and

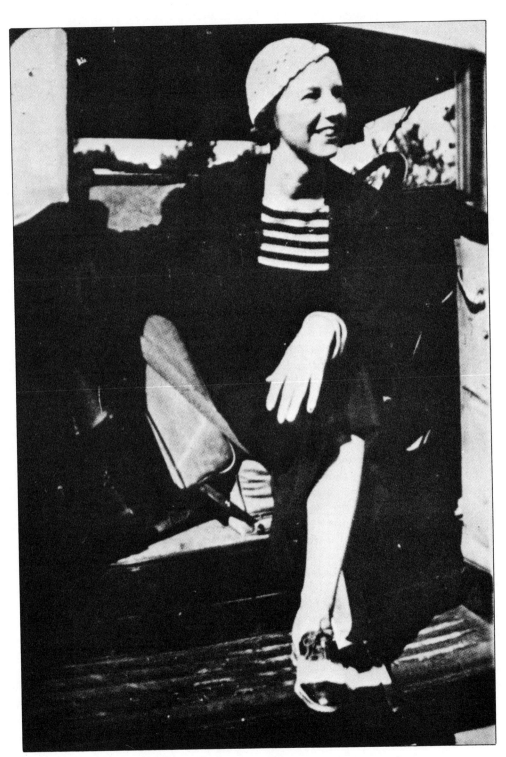

*Anna Kavan. "She is most unlike the popular notion of a
drug addict. Nobody could call her vicious."*

locks the cup in a pigeonhole among thousands of identical pigeonholes in a wall at the top of a cliff overlooking the sea. The winter sea is the color of pumice, the sky cold as gray ice, the icy wind charges straight at the wall making it tremble so that the silver cup in its pigeonhole shivers and tinkles faintly. The wind is trying to tear to pieces a few frostbitten flowers which have not been left for Julia at the foot of the wall. Julia is also driving with her bridegroom in the high mountains through fields of flowers. They stop the car and pick armfuls of daffodils and narcissi. There are no flowers for Julia in the pigeonhole and no bridegroom either.

"This is her syringe, her bazooka she always called it," the doctor says with a small sad smile. "It must be twenty years old at least. Look how the measures have been worn away by continuous use." The battered old plastic syringe is unbreakable, unlike the glass syringes which used to be kept in boiled water in metal boxes and reasonably sterile. This discolored old syringe has always been left lying about somewhere, accumulating germs and the assorted dirt of wars and cities. All the same, it has not done Julia any great harm. An occasional infection cured with penicillin, nothing serious. "Such dangers are grossly exaggerated."

Julia and her bazooka travel all over the world. She wants to see everything, every country. The young man with kinky hair is not there, but she is in a car and somebody sits beside her. Julia is a good driver. She drives anything, racing cars, heavy trucks. Her long hair streams out from under the crash helmet as she drives for the racing teams. Today she is lapping only a fraction of a second behind the number one driver when a red-hot bit of his clutch flies off and punctures her nearside tire, and the car somersaults twice and tears through a wall. Julia steps out of the wreck uninjured and walks away holding her handbag with the syringe inside it. She is laughing. Julia always laughs at danger. Nothing can frighten her while she has the syringe. Sometimes she thinks of the kinky-haired man and wonders what he is doing. Then she laughs. There are always plenty of people to bring her flowers and make her feel gay. She hardly remembers how sad and lonely she used to feel before she had the syringe.

Julia likes the doctor as soon as she meets him. He is understanding and kind like the father she has

imagined but never known. He does not want to take her syringe away. He says, "You've used it for years already and you're none the worse. In fact you'd be far worse off without it." He trusts Julia, he knows she is not irresponsible, she does not increase the dosage too much or experiment with new drugs. It is ridiculous to say all drug addicts are alike, all liars, all vicious, all psychopaths or delinquents just out for kicks. He is sympathetic toward Julia whose personality has been damaged by no love in childhood so that she can't make contact with people or feel at home in the world. In his opinion she is quite right to use the syringe, it is as essential to her as insulin to a diabetic. Without it she could not lead a normal existence, her life would be a shambles, but with its support she is conscientious and energetic, intelligent, friendly. She is most unlike the popular notion of a drug addict. Nobody could call her vicious.

Julia who loves flowers has made a garden on a flat roof in the city, all around her are pots of scarlet geraniums. Throughout the summer she has watered them every day because the pots dry out so fast up here in the sun and wind. Now summer is over, there is frost in the air. The leaves of the plants have turned yellow. Although the flowers have survived up to now the next frost will finish them off. It is wartime, the time of the flying bombs, they come over all the time, there seems to be nothing to stop them. Julia is used to them, she ignores them, she does not look. To save the flowers from the frost she picks them all quickly and takes them indoors. Then it is winter and Julia is on the roof planting bulbs to flower in the spring. The flying bombs are still coming over, quite low, just above the roofs and chimneys, their chugging noise fills the sky. One after another, they keep coming over, making their monotonous mechanical noise. When the engine cuts out there is a sudden startling silence, suspense, everything suddenly goes unnaturally still. Julia does not look up when the silence comes, but all at once it seems very cold on the roof, and she plants the last bulb in a hurry.

The doctor has gone to consult a top psychiatrist about one of his patients. The psychiatrist is immensely dignified, extremely well-dressed, his voice matches his outer aspect. When the bomb silence starts, his clear grave voice says solemnly, "I advise you to take cover under that table beside you," as he himself glides with the utmost dignity under his impressive desk. Julia leaves the roof and steps onto the staircase, which is not there. The stairs have crumbled, the whole house is crumbling, collapsing, the world bursts and burns, while she falls through the dark. The ARP men dig Julia out of the rubble. Red geraniums are spilling down the front of her dress, she has forgotten the time between, and is forgetting more and more every moment. Someone spreads a gray blanket over her, she lies underneath it in her red-stained dress, her bag, with the bazooka inside, safely hooked over one arm. How cold it is in the exploding world. The northern lights burst out in frigid brilliance across the sky. The ice roars and thunders like gunfire. The cold is glacial, a glass dome of cold covers the globe. Icebergs tower as high as mountains, furious blizzards swoop at each other like white wild beasts. All things are turning to ice in the mortal cold, and the cold has a face which sparkles with frost. It seems to be a face Julia knows, though she has forgotten whose face it is.

The undertaker hurriedly shuts himself inside his car, out of the cruel wind. The parson hurries toward his house, hatless, thin gray hair blowing about wildly. The wind snatches a tattered wreath of frost-blackened flowers and rolls it over the grass, past the undertaker and the parson, who both pretend not to see. They are not going to stay out in the cold any longer, it is not their job to look after the flowers. They do not know that Julia loves flowers and they do not care. The wreath was not put there for her, anyhow.

Julia is rushing after the nameless face, running as fast as if she was playing tennis. But when she comes near she does not, after all, recognize that glittering death-mask. It has gone now, there's nothing but arctic glitter, she is a bride again beside the young man with brown hair. The lights are blazing, but she shivers a little in her thin dress because the church is so cold. The dazzling brilliance of the aurora borealis has burnt right through the roof with its frigid fire. Snow slants down between the rafters, there is ice on the altar, snowdrifts in the aisles, the holy water and the communion wine have been frozen solid. Snow is Julia's bridal white, icicles are her jewels. The diamond-sparkling coronet on her head confuses her thoughts. Where has everyone gone? The bridegroom is dead, or in bed with some girl or other, and she herself lies under a dirty blanket with red on her dress.

"Won't somebody help me?" she calls. "I can't move." But no one takes any notice. She is not cold any longer. Suddenly now she is burning, a fever is burning her up. Her face is on fire, her dry mouth seems to be full of ashes. She sees the kind doctor coming and tries to call him, but can only whisper, "Please help me. . . ," so faintly that he does not hear. Sighing, he takes off his hat, gazing down at his name printed inside in small gold letters under the leather band. The kinky-haired young man is not in bed with anyone. He is wounded in a sea battle. He falls on the warship's deck, an officer tries to grab him but it's too late, over and over he rolls down the steeply sloping deck to the black bottomless water. The officer looks over the side, holding a lifebelt, but does not throw it down to the injured man; instead, he puts it on himself, and runs to a boat which is being lowered. The doctor comes home from the house of the famous psychiatrist. His head is bent, his eyes are lowered, he walks slowly because he feels tired and sad. He does not look up so he never sees Julia waving to him with a bunch of geraniums from the window.

The pigeonhole wall stands deserted in the cold dusk. The undertaker has driven home. His feet are so cold he can't feel them, these winter funerals are the very devil. He slams the car door, goes inside stamping his feet, and shouts to his wife to bring, double quick, a good strong hot rum with plenty of lemon and sugar, in case he has caught a chill. The wife, who was just going out to a bingo session, grumbles at being delayed, and bangs about in the kitchen. At the vicarage the parson is eating a crumpet for tea, his chair pulled so close to the fire that he is practically in the grate.

It has got quite dark outside, the wall has turned black. As the wind shakes it, the faintest of tinkles comes from the pigeonhole where all that is left of Julia has been left. Surely there are some red flowers somewhere, Julia would be thinking, if she could still think. Then she would think something amusing, she would remember the bazooka and start to laugh. But nothing is left of Julia really, she is not there. The only occupant of the pigeonhole is the silver cup, which can't think or laugh or remember. There is no more Julia anywhere. Where she was there is only nothing.

PSYCHEDELIC
PIONEERS

Before the 1950's, psychedelic research was performed almost exclusively with mescaline, the active agent of the Native American sacred cactus peyote, and mainly concerned the drug's startling visual effects. Anthropologists began observing ceremonial use of peyote by southwestern Indians during the 1890's, but peyote occasionally reached bohemian society where Havelock Ellis, Aleister Crowley, Mabel Dodge Luhan, and Antonin Artaud tried it. Nonetheless, peyote was generally regarded as a bizarre narcotic of the Indians and was rarely used outside of their tribes. The magic mushrooms of Mexico were considered a myth. It was the discovery of LSD in 1943 by Albert Hofmann in Switzerland that catalyzed the psychedelic era.

A synthetic substance derived from ergot of

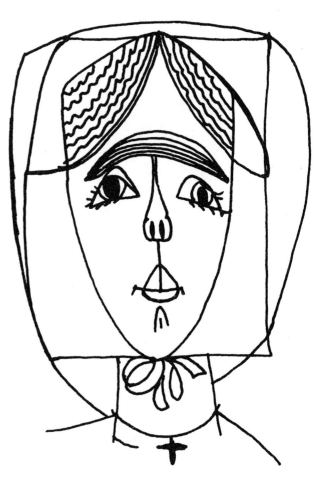

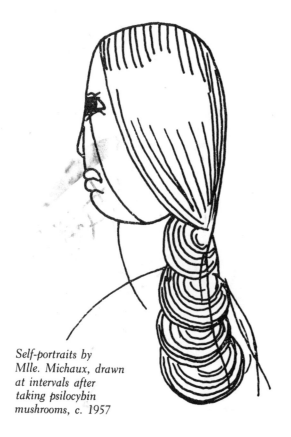

Self-portraits by Mlle. Michaux, drawn at intervals after taking psilocybin mushrooms, c. 1957

rye, LSD was the modern, pharmaceutical relative of the shamanistic plant drugs that had been used for over thirty-five centuries in religious and healing ceremonies. LSD was the first mass-produced, dose-controlled psychedelic. Extremely small doses expanded consciousness without the sometimes unpleasant side effects of plant alkaloids. The psychiatric profession called this class of drugs "psychotomimetic" ("mimicking psychoses"). Although positive results were obtained in treating alcoholism, drug addiction, sexual dysfunction, and some forms of criminal behavior, LSD, mescaline, and psilocybin (the active agent in magic mushrooms) were considered too dangerous to be given to normal people with common neuroses. Gradually this view changed as some psychiatrists and clinicians began testing the drugs on themselves, and then on their friends and associates, because psychedelics appeared to encourage self-knowledge and release creativity. The concept of "psychotomimetic" gradually gave way to "psychedelic" ("mind-manifesting," the term coined by Humphry Osmond in 1957). Aldous Huxley's mescaline books (*The Doors of Perception*, 1954, and *Heaven and Hell*, 1956) presented his cautiously utopian viewpoint grounded in mystical and aesthetic awareness, and greatly influenced the small group of California psychiatrists and their patients who pioneered psychotherapy with psychedelic drugs during the 1950's.

Five of the accounts in this section were written by women who lived in the Los Angeles area. Anaïs Nin felt her "senses were multiplied as if I had a hundred eyes, a hundred ears, a hundred fingertips." She understood the emotional realm of women more clearly than before, but concluded that drugs were too passive an access to the imagination. Laura and Aldous Huxley were the prototype of a couple for whom psychedelic experience was part of the evolution of their relationship. They worked together on analytic techniques, particularly the process of communicating during altered states while acting as guides for each other's inner voyages. The ego-dissolving impact of a psychedelic drug taken at a moment of emotional vulnerability is dramatically presented in Joyce James's "Shouted From the Housetops: A Peyote Awakening." Para-

psychologist Constance A. Newland (a pseudonym) underwent a series of LSD trips in conjunction with psychoanalysis, vividly described in *Myself and I*. Her book demonstrated the way psychedelic drugs speed up the therapeutic process.

Adelle Davis, the leading American nutritionist of her time, was the first woman to publish a full-length book on her LSD experiences. *Exploring Inner Space* (1961), written under the pen name Jane Dunlap and not included here, is an account of Davis's five LSD sessions in 1959, conducted under the supervision of a psychiatrist. She experienced the stages of species evolution and interplanetary travel; subsequent to these experiences, her writing blocks dissolved and her relationships with her husband and children improved markedly. Her young daughter called it "the drug that makes Mommy terribly nice for a whole month." World-renowned medium Eileen J. Garrett, director of the Parapsychology Foundation, used LSD to investigate parapsychological phenomena, finding it "a serious method by which one reaches the deep levels of the unconscious self."

Valentina and R. Gordon Wasson played a significant role during the early years of the psychedelic era by discovering, after decades of research and travel, ritual use of the magic mushroom by Mazatec Indians living in a remote part of Oaxaca, Mexico. In 1957 Valentina published an account of her extraordinary mushroom trip with her daughter, in which they felt transported to different places and time periods. A momentous part of the Wassons' discovery was their introduction of the elderly Mazatec shaman woman, María Sabina, to Western culture. Through publicity in *Life* and the release of a record album of her mushroom chant, the *curandera* (Spanish word for a female shaman) be-

came a living legend to the young beats and, later, hippies who retraced the Wassons' path to her remote mountain village, seeking the magic mushroom high.

The Wassons' discovery also awakened interest among anthropologists. In the next decade Marlene Dobkin de Rios, Barbara Myerhoff, and Joan Halifax, among others, observed and participated in native shamanistic drug ceremonies in Mexico and South America. Most interesting to them was the importance placed on the diagnostic and healing value of the drug plants when consumed in age-old rituals. Psychedelic therapy with the dying was first suggested by Valentina Wasson, and later performed by Laura Huxley and Joan Halifax. By their writings and example the psychedelic pioneers of the 1950's influenced the growth of alternative medicine and holistic health in the 1970's.

Consciousness-expanding drugs were legal for research when Nin, Huxley, and others took them. There was as yet no psychedelic movement, media hysteria, or public outcry. The situation changed in the 1960's, prompting Margaret Mead, dean of American anthropologists, to view with alarm "a flood of poorly conceived legislation which could interfere with both academic and religious freedom."

MARÍA SABINA
1896–

Eighty-six-year-old María Sabina is the embodiment of a shaman woman. Her great-grandfather, grandfather, and father were all shamans of *teo-nanacatl*, "the flesh of the gods," the sacred mushroom that gives visions and transports the eater to "the world where everything is known." Their mushroom culture has survived underground for four centuries, since being outlawed by the sixteenth-century Spanish conquistadores.

When she was four, María Sabina and her sister ate psilocybin mushrooms for the first time near their village of Huautla de Jiménez in Oaxaca. She mind-traveled through many luminous landscapes to speak with childlike mushroom deities who offered her friendship and protection. The role of *teo-nanacatl* priestess was her destiny; when she was eight she performed her first healing ceremony by ingesting the mushrooms and asking them how she could help her dying uncle. *Teo-nanacatl* permitted many more cures. María Sabina married twice, bore twelve children, and continued to practice her mushroom healing art, for which she was envied and distrusted as well as respected and honored.

Early in 1955, the *curandera* for the first time shared the rites of the divine mushroom with members of an alien culture, American ethnomycologist R. Gordon Wasson and photographer Allan Richardson. The event was recorded in *Life* and the *curandera*'s fame spread through Western society. Beat author Bonnie Frazer [Bremser] wrote that many of her circle sought the magic mushroom lady. Throughout the 1960's, young psychedelics users made pilgrimages to Huautla de Jiménez, hoping to meet and trip with the "wise in the way of plants woman." In the 1970's, Anne Waldman further popularized María Sabina's psychedelic healing art by adapting the mushroom chant to her own poetry performances.

The following is a brief portion of a mushroom ceremony, or *velada*, with a few family members and friends in 1956. The *velada* in-

cludes dialogue, humming, bantering, lulling, incantations, and chanting. With the whole force of her culture behind her, María Sabina presides over the ceremony, using many different voices as the mushroom speaks through her. The power of the *velada* is the power of ancient ritual, in which a group passes time together in an altered state of consciousness during a crisis, each person voluntarily surrendering individual differences in order to commune with the mushrooms and discover the resolution to the problem.

María Sabina at home in Huautla de Jiménez. "I'm a wise in the way of plants woman."

Mazatec Magic Mushroom Ritual Chant

I'm a saint woman
I'm a saint woman
I'm a spirit woman
I'm an atmosphere woman
I'm a day woman

I'm an atmosphere woman
I'm a day woman

I'm a waiting woman
I'm a trying woman
I'm a crying woman
I'm a speech woman
I'm a creator woman

I'm a doctor woman
I'm a wise in the way of plants woman

I'm the moon woman
I'm a doctor woman
I'm an interpreter woman

I'm a creator woman

I'm a clean woman
I'm a ready woman
I'm a Saint Peter woman

I'm a clean woman
I'm a ready woman
I'm a waiting woman

I'm an atmosphere woman

I'm a day woman
I'm a creator woman
I'm a doctor woman
I'm an interpreter woman
I'm a Christ woman

I'm the morning star woman
I'm the moon woman
I'm a heaven woman
I'm a doll woman

That's the way it looks when I go to heaven

They say it's like softness there
They say it's like land
They say it's like day
They say it's like dew

VALENTINA WASSON
1901–57

Moscow-born Valentina Pavlovna Wasson fled to the United States with her family during the Russian Revolution. She became a pediatrician and married R. Gordon Wasson, then a journalist, later a financier, and ultimately a pioneer of ethnomycology, the study of the cultural use of hallucinogenic mushrooms.

Valentina initiated her husband's interest in mushroom lore. She had grown up gathering and eating the fungi of her native land. During their honeymoon in New York's Catskill Mountains in 1927, her husband recoiled from eating a dish she had prepared from the local varieties. The contrast of their mushroom attitudes stimulated years of intense dialogue and research. They coined the terms "mycophobes" for those who feared mushrooms, and "mycophiles" for lovers of mushrooms. While practicing as a pediatrician and raising a daughter, Valentina found time to join Gordon in pursuing through travel and cultural studies the impact of mushroom usage, particularly the role of the mind-altering varieties, in Western literature, art, and religion.

Following the lead of an obscure pamphlet, the Wassons began making pilgrimages to Mexico. In 1953 they met María Sabina, shaman of the magic mushoom. Two years later Valentina and her eighteen-year-old daughter Masha be-

Valentina and R. Gordon Wasson in Huautla de Jiménez,
1955. "I noticed that my husband's red plaid sports shirt
was glowing with a peculiar intensity."

came the first women of an alien culture to par-
take of the magic mushrooms in the sacred
ceremony of the Mazatec (Mixeteco) Indians.

In 1957 Valentina's account of her unique
experience appeared in a Sunday newspaper supplement in the same month that her husband's
article was published in *Life*. A few months later
the Wassons published their landmark study,
Mushrooms, Russia and History, filled with refer-
ences to mushroom worship and symbolism since
ancient times. Valentina died that year, but Gordon continued their work, publishing *Soma* and
other highly regarded volumes that fulfilled their
lifelong quest.

I Ate the Sacred Mushrooms

I was lying in my sleeping bag on the damp earthen
floor of an adobe hut, my face turned to a crumbling plaster wall. A few minutes before, I had
eaten five pairs of the supposedly sacred mushrooms. (They are always spoken of in pairs.) I was
struggling to keep control of myself but I knew full
well that with every minute I was being pulled
deeper into another completely unknown world. I
was going to experience a self-induced bout of
schizophrenia.

Although my husband had piled every available
cover on top of me, I still felt cold. Dreamily I
asked myself how they had managed, from one mo-

ment to another, to hang that beautiful wallpaper right under my nose. I admired the shimmering silvery green color of its geometric designs. Then it faded away and I was looking at the dirty plaster wall again. Suddenly I was frightened. But it was too late to turn back.

In the past few days my husband and Allan Richardson, our photographer, had participated in the sacred mushroom ceremony under the guidance of a local *shaman*, who is a combination priest-medicine man, in this case a woman, practicing the ancient cult of the Mixeteco people. After taking part in the rites and eating the mushrooms, both of them had seen staggering visions, all in 3-D and in fantastic Technicolor. They enjoyed the feelings of supreme happiness and well-being that explain the age-old power these "sacred mushrooms" exercise over this remote and primitive people.

What I now wished to know was: Are the mushrooms merely a dramatic "prop" with the vivid mental images really produced by auto-suggestion or some other primitive psychological ruse? Or do the mushrooms themselves contain some powerful hallucinatory drug as yet unknown to science?

As a physician I am usually content to leave this kind of experiment to more adventurous inquirers than myself. You have to be rained-in—in a place like that Indian Mixeteco village—to know how desperate you can get for diversion. Our daughter Mary (we call her Masha) and I had arrived six days before for a 24-hour visit to help Gordon and Allan wind up their work in ethnobotanical research.

A wobbly, single-engined plane had dropped us onto a tiny clearing and promised to come back the next day. No sooner had the plane disappeared than the fog rolled in and it began to rain. The trails were ankle deep in gummy mud. We were marooned with a large family of Mixeteco Indians—kindly and courteous, but limited in conversation—in a small adobe hut. Rain leaked constantly through the thatched roof. The dirt floor was full of puddles. There were no windows. Light flickered from a single kerosene lantern. We were damp, chilled through and miserable. We spent most of the time huddled in our sleeping bags. A few hallucinations, we decided, would be a great help. Why not try the mushrooms?

Our hostess, a school teacher, is one of the few educated villagers. She disapproves of the mushroom rites and is frightened of them. We did not tell her what we were going to do. After lunch, my husband obtained nine pairs of the sacred mushrooms, put them into a bowl and served them to us. I took five pair and Masha took four.

It was a revolting dish. They were moist, greenish and very dirty. I bit into one and gagged. It tasted like rancid fat. Masha and I chewed the rest slowly and swallowed with difficulty. My husband got out his notebook and prepared to record whatever we were about to say or do.

For some queer, obstinate reason I had made up my mind not to give in easily to this seductive alien drug. I strode back and forth vigorously, breathing hard. The early symptoms were mild but not unpleasant. Masha complained of a headache. I felt a little unsteady on my feet and muttered that it felt like a champagne hangover. I was seized by a great fit of yawning.

Masha suddenly declared that she saw a nest of bright blue boxes piled up in the corner of the room. There were none. I looked at her scornfully. After half an hour I took my pulse. It was a slow but regular 65. I lay down on the floor. Masha said she saw hens and chickens. It was true there were several stray fowl running about underfoot in the house, but none were visible at the moment.

I noticed that my husband's red plaid sports shirt was glowing with a peculiar intensity. I stared at the crude wooden furniture. The cracks and knotholes were changing shape.

Masha cried suddenly, "I feel like a chicken!" We both burst into peals of laughter. I thought it was a very funny remark. I half closed my eyes. I turned my face to the wall. I had a brief sensation of looking at beautiful wallpaper. Then the walls suddenly receded and I was carried out—out and away—on undulating waves of translucent turquoise green.

I don't know how long I traveled. I arrived in the Caves of Lascaux in the Dordogne, in France. We had visited France before and I immediately recognized the vast vault of stone above me, the early cave dwellers' beautiful primitive paintings of horses, bison and deer on the walls. The paintings were even more beautiful than in real life. They seemed suffused with a crystal light. But I was disappointed. I was born in Russia and I have not seen my native land since 1918. I had hoped to be carried there in my visions.

I now lay limp and warm in my sleeping bag. My mind was floating blissfully. It was as if my very soul had been scooped out and moved to a point in heavenly space, leaving my empty physical husk behind in the mud hut. Yet I was perfectly conscious. I knew now what the *shamans* meant when they said, "The mushroom takes you there to the place where God is."

I abandoned my visions to sit up and smoke a cigarette while I told Gordon and Allan what I had experienced. Then I returned impatiently to the land of the sacred mushrooms.

I was now in eighteenth-century Versailles, the fabled French court of Louis XV. A grand ball was in progress. Hundreds of beautifully gowned couples danced the minuet in train and powdered periwig to the music of Mozart. Overhead glittered a magnificent crystal chandelier. Fiery flashes of green and blue light spattered from its hundreds of prisms.

I was struck again by the magnificence and intensity of the colors. Everything was resplendently rich. I had never imagined such beauty. On a shelf near the door to the ballrooms stood a tiny pair of elegant miniature china figures dressed in eighteenth-century ball gowns. Looking closely I saw they were my sister and myself. We were dancing the minuet, too.

From a distance I heard my daughter Masha say impatiently, "Oh, Father, I'm having too good a time to bother talking to you!"

But I was aloof. I was now alone in the splendor of a Spanish church. The dark woodwork was elaborately carved. The stained glass windows were showering radiant light. Before me was a towering crucifix. I tilted my head back to see the top but it stretched away into the sky. It was so high I couldn't see the upper part of the figure on the cross. I said aloud, "Am I unworthy to see Him?" Yet doubt and anxiety never crossed my mind. Everything was crystal clear and exquisite.

At a quarter to five—90 minutes after swallowing the mushrooms—my pulse was 56 but still steady. My temperature was 99.8. I had no feeling of sadness, yet tears rolled from my eyes. My hus-

band recorded that my pupils were extremely dilated and failed to respond to the beam of his flashlight.

Masha and I both heard the call to supper but said impatiently that we didn't wish to be bothered. I was now sitting in a showy box at the Metropolitan Opera House, watching a performance of the ballet, "Les Sylphides." At the end of the program I took off into the skies with several of the dancers. Then I was bending over a huge, deep blue Chinese vase, inspecting several handsome gold dragons crawling around at the bottom. I was not afraid. It was much, much too remote. I sat up and told Gordon about it.

Then I was in a strange country. I saw picturesque tiles. "Holland!" I exclaimed to myself. "What nonsense—I wish to be in Russia!"

I was in Russia. The tiles were framed about an old peasant stove. Children in colorful pre-World War I costumes were dancing around the room. Everyone was laughing and gay, singing old songs.

Suddenly I was quite out of the picture. I was looking at a beautiful piece of cabinet jewelry. It was a large, rectangular box, made of black Chinese lacquer. A map of China was outlined on its surface. Cities, rivers and mountains were depicted in rubies, sapphires and emeralds. I seemed to be examining it through a strong magnifying glass. It was breathtakingly beautiful. The vision, like the others, rolled past.

The hours had passed imperceptibly. It was 8 o'clock in the evening when the hallucinations ended. Masha and I both felt hungry. We accepted our hostess' offer of a cup of aromatic hot chocolate and some sweet rolls.

Masha and I exchanged notes. She told me that her dreams had consisted of all the happy memories of her life, beginning from birth and carrying through in rosy succession to her present freshman year in college. She said she was constantly in the company of relatives and friends and in the places she loved most. "The world was little and beautiful, and I was on top of it," she said. We also agreed on being completely awake during our incredible dreams.

Soon I was overcome by the same fit of strong yawning that had preceded my submission to the powers of the potent sacred mushroom. I fell asleep. It was the deepest, soundest, most refreshing sleep of my life.

I awoke clear-headed, alert and happy with no trace of aftereffects. It was raining and bitterly cold. The village was still wrapped in a thick, gray blanket of fog. The Indian children, tightly wrapped in their thin cotton shawls, crowded in at the door, staring at us in wonder. I set about writing down my notes of that weird and wonderful experience.

ALICE B. TOKLAS
1877–1967

Alice B. Toklas in the 1930's. "Almost anything Saint Theresa did, you can do better."

Although it was sent in by a friend (avant-garde artist Brion Gysin) and Alice B. Toklas claimed to have no idea of the ingredients until her cookbook was about to be published, a recipe for baking marijuana brownies brought her unexpected fame in her later years. The lifelong companion of writer Gertrude Stein was a gourmet cook who had helped create memorable soirées for the artists and writers of Paris in the 1920's and 1930's.

The notoriety of marijuana in 1954 caused the recipe to be censored from the American edition of *The Alice B. Toklas Cookbook*, but it was printed in the British edition because cannabis was still in the official pharmacopoeia. By 1960 it was permitted in the American paperback edition. Socialite and gourmet Poppy Cannon called it "the recipe of the decade." It was modeled after Arabian *majoon*, formerly used by members of the French "Hashish Club" and the characters of Louisa May Alcott's "Perilous Play." In 1968, Peter Sellers and Leigh Taylor-Young starred in *I Love You, Alice B. Toklas*, a popular movie plotted around the eating of marijuana brownies.

Hashish Fudge

(WHICH ANYONE COULD WHIP UP ON A RAINY DAY)

This is the food of Paradise—of Baudelaire's Artificial Paradises: it might provide an entertaining refreshment for a Ladies' Bridge Club or a chapter meeting of the DAR. In Morocco it is thought to be good for warding off the common cold in damp winter weather and is, indeed, more effective if taken with large quantities of hot mint tea. Euphoria and brilliant storms of laughter; ecstatic reveries and extensions of one's personality on several simultaneous planes are to be complacently expected. Almost anything Saint Theresa did, you can do better if you can bear to be ravished by 'un évanouissement reveillé.'

Take 1 teaspoon black peppercorns, 1 whole nutmeg, 4 average sticks of cinnamon, 1 teaspoon coriander. These should all be pulverised in a mortar. About a handful each of stoned dates, dried figs, shelled almonds and peanuts: chop these and mix them together. A bunch of *cannabis sativa* can be pulverised. This along with the spices should be dusted over the mixed fruit and nuts, kneaded together. About a cup of sugar dissolved in a big pat of butter. Rolled into a cake and cut into pieces or made into balls about the size of a walnut, it should be eaten with care. Two pieces are quite sufficient.

Obtaining the *cannabis* may present certain difficulties, but the variety known as *cannabis sativa* grows as a common weed, often unrecognised, everywhere in Europe, Asia and parts of Africa; besides being cultivated as a crop for the manufacture of rope. In the Americas, while often discouraged, its cousin, called *cannabis indica*, has been observed even in city window boxes. It should be picked and dried as soon as it has gone to seed and while the plant is still green.

ENID BLYTON
1897–1968

Enid Blyton, the most prolific modern British writer of children's books, related a nitrous oxide (laughing gas) experience she'd had in a dentist's chair. Her account appears in a letter printed in Barbara Stoney's biography, *Enid Blyton* (1974), where it is noted that the author later changed the date of her experience from c. 1915 to c. 1955.

The sensation of going through "vibrating *waves* of light" describes the characteristic rush following a big suck of laughing gas into the lungs. Her feeling of learning "the secret of Everything" and being totally incapable of hanging on to it has always been the most remarkable of nitrous oxide's mental effects. Blyton's account demonstrates the propensity of laughing gas to occasionally provide (when dosage and condi-

tions are right) a full-blown psychedelic trip, with all the classic Jamesian elements of mystical experience—"great and holy and ineffable."

But Blyton does not regard her experience as religious or mystical, only "something amazingly produced by the gas."

Enid Blyton. "Then I knew I was going to hear the secret of Everything—"

From Enid Blyton: A Biography

I feel I would also like to comment on your *'presque vu'* reports. For some reason I had not heard the experiences called by that name, but it is really a very good definition. I have only had this experience, in my teens, under 'laughing gas'. I have had gas many times, but only once did I ever experience *'presque vu'*—and then it was in one respect different from the things you report in that instead of *'almost* seeing', I *did* see and grasp everything, or so I thought!—and then lost it. This is what happened. I have never forgotten it and its extraordinary clarity has always remained with me. I found myself (apparently bodiless but still firmly myself) being drawn through space at a speed so great that I thought I must be going at the pace of light itself. I seemed to go through vibrating *waves* of light, and thought that I must be passing many suns and many universes. (I love astronomy, hence my suppositions, I suppose!) Finally, after a long, incredibly long journey in an incredibly short time I arrived somewhere. This Somewhere was, as far as I could make out, in my dazed and amazed state, a place of wonderful light (not daylight or sunlight)—and I saw, or knew, that there were Beings there—no shape, nothing tangible—but I knew they were great and holy and ineffable. Then I knew I was going to hear the secret of Everything—and Everything was explained to me, simply and with the utmost lucidity. I was overjoyed—filled with wonder and delight. I knew the reasons behind existence, time, space, evil, goodness, pain—and I rejoiced, and marvelled that no one had guessed such things before. Then I knew I must go back to my body, wherever it was, through all the long eras of time and vastness of space, and as I left in sorrow, my spirit cried out, or seemed to cry out 'Let me tell everyone this wonderful thing I know, this secret that explains everything and will bring such rejoicing and happiness!' And as I went back down aeons of time, I was told I must not divulge the secret and I cried out why—and as I went, I was told why, and I said 'At least let *me* always remember', but no, I was not even to be allowed to remember even one small detail myself, and I cried out again—'But why may I not remember?' And then, just at the very moment when I returned to my body in the dentist's chair, I was told why I must not even hug the knowledge to myself, and it was such a logical and wonderful reason that I accepted it joyfully, in the fullest understanding, and found myself opening my eyes, and smiling happily in the chair, completely overcome with what I thought had been a true and overwhelming revelation. That is the only *presque vu* experience I have had, and as you will agree, it was more than *presque vu*—it was '*complètement vu*'—and yet ended by being completely lost. I can still get back the feeling at the end of it of acquiescing joyfully in my forgoing of the secret, and yet hugging to myself the certainty that 'all's well with the world', despite everything!

This experience has nothing to do with religion, it wasn't a 'vision', only something amazingly produced by the gas—but I kept hold of my identity all the time, and did not lose the reporter sense of the practised writer, who instinctively retains all that is essential to her true 'news-story'. I have told only two or three people of this experience, as I did not think it sounded believable.

ANAÏS NIN
1903–77

Diarist and experimental novelist Anaïs Nin, celebrated for her deep probes of female psychology, was equally interested in the process of artistic creation. Intrigued by what she had heard about LSD, she seized an opportunity to experiment with the drug under a psychiatrist's supervision in his Los Angeles office.

In one of the most superbly described trips in psychedelic literature, Nin articulates a flowing series of richly detailed, colorful, constantly changing images and emotional transformations. She imagines herself as Alice in Wonderland, the Little Prince in outer space, a comic spirit of "Russian-opera extravaganza," a Balinese dancer, and "an ordinary weepy female." "The secret of life," she decides, is "metamorphosis and transformation."

Afterward she decided that "this world opened by LSD was accessible to the artist by way of art." She believed the repression of sensuality and emotion in English and American cultures was one reason for the popularity of LSD tripping in the West. But she feared that continual use of psychedelics would dull natural access to the subconscious, the source of creativity.

Anaïs Nin in New York. © 1982 Jill Krementz.
"I thought I was the quickest mind alive and the quickest with words, but words
cannot catch up with these transformations, metamorphoses."

From The Diary of Anaïs Nin, 1947–1955

I had just read Aldous Huxley's *The Doors of Perception* but it did not impress me as much as Gil Henderson's talk about the visionary effects of LSD. He had participated in an experiment with Dr. Oscar Janiger. He painted an American Indian doll before taking LSD and then again after the ingestion of the drug, and the difference between them was astonishing. The first version was rigid and photographic. The second impressionistic, emotional. Gil asked me if I wanted to participate in an experiment because Dr. Janiger was hoping a writer would be more articulate about the experience. There were to be two other subjects there, a biologist from UCLA and another painter. Gil would be my sober pilot, that is, a person who has taken LSD before and now stands by to help one and guide one if necessary.

It seemed strange to be coming to a psychiatrist's office for such an adventure. Dr. Janiger took Gil and me into his private office, which was lined with books and very dark. I had little time to form an impression of him, for he immediately dispensed a number of blue pills, five or eight, I do not remember, with a glass of water. Then he conducted us to the waiting room, where the biologist sat already with a pad on his knee, pen in hand.

At first everything appeared unchanged. But after a while, perhaps twenty minutes, I noticed first of all that the rug was no longer flat and lifeless, but had become a field of stirring and undulating hairs, much like the movement of the sea anemone or a field of wheat in the wind. Then I noticed that doors, walls, and windows were liquefying. All rigidities disappeared. It was as if I had been plunged to the bottom of the sea, and everything had become undulating and wavering. The door knobs were no longer door knobs, they melted and undulated like living serpents. Every object in the room became a living, mobile breathing world. I walked away, into a hallway opening into several small rooms. On the way there was a door leading to the garden. Gil opened it. The dazzle of the sun was blinding, every speck of gold multiplied and magnified. Trees, clouds, lawns heaved and undulated too, the clouds flying at tremendous speed. I ceased looking at the garden because on the plain door now appeared the most delicate Persian designs, flowers, mandalas, patterns in perfect symmetry. As I designed them they produced their matching music. When I drew a long orange line, it emitted its own orange tone. My body was both swimming and flying. I felt gay and at ease and playful. There was perfect connection between my body and everything that was happening. For example, the colors in the designs gave me pleasure, as well as the music. The singing of mockingbirds was multiplied, and became a whole forest of singing birds. My senses were multiplied as if I had a hundred eyes, a hundred ears, a hundred fingertips. The murals which appeared were perfect, they were Oriental, fragile, and complete, but then they became actual Oriental cities, with pagodas, temples, rich Chinese gold and red altars, and Balinese music. The music vibrated through my body as if I were one of the instruments and I felt myself becoming a full percussion orchestra, becoming green, blue, orange. The waves of the sounds ran through my hair like a caress. The music ran down my back and came out of my fingertips. I was a cascade of red-blue rainfall, a rainbow. I was small, light, mobile. I could use any method of levitation I wished. I could dissolve, melt, float, soar. Wavelets of light touched the rim of my clothes, phosphorescent radiations. I could see a new world with my middle eye, a world I had missed before. I caught images behind images, the walls behind the sky, the sky behind the infinite. The walls became fountains, the fountains became arches, the domes skies, the sky a flowering carpet, and all dissolved into pure space. I looked at a slender line curving over into space which disappeared into infinity. I saw a million zeros on this line, curving, shrinking in the distance, and I laughed and said: "Excuse me, I am not a mathematician. How can I measure the infinite?" To Dr. Janiger, who was passing by, I said: "Without being a mathematician I understood the infinite." He did not seem impressed. I saw his face as a Picasso, with a slight asymmetry. It seemed to me that one of his eyes was larger, and this eye was prying into my experience, and I turned away. Gil was sometimes there, but now I became aware that he was a child, that he had a big round face with a grin. Now I was standing on the rim of a planet, alone. I could hear the fast rushing sound of the planets rotating in space. Then I was moving among them and I realized a certain skill would be necessary to handle this new means of transportation. The image of myself standing in space and trying to get my "space legs" amused me. I wondered who had been there before me and whether I would return to earth. The solitude distressed me for the first time, the sense of distance, so I asked Gil very vehemently: "Are you sure that I will find my way back?" Gil answered reasonably: "Of course, I found my way back. I'm here." He asked me if there was anything I wanted, a glass of water or a sandwich. I answered: "I want a pagoda." And after a while I added: "I realize this is an unreasonable request." I returned to my starting point. I was standing in front of an ugly door, but as I looked closer it was not plain or green but it was a Buddhist temple, a Hindu column, a Moroccan ceiling, gold spires being formed and re-formed as if I were watching the hand of a designer at work. I was designing red spirals which unfurled until they formed a rose window or a mandala with edges of radium. As each design was born and arranged itself, it dissolved and the next one followed without confusion. Each form, each line emitted its equivalent in music in perfect accord with the design. An undulating line emitted a sustaining undulating melody, a circle had corresponding musical notations, diaphanous colors, diaphanous sounds, a pyramid created a pyramid of ascending notes, and vanishing ones left only an echo. These designs were preparatory sketches for entire Oriental cities. I saw the temples of Java, Kashmir, Nepal, Ceylon, Burma, Cambodia, in all the colors of precious stones illumined from within. Then the outer forms of the temples dissolved to reveal the inner chapels and shrines. The reds and golds inside the temples created an intricate musical orchestration like Balinese music. Two sensations began to torment me: one that it was happening too quickly and that I would not be able to remember it, another that I would not be able to tell what I saw, it was too elusive and too overwhelming. The temples grew taller, the music wilder, it became a tidal wave of sounds with gongs and bells predominating. Gold spires emitted a long flute chant. Every line and color was constantly breathing and mutating.

It was then I began to experience difficulties in breathing. I felt immensely cold, and very small in my cape, as if I had undergone an Alice in Wonderland metamorphosis. I told Gil I could not breathe, and he took me to the doctor. The doctor calmed me with words. I had asked for oxygen. He suggested I lie down and cover myself well. Gil was seated near me, grinning. I asked him if he had had difficulties breathing. I still had the impression I had been among the planets. I remembered the illustration from Saint-Exupéry's *Little Prince*, the child standing all alone on the edge of the planet. I lay down and covered myself. I was smoking a cigarette. I looked at the curtains of the room and they turned to a gauzy gold. The whole room became filled with gold, as if by a strong sun. The walls turned to gold, the bedcover was gold, my whole body was becoming GOLD, liquid gold, scintillating, warm gold. I WAS GOLD. It was the most pleasurable sensation I had ever known, like an orgasm. It was the secret of life, the alchemist's secret of life. From the feeling of intense cold, as if I were chloroformed, of loss of gravity of the legs, and diminution in size, I passed to the sensation of being gold. Suddenly I was weeping, weeping. I could feel the tears and I saw the handkerchief in my hand. Weeping to the point of dissolution. Why should I

be weeping? I could see Gil smiling, and realized the absurdity of weeping when traveling through space. As soon as the concept of absurdity struck me, the comic spirit appeared again. It was another Anaïs, not the one which was lying down weeping, but a small, gay, light Anaïs, very lively, very restless and mobile. The comic spirit of Anaïs was aware of Gil's predicament: "Poor Gil, you are out with an ordinary weepy female! What a ridiculous thing to spoil a voyage through space by weeping. But before we go on, I want to explain to you why women weep. IT IS THE QUICKEST WAY TO REJOIN THE OCEAN. You liquefy, become fluid, flow back into the ocean where the colors are more beautiful." The comic spirit of Anaïs shook herself jauntily and said: "Let's stop this weeping. Everything is more wonderful under water (than in space?). It is alive and it breathes." Space was lonely, and empty, a vast desert. After the feeling of GOLD I had a feeling of danger. My world is so beautiful, so beautiful, but so fragile. I was pleading for protection of this evanescent beauty. I thought I was the quickest mind alive and the quickest with words, but words cannot catch up with these transformations, metamorphoses. They are beyond words, beyond words. . . . The Oriental cities vanished and the infinite appeared again, but now it was bordered on each side by celestial gardens of precious stones on silver and gold stems. Temptation not to pursue the infinite, but to enjoy the gardens. Space is definitely without sensuous appeal.

The comic spirit of Anaïs stood aside and laughed at so much Russian-opera extravaganza. But the other Anaïs maintained her pose as a Balinese dancer with legs slightly bent, the tips of the fingers meeting in a symbolic gesture of pleading. I could feel the weight of the brocade.

I watched a shoreline of gold waves breaking into solid gold powder and becoming gold foam, and gold hair, shimmering and trembling with gold delights. I felt I could capture the secret of life because the secret of life was metamorphosis and transmutation, but it happened too quickly and was beyond words. Comic spirit of Anaïs mocks words and herself. Ah, I cannot capture the secret of life with WORDS.

Sadness.

The secret of life was BREATH. That was what I

always wanted words to do, to BREATHE. Comic spirit of Anaïs rises, shakes herself within her cape, gaily, irresponsibly, surrenders the abstruse difficulties. NOW I KNOW WHY THE FAIRY TALES ARE FULL OF JEWELS.

After my experience with LSD I began to examine whether it was an unfamiliar world, inaccessible except to the chemical alterations of reality.

I found the origin of most of the images either in my work or in literary works by other writers.

In *House of Incest*, written in 1935, objects become liquefied and I describe them as seen through water. There is a reference to Byzantium and I was brought up on volumes of *Voyages Autour du Monde*, which had images of Cambodia, Thailand, Bali, India, and Japan, and which remained forever in my memory. I have listened to countless recordings of Balinese music, tapes made by Colin McFee.

Images of split selves appear in *House of Incest*.

The image of loneliness on another planet is derived from my frequent reading of *The Little Prince* by Antoine de Saint-Exupéry.

In *House of Incest* there is mention of crystals, precious stones: "The muscovite like a bride, the pyrite, the hydrous silica, the cinnabar, the azurite of benefic Jupiter, the malachite, all crushed together, melted jewels, melted planets."

The sensation of becoming gold is one I had many times when sunbathing on the sand; the sun's reflection came through my closed eyelids, and I felt myself becoming gold.

I could find correlations all through my writing, find the sources of the images in past dreams, in reading, in memories of travel, in actual experience, such as the one I had once in Paris when I was so exalted by life that I felt I was not touching the ground, I felt I was sliding a few inches away from the sidewalk.

Therefore, I felt, the chemical did not reveal an unknown world. What it did was to shut out the quotidian world as an interference and leave you alone with your dreams and fantasies and memories. In this way it made it easier to gain access to the subconscious life. But obviously, by way of writing, reveries, waking dreams, and night dreams, I had visited all those landscapes. The drug added a

synthesis of color, sound, image, a simultaneous fusion of all the senses which I had constantly aspired to in my writing and often achieved.

I reached the fascinating revelation that this world opened by LSD was accessible to the artist by way of art. The gold sun mobile of Lippold could create a mood if one were receptive enough, if one let the image penetrate the body and turn the body to gold. All the chemical did was to remove resistance, to make one permeable to the image, and to make the body receptive by shutting out the familiar landscape which prevented the dream from invading us.

What has happened that people lose contact with such images, visions, sensations, and have to resort to drugs which ultimately harm them?

They have been immured, the taboo on dream, reverie, visions, and sensual receptivity deprives them of access to the subconscious. I am grateful for my natural access. But when I discuss this with Huxley, he is rather irritable: "You're fortunate enough to have a natural access to your subconscious life, but other people need drugs and should have them."

This does not satisfy me because I feel that if I have a natural access others could have it too. How did I reach this? Difficult to retrace one's steps. Can you say I had a propensity for dreaming, a faculty for abstracting myself from the daily world in order to travel to other places? What I cannot trace [is] the origin of seemed natural tendencies which I allowed to develop, and which I found psychoanalysis encouraged and trained. The technique was accessible to those willing to accept psychoanalysis as a means of connecting with the subconscious. I soon recognized its value. My faith in it is unshaken. But then there is also the appetite for what nourishes such a rich underground life: learning color from the painters, movement from the dancers, music from musicians. They train your senses, they sensitize the senses. It was the banishment of art which brought on a culture devoid of sensual perception, of the participation in the senses, so that experience did not cause the "highs," the exaltations, the ecstasies they caused in me. The puritans killed the senses. English culture killed emotion. And now it was necessary to dynamite the concrete lid, to "blow the mind" as the LSD followers call it. The source of all wonder, aliveness, and joy was feeling and dreaming, and being able to fulfill one's dreams.

Even the art of reading, lost to America, was a constant nourishing source which revealed countries I wanted to see, people I wanted to know, experiences I wanted to have. How cruelly the weight of ordinary life, *la condition humaine*, weighed upon America, with everything forcing you to live in the prosaic, the shabby, the practical, the quotidian, the down-to-earth, the mediocrity of political life, the monstrosities of history via the media, because they believed this was contact with life, and it was the very thing which destroyed the contact with life.

So the drugs, instead of bringing fertile images which in turn can be shared with the world (as the great painters, great poets, great musicians shared their abundance with the unfertile ones, enriched undernourished lives), have instead become a solitary vice, a passive dreaming which alienates the dreamer from the whole world, isolates him, ultimately destroys him. It is like masturbation. The one who wrestles his images from experience, from his smoky dreams, to create, is able then to build what he has seen and hungered for. It does not vanish with the effects of the chemical. The knowledge gained without the drugs, as, for example, my feeling for color learned from watching the painters when I was posing for them, is a permanent acquisition. It became part of my being, it was applicable to my travels, to my image of people. It was or became a new faculty, part of my sensory perception, available, but the effort I made to learn was also the strengthening of the ability to create with a sense of color, to create houses, clothes, visions of cities, enjoyment of color not only as a passing, ephemeral, vanishing dream, *but as reality*. And that is the conflict. The drug effect does not strengthen the desire to turn the dream, the vision, into reality. It is passive.

I have to go on in my own way, which is a disciplined, arduous, organic way of integrating the dream with creativity in life, a quest for the development of the senses, the vision, the imagination as dynamic elements with which to create a new world, a new kind of human being. Seeking wholeness not by dreaming alone, by a passive dreaming

that drugs give, but by an active, dynamic dreaming that is connected with life, interrelated, makes a harmony in which the pleasures of color, texture, vision are a creation in reality, which we can enjoy with the *awakened* senses. What can be more wonderful than the carrying out of our fantasies, the courage to enact them, embody them, live them out instead of depending on the dissolving, dissipating, vanishing quality of the drug dreams.

I will not be just a tourist in the world of images, just watching images passing by which I cannot live in, make love to, possess as permanent sources of joy and ecstasy.

LAURA HUXLEY
1917–

Laura Archera Huxley was born and raised in Italy. She studied music and came to the United States as a concert violinist before World War II. In California in 1948, she met the brilliant English writer Aldous Huxley and his wife, Maria. Archera read *The Doors of Perception* (1954), Huxley's eloquent appraisal of mescaline and LSD as tools for understanding the mind. In 1955, she received Huxley's written account of Maria's last days, describing his use of hypnosis to alleviate her discomfort.

After Maria's death, Laura and Aldous guided each other on psychedelic trips and experienced psychic bonding. They were married in 1956. Seven years later when he was dying of cancer, Aldous requested LSD and Laura administered it. Her eloquent account of this event anticipated the practice in the past fifteen years of giving psychedelics to the terminally ill. All of this is documented in Laura's book of her life with Huxley, *This Timeless Moment* (1968), from which the following excerpt is taken.

Laura Huxley. "The round, white bowl with little pieces of vegetable was to me the cosmos, round and infinite."

From This Timeless Moment: A Personal View of Aldous Huxley

The morning of my first psychedelic day, more than my own state of mind, I remember Aldous's delighted anticipation. He gave me a glass of water containing the mescaline. After a while—maybe half an hour—I became a little nauseated.

"You are on your way," he said, smiling.

Nausea is usually expected from mescaline. It lasts only a short time, after which the experience begins. I was "on my way."

I was lying on the sofa in the living room. Suddenly another human being, also lying down, came into my consciousness—*became* my consciousness: a baby I had seen a few days before. It was a recent experience, fresh in my memory—only now it was not a memory, it was the experience itself, perceived and felt with an intensity a thousand times greater than when it happened. Before, I had only been moved by the event; now, the event and I were almost one.

The previous week Ginny and I had visited an orphanage in Tijuana: eighty-six infants left there by women unable to keep them—six nuns to care for them all. The nuns were magnificent. With the most meager financial resources they had the daily care of eighty-six infants—washing diapers, preparing food, cleaning and bathing. I see them now doing their work in a happy, spirited manner, running from one end of the hall to the other. But there is no time left for the nuns to take the children in their arms. Imagine the time required just to wash and fill eighty-six bottles six times a day. . . .

The children were left hours and hours lying in their cribs, small, alone, and undergiven—alone and undergiven before they were born. Lying there, untouched. Some cried, others had already given up crying and had receded into an echoless silence, without light. A few were sleeping peacefully; many were staring, staring. One child had made a deeper impression on us than all the others; Ginny had baptized him "the violinist." He was about ten months old. Silent, the wide dark eyes open and unblinking, set in pale blue skin, he seemed more than the others alone. He kept his left hand up in the air as though he were holding a violin; the long fingers incessantly moving as though searching the notes on the string. In comparison to the small emaciated body, his hand was big, ideally formed to play an instrument. The fingers, moving in solitary space, were searching, searching, it seemed, for a contact with somebody, a human contact which could have come, at this time in life, only through touch. There was no one to touch. He had been given life, but no contact with life. Immersed in a sea of loneliness the little boy kept his arm up high, moving his fingers, hoping—vainly hoping. Would the little fingers ever find someone to touch? Would they find someone *in time*, before they would accept the present separation as life's essence? Or would death lift the oversized incubus imposed on the little creature?

As I entered the psychedelic state these feelings-thoughts invaded me with an indescribable intensity. I broke into a desperate sobbing. Simultaneously present with the loveless destiny of the little violinist, my own childhood, filled with love and care, seemed an offense to the unlamenting infant. Why? Why such injustice? Why so much love showered on one and none on that other equally guiltless creature? His little, long, white fingers incessantly moving in emptiness, vainly searching for a human note, became to me the essence of humanity's loneliness and despair. I don't know how long I sobbed. Aldous was very near and very quiet. I sobbed until I could not breathe. I had to sit up to take some air. But my breath was practically stopped by what I saw—what a spectacle! Framed in the Spanish window, which gave it a powerful perspective, there was a new country—the garden. And right by the window a rich climbing bush of a rose of Portugal. Tenderly sensual, generous, and unafraid, the roses were smiling at me. But among the roses was an object, an everyday object suddenly now so powerful and magnificent and dangerous— dangerous, not for me, but for the roses! It was the ladder, the metal ladder, obviously forgotten by the gardener. Inconceivably brilliant and clear, it leaped at me like a virtuoso's *arpeggio* of a wind instrument; all the while, unaware and perfect, the roses were exuding their fragrant melody on strings. The ladder was beautiful, but hard and piercingly cruel. One should not let it be so near the roses— how could they coexist? Undulating, triumphant, and free, the roses did not realize, did not fear, the cruel object on which someone will climb with garden shears . . . The roses know better—they live in this timeless moment.

In the psychedelic session, thoughts-feelings occur with such rapidity as to appear simultaneous; the conflict of the rose of Portugal and the metal ladder brought feelings and thoughts of all kinds and degrees, but the conflict remained for me unsolved. I was not able yet, as Aldous was, to reconcile the opposites.

"Beauty and horror, beauty," he repeated, "and horror. And then suddenly, as you come down from one of your expeditions in the mountains, suddenly you know that there's a reconciliation. . . . A fusion, an identity. Beauty made one with horror in the yoga of the jungle. Life reconciled with the perpetual imminence of death in the yoga of danger. Emptiness identified with selfhood in the Sabbath yoga of the summit."

Another image of that day is still marvelously vivid in my mind: a dirty soup dish. After a few

hours—or centuries?—Aldous had given me a bowl of vegetable soup, beautiful and delicious. When I finished it, Aldous made a move to take the bowl and wash it. I held on to it as though he were taking my most precious possession.

"Please don't, Aldous."

The round, white bowl with little pieces of vegetable was to me the cosmos, round and infinite, punctuated by light exuding planets and stars of fiery orange and translucent green. Aldous smiled; he knew what one can see in a dirty dish when the doors of perception are cleansed.

At the end of the day Ginny fetched me and drove me home. I was wide awake the greater part of the night—pleasantly awake. I had a few very clear images with my eyes closed. One of these images came back again and again. It was this image that gave me, several months later, the style and color for the house we bought and decorated after our marriage. The strange part of it is that only years after did I realize that my decoration had been inspired by that image.

HARRIETTE FRANCES
1925–

The artist Harriette Frances participated in the Menlo Park LSD studies in the early sixties. "I began to feel the dissolution of my Ego, my sense of self," she wrote, "and fought for a time against relinquishing control of my known self to the unknown subconscious part of me and this conflict resolved itself in my 'death,' when I leaped into the unconscious and began the painful exploration of my subterranean landscape."

Six weeks after her LSD experience, she made this series of drawings, which Stan and Christina Grof (in *Beyond Death*) called "a sequence resembling shamanic initiation."

CONSTANCE A. NEWLAND

Constance A. Newland (the pseudonym of an actress, now a respected parapsychologist) underwent an intense personal transformation during twenty-two LSD sessions in her psychiatrist's office. Her acid-heightened analysis focused on her sexual dysfunctioning and revealed an amazingly active subconscious.

Myself and I was the most popular early LSD book, and remains an important document of LSD-assisted psychotherapy.

From Myself and I

Arriving promptly at Dr. M's office, I was given three small blue pills, no larger than saccharine tablets, which I swallowed down with some water out of a paper cup—a prosaic passage into the unconscious. Even more prosaic was the suggestion that I look through some magazines during the half-hour required for the drug to take effect.

For about fifteen minutes I leafed through a digest, feeling so normal I began to worry lest I was one of the small percentage of persons on whom the drug has no effect. A few moments later I became aware of the smell of gas (the kind used by dentists for oral surgery) which dissipated almost as soon as I noticed it. I wondered briefly about that vagrant odor but then decided it must have wafted in from the next suite of offices, which housed a group of dentists. I had particularly noticed those offices because I had a fear of dentists, accumulated steadily over the years. Having found a nice and natural reason for the smell, I promptly forgot about it.

At the end of the half-hour I felt a slight dizziness, as if I had had a bit too much to drink. It was then that Dr. M joined me. He asked me to lie down on the couch and gave me an eyeshade to put on. Feeling rather foolish, I put it on and lay down,

whereupon Dr. M covered me with a blanket. The blanket seemed unnecessary but I accepted it without comment. I could hear Dr. M adjust the record player and after a moment symphonic music filled the room. The music seemed unnecessary too, and I told Dr. M so. I explained, cheerfully, that I was a moron musically; my tastes were limited to *un*progressive jazz like show tunes and torch songs; if Dr. M expected classical music to evoke any emotional response in me he would be disappointed. Dr. M ignored my remark and continued to play various kinds of classical music throughout this session and all of the sessions to come.

I lay for some time expecting something visually interesting, strange, to appear in my mind's eye. Nothing did. I saw only the grayish-black which I usually see when my eyes are closed. At length Dr. M asked me what was happening.

"Nothing."

"Please don't say 'nothing,'" Dr. M reminded me.

"Sorry!"

I struggled to feel or remember any sensation I might have had since taking the drug. The only thing that came to mind was the momentary smell of gas. Feeling rather foolish, I reported it. Almost immediately the smell returned. Powerfully. Dr. M asked what the smell of nitrous oxide might mean to me. I did not know, except that over the years my teeth had grown so acutely sensitive (only at the dentist's office), I could not endure even a prophylaxis without being given gas. More recently I had permitted the substitution of a powerful tranquilizer, in addition to novocaine salve rubbed over my gums and teeth. As I talked the smell of gas so intensified that I felt it would anesthetize me. Dr. M suggested that I let it anesthetize me. I tried but instead of blacking out I found myself suspended in a kind of gray-black limbo. Eventually Dr. M. asked again: "What's happening?"

I did not want to say "nothing" again. I searched for some mental impression, emotional reaction, physical response. Anything. Finally, lamely: "Well . . . my left knee is twitching."

"Let it twitch."

Feeling extremely foolish, I let it twitch. After a

moment my other knee began to twitch. Then my legs started to twitch . . . more than that . . . they began to shake . . . and so did my arms. Before I could report what was certainly a visible phenomenon, my whole body was shaking. Violently. *Of itself.* Extraordinary sensation: it was as if I were observing this reaction of my body dispassionately, even curiously.

"Why am I shaking like this?" I asked Dr. M or myself or my body, which was still shaking violently.

For answer, my teeth began to chatter. Why? Because I was cold. Suddenly, unexpectedly, I was very very cold. Through my chattering teeth I told Dr. M that I was freezing and would like another blanket.

"Let yourself freeze," he replied.

The conscious part of me (which was quite disconnected from my shaking, shivering body) began to laugh then because what was happening was so funny and so Freudian . . . ! The specific problem I had set for myself was of course my *frigidity*: and here I was, quite literally *frigid*. It was too pat, too pat and too funny—

But the cold was so real. So very real that I heard winds roaring around me. Wild winds. Somehow I was caught up in one of those wild whirlpools of wind. . . . I could see my body swirling off into space . . . caught up in the very vortex of a whirlwind . . . growing smaller and smaller . . . microscopic . . . as if all the space within the atoms of me had been swept away in the wind. . . .

But the wind had somehow now become . . .

. . . water . . .

. . . yes . . . I was in a great whirling water . . . sinking deeper and deeper down . . . rather a lovely sensation, being drawn into the depths of this dark dark ocean . . . down to the very bottom. But there I lost myself. I looked curiously around the ocean floor to see if I could find myself. I could and did. I was—

—a clam.

One closed-up clam, alone, at the bottom of the sea.

I heard myself laughing loudly: it was so funny and Freudian again. I was one closed-up clam, which was of course another expression of frigidity. Closed-up, non-feeling—

Dr. M cut sharply through my laughter:

"Why do you see yourself as a closed-up clam?"

My laughter aborted. The conscious part of me realized that Dr. M had asked a pertinent question for which I had no answer. Why *did* I see myself as a closed-up clam? I waited, half-expecting some new imagery to furnish forth the answer. I saw nothing but gray-black, for what seemed an endless time.

Unexpectedly Dr. M removed my eyeshade and asked me to look into the mirror he was holding in his hand. I refused, almost wildly—and shut my eyes tight. Dr. M asked again that I look into the mirror and I heard myself cry out:

"I won't look at myself! And you can't force me to open my eyes. I hate my face and I won't look at it, I won't, I won't!!"

(Only several weeks later did the full impact of this episode hit me. One of the chief purposes of psychotherapy is to look at one's self, to discover one's self. In the symbolic form of looking at my face in a mirror I had refused, even to the point of shutting my eyes tight. Literally.)

Dr. M took the mirror away and I replaced the eyeshade. Silence until Dr. M asked: "Why do you hate yourself?"

"I don't hate myself. I just . . ."

"You just what?"

"I just . . . don't know how to love. That's the big twentieth century sickness, isn't it? People can't love. Psychiatrists' cliché number one. And psychiatrists' cliché number two: if you can't love yourself, you can't love anyone else."

I realized I was jibing at Dr. M. Why? I had come for his help. Even as the conscious part of me thought this, I heard the other part of me go on in a tirade against psychotherapists and their pigeonhole terminology. Labels for everything, cures for nothing. When my resentment had spent itself, Dr. M commented that I had probably spent my life in intellectual rather than emotional exercise. I snapped back that I had come to him with exactly that problem which a great many people have. But not everyone. Not my husband. My husband had known how to love. He had always been there for me, full of love and understanding. He had been a rock. A rock.

Crazy unexpected laughter came welling up out of me and then I said: "Yes, he was a rock. A rock, all soft inside with cancer."

I gasped at what had surged up from the unconscious part of me. As a writer, writing with only conscious awareness, I would never have found those words.

I went on to speak of my husband's sudden swift death of a cancer no one had suspected. He had always seemed so strong. But within him, obviously, the pressures of his life had been too severe. For many of those pressures I had to accept the guilt. . . .

As I spoke, pain. Terrible pain which after a time localized in my breasts. I understood the relationship between this pain and my husband's death. I felt guilty for his death and wanted to die of cancer too. As retribution.

Dr. M asked me not to intellectualize but to "go with" the pain and see where it would lead. For a long time the pain remained static in a void of gray-blackness. Gradually an image took shape in the gray-blackness: a white marble statue of a nude woman with two gaping holes where her breasts should be; through those gaping holes shone a brilliant blue sky.

I felt as if I recognized the statue. . . . Had I seen it somewhere? . . . No . . . I remembered now . . . someone had told me that after the Second World War, there had been erected in the center of a German city, totally blitzed . . . a huge statue, visible from every part of the city . . . of a woman with gaping holes instead of breasts. The statue had been christened The City without a Heart.

I understood now. This image I had created in fantasy was meant to be a symbol of—myself. I was a Woman without a Heart, who could feel neither love nor sex.

But why?

I struggled to see some sort of answer.

Limbo.

In the limbo, the music of which I had been unaware began to envelop me. Romantic music, many violins. I found myself caught up in those violins . . . which began to itch . . . itching violins? . . . yes . . . I was surrounded by . . . or I *was* those violins itching more and more strongly until . . . somehow . . . the itching became *sexual*? . . . Yes, this was a sexual itching rather like the sensation of a clitoral orgasm. Extraordinary. I *was* those violins which were also an itching and a clitoral orgasm.

(I wish I could convey how real is this sensation of becoming something or someone other than one's self while under the drug. This experience can be wonderfully pleasant, as these violins were; or it can be hideous and terrifying, as later sessions will show. But it is always extraordinary. To retain one's own identity, yet to become another being or animal or object: the process seems related to the primitive concept of metempsychosis or to the present concept of psychosis where one believes himself to be Napoleon or Cleopatra or a glass vase which will shatter if it is touched.)

This experience seemed an extremely important one which I should report to Dr. M. I started to speak—and found that I could only stutter. I stuttered a few words about "sexual itching"—and then found I could not speak any words at all. I was, for the first time in my life, vocally paralyzed.

"Don't try to talk. Just go with those feelings."

I heard Dr. M speaking as if through layers of time. I stopped struggling for words—and immediately was flooded with strong desire for—Dr. M. Oh no no. I did not, NOT want to suffer through a transference to Dr. M. I had experienced one transference already to my analyst which had been as genuine and frustrating a feeling as unrequited love. No more transferences; no more Unrequited Love!

But even as I protested I felt more and more desire for Dr. M . . . unsolicited, unwanted yet delicious sensation . . . which continued to grow and grow until . . . so unexpectedly! . . . the pressure of a full bladder cut across and obliterated my desire. That full bladder pressure intensified. Painful now. And extremely embarrassing.

Silence.

At length Dr. M asked what was happening. I wanted very much to explain but although I was now physically capable of talking, I was mute with embarrassment. I knew the reason for that. As a child I had been a chronic bed-wetter. During my analysis I had been told that bed-wetting is an indication of a strong disturbance in childhood, usually of a sexual nature. I had tried again and again in analytic hours to discover that childhood disturbance, sexual or otherwise, without success. I had never learned the reason for my bed-wetting, nor had I overcome my sense of shame about the toilet functions. Because of that still present shame, it took an inordinate time to tell Dr. M about the bladder distress I continued to feel. When at long last I reported it, I heard a question leap out of me, totally unpremeditated:

"Is an orgasm like *wetting* someone? Is that why I don't have an orgasm?"

"I don't know. Is that why?"

Gray blankness again. I tried to find an answer to the question in the blankness but none came. Gradually the full-bladder distress dissipated and I was left, emotionless, in a gray-black void.

And then I was told that the session had ended.

I could not believe five hours had passed, yet I felt I had been living in eternity. I was to discover that this elasticity of time is one of the most distinctive features of the LSD experience. Einstein's relativity becomes the fact: a minute seems endless while five hours pass in a trice.

I left Dr. M in a state of enchantment: the intervening week seemed hardly enough to classify and comprehend the wealth of imagery and sensation which had appeared in this five-hour trice.

JOYCE JAMES

Joyce James's first psychedelic experience demonstrates the potential of a single, high-dose session. In the company of her husband and another couple she ingested peyote in a concentrated liquid. It was not uncommon in the early 1960's for married partners to trip together in both clinical and recreational settings; often after the scrutiny of a psychedelic the dyad would get tighter or come unglued. Here the heightened sensibility of the author causes her to flee the group after a casual, but characteristic, put-down remark from her husband. As she sits on the roof in self-imposed exile, "with racing mind forming picture after picture of our 'marriage,'" she endures one of the most harrowing trips in altered-state literature. Ultimately she accepts herself as creator of her negativity.

The *Psychedelic Review* published this "peyote awakening" in 1964, describing the author as a teacher of semantics. The first half is reprinted here.

From "Shouted From the Housetops: A Peyote Awakening"

Back at The House; three of us, with one other—Marolyn, a friend. It was the weekend of Easter, and the early evening of Good Friday. It was also just one year ago that we had commenced the deeper meditation of Yogananda's initiation into Kriya Yoga.

As Monty had recommended, we had eaten lightly, nothing more than an apple. From the jar of liquid he poured us each a thumbfull. Considering all the claims that were made for it the amount seemed scant enough, but holding that brown-green, soupy mud where once one could smell it, one's nose of itself would rear nostrils aback, with refusal. Oh but it was bitter! Unbelievably alien to the human taste. One's whole body was affronted. We thought that perhaps if mixed with honey and slowly rolled on the tongue, at least we should be able to swallow it. No sense of anticipation remained, there was no prelude to awe, but the act of

Peyote Awakening. "Oh, poor poor Eve! That apple choked her daughters all through time, so abysmally wretched with the good and evil phantasy" (Joyce James).

sipping that brew was a total experience in itself—
the reluctant gagging.

"Sure must need something pretty badly to endure this . . . ," I thought. Slowly, and very surely,
we extracted from our senses the condensed savor of
all the bitterness there is in life, slow distilled to
almost unassimilatable lees of taste. And the honey,
with its polarity of sweetness merely seemed extension of the slow drip poison dreg of bitter.

Down at last. I was disappointed—phooey, there
seemed nothing to this stuff. I might have known it
wouldn't work on me. I felt no change. I do not
know my expectation, something like champagne
perhaps—a deeper sensing of beauty, an intensify-
ing of color, and significance in form—less that
dulling of perception that drunkenness can bring.
Oh ignorant. Naive.

Bodies still, and waiting; after some time Don
claimed some new sensation at the base of his skull.
It seemed like idle conversation, for I myself was
not aware of any change, except I did not feel so
pleasant or indifferent as I had, and a light remark
from Marolyn, with her usual mocking humor drew
from me overweighted, snapped rebuke. My contempt was quite apparent, surprising me at least, so
unguessed its existence and extent before. But Don,
in voice so thinned and cruel with answering dis-
gust replied for her to me in accent from the gutter—"Jesus Myrtle! Ain't you the little lady
though."

Some such thing, but his expression as he flung
it, his lip a writhing of disdain, was a dispropor-
tioned embittered consignment to derision. Never
had I heard him speak that way in all our lives together. The cause I did not understand, but my response was immediate and frightful to me. That
voice of his that darted venom hit like frozen falling
into water. Shock rippled unsuspected depths of all
my being, encountering underlying other shock of
knowing that all along such hate had been before,
never acknowledged, suppressed, denied; counter-
pointing, chording, leaping scales of expanding recognition. I knew such freezing anger, I could not
describe; such indomitable, rigid anger, and cruel
shock and pain that I was battered—and forever re-

moved from ignorance of our relation. Why—he
had only hated me as the woman, any woman—and
had negated my rights to become one; suppressing
me had practically turned me into a boy—neutered
me in fact. Gone forever the humble pleading to
God to try to reflect my husband's elevation, incor-
porate within myself the superior nature ascribed to
him. Now I knew. He was an affront to nature
while refusing of its existence should it manifest as
woman. Oh, what the mother of such a boy? And
who actually was this stranger with whom I'd ridden
dreaming nightmare for so long?

Final and irrevocable, that anger loosed in
me—and fatal—for it embodied death. Heart bursting into mind's reflected anguish the churning of
my diaphragm lashing on torment, the sudden
weakness of the knees under sickened, goaded body,
I spoke:

"Aaagghh. I had better leave this place Don
Naylor, or I'm afraid I would kill you. . . ."

And I groped out of the house, nauseous,
wracked with the burgeoning vision of our state together. Unbelievable! Yet somewhere, somewhere,
I had always known this. Oh why so unconscious
that fear, that hate of him, smothered in guilt and
delusion?

I left them in the warm hearth room, all firelit
and calm—in just those few seconds an exile.

"Ah, I am really alone then. The outcast, the
nonbelonger, and have I not always known it?"

And a subtle change in sense occurred. That
hate was true, my answering leap of violence real.
Fear had always been. Now I saw the veils were
lifting, and the view was black and wasted. Nausea
mounted. Thirteen years' experience became as
naught—or—cycled round again to that other night
of life, when "they" had told me I was not their
own. Sickening as that shock had been, aftermath
had brought relief—"at last the things that are, are
seen as so, and desperate though they be, they are
not so fearful as delusion." Now again that grimness
of relief, with vision freeing from the webs stranded
on mockery. My God! How that man did hate—
and it wasn't even hate for me—only intervening
phantoms interpolating image and reality. Ah, how

blinded my poor, weak eyes. ("Jesus Christ". . . . I'd said it myself, that I would not marry any other than He!) And what of him, was he blind too, or did he really know? Oh dear God. NOW is upon me! Again! For I see as clearly. We are blind.

And helpless. These words that take a page and half an hour to write them take no motion of time for their living—lived as they are outside it. In less than the reach of a footstep, the fast racing knowing of how things have been for a lifetime!

Falling now, so weak with wrack and shame, but on up to the roof, "I'll be alone this night, whatever it should bring. At least is less danger apart."

And up the slow stairs, in utter aloneness, I stepped on the roof to the deck—reached the mattress—prostrate I was ill. Nausea flooded up the bitterness of down savored drug, throwing up the apple that had comprised my dinner. Oh poor, poor Eve! That apple choked her daughters all through time, so abysmally wretched with the good and evil phantasy. It bubbled like a fountain in my throat, the grief.

Body quietening, I lay with racing mind forming picture after picture of our "marriage." Came vision with new emphasis, informing as a dream, and I shuddered at the cruelties hidden but implicit. I could not weep—weeping is a part of the sad scenes that it mourns, an extension of the past with some hope for its future—but I saw only a past that had never existed, replaced by realities that had never been dreamed; crouched like a stone under the moon-deflecting screen. Like a sad, sad stone.

Laughter floated the roof, came drifting over the garden. They all seemed happy enough down there! I cannot tell you to what depths my spirit dropped—deep, deep fathom-plummet beyond all reach of feeling. Anger and sadness, hot-lipped words; they were so far away. They were of the living and no life moved in me except for my body breathing the life of its own. I was nearly shocked to death and beyond characteristic of the living.

The night drew on and their voices murmured above the trees. Sometimes music played, and I alone—on the top of the house—was a part of the house for all the feeling left to me. I do not know how long I sat, and after a while found my legs of themselves had folded into lotus, seat of many a morning's quiet, and that I was not so sad as then. Dropped away the daily life that had distraited so— little but the moment and the knowledge that I had no life, and likely never did, was peace enough. It was a certain knowing—and that is all we pray for: certainties. I raised my head to the moon sky and met the silent core of Self inside on which all things turn, but is lost to the mundane vision by overflow of dream. It is itself the dreamer also, and not the one in dream. Self is a quiet thing, a strong thing, and it is all there "is." Free of dreams, free of the see-saw of the thoughts of them, it is neither good or bad. It just is.

And for a while, it was.

I heard the slow walking of someone under the trees, and although it was quite distant the hearing was acute, as I had not experienced hearing in years. Someone moving nearer to me and on up the stair. In the doorway, head against the moonlight and looking as I had seen him look the last time he was "He" and real, there stood my old friend Monty.

He quietly sat himself beside me—understanding in his manner, and in his self-containedness was reflection of my own.

"Oh" (In my everyday mind—like a mind going on at the foot of the stair.) "Then I must seem as he. This is the answer to that question of how must he have felt? Ah, it is a far country that manifests so."

A sense of shock for myself this time, in the little conscious mind that existed with this other Self, for now I also knew the distance traveled from that daily world existence. As if the outer skin purports to be the person, but when the skin is made transparent and the Being inside is seen, one learns what was the skin only, with a pockmark seam of pain of unguided belief that has nought to do with the inner self, and is merely a record of the dream—and that the Self was never known.

There is the split in the mind.

"Are you well?" he asked, and I answered,

"No, my soul is sick to death."

He looked very kind there in the moonlight, and utterly remote. As remote as anyone actually is, and as he had formerly appeared to me, when I adored what had then been far beyond me. I understood. In the quiet of my soul before it plunged hell-bound on the soaring way to heaven, I understood, regarding him without the love which he evoked before—for I was far away from love.

Bard-oh! Bard. Sing to him who passes now
quietly slipped from mooring of his clay.
Bardo! Bard pray now. Pray forever that
he may, now and forever bridge the stream
from life to death, unslain by knowledge of
his own lie in breath-taking pictures constantly
pray for him now all is one.
Now he descends into Bardo! Bard, oh pray!

And the sound of my own voice astounded me. A deep booming ring from the bottomless tomb. It was myself, that tomb!—with voice as low and endless as all the bounded earth that comprised my form; a voice that used up ravening strength to merely utter of itself. I observed its force of travel in every muscle, nerve and tissue, before it transformed the ether into corresponding sound. God! What a journey. Each sound, each thought, each word was the echo of a lifetime of existence, choice and action. All history went to form one sound! No utterance is made but it employs totality. A fact existing without our notice in our usual slow-body-consciousness. My own voice frightened me come issuing from the grave. I had never heard my voice before! Buried in my body! So obvious a state I did not know how I had so long successfully evaded it. The days of my life had been mostly death! Was I now alive?

Implication of a judgment yawning now before me as the soul stands free of its tomb, this which was happening to me: for great changes are taking place in this little structural universe of myself. . . .

Sitting rapt as lotus, there before me was the person calling himself "Monty." No one I had ever known! Oh God, the world as I know it is slipping from me, what is taking place? This . . . this form beside me, who was he, and ahhhhh . . . who am I? So long I have asked that question, gone the

years I thought I knew. Just another dream-filled period obscuring deep issues that have those few times caused me to ask it. . . . Heaven above, I ask you now! WHO AM I?

For fearful was my vision, racing was my vision. The moon and stars were nearer and leaping on the sky. Centuries were flashing in those sky journeyings. Light was changing now for me, the light that was in things. Encountered central core blue flame, my eye that struck the wood beam, and up to the stones that, glowing too, filled me with rising horror of recognition—the world of dream was loosed from sleep and the world of dream was real! I could not jump to the sleep of the day and flee it all behind. In every thing the cold blue fire—moving, moving on itself. Appalled, I felt the mounting rushing speeds inside, far below was my plodding mind, duly recording the doings of a consciousness far beyond itself; still down there in a familiar world. I had left that world behind for another and another and even then another. . . .

"Shouted from the housetops" that were our own heads.

Christ told us, long ago.

"Oh, I'm afraid," I moaned to him beside me. "Please don't leave me now."

"I shall stay with you, but don't you know you're cold? Let me fetch you a blanket."

"No! No, please don't go. Cold! What is that to me?"

I shrugged a shoulder and it seemed an hour, so complex and lengthy that procedure.

I was beyond the hold and protection of a body. I raised my head to look at the town, and the lights were demon's eyes. Hell-firelit evil holes, burning in the night that did not veil the pit beyond.

"Oh God! . . . Does no one know how things really are? Doesn't anyone see the terror and the evil?"

Wherever vision turned, eyes. Everywhere were eyes, and things were contained within the eyes; not the eyes contained in them. Everything had vision, saw with the countless sights—of thousand-eyed gods.

"You experience yourself," he said, "there is only you."

But I could endure no longer and lowered lids to turn their vision in to encounter loathsome horror at the pictures spawning, swarming in towards me. They opened with a bang! my eyes. I was wearied to death and broken-hearted.

"I should never have done this, never have come."

"Perhaps it is a good thing" was his only answer, and our voices sounded as thunder, and as timeless.

Now I was approaching another effect. I will not waste words defining terror. Terror is at least this side of life, and I had ventured far beyond it and all antidote. Now I was alone and adrift in infinities—lost in the universe of myself, vast and teeming, and in no thing different from the one we call outside. There is no outside.

"Speak. Speak. Confess before it is too late."

The harrowing vision and the overwhelming realization that all around were other worlds, other beings, other kinds, became too much for me—and inner resources overtaxed, I moaned again,

"I should never have come."

I was in another place. Vistas opened on new world terrors in the ether, showing infinite departures of various heavens and gaping hells, either kind inspiring dread and none of which I had the freedom to avoid—not while their maddening interpenetrations had their way with me.

"Look at me!" he said, for desolation was covering the end of the earth.

"Look at me, and be still."

And I looked. Looked and took measure of his calm. Yes, it reassured me for the instant. His face was the most beautiful thing I had ever seen, scarcely known in its perfection, and certainly it was a beauty betokening little of the human. What there was seemed only signature of the way that he had come, a mapped indication of his forces. I saw the face that had walked with me the desert—but now I saw with an inside view! No more a girly-worly-worldly eye titivated by the vision of a beautiful young man. This was the ageless perfection of a very old 'soul', in a body held perfect, unmarred by the ravage of timing passion. This was impersonal face, and so it had been before. It shamed me what

I had made of it only so recently. He . . . he had been kind, in the face of that blind, angry figure. So blind, so angry, and empty. Incredible, that one could be so sightless and so hungry! Then, possessed by his calm, by his utter repose, I gazed at him as if to meditate.

And there on the roof, and out of my head, the heavens rent their veils and vision came clear. I saw Monty (as he must have meant it previously when he said he "saw" me) and I sobbed afresh at the sight. Cleansed my eye, released from the clutches of corpus that had only thought to interminglemangle, there was the hope—the human encounter with the human soul. (Pandora stalks eternal fruit sown seed of Hope. Ageless Pandora walks the heart. There will always be the baulks to open.) I gazed and was humbled forever as I saw the unsheathed face of the Being cleared of all his veils. A great one. An old one—and I bowed before him. He smiled. He knew, and raised the tear-stained head. Light was truly all round him. For an instant my gaze held clear, but shame overcame and I hung my head. The light was a great wide halo—from toe to the head to the sky, and the light was myriad rays *divided*, and each pulsing ray was the soul of a man. The multiple light of all men's souls was forming the halo, like great shimmering wings, converging his center which held them contained.

"Everyman must come through Me. For I am the Way, and The Light of the World."

Thundering, awestruck recognition of the Christ spirit, resident within him. That is the path that Everyman must travel!

I know why people grovel and touch the head to the ground before the radiance of The Light made human. One knows one's humblest state on the scale of spirit married to form.

And as I, humble, worshipping, was ready to prolong, from every part of consciousness the words blared forth as trumpet:

"DO YOU SEEK TO WORSHIP ME IN ONE OF MY CREATURES? OPEN YOUR INNER EYE!"

I lowered lids, and there with the completest

understanding saw the center of creation—The Light of The World issuing from Itself the Center, eternally departing triad, like a universe of fleur-de-lys, golden moving of the lotus which is ever a becoming.

"I AM NO ONE, BUT ALL. . . ."

And light was sound, issuing forth to penetrate the ether, welding sound to thought, and thought to form, apprehended by the impact of any eye. And as the sun to earth is, to the sun is this inner model of a universe.

I opened my eyes to look at the one I'd called "my friend," as had Arjuna called Krishna, while unseeing and deluded. So recently with the eye of woman had I yearned for his form, now "I" saw—not with the web of circumstance that calls itself Joyce, but "I," my Self. (Joyce is of the world, and time. Perhaps "I" should not have been so hard on her, had 'I' not just then learned of her separate existence, to our mutual embarrassment. One need not negate the other, for both are quite dependent. Perhaps always at the first, it is that movement from one state causes shame in another—but the novelty of one cannot deny the old, else one has not conjoined one's understanding.)

Gaze shifted once again—his form was changing there before me.

Strange sound issues forth from me. Blue core flame in him reveals to me the skull. Gone the face, gone the being I know somewhat.

"I'm looking through you! I see your skull, your fleshless eyes. Now too they vanish. I look beyond. I'M LOOKING THROUGH YOU! Through a hole in the web of our world! The world is gone. I pass through you and see . . . the universe! The galaxy! The All There Is in motion, orderly, predictable. The vague shadow of your circumscribing skull is as easily a world. Gods, demons, fathers, mothers, devas, prophets, angels, worlds and stars; landscapes, saints and deities of oceans—all the forms of every kind that have inhabited the mind of man on earth, all slowly suspended in the world dance of an atom of infinity, turning on the spheres of themselves. Forms their total composition the features of a Being, eyes of distant suns and moons, gaseous clouding forehead, upholding all the stars of ever were or shall be; the atoms of the galaxies form gigantic head and mouth that terrifies with appetite spewing forth and gathering in all the hordes of souls and men and god and planet.

Not so much The Lord of All—for He Is All There Is, cosmic man or cosmic mountain, the many levels of existence through which all must climb.

"A god."

"A God? The God?"

"No. He Is All. Nameless, formless and terrible, composed of nought but all there is, and isn't—slowly interweaving the traces of its forms. A mountain of being in your head! Monty! A mountain are you!"

Awe-struck my gaze sped on, in this moment of my life taking place outside of time. Looking through the "whole" in the universe. (As Thomas before me had looked at the hole in his God and saw the whole of everything. I do not play with words—do you see how the words do play with us—and the sleepy minds that do confuse their meanings?)

And with all my being transfixed in the moment that answered the quest of my life, I shuddered in my soul, for Grace carried even further and with new velocities of divining sight I saw our universe sphering on its destiny, dissolving in the ether of some inconceivable infinity of future, and then another vortexing of itself in the place made absent—then another, and another. . . .

Deeply my warning spirit chastised:

"WHEN WILL YOU OF THE UNCLEAN EYE BE SATISFIED? YOU ARE TOO BOLD. IN THE BEGINNING WAS THE WORD, AND THE WORD WAS WITH GOD!"

Shame anguished me. . . . "I haven't the right," I whispered, "I haven't the right, I know," and turned away the paltry gaze that faltered on eternity. The Word was not mine. My own word had never been with God.

But I had! *seen* the Beginning.

MARGARET MEAD
1901–79

Margaret Mead, America's preeminent anthropologist, assessed the national controversy over psychedelic drugs in her regular column in *Redbook* in 1968. Using examples from both Western and primitive cultures, Mead discusses puritanical reaction to nontraditional expressions of religious and personal freedoms.

Margaret Mead. "Puritanical Americans disapprove of all drugs of this type."

Psychedelics and Western Religious Experience

Users of LSD claim that with it they have valid mystical experiences, comparable to those previously known by holy men and saints. Is there any clear difference between the two experiences? And if not, what right has society to deny anyone this new access to age-old spiritual experience?

The question of validity has troubled every religious group that has accepted the possibility of mystical experience. As in the case of miracles, visions are subjected to the most intense and severe scrutiny. Those who claim, or have claimed for them, a unique relationship to God may be admitted to sainthood only a very long time after the event. Joan of Arc was burned at the stake as a witch in 1431 and was not canonized until 1920. In the Western Christian tradition, validity turns essentially on the relationship between an individual's mystical experience and the religious beliefs of others. That is, it is the miracles, the stigmata and the visions that come to have relevance to the community of the faithful that are judged, in the end, to be valid. In this sense the question of whether or not LSD users have *valid* mystical experiences is beside the point.

The central issue is that LSD changes the state of consciousness of the user for a shorter or longer time. Puritanical Americans disapprove of all drugs of this type, even mild ones like nicotine and alcohol. Moreover, they take the stand that individuals' private lives are within the jurisdiction of public legislation. At present their zeal for total abstinence is concentrated on drugs. It is expressed also in the refusal to regard addiction as an illness instead of a crime or a sin.

The problem of LSD is further complicated by the claim that it produces a state comparable to psychosis and that controlled experimental use of this drug can give psychiatrists new access to an understanding of their patients. For many persons it is only a short step from this claim to the belief that young people, students, are being allowed to take a drug that may make them insane. Instances of disturbed individuals who have committed crimes or who have suffered irremediable injury while under the influence of LSD have strengthened this fear.

At the same time there are others who claim that certain drugs such as marijuana, mescaline and now LSD open the doorways of perception and give the user an extraordinarily vivid sense of himself and his relationship to the universe. This was the viewpoint of Aldous Huxley in his book *The Doors of Perception*. In his utopian novel *Island*, he pictures the use of psychedelic drugs in a regular form of initiation of young people to a more sensitive realization of themselves and their place in society. That is, in *Island* Huxley attempted to construct a new religion in which these drugs play a carefully controlled part.

In his interpretation, psychedelic drugs become adjuncts to religious experience comparable to but more effective than fasting, isolation, prayer, meditation and highly controlled exercises in breathing or in taking special physical postures. The means are new, but the quest for religious experience is part of an ancient tradition in which the individual who feels a vocation makes a long, disciplined effort to attain a closer relationship to the supernatural. Even when the vision comes to an unbeliever like Saul of Tarsus, who neither sought it nor prepared for it, the experience is within a living tradition.

Certain cultures—for example, Balinese culture and the peasant version of Haitian culture—have encouraged religious-trance experience for many individuals. In these societies people take a great many precautions in selecting and ritually training those who will engage regularly in trance and in controlling where and under what circumstances trance may be induced. Individuals who go into trance at the wrong time and in the wrong place are exhorted to stop these activities or stay away from the community.

It is quite possible that the use of psychedelic drugs, whether in an old or a new religious context, may be able to facilitate mystical experience. But all that we know about religious mysticism suggests that very careful disciplines and rigorous forms of training would have to be developed on which those who used the psychedelic drugs as an adjunct to

religious experience could draw. It also seems clear that in our own American tradition, one test of whether such a development was in fact a religion would be its social relevance. For unlike those Eastern religions in which mystical experience is a purely individual spiritual belief, Western religions contain the expectation that religious experience benefits not only the visionary but also others who share his faith. With this expectation the solipsistic aim of the LSD user, whose interest is wholly introspective, is out of key.

The panic roused by the widespread and uncontrolled individual experimentation with LSD is precipitating a flood of poorly conceived legislation. One unexpected by-product of these laws may be a new kind of interference with the regular religious exercises of the American Indian Church, in which peyote is used. In this situation the prohibitions become an unjustified interference with religious freedom.

It must also be recognized, however, that there is no necessary relationship between the use of drugs and religious experience. The ordinary LSD "trip" has no more necessary relationship to mystical experience than the drinking of ten cocktails has, after which many people experience various alterations of consciousness.

From one point of view the battle between those who wish to enlarge their experience through the use of LSD and other drugs and those who are exercising all their powers to prohibit this use is a very old one in Western cultures. On the one side are those who believe that control over consciousness is crucial to human living and that loss of control inevitably leads to the emergence of dangerous, bestial impulses. On the other side are those who believe that control of consciousness is itself inimical to true spirituality.

These two views, the Apollonian and the Dionysian, represent an ancient conflict within our cultural tradition. But now, as in the past in our own society, puritanism, which is not a necessary aspect of the Apollonian conception of life, embitters many on both sides who are trying to come to grips with the deeper issues of the handling of human potentialities.

Anita Hoffman. "Hardly anyone on the train, and no way for anyone to guess that we were carrying four thousand joints of grass between us."

BEATS &
HIPPIES

On LSD in the Gulf of Mexico, 1966

The Beat Generation of the 1950's and early 1960's, a subculture of writers, artists, and adventurers, challenged the values of an affluent, conformist society. In the tradition of the bohemian undergrounds that had spawned the major revolutions in the arts, the beats experimented sexually and used drugs to release creative and visionary powers, as a statement of their individualism, and to defy the prevailing cold war, bombshelter mentality. Their heroes were mad poets, crazy Zen monks, and black jazz musicians. From the latter they gained familiarity with reefer, girl, and horse (marijuana, cocaine, and heroin) and developed a "spontaneous bop" writing style based on the improvised jazz riff. In their far travels the beats drank yagé in Colombia, smoked hashish in Morocco, and volunteered for early LSD experiments. Their style was

labeled "beatnik" and dismissed by the mass media. Academic critics condemned beat literature as incoherent, but *Howl, On the Road, Coney Island of the Mind, Naked Lunch, The Love Book*, and *Memoirs of a Beatnik* were widely read by the young. The prototype hipster was an urban shaman who manifested his or her cool with a junkie's detachment, a pot-smoker's humor, and a peyote-eater's visionary awareness. This image had a potent effect on the next, much larger and more drug-oriented counterculture.

The women of the Beat Generation made every scene from North Beach to Greenwich Village, from Oaxaca to Tangier, from the Left Bank to Athens. The psychedelic pioneers of the previous section were mostly turned on by psychiatrists, but the young women of the Beat Generation scored drugs from street dealers, sometimes in foreign lands. Although there was some experimentation with cocaine and heroin, their favorite drugs were Mexican marijuana and peyote. Whatever her social class, each of these 1950's women had the same quest: to get high, to break through her cultural conditioning and gain new perspectives.

The style of the quest was different for the beats than for the psychedelic pioneers. Valentina Wasson had eaten psilocybin mushrooms supplied by a *curandera* while on a scientific expedition to Oaxaca; Bonnie Frazer [Bremser] flew there with her fugitive husband, scored a shoe box of the mushrooms from a local youth, and ate them in her hotel room. Constance Newland had taken LSD with her psychiatrist to analyze her sexual problems; Lenore Kandel took psychedelics with her lover to explore their hedonic levels. Adelle Davis in Los Angeles and Kay Johnson in Greece each probed myths of femininity with LSD, but used vastly different language. Anaïs Nin wrote of the inner turbulence of LSD, and Diane di Prima of its social manifestations.

LSD was a catalyst in the evolution from beat to hippie. In the first half of the 1960's, a small number of outsiders grew into a widespread and visible counterculture composed mainly of young middle-class dropouts. The acid trip was the most intense of the shared experiences, a sensory and psychic extravaganza in which hallucinated hysteria, psychic awareness, and cosmic giggles could all occur within the space of a minute. Marijuana remained a staple mind-alterant for the hippies, and it was more readily available than during the time of the beats. But LSD was the strongest psychoactive substance. Its widespread use, along with other synthetic and natural mind-altering drugs, triggered psychic, social, and spiritual change in this segment of society.

Ellen Sander recreates the beginning of the hippie era, when the reliable dealer of soft drugs became a folk hero. Sometimes women took this role, but usually men did. Although women directly participated in every aspect of the counterculture and consumed drugs as frequently as men, male chauvinism continued to prevail in relationships within the hip power structure. Sander shows how the rituals of obtaining and doing drugs proved democratic and sexually equalizing experiences.

Their epic binge of peyote eating in an Arizona national park places Jocelyn's *Tripper*, not included here, and her tribe of urban dropouts in the traditions of Native American tribes and nineteenth-century utopian collectives.

The polarization between persons who tripped and those who didn't is examined by Linda Rosenkrantz, whose characters move in New York art circles. Sharon Rudahl's protagonist navigates Manhattan's Lower East Side with her head full of acid, experiencing in the course of an afternoon tantric bliss with her psychedelic lover and emotional depression with her junkie lover. New York is also the setting of Anita Hoffman's memoir. How dope and politics mixed in the 1960's to create a surrealistic band of media guerrillas known as the Yippies is dramatized through a stoned heroine who finds herself on a crowded Manhattan subway carrying four thousand joints to be mailed to politicians.

Educator Garnet Brennan's private use of cannabis suddenly became a public scandal in 1967. The accelerated waves of sixties' politics carried her to confrontation and brief fame.

Despite some doctors' warnings (later proven false) that the children of LSD users might suffer from genetic deformity, some women did take acid during their pregnancies. Though not reprinted here, Karen Harvey's interview in *Ecstatic Adventure* (1968) and Rena's unpublished journal, *Ecstatic Evolution*, discuss psychedelic augmentation of the birth process and conception.

A century after Alice entered Wonderland by drinking opiated medicines, eating mushrooms, and conversing with a hookah-smoking caterpillar, the song "White Rabbit," written and sung by Grace Slick of the Jefferson Airplane, topped the music charts. Rock critic Richard Goldstein called it "the hippie national anthem." "Feed your head," the song's refrain, are the words of the Dormouse to Alice as well as the serpent to Eve, and of the shamans of many tribes and cultures to those seeking to know (some would say escape to) other realities.

"The main reason for 'White Rabbit,'" said Slick in 1967, "is to write a song that's up front about drugs. . . . Alice winds up in a place her parents don't know about and that she has to experience and understand herself." A decade later Slick conceded that many people may have misinterpreted the lyrics. "'Feed your head' doesn't mean take every fucking drug that comes along," she told an interviewer in 1977. "'Feed your head' means read. . . . Listen and read."

Grace Slick performing in 1967. "Feed your head."

Janis Joplin, another freewheeling rock 'n' roll vocalist of the period, drank Southern Comfort and did heroin in the tradition of blues singers, dying of an overdose at the age of twenty-eight. The upper-and-downer syndrome that proved fatal to Hollywood superstars Judy Garland and Marilyn Monroe, among others, was scrutinized in Jacqueline Susann's 1968 best seller *Valley of the Dolls*.

Several female social scientists produced outstanding works. Jean Houston coauthored with R.E.L. Masters a classic textbook, *The Vari-*

eties of Psychedelic Experience (1966). Bonnie Golightly collaborated with Peter Stafford on the highly acclaimed *LSD: The Consciousness Expanding Drug* (1967). Lisa Bieberman, a force behind the Psychedelic Information Centers, published a long-running newsletter.

During a decade that featured political assassinations, the Vietnam War, civil rights struggles, and student unrest, the growing use of mind-changing drugs, the social rebellion of the hippies, and the politics of "flower power" were elevated to a national threat. Alarmist medical warnings were announced. The highly publicized tragedy of Diane Linkletter's suicide was attributed to acid, although she was not tripping when she killed herself. LSD was declared illegal in 1966, and almost all scientific research was suspended.

Nonetheless, several million people opted for consciousness alteration with this highly publicized and widely available mind drug. Journalists Joan Didion (in "Slouching Toward Bethlehem," not reprinted here) and Rasa Gustaitis *(Turning On)* assumed the role of anthropologists as they explored the psychedelic milieus of California's Haight-Ashbury and Big Sur in the late 1960's.

The police moved to suppress the most visible underground of illicit drug users since the days of Prohibition. Many people were arrested; others dispersed in the wake of the narcs, the scene-crashers, exploiters, entrepreneurs, burn-outs, and the influx of hard drugs like speed and heroin. The psychedelic movement ended with the 1960's, closing with the Woodstock Festival and the crime spree of the acid-brainwashed women of the Charles Manson gang. As the latest underground was dispersing and being absorbed by mainstream society, so were its patterns of drug use and abuse.

BONNIE FRAZER [BREMSER]
1939–

A few years after Valentina and Gordon Wasson discovered that magic mushrooms were ritually used by Indians living in a remote Mexican village, Bonnie Frazer and her fugitive husband, poet Ray Bremser, arrived in that same "mainstreet mushroom town." The articles by the Wassons served as a signal to the Beat Generation. By 1959, writes Frazer, "one-half of the people I know who have gone to Mexico have made the thirty-hour trip up into the mountains to get to Huautla, everyone knows about it."

Frazer, daughter of a State Department official, was a graduate of exclusive girls schools who adopted the underground life-style of her husband. *Troia*, the title of her book, means "adventuress and prostitute." The freedom to get high represented for her a victory of the spirit. The couple scored a shoe box full of psilocybin mushrooms from a young Indian boy. The author ate the mushrooms continuously, not wanting to come down, valuing more "the large time cycle change of life" than the specific experiment.

From Troia: Mexican Memoirs

We are off on our mushroom visit (projected length two months—actual length ten days) and we both know it is going to be fun, paradise in fact to plan (pot high of course) such a great adventure.

We traveled a day and a night to get up to the mountains. It appears only a fifty mile drive by the map but the trip takes thirty hours, the bus seems to go too fast even at that, and each hundred foot turn in the road threatened to be the end of the line. There were two bus drivers, and my attention

focused on one of them. But why am I interested in people? Life is as it is, I am tired of smelly rules.

Mainstreet mushroom town runs along the side of the mountain, parallel streets are up or down the mountain, but not evident. Main street is a dirt road, and the road we arrive on in the bus becomes main street, and the market is perched on a precipice which faces west. The morningtime market as we arrive offers no more welcome than any of the other inhabitants, no one curious about us, no one even notices except a little boy who came up and asked if we wanted to buy mushrooms and Ray said yes and found out where the one hotel in town was, at the east end of the village. The road runs level as it is confined in the village and starts going up and

Dust jacket of Troia. *"I ate a lot, immediately, having great faith (all of these organic highs are religious, don't ask me chemical effects)" (Bonnie Frazer [Bremser]).*

down again immediately as it gets past the hotel. We check in—the prices are very high and the conditions primitive; not that I mind, in fact I grew to love it, and would have liked to stay there forever. The wooden stairs of the hotel passed upwards connecting balconies that grew more rickety the higher they got. We were on the second floor. The door was fastened by a padlock, but immediately in the room we discovered many knotholes which would make the living communal.

It is a great thing to start out on a trip with enough money. We indulged in a new kind of tourism, and hunted out the most ideal places, every once in a while returning to the hub Mexcity, oh Mexico time snake, where I have to exert myself to raise as much money as possible quickly so we can get away and be safe again. I found out later that this is a cycle many Mexican prostitutes do with their boyfriends: fierce work, extended vacations, though I know none who got so elemental as us. We grew not to fear too much running out of money at the end of the line, because hitchhiking was possible, but then anything had possibilities of fear; there are always the police around.

Huautla. You learn to say these names, learn to say them passing through; approach a town and there is the rumor of its name, and when you are through it you have learned it, and it is usually beautiful too. Ever find it hard to accept that a dream place exists, like the peyote church in Brooklyn? That's how I felt about Huautla, and forgot about Seraphita with the street score, figured that was more hip anyway, and as long as we had them might as well start eating. I ate a lot, immediately, having great faith (all of these organic highs are religious, don't ask me chemical effects), and immediately the bright day hotel window draws sounds of saxophones, clarinets, flutes and danzon drums of the Indian hillside road top. The music quickly begun stops, a few beats of a march, we rush to the balcony and see the band, it is rinkytink dissembled, all sizes of men in white wrapped on trousers unanimously blow one bagpipe chord strong which peters out into creative frills and tootles according to each man's inability to control the register. That's how jazz began—a happy, full-of-

joy music starts shyly and then jumps by the hotel road below, exactly rhythmed to the bounce of Indian foot parade going by, at that moment the most beautiful expressive music of love ever heard, and then we see what it means; a girl in a white dress, arm held by a man in extra white shirt and wrap between the leg pants, actually defined by the joy on his face as the bridegroom. They are modest, they are beautiful, the band plays their regal hopped up walk through town, a bebop Indian waltz. That was the first mushroom experience: everyone in that walk through town loved them who loved each other, and I thought I saw the bride look up at our balcony.

Another day dawns and I contemplate the sun moving, or the earth moving-relativities of shadow and light that make the window a half creeping of brightness, the rest still the blue birth of dawn, early in the morning. There comes to my head sad musics of a saxophone contemplating (musing) and in all the mountain heights I am puzzled where such a sound is coming from. I rouse Ray and we decide it comes from the graveyard down the road; it trails a cleft of greenness in the mountainside. This is the first truly pastoral music I have heard in my life, and it sings the blues, many mornings in Huautla, someone singing dawn to those already gone, such dedication of individual emotion, this blue and beautiful music, the mushrooms start to tell me something of life: whole nother conception of living, again.

*   *   *

The mushrooms look like mushrooms. . . . We bought a kilo (about two pounds) for eighty pesos (about six dollars), a shoebox full; they are dried to brown black witheredness. Big and small, their thin heads project from the center like dried flowers, but more organic, brownish black, they look like the earth itself, and we spend a couple of hours tearing the stems off and throwing them away; I eat as I work, Ray is timid of them (too organic) but eats enough to get high. I go crazy and eat about a pound of them while we are in Huautla, knowing that I will worship the effects, the taste is something to be ignored, I keep eating, every time we return to the room I eat mushrooms. I ate so many mushrooms I was never able to describe or remember the immediate feeling of their effect coming on, but know looking back that I was high for months (this is the way peyote hit me too—I can say a few beautiful high experiences, but the effect is a large time cycle change of life: how I get my religions) and the stomach gurgles in digesting these rinds of pure clean hilltop earth.

ELLEN SANDER

In *Trips*, Ellen Sander, one of the leading rock journalists of the 1960's, describes the counterculture from the inside. She evaluates the role of drugs in the emerging hippie scene in New York's Greenwich Village and Lower East Side in 1964–65. One of the central characteristics was the relatively easy availability of marijuana and psychedelics. Scoring a lid, sharing a joint, doing acid often unified young men and women seeking neurological liberation and self-reward. Sander traces the influence of mind-altering drugs on music, the folk arts from paraphernalia to clothing, and natural foods.

From Trips: Rock Life in the Sixties

They were lean days, it was scufflin' times. We were threadbare, hungry in so many ways, but basically happy, all of us in the first home we'd ever found, among peers, kindred minds, and a growing sense of something, somewhere, somehow getting better and that we had something to do with it all. We just lived the shit out of the times, soaking up days and nights of experience.

We were getting turned on in so many ways, lit up to new experiences, discoveries, adventures, music, all of which had something very tangibly related to the drugs available. The drugs were enjoyed, used, abused, taken, given, bought, sold, and stolen. We never questioned them, we did drugs because they were there. They felt good, they were fun, and they were a part of our existence. They helped us over some mighty humps and they stood in the way of others. Most of all they were a stone groove, for making and hearing music, for making love, for getting silly or serious and down to it among ourselves.

High and grooving for the first time, we were above the narrow-minded puritanism that held them illegal. Legal for us was what we chose in good conscience. Smoke sweet and high, it couldn't hurt. And out of this the mutual contempt between us and the heat was born, developed, and grew. It seemed such a humorless, pleasure-denying society, one that took its kicks behind excuses. We had no excuses, we were just getting as high as we could in every conceivable way and out of it a whole scheme of commerce—dealing—developed.

Grass, hashish, acid, and pills were cool, we knew their limits. Cocaine, it was so fine, a breathtakingly exhilarating high, too expensive to keep enough around to do any harm. Not in the shape *we* were in, for Chrissake! Bumming coin from one another, chipping in for Chinese takeout or pizza, cooking brown rice and seaweed, short on everything but dope.

For anything really important there was money, or other means, around. Any trip that got you off was cool, the higher the better, the happier the better, the funnier, the freer, the more and the more and the more. It was for now, for nothing else but now, for us, for our thing; no other dimension of time, space, or responsibility existed. The past was a bummer, the future completely uncertain, and nobody would then really admit to feeling secure as to whether or not the future would even be. If there was to be a future, we would create it out of the flat-out-balls-against-the-wall good time we were having in the great now. The pageant that was our lives had no past and no future, it was always in the process of becoming. It was not goals that stimulated us, it was the experience of being and becoming, the journey there rather than the end haul. We had no precedents that we knew of, we made it up as we went along, anything that proved uncool fell by the wayside of our circus.

We were certainly aware of the hassles. Paranoia fired our thinking and imagination into outrageous hooliganism. It got so that we could just smell trouble coming. A signal would go round the street like electricity whenever the heat was on. They had their informers and we had ours. The only difference is that they were running scared and we weren't.

No matter how hard come by, dope was always shared. Before 1965 it was relatively scarce on the East Coast, which created a situation where the really cool dealers emerged as community heroes. If you could handle it, you bought some; if you couldn't, there was always a free taste around. It was part of taking care of one another. There is something about supplying a brother's delights that just doesn't compare with the kind of competitive relationship you'd have to assume outside of the scene, off the street. It was just a better way to live, and nobody was looking back.

"Hang together or hang separately" was an expression passed around and examined in the light of what we were doing. Pete Seeger's agreeable "Take it easy but take it" was a greeting, a farewell, a verbal contact point. New language developed, a colorful, living language, growing, changing, borrowing from the songs and style and contributing to them. Everything we had to do with one another was reciprocal, cyclic, change feeding on itself and causing more in an upward spiral of change whose end was not known or cared about as long as it got higher. The vernacular of the day was a sign between us as the two-fingered V became, the parting "peace" and the special frivolous gypsy-injun way we dressed and lived.

Clothing was warmth and body decoration expressing a love of beauty, individuality, and humor. A leathercrafter in from Colorado would go around the Village in a black-and-brown suede jacket he'd made, beautifully tailored with a huge question mark welted into the back. His old lady would walk beside him, the back of her identical jacket adorned with an exclamation point. Zap-pow. Walking comic book.

Clothes were inspired by traditions we assimi-lated, fieldhand funkiness, nomadism, tribalism, and whatever hybrid that mixture produced. Before department store hippie garb was around, some discomfort with the gear he was wearing would give a cop in the ranks away instantly.

* * *

Every head in the village with access to tools would come up with some variety of handmade hash pipe, and head shops carried little screen discs to place in the bowl so no burning embers could come through the shaft.

Roach holders, which had humble origins as paper clips, bobby pins, hair clips, toothpicks, or split matchsticks, eventually became an art form. There were elaborately looped ones you could wear around your neck arousing no suspicion because they were so decorative, and little hand-wrought pincer-type devices with amulets at the base. Surgical sutures worked beautifully and were so big they rarely got lost. Roach clips are used on the very end of the joint, to hold the roach so that every bit of grass could be smoked. The main trouble was that by the time you were ready to use one, you were so stoned that you forgot where you put it, having been at least that stoned the last time you used it. So a suture made a pretty good table model. Alligator clips were handy and had the added advantage of being a necessary piece of electrical equipment any road manager should have on supply.

There were imported stash boxes, lava lights, posters finely detailed for stoned examination, lovely small glass beads to string and wear or give away, and all manner of pretty toys to enjoy while stoned.

If Congress had any idea of the extent of the marijuana market, for both drugs and paraphernalia, it would legalize grass instantly.

Because of the increased sensual awareness being high produces, artificial food tastes artificial. And because being high widens perspectives on physical as well as mental well-being, organic and genuinely nourishing food becomes more attractive, clean air becomes more important (smelling pollution stoned is immensely depressing), pure water is appealing, and a physically stimulating life becomes more attractive. Staying as high as possible under the most pure and comfortable (and uncomplicated) circumstances takes on a singular importance.

The drug scene grew geometrically. The first people into drugs were those with nothing to lose by it. Ghetto kids honestly believe that as the man kept the Indians stupid with fire water, he was keeping the blacks complacent with drugs. For us, hardly ghetto kids, except perhaps in an emotional sense, it was a way into ourselves, one of the first steps on a road that led to many fascinating journeys through the mind, that set the imagination roaming in hidden or forgotten corners and conjured up subliminal scenes that snaked surreally through the consciousness. Bob Dylan was the first and the most talented artist to articulate these hallucinations that were not hallucinations at all: they were there, they fit, they moved and went off into a blackness resolving deep in a moist mysterious level of thinking. He had a hold on our minds that was religious and he'd set them afire with kaleidoscopic chain reactions to his visions, which were always precise and revealing.

Defiance of the law, or any kind of authority for that matter, was merely a byproduct of what we were doing when we got into drugs. True, the surreptitious nature of obtaining and using drugs was a part of the romance, but the real point was getting high. "If it feels this good, it can't be all bad," we reasoned; either we're crazy or the law is, and between us, it was working out quite all right. We lived beyond the law, above it, just out of reach of it. It was obvious after a while that millions were turning on with soft drugs, that dealing (pushing is a rather irrelevant term because the demand, without exception, always exceeded the supply) was an honorable way of life. By sheer force of the quantity and stature of the people that were turning on, the law would be overpowered. It was just a matter of time during which one had to be particularly careful and develop a keen intuitive sense of trouble about to happen. Keeping the grass coming while avoiding a bust stimulated our inventiveness about survival and kept us sharp. We would stick it out.

Heads came out of the woodwork. Young lawyers (Lenny Bruce always said grass would eventually be legalized because all the law students he'd ever met were heads) who smoked grass became specialists in defending pot busts, which were usually effected with a plethora of errors and torts; druggie doctors would straighten out medical facts and squelch widely publicized rumors about drug complications such as the relationship of acid to chromosome damage, about which there is an overwhelming amount of doubt. Heads would open head shops with psychedelic merchandise, some would open health food restaurants (no cigarettes allowed inside), freaks would invent toys to play with while stoned. The whole look of fashion changed from the street level on up: where once a flash car was a symbol, it became a Volkswagen bus; where once it was blue suede shoes, it became knee-high moccasins with soft leather soles through which it could be discovered how much one's feet could feel as one walked. Attire gradually became exhibitionism of the most generous sort; to be a thing of beauty for stoners to groove on was a concern of audience and performer alike, and both were so much on the same trip that the music became a language of heads. Whether or not the lyrics were specifically (however surreptitiously) about drugs, it was head music, music to turn on to, music to fill the new spaces in one's mind that drugs unlocked.

KAY JOHNSON

Poet and painter Kay Johnson was living in Greece in a circle of expatriate beat writers and artists when she took a high-dose, ego-shattering LSD trip and subsequently produced a psychedelic visionary poem on the scale of George Andrews's "Burning Illumination" and Allen Ginsberg's "Lysergic Acid." "LSD-748" (because of its length only the final part is reprinted here) describes a voyage through the evolutionary gene pool, a search for ultimate identity, and a quest for the mother goddess.

According to her note, the title of Part IV is derived from *The Tibetan Book of the Dead* and refers to "a synthetic mystical experience in the Hallucinatory Region of Second Bardo, Region of Vision 3: 'Fire-Flow; internal Unity; eyes closed; emotional aspect.'"

From "LSD-748"
IV. FIRE FLOW

negative force. i need it. i want it. where is it?

where are you Negative Force? running down a street to the point of climax? down the funnel and out the other end, down into orgasm, down to the point of a tear; ah god my violence, god my destructive kicking feet,

                        where is it now?

all lost? come, come here; i want you in this poem; come little female, come eve, come negative force, what image can i hold for you to be intrigued and jump in? how can i turn the image upside down; look, you are not a funnel, not force falling to the pinpoint orgasm of a tear;

you are not wasted, you are not exploded on somebody's floor come negative force i cry, i evoke, and the landlady cries out in the yard, she calls i come we speak about water i have no water; we kiss, we hug, she looks worried about me as usual am i ok? how did it come she answered my cry for negative force, as if she heard; oh god, the terrible and wondrous connection of all things, i evoke negative force, the woman from myself, and the woman in the house next to mine not knowing why cries and answers; god these coincidental occurrences in your personal lives—these mysteries—these things, these happenings, these inexplicable . . . I evoke negative force!

the mother of the world! it comes in a thousand forms! how dare i say where does one thing end and another begin? my drawers are emptied; the chest fell down;

this happened in New Orleans;

the ice cubes melted; i became water; water is silver; is all; is moon is negative force; is glue what holds everything together; all the solid

constructions and form; this negative force; this live love doth paste and hold; it stands in it; this is the blood; the glue of the world; the womb of the mother and her love; the chaotic principle; thou art the great container the big glass jar; the container of all;

thou art a christmas tree of oilcans and circular things for holding—as the womb holds the male member;

yet yesterday i called you SUBSTANCE, how can this

                                    be?

yesterday *you* were substance and feeling; you were the female soul substance contained by outline; by splitting from yourself, you became both male image and

                                            female

substance; god dividing; oh god; god god god, what happens? not adam dividing from his rib; his rib being female and coming to stand falling beside him into the fall of the many

thousand things, coming from the one, oh god, no, but you; you being female;
oh goddess oh mother, floating in you, how i am at one with myself! my hair on the wind;
the wind in my heels; the water under my step,
how i am at one in you, how your tears in my eyes are joy—are lights on your tree
how can i celebrate all the things you are to me?
Listen, the dirt under my nails—all negative forces, the dog-shit on my kitchen floor, the
smell of organic shit, the dog shit i leave in piles on the studio floor 'til it molds and can't
clean up; it is you; it is what i do when I don't know why i do and when i can't not don't do
it, but to construct myself—and the dirt on my arms and the absence of baths and the wax
in my hair, it is you; ugliness, it is you; dust, it is you; shit smells, it is my praise of you;
overflowing ashtrays—it is my fountain of love for you; i float in you; i am sustained
by you; i dare not wash you off; i dance for you; i see your image in a girl, and i
become water, my towers melt and my drawers; all turns to flowing and relaxation and
effortlessness, and i make fish movements with my hands my body gets fluid and supple,
when i see your form, and i dance for you,
not the movements of the woman to the man; not the grinding, but more—fluidity of
fingers, all supple movements that are enticing tendrils of your hair
all psychic excitement, that which is irrational and moving, all impulse, all fear dissolved
in trusting for you are that which buoys up, you are the water, i am the door of your
flowing
in you i float from trusting, and you do not fail to be deep, you are deep water, you are that
of which i am unafraid, you are the depth wherein is no harm nor sharp stone you are the
deep center of my diving, i move in you and have my being,
and you widen out, you are world and food at every point of compass to me now, that,
when i evoke you, you come, the prayer is answered
i am in you; in the response is evident, is self-evident, is feeling emotion, the flowing of
locked ice; not broke; not breaking; but water deep and warm as blood, i walk into the water
that is home; it is not death as i thought; although to find you, Hart Crane took off his
coat—and jumped, Virginia Woolf walked in in in, and out—into the water that was
death, but death i have you now in life, death, you womb,
death the mother out of which i came; into which i enter in dream; the blood the soul the
symbol tongue; the center of the world; a place of feeling only; a state of being; i cry here
now; a howl of joy i am born again; daily this must be; white goddess; black negro wife
great grinning mouth with teeth—you are the womb in which i am the tongue; my great fat
love pricks from between your lips; i merge—emerge, i come out from the spider of the
past; in you; i am the mailman; you are the postoffice of my love; all my letters were to you;
who did i mail them to? i am the letter and to you is all written; i am the arrow; and you

are the wound, i am the mosquito and you are the great iron ox,
What's impossible is what we do, you and i, i and you, i am the figure I, you are the
mouth of the pail, i am the key, laid across your lips, i am the finger of silence at your lips,
within you is the shadow of the cavern of the Arc de Triomphe in Paris,
You are the bridges of the Seine, all that caves, curves over, enfolds me, i am the eternal
water moving through your door you are the real, i am the unreal,
i am thy shadow on the water, but listen, if i be Herclitus' river, if i be eternal movement
and the flowing under and through you, how is it that though i am at each moment other
water than i was, yet still you are the order on me, how deep does the shadow of the arch
fall through the dream, what is lost is what i am, lonely arches, stone cold arches of Paris,
how I ached for your loneliness, i am your other half, completing you at the rip of the
seam of syntax, on another plane: for the shadow is a substance other than the bridge, than
coldness, than water, i am that hint of your completion, my frozen mother, my corpse in
parcels, my death in the water, all packages undone, oh the loose string—the broken is
whole, the golden bowl is loosed, you pour, i pour, who can know which is which
anymore, you are the power and the laughter, you are the madness, love, you are the
possession that possesses lovers, i know all now, what you are you are the falling into, you
are the fall, you are the depth of the water in which i cannot drown my only fear is fear of
shallow water, the beached white whale, the heart, stranded & drying, how you seeth the
dark night of the soul, how you are the ointment for dryness, oh Mrs. God, how i dare not
publish you in a catholic magazine fit for the tightness of virgins, how the Virgin is male,
is Narcissus, the chaste, the holy, how you are the loose the wide the cave the hump on
the camel; the Washtub of the World, the Everything! how i love you as a washtub, how i
am your old grey washer-lady, rubbing the clothes up & down, how listen every move i
make, are the bells of my sounding to you, are the chimes of my prayers within your
womb, my heart is your Chinese gong:
all loves i ever loved were you, hidden there within my own tear,
That which dissolves, that which ferments, that which turns, the catalyst who is unmoved
within my moving, i can't tell which is which, which side up we are or down, one
becomes the other, the tree and its image in the water, i am the power of the worship of
Ramakhrishna for you, Listen, i have written you novels,
I have called your name in a hundred ways and you never came, I have named you
Loneliness, i have named you Fur and Hair—I have named you the moving through
windows and doors, i have named you music, i have called you Theme,
i have seen you strung through my life like a silver polar axis of which i am the flesh, you
are Meridian, you are Imaginary Line—you are all force invisible which has no temple

built to house it but my crying . . . you are the order of my soul, you, chaos! I'll never give
you away! Be then the knot in my hair, the coiled spring of my bed, the dust of which i
was afraid . . . inhabit black leather jackets, hung like skins of you, be the liver i cook and
eat for strength, be all food to me, oh lady of Chance, oh Fate, oh Change herself, of
which man is afraid, oh disrupter of order, oh melter of ice-cubes, oh holy water, oh
enemy of the refrigerator! oh holy stove! god in the shape of fire, the female tongue, the
liquid penis of the world, the color red, the sound of gongs and bells, the smell of human
dirt between the toes, all things funky and ab-original, thee whom i love,

how shall we court then, the two of us, like two lesbians, he with the pinched nose? he
the owl of a dead wisdom? what shall we say to Socrates? what shall we say to those
possessed by a lack of enthusiasm? how shall we speak to the spectacular, the owl eyed? he
who ruffles his feathers? the god gone mathematical, how shall we love him?
how shall we love the ice-cube then,
how shall we preserve in luminous virginity, his tray for him? how shall we then partition
his heaven? how shall we count his lambs? how shall we string the hairs of his head to a
harp, and make a weird song from his geometrical precision? yet music is this, music is the
union of god with god, the geometrical with the lucid, the bass with the treble, the drum
and the violin, the flute and the french horn, now we are similar goddess from worship i
ascend, a pair of us now, shall we be two dancing girls in the court of man, he'll never
know which is you and which is me, we heavenly twins, we two, beyond the grasp of
Baudelaire—we being the A and the E that Yeats could never fathom, with all his man-
powered system, we being the force that turns the wheel, like water and wind, wind and
water in the dark lake making a stirring in the center of the pool, he who jumps in first is
cured, we are the moving of the water with the wind, the dancer and the dancing, guest
and host united in one mouth, the act of eating, goddess, this personal life, this limited,
this relative, how do you make it you? how do you rip the syntax, how do you bestow the
Jacob's ladder, how do you move—in and out of the dimensions? me so close to you, like
skin, it takes me too, i am transcended, i am visible, yet i am invisible too, what is motion
in me, this motion that moves the visible, the invisible motion that moves the leaves, the
force and the power, who can prove you? who can measure you? who can ohm your watt
and capture your decibel? who can merge you in a mill and make you power, oh genie of
the bottle, how you so strangely lend invisibility to relativity, the absolute itself, invisibly
moving through our limited relative! how do you do it?
how can you be so humble that you become, the very fire cracker snap between my fingers
& what is it? that quick movement of the foot of the thumb against the ring finger, and
there you are, a mantra of sound! now my body is your container, i am thy Ocean now.

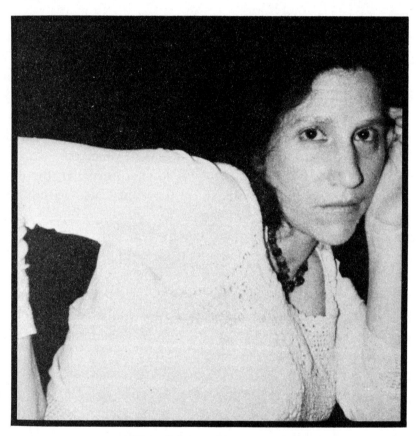

*Diane di Prima. "We sat constantly
on this powder keg at Millbrook, dissuading ecstatic first-time trippers from
calling their wives in Virginia."*

DIANE DI PRIMA
1934–

Beat Generation poet Diane di Prima has remained closely involved with countercultural life-styles and issues. Since the 1960's her work has treated personal transformation in mythological terms, and explored the ecological and social ramifications of consciousness expansion.

In *Memoirs of a Beatnik* (1969) she observes a drug scene in which scoring as little as five dollars worth of marijuana was a potential bust. In the mid-1960's she lived for a time in Timothy Leary's Millbrook commune. Her previously unpublished memoir of this would-be psychedelic utopia is a New Age comedy of manners.

Di Prima's *Revolutionary Letters* (1971) testifies to the political awakening of a segment of the psychedelic movement. "Revolutionary Letter #39" depicts an archetypal event of the period: the ingestion of LSD at a life festival or be-in.

From Memoirs of a Beatnik

GREENWICH VILLAGE, 1953

There were more and more drugs available: cocaine and opium, as well as the ubiquitous heroin, but the hallucinogens hadn't hit the scene yet. The affluent post–Korean War society was settling down to a grimmer, more long-term ugliness. At that moment, there really seemed to be no way out.

As far as we knew, there was only a small handful of us—perhaps forty or fifty in the City (NY)—who knew what we knew; who raced about in Levis and work shirts, smoked dope, dug the new jazz, and spoke a bastardization of the Black argot. We

surmised there might be another fifty living in San Francisco, and perhaps a hundred more scattered throughout the country: Chicago, New Orleans, etc., but our isolation was total and impenetrable. . . . Our chief concern was to keep our integrity . . . and to keep our cool.

The Holidays at Millbrook—1966

Thanksgiving Day dawned clear. I got up later than usual (8:30 or so) and made it down to the kitchen, grimly resolved to eat a breakfast, DO NO COOKING, and leave again for a leisurely day at home. After cooking all three Millbrook meals for some 50 people for over a month, I had had it with the spacious and picturesque kitchen, and the eternal Beatles on the kitchen phonograph.

When I got to the "main house" I found that Kumar, our Hindu poet friend, had already arrived from New York with hashish and gossip, and many other people were converging from Massachusetts, Washington, and farther afield. The parking lot beside the big house, with its great gouges and holes—from the legendary trip when Timothy & Co. had decided to get rid of all the pavement in the world, starting in their own back yard and heading down the Taconic State Parkway—was full to capacity with everything from old pickup trucks to a solitary silver Porsche, and the house was filling rapidly. It was clearly necessary to do some cooking—none had been started yet—and I had a sinking feeling that I wasn't going to escape, after all.

Sure enough, Alan had volunteered to cook one of the four huge turkeys, and he conned me into "starting" it for him. Naturally, I looked up from the first motions to find him gone, and wound up cooking the turkey, and several gallons of cranberry sauce, and a cauldron of candied yams, while Alan made off for parts unknown. It was a soft, warm day, doors and windows were open, velvet draperies blowing, and wind; goats, dogs and children all wandering in and out.

There was a football game before lunch on the lawn in front of the main house. Timothy loves football, baseball, softball—has a big rah-rah streak which some find very lovable—and is constantly pressing his guests into some strenuous sport-like activity, which leaves them usually with sprained backs and sore leg muscles and sour dispositions—until the next round of drinks, food, meditation, or grass sets them up again. The more ornamental girls gathered round to cheer. The rest of us went on with the cooking.

I noticed that Alan had managed to escape the football game as well as the turkey. Found out later that he had retired to sweep the back porch of the pseudo-Swiss chalet that he and I lived in with the children—a really charming little building of wood and stone, known to Millbrook inmates as "the bowling alley" (it had indeed been built, with its myriad stone balconies and three-inch-thick shingles, as a bowling alley and billiard room for the first owner). Whenever things get to be too much for Alan, he sweeps.

He showed up for lunch, though, which was baked Virginia ham, split pea soup, beer and other goodies set out on the front porch of the main house, and in the main dining room. The kids wheeled their tricycles up and down the porch while we ate, looking out over the sweep of the lawn turning brown from the recent frosts. Alexander, my three-year-old, drank a half a can of beer and fell out on a mattress in the main dining room and slept till dinnertime.

The light came in, and faded, and I was still in the kitchen. A familiar feeling. Around 5:30, Jean McCreedy, Tim's secretary, came in and offered to candy the yams in my stead if I wanted to rest before dinner. I went back up to the bowling alley dead tired, to change clothes.

DeeDee Doyle was up there, reading and reminiscing. DeeDee was a California speed freak and old friend, who had sought refuge with us a few days before, when her old man had gone a little too berserk, even for her. She was wanting "something pretty to wear," and so we pulled gowns and capes and old shawls out of the closet and spread them about, and I put Bob Dylan on the phonograph.

DeeDee picked a costume, complete down to rhinestone pins and necklace, and put up her hair while she told me how years ago she had given Dylan a book of Michael McClure's, and how it had turned him on. Dylan later bought McClure an auto harp which changed his style for a while: he sang his poetry readings, wrote songs, grew his hair. Dylan had wanted her to live with him, "but I chose to go with Bad Bruce," said DeeDee a little sadly, making up her eyes.

I pulled on a coral gown and black velvet cape, braided some pearls into my hair, stuffed all the remaining clothes back into the closet, and returned to the main house to go to the john. (The bowling alley had no toilet facilities—no running water at all, in fact—nor any heat, except for a very small fireplace, more decorative than functional, which, during the winter ahead, usually managed to heat the huge room we lived in to about 40 or 50 degrees.)

At the main house I found Bali Ram. Bali is a Nepalese temple dancer. He had come to the States a few years before with Bill Haines, who was then arranging tours for groups of eastern dancers, musicians, etc. Bill was now head of the Sri Ram Ashram, a motley crew who occupied the second floor of the Millbrook main house at this time. The Ashram had 28 members, mostly young longhairs, to whom Tim had recently given asylum when they were thrown out of their former home, the Ananda Ashram in Monroe by the staid older members of that organization. The older members owned the land, and controlled the board of directors; the younger members had come to work the garden and pass the summer. They decided to stay and squatted, more or less, till the arrival of a large number of police and private detectives made it unfeasible for them to remain. The Sri Ram Ashram boasted several colorful and talented members. There was Jean-Pierre Merle, grandson of Raymond Duncan, and third-generation vegetarian: a skilled painter, sandalmaker, potter, and flute player, a slight young man who looked positively frail till you saw him in action. There was Tambimuttu, the Indian-British poet with a strong English accent, a friend of Auden &c., and founder of the little magazine of the '50s, *Poetry London-New York*. And there was Bali.

Bali was in full costume, about to begin a dance recital in the "music room" when I came in, and I immediately sat down to watch. He is a great dancer, and today he danced the dedication to Shiva—with which he opens all his concerts—particularly well. He changed, did a narrative dance from the Mahabarata, changed again, and danced the Nataraja, which I had never seen before. In it, he actually portrays Shiva doing his dance of the destruction of the cosmos, and ends in the pose on all the statues of the dancing Shiva: one hand raised in the "have no fear" mudra, the other pointing to his lifted foot, which represents liberation/enlightenment. I have never found any of Bali's dancing as moving as I did today. (Bill Haines told me later that Bali had been dedicated to Shiva as an infant, and given to the temple at the age of six, to begin his training.)

After the dance recital, nearly everyone was as out of it as I was, no one seemed to want to move, or talk. Allen Ginsberg took out his finger cymbals, and he and Peter began to sing a *kirtan*, starting with the "Hare Krishna" mantra that nearly everyone there knew. I stole that opportunity to try and make it back up to the bowling alley to gather up Alan and whomever else might want to come and sing. But I was to have a rude shock.

I left the music room by the sliding doors that open onto the main entry hall of the house, and there in the hall narrowly missed being knocked down by a giant of a man who was literally hurling himself about, from banister to wall, barely missing the huge gilded mirror and shouting "I have been Vi-o-la-ted!" over and over again to an astonished and immobilized audience.

Turned out that he was one Ted Cook, Canadian reporter, who, while being wined and entertained by Timothy in his study on the third floor, had inadvertently imbibed a large quantity of acid. It seems Timothy had offered him the choice of some perfectly straight bourbon or scotch, but he had secretly decided on the sherry he had seen in the cabinet, and when everyone else was otherwise occupied he wandered off and helped himself to a good-sized glass of same. The sherry happened to be one of the three bottles of liquor which held our new stash.

And now it seemed he was very shook up. Well, it served him right, I figured. Not simply because it ain't cool to drink liquor which ain't offered, but—

dig this—he had done a full-length movie about acid for CBC or something without ever having touched the stuff. That old black karma, catching up with him. I ducked as he made another howling lurch for the stairs and went on back to the bowling alley.

By the time I came back to the main house with Alan and our friend Zen (who lived downstairs from us in the bowling alley, where he devoured large quantities of morning glory seeds almost daily, and played his trumpet) *kirtan* had broken up: the howls and curses of Ted Cook had proved to be too much for everyone. Most of our guests were milling about aimlessly, making small talk and waiting for dinner, while the more competent—and the more paranoid—members of the community crashed around outside, coatless and flashlightless in the winter twilight, trying to find Ted Cook who had burst out of the house, surging through the masses of folk around him.

The general fear was that he would find his way to the highway (a good half mile away) and all hell would break loose with the local folk. We sat constantly on this powder keg at Millbrook, dissuading ecstatic first-time trippers from calling their wives in Virginia, tromping resolutely by the side of energetic ones who had decided to go for a long hike, feeding yoga, breathing exercises, niacin, or thorazine to persistent bad-trippers—handling any and all drug crises as best we could alone.

Dinner was finally ready. I made a quick run back home with Ed, to wake up Mini, my four-year-old, who had consented to take a nap on my sworn oath that I would get her up in time to eat. The shouts of Ted Cook could be heard in the distance as we went up the path to the bowling alley, and I heard myself muttering, "If this is Thanksgiving, what will Christmas be like?"

At the bowling alley there was also a heap of presents that had to be brought back to the main house, Alan having, the day before, bought a gift for each of the eleven Millbrook children. There was absolutely no money at Millbrook at this time—times of total financial drought alternated there always with times of dizzying plenty—but that didn't stop Timothy, who handed us a blank check and told us to fill it out for whatever amount we needed. And so, Alan had decided that presents were in order, and had bought sweaters, toys, mittens, etc., at the huge shopping center in Poughkeepsie at the same time as the turkeys, yams, and other goodies.

Ed carried Mini, who was still half asleep, and an armload of packages, and I lugged a huge shopping bag full of presents back to the main house.

Dinner was very good and very luxurious, in the way that feasts always feel luxurious when the house is full and there is more than enough of everything. I heaped a big paper plate for myself and stashed it in a cupboard, and then I went to check out the rest of my family.

Found Jeanne, my eight-year-old, asleep in Suzie Blue's room on the top floor, her hair full of pincurls. She had been planning on a dazzling and glamorous entrance at dinner time. I woke her just enough to ask if she wanted to come on downstairs and join the festivities. But just at this point, Ted Cook, who had been captured in the ruined formal garden behind the "meditation house" was standing among the extra turkeys in the butler's pantry, alternately shouting horrifically in some abrupt, violent fright, and murmuring beatific nonsense at those who were trying to calm him. Jeanne listened to the noises from downstairs for a while, and decided judiciously to stay where she was. She asked me to bring her a dinner, which I painfully did, handling cape and gown and tray most clumsily on the stairs. She and Suzie settled themselves in, cozy and snug, getting high and watching television.

I finally got around to eating, settled halfway up the first flight of stairs in the entry hall, as the dining room was way too crowded. Alan passed by, looking totally out of his mind. He was working on his third plate and his sixth glass of wine. I told him what was going on upstairs, which hugely delighted him, and he went on up to join Jeanne and Suzie in front of the TV version of *Jason and the Argonauts*.

Soon after this, we had the *kirtan* that Ted Cook had interrupted before dinner, and Ted Cook brought it about. He had wandered out of the butler's pantry and settled down on a black trunk in the small entry hall, his trip still struggling between good and bad. Allen Ginsberg followed closely behind and sat down on the floor next to him. The hall was small, cold and drafty, and the floor was tiled and very hard. Allen began to sing mantras to Ted, and slowly a crowd gathered in spite of the discomfort. We brought cushions and our dinner plates, and sat on the ground or in each other's laps, squeezed into that tiny space.

We sang for over two hours: "Hare Krishna," "Hare Om Namo Shivaya," "Om Sri Maitreya"— one after another of Allen's favorites. Kumar, our Hindu friend, with Naomi, one of his two women, me and the kids, Howie from the Ashram, Karen Detweiler, a young blonde witchgirl who kept a cauldron in the Millbrook forest, Judy Mayhan, our blues singer, Jackie Leary, Tim's son, and many of the Ashram people—all joined together in singing for this strange, frightened man whom no one of us had known two or three hours before. He slowly relaxed; his Buddha-nature began to shine forth— reluctantly at first, and then stronger as our energy built. He finally became perfectly joyous, joined us in singing a Shiva mantra over and over, and after a long time was able to wander about and join in the throng in which a good third of the guests were probably as stoned as he.

I had learned a lot from watching the kindness and understanding that Allen had so spontaneously held out to a fellow creature. That *kirtan* remains to this day the most moving I've ever been in. But the day was to hold one more heavy learning experience for me.

I heard from Joel Kramer that Tim, who hadn't been downstairs to eat at all, was on a high dosage "session" (usual Millbrook terminology for tripping), and that he "had to be seen to be believed." I was naturally a little curious to know what that meant—to see what Tim was into. So I went on up to the third floor, first stopping in Suzie Blue's room to ask Alan if he had seen Tim since he turned on. Alan nodded and said, in his best rhetorical style, "I'll never be angry with him again." When I asked him why, he said simply, "Go in and see for yourself."

I knocked on the door to Timothy and Rosemary's room, and opened it. The space in the room was warped—a funny kind of visual effect curved it somehow, as if it were in a different space-time continuum. I have since talked to other old-time trippers and hangers-around-trippers about this, and they all admit to seeing something similar at some point when they came "cold" upon people who were on a very high dosage of acid. The visual effect is a bit like the "heat waves" that show around a candle flame, or a hot car in the summer sun, or the waves that rise from the hot asphalt of a highway in the desert. I have seen it a few times since. I remember waking one night later that winter when Alan Marlowe and John Wieners were tripping in the bowling alley and seeing the air around them curved in the same way—some kind of high-energy charge that becomes visible. But this was the first time I had ever seen anything like it, and it literally made me gasp.

Stepping into the room was like stepping into another dimension. Timothy looked at me from a million light-years away, from a place of great sadness and loneliness and terrible tiredness, and after a long time he formed the one word "Beloved." I knelt down to where they were sitting side-by-side on the rug in front of a cold, dark fireplace, and kissed him and Rosemary, spent a moment holding their hands and looking into their eyes, and then went away as quietly as I could, leaving them to each other.

It turned out later that the sherry which had set Ted Cook off was what Tim and Rosemary had also had that day. Nobody ever managed to figure out how strong it was. What had happened was this: a new shipment of acid had arrived in powder form. Timothy dumped half the powder in a two-pound coffee can, dumped in a quart of vodka, sloshed it around, and poured it back in the vodka bottle. He then repeated the process with the other half of the powder and a second quart of vodka. After that, to save whatever might be sticking to the coffee can, he poured in a fifth of sherry to rinse it out. It was this sherry that dominated the events of that Thanksgiving.

Revolutionary Letter #39 (1969)

let me tell you, brothers, that on May 30th I
    went to one of our
life festivals
dropped acid in Tompkins Square Park with my
brothers & sisters
danced in the sun, till the stars
came out & the pigs
drove around us in a circle, where we stood
touching each other & loving, then I
went home & made love like a flower, like two
    flowers opening
to each other, we were
the jewel in the lotus, next morning still high
    wandered uptown
to Natural History Museum & there
in a room of Peruvian fauna, birds
of paradise I saw as a past, like the dinosaurs
saw birds pass from the earth &
flowers, most trees & small creatures:
chipmunks & rabbits & squirrels & delicate
    wildflowers
saw the earth bare & smooth, austerely plastic &
efficient
men feeding hydroponically, working like ants
thought flatly, without regret (I have unlearned
regret)
    'WHAT BEAUTIFUL CREATURES
    USED TO LIVE ON THE EARTH'

LENORE KANDEL

Lenore Kandel, like Diane di Prima, has long been a member of the Beat Generation and the San Francisco poetry scene. Her best-known work, *The Love Book* (1965), was for a time suppressed for its erotic sensibility and language.

Lenore Kandel. "one month we touch extremities/ next year a kiss"

Word Alchemy (1967) contains several poems on the drug experience. "Peyote Walk" deals openly with psychedelic lovemaking under the visionary drug peyote. "Blues for Sister Sally" treats the tragedy of drug abuse, which was equally part of the 1950's and 1960's. "The pot bird story" is a light love story fused with marijuana mirth, a jazz poetry riff like "Blues."

Peyote Walk

        1
    VISION: that the barriers of time are arbitrary;
        that nothing is still

    we, the giants of the river and universe,
        commencing the act of
    love, enclosing our bodies in each other's
        wilderness, vast hands
    caressing pinnacles of meat, tracing our titan
        thighs

        one month we touch extremities
            next year a kiss

    the giant prick engorged began its downward
    stroke at years beginning into years end giant
    cunt (a) (slow) (sea) (clam) hips and rotundities
    earth-moving from month to month and
    promises of spring

            orgasmic infinity
            one (!) second long

    EARTHQUAKE!
    FLOOD! FLOOD! FLOOD!

    huge pelvises shuddering
    while worlds burn

        2
    VISION: that the barriers of form are arbitrary;
        nothing is still
    now now now
                moving
    tangled my fingers tangle in
        sticky life threads
                moving
    between my fingers

    a geode, granite walled crystal universe
    I see both sides at once
    how easy why didn't I before

                I AM

    part of the flow

            the lamp the fig and me
            we the redwoods
            us the walls and winds
                    body mine?

    you?
    MOTION

    beingness   my fingers t—
        angle

the only light our vital glow our radiance
turning to you your face becomes a skull
        MY SKULL!

protean the form encloses space and time
        moving

NOWNOWNOWNOWNOWNOWNOWNOW
    NOWNOWNOWNOW

    3
VISION: that yes

        (we) is (god)

Blues for Sister Sally

    I
moon-faced baby with cocaine arms
        nineteen summers
        nineteen lovers

    novice of the junkie angel
lay sister of mankind penitent
    sister in marijuana
    sister in hashish
    sister in morphine

against the bathroom grimy sink
pumping her arms full of life
        (holy holy)
she bears the stigma (holy holy) of the raving christ
        (holy holy)
        holy needle
        holy powder
        holy vein

dear miss lovelorn: my sister makes it with a hunk
of glass do you think this is normal miss lovelorn

        I DEMAND AN ANSWER!

    II
        weep
for my sister she walks with open veins
leaving her blood in the sewers of your cities
        from east coast
        to west coast
        to nowhere

    how shall we canonize our sister who is not
quite dead
        who fornicates with strangers
        who masturbates with needles
who is afraid of the dark and wears her long hair
soft and
        black
            against her bloodless face

    III
midnight and the room dream-green and hazy
we are all part of the collage

        brother and sister, she leans against the
wall
        and he, slipping the needle in her painless
arm

        pale fingers (with love) against the pale
arm

    IV
children our afternoon is soft, we lean against
each other

        our stash is in our elbows
        our fix is in our heads
god is a junkie and he has sold salvation
        for a week's supply

---

the pot bird story

waking half waking mouth open eyes shut and legs
grabbing at each other with breath subsiding as the
juices dry our eyelids flicker up we reach beside the

bed for the artful joint so wisely placed the night before and sip with tender mouths (still cradled in each other's flesh) when suddenly at once eyes gently peering to the window left we see the flash of yellow birds swarm the trees like locusts hopping claw footed over green leaf waysides soft bird-shaped birds as never seen before their egg and butter winging bodies and silver heads and pure surprise
what are they? half wondering if you see them too and small relief as you whisper in my ear, pot birds, you say I don't believe you, I answer sure of your truth as I deny it, what color are they? yellow you tell me and what can I say to that so yellow they are yellower than anything I've ever known and so you see them too and both of us so sweetly high and are you right after all, pot birds? and we sit there warm in bed and watching
they only show up when you're high one right there! two over there! and twenty and ten and yellow each more bird than bird has ever been and dance the tree into yellow bird heaven until suddenly all gone and we arise at noon washing our faces with soft water from a leaky tap each morning waking then with one eye turned toward birds and never finding only empty green and tarnished trees and waking then with love and coffee but neither pot nor birds nor quite convinced of their alliance but wondering and morning sitting over breakfast smoking thin cigarettes for lunch gave quick look at window and they were back a revelation of angels swarming the trees with yellow feather wings the pretty birds leaping limb to limb pot birds, you smiled I nodded and sat there watching the abundance of yellow with the smoke drifting through the interstices of my long long bones

GARNET BRENNAN
1909–

In 1967 Garnet Brennan was principal and teacher of a small public school in Marin County, California, when she became the center of a local scandal that overnight became a national news story. Although her reputation and career were hanging in the balance, Brennan refused to panic. She struggled against the police, the school board, and the media to present her own viewpoint, that of an educated, discreet, middle-aged marijuana smoker who believed she knew the drug's best uses. She argued for the right to privately alter her own consciousness, but was suspended for immoral conduct. Forced out of the education field, she turned to travel and writing. "Marijuana Witchhunt" appeared in *Evergreen Review* in 1968.

Garnet Brennan before the school board, 1967. "Of course, I told them my response would be that I would appeal the case, even to the Supreme Court, if necessary."

From "Marijuana Witchhunt"

My friend Melkon Melkonian was arrested and held in San Francisco County jail, charged with sale and possession of marijuana, a year ago last January. He was having trouble raising the high bail set by the judge and had to stay in jail from January until April before friends put up the bond. I was asked to co-sign for his bond since I was a property owner in Marin County.

Several of us heard we might help his case by signing affidavits attesting to the harmless effects of marijuana and were told to meet in his lawyer's office. There were about twenty-five others waiting there when I arrived. Mrs. Molly Minudri, the lawyer, told us we could not be arrested for supplying the affidavits but that we might have to be "cooler" about using marijuana.

Because there were so many of us, we had to take the affidavit blanks home and fill them in ourselves. I got high, wrote out the affidavit, and delivered it to Mrs. Minudri on September 27. In the affidavit I wrote:

Marijuana is not harmful to my knowledge, because I have been using it since 1949, almost daily, with only beneficial results. It has a relaxing effect when tenseness is present. My depth of perception has been increased; this carries over into times when I am not under the influence of marijuana.

Teaching children is my profession. I have been a teacher for thirty years and at present am the teaching-principal of a public school. During school hours I never feel the need of using cannabis sativa; however, each recess is eagerly awaited for smoking tobacco cigarettes. I do not consider marijuana a habit-forming drug, but to me nicotine is.

I have been smoking one or two marijuana cigarettes every evening; sometimes more if school is not in session. Then I stay up later at night.

I have known some people who have become momentarily nauseated, but neither I nor anyone I have ever known has had a "hang-over" from its use.

This is a true statement.

Another of the teachers at my school, Jeff, also wrote an affidavit stating that to his knowledge marijuana is harmless, but he didn't "cop out"—say that he had used it.

I continued teaching school and thought no more of it. I was the teaching-principal of a three-teacher public school in Marin County, in the small unincorporated village of Nicasio. In our school we have a total of forty-seven children in grades one through eight, though it is really an ungraded school—we teach the children according to what and when they can learn.

Melkon's case came up in court on October 6. Surprisingly, the attorney handed the judge forty-six affidavits from all kinds of lay and professional people. At the time it never occurred to me that my signed affidavit was anything more than a helpful gesture for Melkon.

On the afternoon of the trial a reporter from the *San Francisco Chronicle* called me at school to tell me that the trial and my affidavit were front-page news. He wanted to get all the details straight. I was rather flabbergasted. It was ten minutes before dismissal time, so I said I would go home and call back immediately. I told Jeff this and he said, "Go home at once, this may be something big. I'll lock up for you."

Court had dismissed after 2 P.M.; I was phoned before 3 P.M. When I called back the *Chronicle*, Mr. Raudebaugh, who covered the case at court, told me: "This is big. Don't you know the sheriff's office has been notified, your school board has been notified. Let me come out and take pictures." I pleaded with him to keep my school out of the papers. I didn't want the children to be disturbed by this. He asked for my address and said he'd see me in a few minutes. In near panic, I ran out of my house, got in the car, and drove off, but after only a couple of miles I turned back. This was it, I decided. I had no one to hurt, nothing to lose; come what may, I was ready.

Returning home, I got a paper bag, cleaned out drawers, ash trays, and disposed of all the evidence.

Soon an unfamiliar car appeared. It was the local deputy sheriff, whose sister I had had in school for three years and whose nephew was in my class now. Along with him was an under-sheriff.

"I guess you know why we're here," the deputy sheriff said.

They came into the living room and sat grimly on the edges of their chairs. I was relaxed and very calm. They told me they had been sent by the sheriff because I had signed an affidavit saying I had used marijuana, and began asking me questions which I refused to answer, saying I would have to consult my lawyer first. Using marijuana, they said, was illegal, and then asked if they could search my house.

"I understand that a search warrant is legally necessary for this to be done, isn't it?" I asked.

"Well, yes."

"Do you wish to search illegally?"

They seemed a bit dumbfounded, hesitated, but finally left, saying, "Well, we'll leave it as it is."

In the next two days they tried their best, but no judge in Marin County would sign a search warrant and I've never since been annoyed by any more law enforcement officers. However, my house is "clean." I have had no marijuana in the house, nor have I smoked it. This way I am able to prove that marijuana is not addictive or habit-forming, any more than brushing one's teeth is habit-forming or listening to music is addictive.

Next day, Saturday, I was undecided about what to do. I didn't know whether to call my school board or just wait and see what would happen next. I'd never been faced with a similar dilemma, so I didn't know what was expected of me. I've always had an adage to go by: "When in doubt, don't." So I just waited.

Soon the phone began ringing—calls from as far away as New York and Chicago. When I saw the story on the front page of the morning *Chronicle,* I understood why—my name, school district, county affidavit—it was all there in print.

The sheriff was trying to get a search warrant and my board was meeting. I just sat tight and waited. In the afternoon, a long panel truck with KPIX printed in large letters on the side came up the lane. Two men grinding cameras came across the little Japanese footbridge that leads to my house. They interviewed me on the deck of my house. It was a good interview, easy for me, because I had nothing to hide. All was truth, unadulterated and guileless. The camera continued to grind; the interviewers were kind and sympathetic, although I didn't feel I needed their sympathy.

That evening, watching the news on TV, I saw, for the first time, how things actually looked to the world.

On Sunday, after many pictures, interview after interview, and interminable calls (I completely lost track of who wanted to know what), two members of my school board arrived, looking sick at heart, sad and pale among the cameras and newspaper people. They handed me my notice of suspension so I would be sure not to appear at school the next morning.

That evening, returning alone from an Ellington concert, I found more people waiting for me at home. Interviews by tape went on into the night; even a radio broadcast from my home by telephone for the midnight news. Things were really jumping; I still felt fine and very happy because all the country was being informed about what was happening.

On Monday, I've been told, the school was abuzz; TV equipment, parents bringing children to protect them from me in case I arrived; my school board, two members of the multitudinous county office staff, all making sure that school would go on as usual.

Can my children understand how on Friday evening we lovingly said good night to one another and on Monday morning they had to be protected against me—all because of my telling the truth and trying to help a friend in need? Suddenly, I had become a threat to them. The children and I have been trying to be truthful, guiltless, unharmful to others, and loving. Is this the way it is done?

Mrs. Minudri, now my lawyer, had been advised by Judge Karish that he would give us two weeks to get as many affidavits as we could, so I had many forms to give out. The same day I was to be interviewed by KPIX-TV and was due at 2:30 P.M. at Mrs. Minudri's office. She hadn't arrived but the cameramen and interviewers had.

We had to appear at my school for a board meeting that night so that my fate might be determined. En route we were to stop at the home of

Hugh Hinchliffe, the present chairman of the Ad Hoc Committee for the Repeal of the Marijuana Laws. There we met more cameramen for more interviews. Melkon, Molly, and I were all interviewed and photographed until finally I had to call the school to say we'd be about twenty or thirty minutes late. We were followed by a TV wagon to show them the way.

At the school ground we found the space completely filled with cars, trucks, and masses of parents, hippies, sympathizers I had never met before, and the simply curious.

As we entered, giggling and hurrying into the glare of lights and more grinding cameras, a path was cleared down the center of the room and I was seated in the front row facing a long table with three grim-faced board members, their attorney and secretary. All around the edges were the cameras and the constantly moving men with the long cords and mikes.

The board meeting was already under way when we arrived. Only a few of my parents took part in the discussion, saying what a good teacher I was, how they had liked me and what I was doing, *but*, since I had said what I had, I had broken the law and could no longer be allowed to teach their children.

Some parents, whose children I had previously taught, expressed good opinions of my teaching and begged tolerance and understanding. Several so-called hippies spoke well, some were too highly agitated to express their actual feelings. The deputy sheriff who had come to my house said, "Why do we need this riff-raff from the city to tell us what to do? We already know what we're going to do."

The verbal battle raged back and forth; hypocrisy was thick in the air. I sat quietly listening, tired and cool, just waiting. Mrs. Minudri talked for me superbly. We had agreed beforehand that the final decision would be made in a closed executive session.

After some time, the board, two lawyers, the secretary, a man from the county office, and I retired to another room downstairs where they asked me if I wouldn't just resign. I couldn't bear to do this, so I refused, flatly. We talked for about an hour, very pleasantly and quietly, and decided how things were to be. The assistant county superintendent of schools, who had been there all day, said: "I never visited a better organized school." The three board members moved to a corner and made their unanimous vote to dismiss me from my duties. The lawyers then discussed how to inform the full meeting upstairs of the decision, and how to cut off all further discussion by adjourning the meeting forthwith. Of course, I told them my response would be that I would appeal the case, even to the Supreme Court, if necessary. This was accepted pleasantly.

We filed back into the room with the glaring lights and grinding machines. After a stumbling reading of the prepared statement, we adjourned. All at once, I was pounced upon (like a presidential candidate who had just lost) with seventeen microphones thrust at my face and behind each mike, a man with a question. I merely said: "Of course, I shall appeal." Then: "Under the circumstances, due to the expressed feelings of the people who voted for the trustees, they had no other alternative than to fire me."

We finally maneuvered our way to the door through the downcast looks of my children's parents. I was stopped by one mother with whom I had been very friendly. She and I used to discuss freely with great understanding the problems of her three children who had been in my classes. Now she said: "Oh, Garnet, please don't hate me!"

* * *

It was late in 1949 when I first had marijuana. I was living in Monterey and was invited to visit friends in Big Sur. After dinner, sitting around the fireplace, the man rolled a marijuana cigarette. He always rolled his own tobacco, so I thought nothing of it until he handed it first to his wife, then to me.

I had been curious about marijuana for a long time but had never made the effort to get hold of any. They taught me how to smoke it and it was at once a delight. I really felt like Alice in Wonderland—when I stood up, I kept growing, my arms became long, and I felt I might be able to fly into the Pacific when I went outside. But, of course, nothing around me was abnormal and I was aware of this. The next day was fine; everything was the same. I'm not sure what I expected, but having heard some of the myths about marijuana (which I felt to be untrue), I couldn't be sure. . . .

I never used marijuana while at school, or in the morning before going to school. There was never any need for it. I did find it helpful in dealing with student problems—checking papers, making out grade cards, reports, and cumulative records. I never found it necessary to write derogatory comments on files that would follow a child through life; marijuana always helped me find something good to say about the student. . . .

For me, marijuana has been a fine relaxant, a beautiful cocktail before dinner, a great source of deepening perception, but I would never recommend its use for "mixed-up" people or children. Kids are already "turned on" if they are just allowed to be. I would never recommend its use in excess by anyone. In fact, it is difficult for most normal people to use it in excess because marijuana imposes its own limits when you have had enough. You don't need or want any more. Yet, when you will it, you can use it without the fear that it will ever become the "Boss."

*   *   *

In the meantime, I have received more than one hundred letters of support from all over the U.S., as well as three from boys in Vietnam. Only three letters from retired, misinformed, unenlightened school teachers, were critical. The Craig Biddle Interim Congressional Committee studying Criminal Procedure invited me as a witness, and I was interviewed by Hugh Downs on his "Today Show" in Los Angeles. I have also taken part in several college panel discussions on the subject of marijuana.

Let us hope all this will lead to changes in our laws to bring them more in line with the ideals expressed in our constitution, and strengthen the guarantees protecting the freedom of speech for all teachers. Perhaps it will also help to open the minds of people to confront our changing world with more tolerance and thoughtfulness. May we all come to truly enjoy "Life, Liberty and the Pursuit of Happiness."

LINDA ROSENKRANTZ
1934–

In one chapter of *Talk* (1968), her fine novel of manners about three young, artistic New Yorkers, Linda Rosenkrantz's characters discuss psychedelics. While Emily's listener, Vincent, gives his sympathetic attention, she analyzes her first LSD trip, particularly the metaphysical aspects. Sixties' attitudes about the validity of mind-altering drug experiences are presented in a partly realistic, partly satirical manner.

▬▬▬

From *Talk*

EMILY: You know I've taken LSD. And let me tell you, at a certain point—it's really impossible for you to understand, you might be able to comprehend it in your head, but you can't experience it—all of a sudden my mind was where this boyfriend was, where that best friend was, all of a sudden I didn't *understand* their sickness, I *had* it. I was there, right where they were. If I took it now I could go maybe where Michael Christy is. It's incredible. I for instance thought of Jonquil. Jonquil my cat: instant tears, instant total emotional value of the thought. My mind the next moment is on that bathing suit on the line and it's hysterically funny to me that the bathing suit is drying there, and I can feel the pull, the water going into the air.

VINCENT: My God! How fantastic!

EMILY: The next thing I'm a mother in her loneliness, and there's a whole kind of gloomy feeling, but there's no working yourself into, it's instantly touching all the notes of the instrument.

VINCENT: Then when you talk about love, you're talking about like total empathy and compassion.

EMILY: No, not compassion, because compassion is to a certain extent identification and a kind of

Linda Rosenkrantz. "I was intimately a part of every pulsebeat of every sun that came up on everybody's life."

tolerance. This was feeling that my blood wasn't the blood that made up Emily Benson and the cells that were all locked inside her life; it was an extension of humanity, like I was part of Marsha, we weren't separate people, we were all part of each other, somehow sliced off by maybe a knife.

VINCENT: Right.

EMILY: But that everything was touching and I was intimately a part of every pulsebeat of every sun that came up on everybody's life. There was a huge opening of the sky, I saw God, I had a tremendously mystical experience. I was deeply moved, deeply in love. And when I say love, it's not like on the level we know from analysis. It was the absence of all anger, the absence of all conflict.

VINCENT: But that's what you're working toward in analysis.

EMILY: No no no, that's not what you get from analysis. Analyzed love is not the absence of all those things, it's after dealing with them. Under LSD, they didn't even exist. You see it wasn't a love in which there was *present* such-and-such, but rather an *absence* of anger, of aggression, of conflict, of identification, of need, of unfulfillment, of frustration—all those things we feel go into love, because love is based on so much else. I don't think love is some kind of pure fucking quality, you know. Actually, the only thing that comes close to expressing the kind of feeling I had is *Seymour, an Introduction* by Salinger, that's the only thing that approaches it. It has nothing to do with thinking things out. It's like if you're in a warm bath, your reality is that the body is in warm water.

VINCENT: I know.

EMILY: Yeah, you get it, darling.

VINCENT: But I think you can also arrive there in other ways.

EMILY: I've been there, but only under the most extraordinary circumstances, the most temporal.

VINCENT: After you come down, is the experience very meaningful? In other words, do you think I should take the trip?

EMILY: The LSD trip? I don't know, a lot of people have asked me that. I'll tell you, Vinnie, the ex-

perience was fantastically extraordinary, and I would never undo it.

VINCENT: That's good.

EMILY: I would never undo it, but I would never tell you to do it.

VINCENT: I'd be afraid of the cataclysm, the black depression coming in on me. I've had enough of that.

EMILY: I had blackness then like I've never known blackness in my life, because when I started coming down, and I saw I'd written all over Philippe's body and on the walls with a ballpoint pen *This stone is love, God is in this pebble*, and I really knew when I wrote it what the fuck I was talking about, and then I started to come down and I said who wrote this?

VINCENT: Oh my poor darling.

EMILY: And all of a sudden I said my mind, I'm losing my mind. There's nothing more frightening. Like no matter how drunk you are, how insane, there's always some core that you know in yourself to be you?

VINCENT: Right. And you lost that.

EMILY: And that went. But if you could take it with a doctor, then I'd say definitely take it.

VINCENT: Actually, truth is both those things, you've got to accept both that huge love and the total absence. One is no more true than the other.

EMILY: You know I'm not at all sure, Vinnie—this is a very strange thing I'm coming to—I'm not at all sure that the way it's worked out socially, in terms of civilization, I'm not so sure that men and women *can* love each other and grow families, that naturally these things work out.

VINCENT: Civilization is completely artificial, I've always said that.

EMILY: The working out of structure is a decision and civilization surviving is a decision.

VINCENT: And even love isn't natural.

EMILY: I'm not sure it is. Not that it's strictly synthetic, but I'm not sure it's a built-in thing, that whole marriage system of society our lives are based on. Even yours.

VINCENT: Is it out of your LSD you're talking now or are you jumping?

EMILY: I'm jumping.

VINCENT: Oh, jumping. Because I don't want to go off into marriage, that's a whole other discussion. I want to stay on what you learned out of your LSD experience.

EMILY: I'm not a pragmatic person, so I can't say that it had a use. I only know that the only time I've ever gone beyond any point of identity in terms of Emily Benson was then.

VINCENT: But now, when you look at reality, has it made a new imprint on you? Do you see things in a different way? Do you feel more religiosity? I sound like David Susskind.

EMILY: No, but you asked me about the religious part. First of all, in a crazy way, I don't want to use the word religious, but you know that from my father I have a mystical side to my mind, my nature. And I'll tell you, Vinnie, the phoniest thing, the Zen koan at the beginning of *Catcher in the Rye*—I really love Salinger very much, I'm very hooked up with him—it says we know the sound of two hands clapping, what is the sound of one hand clapping? Now that's a very kind of trite thing, it's pat, but I really get it and I get all the vibrations. You know I called Marsha up when I was under LSD and she said I was talking pure poetry.

VINCENT: Really?

EMILY: A child is crying in the wall. You know the idea that flowers cry when they're picked? Well the sensitivity was so great that if the flower *was* picked, I could hear it crying. I didn't identify with the flower, I *was* the flower. And it wasn't like I'm such a sensitive person or anything, it was simply that the power or the chemistry of the mind reached a certain level. I remember pouring a glass of milk, and as I did, I experienced myself being poured into the glass. The milk was part of me, an extension, that's what I mean by mystical.

VINCENT: Incredible.

EMILY: I shouldn't really say mystical, because the word evokes a whole mysterious realm of associations, whereas this was absolutely logical. Say for instance right now we both look up: we both see a certain kind of blue sky, a certain kind of star,

and it makes a certain kind of sense, so that if we each sat down to paint it, the paintings would correlate to a great degree. But if we both took LSD, the art would instantly change. That's what pre-Columbian art is all about, you know, because those guys weren't straight, they were chemically different, and the whole distortion of style was just a reflection of what they saw. The reality of the landscape is completely determined by the people who see it.

VINCENT: Of course.

EMILY: Like when a madman on the street says get away from me, it's because he sees a person with a knife trying to kill him. It's not that he's a lunatic seeing a mirage; he actually, for his own mind, sees it. It's completely real. That's why the word mystical is misleading. You know, Vinnie, I really believe that the nature of the fucking sands would change if the chemistry was a little bit different in all our heads. For instance, if *my* chemistry was different, I might see that this sand wasn't sand. Look, I'm going over to it right now, I'm walking to the sand and I'm going to the LSD experience. I'm getting canyons, and these little things that dip in all of a sudden become miles dipping in. The top becomes sunbaked peaks, and these specks become arid plants growing.

VINCENT: No kidding!

EMILY: And the white becomes illusions of clouds floating on top. All kinds of things start to happen if I let my mind go. I don't associate just sand is sand, like I've always seen sand and I know it because I'm secure that that's sand. All the security is taken away from everything. Suddenly I've never really seen sand before—and I haven't, because my eyes have changed, the retinas.

VINCENT: But isn't that flirting with the psychotic? Isn't it like a psychotic interlude? I'm scared, Emmy.

EMILY: Of course, it induces a false psychosis, that's what the drug is all about. But the term psychotic means a flight from reality, and the reality, as I just said, is based upon what we all define it to be. If we took those limitations away, a psychotic would just be someone on another level.

VINCENT: Why *don't* we take them away?

EMILY: Why don't we? Because we have to function within orders, within laws, within rules of society, whatever it is people say we have to function in. You know that as well as I do.

VINCENT: You're brilliant, Emmy. But look at the sand. You *know*, when you walk over there it's not a canyon.

EMILY: Why isn't it? Because I know all about sand, I've walked on it since I was a child, I know you can walk on it and you're not going to sink. But if you never have walked on sand before . . .

VINCENT: So you're saying you have to go back to the innocence of not knowing.

EMILY: Back to a total innocence of not knowing.

VINCENT: And if you were on LSD and you walked over to that sand, you might feel you were sinking?

EMILY: I could feel that the sand might be a grave beginning to open.

VINCENT: In other words, you don't really believe that there are objective limits.

EMILY: No, I don't believe that we, who are all sane, know all there is to know about that sand. I think that if we took LSD right now, we'd know something else about it. The thing is, if we were babies, we couldn't say what we felt about it; we'd just have a certain kind of feeling about the sensation. We couldn't articulate it, right?

VINCENT: Yah.

EMILY: And it wouldn't be the same for both of us. Maybe for me it would be dirt or shit and for you it would be some kind of cream like your mother used or hair or what it feels like to touch your clothes. Whatever these things are, they wouldn't become sand right away, with a word.

VINCENT: Look, I understand that under LSD, I might experience this coffee cup in huge, monumental fashion; I just wonder if there isn't a reality outside that. I mean I can make this into a thousand bigger or different qualities, but after all it *is* porcelain, it *is* four inches in diameter, and it *can* hold maybe half a pint of liquid. Aren't those limits that exist outside any potential it has in our psyche?

EMILY: Yes, but those limits are absolutely infinitesimal.

VINCENT: What do you mean?

EMILY: That the possibilities are infinite, whereas the limitations are infinitesimal; that this is porcelain, that it weighs half a pound, that it holds half a pint, these qualities, confronting the possibilities of it, are minute. They're *nothing* to what it could possibly be. You know that Marsha, for example, would never take LSD.

VINCENT: I know she wouldn't.

EMILY: She's terrified of all drugs. She needs her controls, she can't give them up. Of course she will someday.

VINCENT: You think she'll take LSD?

EMILY: No, I think someday she'll surrender, she'll love.

SHARON RUDAHL
1947–

Acid Temple Ball is a tour de force of psychedelic erotica. The heroine makes love under the influence of eight or so different drugs and drug combinations. The book is set in Manhattan's East Village and San Francisco's Haight-Ashbury during the middle and late 1960's.

On LSD, the heroine sees an ordinary apartment as a temple where "a pageant of the Eastern Gods is unfolding." She and her lover Jesse are Shiva and Shakti in the yab-yum position. But the illness of her junkie lover Davy terminates their high.

Acid Temple Ball was written under the pseudonym Mary Sativa. Sharon Rudahl is a prominent underground cartoonist.

From Acid Temple Ball

I walk into Davy's place and find them both there, one is dark, the other fair, already friends after a week. Today Jesse and I are going to take acid,

Sharon Rudahl. "I am our one locked body moving in its perfect, necessary dance."

something we haven't yet had a chance to do together. It is early morning and I needn't go home . . . till seven or eight—I'll still be high, but not uncontrollably so. Offer to Davy that he join us, but he has to go discuss a movie script and hustle dope. For every two bags of heroin he sells he gets one free. A nasty system, but he always refused to sell to me, gave me some free whenever I really needed it. Jesse and I each take one of the little sky-blue pills, acid has been coming in the loveliest colored pills the last year or two. Pink, purple, orange, various shades of blue. Pressed by expensive machines for mass distribution.

I bustle around fixing some breakfast for Davy, who never eats enough; he's getting the really pale emaciated look of junkies. Nothing for me and Jesse, the drug will hit harder and quicker, with less chance of nausea, if our stomachs are empty. I dig tripping after a three or four-day fast. We get off quickly; after only twenty or thirty minutes, the dishes I'm washing become fragile and transparent, I turn off the water and flop down on Jesse's Salvation Army mattress.

Davy pats me on the head, shakes Jesse's hand, and goes out.

"Don't set the place on fire or anything, you two. I probably won't be back till evening." Jesse is laughing as Davy closes the door.

The pale bluish light from the windows becomes rich with hints of color, breaking into strips and ribbons, then brighter color within the ribbons, moving and forming glowing patterns. Complicated medieval stories forming and unforming. I sit near the window, watching entranced. The light is calling out to me, brighter and brighter. I raise my arms to it and feel myself drawn out, flowing. Brighter and brighter but not light enough.

Too blue, too grey. I go around the apartment, lighting candles, turning on lamps. The room shifts from blue to red and back to blue. Jesse's flesh is melting and merging like colored lights. I peer through the patterns at him, he smiles. The smile opens, shooting darts of light in spreading whirlpools in the room. Moves his hand before my eyes and leaves a trail of golden, dripping images, like a harpsichord arpeggio.

Time is a train hurtling between brief stops, before and after are short-circuited. I touch his cheek and lose the sensation before I can remember touching. Repeat and repeat, but feeling is in a different world than my mind now. His face is a whirlpool of inlaid images, growing more and more complex as I look into them, flowering infinitely. He holds me in his arms and laughs.

"Pretty heavy, huh?"

"Get undressed, Jesse, I want to look at you." He takes off his jeans and cowboy shirt, less awkward than I am, fumbling clumsily at ridiculous complications of zippers and stockings. I get hung up with my dress over my head, grooving on the light coming through the woven fabric, each pinpoint of light opening into kaleidoscopes of color. Jesse helps me and pulls me down to him.

"Hey, you doing all right?"

"Fine, baby. Jesse, beautiful Jesse, you're really here."

"Why don't we go out after a while and you can show me New York?"

I told Jesse once about how long it took me to get used to being on the streets in New York while I'm tripping. Now I do it all the time, I.D. in pocket and making sure I'm clean of drugs; even if I am found gibbering in a trash can, what difference does it make? And just not being paranoid about being picked up by cops makes it much easier. Shit, if I can't trip on the streets, what am I tripping for?

Digging this special excursion into super-reality and the extension of all senses means being able to face and enjoy anything under its effect. It's gotten so I'd rather do something unpleasant while tripping than while straight: it will still be unpleasant, but at least I'll be tripping. But now I want to blow my mind a little on just being high with Jesse, beautiful silky Jesse, covered with swirling tapestry patterns and a marble mosaic derived from his veins and pores. Faint pale green and pink and golden stones set together to form his cool firm flesh.

"We'll go out in a little while, Jesse, O.K.? I want to be here with you now."

My mind is rambling through vast deserted gardens, fragrant with perfumed opium, a sense of birds fluttering above us, a statue of the god set before a fountain of light. I hold a candle in my hands, feel its warmth, feel a rainbow of hot to cold as I move one hand above the candle, closer and farther away. Watch Jesse's body forming and unforming in the candlelight. I drip the hot wax on my hands and feel no pain, play at peeling it off, little impressions of my flesh, fragile, crumbling in my hands.

"Don't hurt yourself with the wax."

Perhaps I have burned my hands. There are red spots where the wax was. Of course there are blue and pink and green and yellow spots, too. Moving around. I put the candle down.

Davy's little black cat is crawling around on our naked bodies, it knows we are as harmless as saints in the forest. Lovely and furry and gentle it purrs at us and rubs its head against our bodies. I stroke my breasts against its fur and kiss its head, take its ear in my mouth. The cat lies perfectly still, purring. The cat is as important to me as a brother, now; I have unlimited regard for its individuality. It is fearless and supple, not so much contact high as permitting us to enter its reality. Perhaps I am even simpler than a cat, now, perhaps I am merely a stone or a flower it has no reason to take seriously. Yet I can call it to me with a small gesture of my hands or a look of my eyes.

"Is it O.K. if I put on some music, Jesse?"

"Sure. Rock?"

"I don't know, I'll think about it." I think about it squatting naked at the pile of records, getting hung up looking at the cover of each one, figuring out what it is, what the emotional content of listening to it would be. I want to hear four or five at once. Jesse comes over and rubs his chest against my back.

"Hey, just choose one."

I pick a cover that appeals to me, an earthmotherly face, flowing white garments. Indian music. Jesse puts it on the turntable for me.

Intricate golden notes fill up the atmosphere of the room, create their own dense, rippling space. My body, arms and hands move to the music; dripping colored afterimages, like trailing iridescent ribbons, follow every gesture. Jesse's body is golden and smooth, each curve responding to some subtle ideal of form. He and the room take on the quality of the music, ceremonial and erotic, the deep mystery of images complete in themselves.

A pageant of the Eastern gods is unfolding as I dance naked towards his naked body. The wheel of creation and destruction, things of surface and illusion dying into purer being. We are the perfected. Changing yet unchanging in annulled time. I dance toward him and each moment is lost, unremembered. The surface of his body is smooth and cool as metal, as stone. He sits cross-legged, motionless, radiant and removed, the child-like smile of absolute knowing, knowing beyond words, peace that is not static but flowing. He and change are embraced in rapture, he contemplates his birth and death with a golden smile.

Reverently, I touch his shoulders and chest, the tight bud of his penis, touch it lightly, watching it swell and rise, filling with its own energy, coming forth huge and erect, rooted in his peaceful body. It sways with the music and the passion and energy pouring into the room. I dance to it, invoke it, stroking lightly with my hands and lips.

Lightly he takes my shoulders and I climb on to his lap, crossing my legs behind his back. The record changer is playing the last half of the record over and over, in response to our needs. But always unfamiliar and now, infinitely complex. I am wet and open, I am cool and removed, creator of worlds. His prick is huge and living in me. I feel its veins and the pulsing of blood, it fills me and makes me solid and complete. I sit on his lap, his hands are on my hips, moving me gently to the music, I dance with my arms and hips, twisting slightly to the complex beats of drum and flute and sitar. We are carved from stone, we are molten gold. His hair shoots sparks of joy on my cheeks and shoulders. Peaceful and whole together we dance, our movements sliding his vast hard phallus into my depths, fluttering, sucking into me, then slightly withdrawn, hard and smooth in short jolts deep in me, the swollen pounding head swaying as we rock slightly from side to side. Around us, worlds are born and fall, images dance with us, strange animals and shapes echo our desire and glow brighter with stabs of pleasure. I look into his eyes, cool glittering blue and grey and gold, my face not touching his, breathe his breath, he is a mirror reflecting some other form of me, I am his cock deep inside myself, I am our one locked body moving in its perfect, necessary dance.

I touch his glittering hair and feel my own fingertips, feel the music playing in my cunt, rock and twist and shudder flowing uncontrollably through our bodies. Only the slightest movements, enough to keep desire swollen and tight, constant and intense, constant flowing lust and satisfaction, hungry and filled, his hardness rocking in me, each movement a gesture carved in stone. I am the earth from which he flowers, he is the river rushing into me, every muscle and vein confirmed and created to this dance. Time is dead; we are the sacred image.

* * *

We become satisfied, our mood shifts; we want to go out, see things, do things. Something ecstatic and revealed remains ringing in my thighs and arms, a sense that we are beautiful and whole, going forth to shed light. Rescue the record, dress painfully, careful to be warm, to take care of our distant flesh. It is still bitter and windy outside, though we probably won't feel it. Laughing, delighted with ourselves for having succeeded in getting ready to go out; step outside, close and lock the door. Many difficult operations to figure out, manipulations and conventions. Walking, putting one foot in front of the other, the ball of the foot, and then the heel, shift weight, and you're off. Doing fine, the wind blowing past our heads, remembering what red lights are for, but forgetting how long they can last. Lighting a cigarette in the wind, careful not to start laughing. Faces that are friendly and faces that are forbidding, opening like hidden windows and then drifting past before we can look inside. Sometimes it is hard not to follow. A bum reaches out and we give him all our change, little as it is. Now we won't have to decide again if we have or should give money.

Colors glowing through a fine misty rain, people like delicate ink drawings, elongated, striding ridiculously. Lights and hallucinations shimmer on the damp streets. We walk and walk, not remembering we have walked, forgetting where we are, fording rivers of savage traffic, staring in windows lighted softly in the afternoon twilight. Places I have been, different times and cities flash by me, as though I walked in one place before a vast lighted screen.

We walk and walk, the mist becomes darker, I begin to feel hunger and cold. Heading back toward Davy's place, able to read signs now, eager to get warm, to sit down and eat something. We go to a little gourmet store on Second Avenue, it is warm and light inside, full of friendly knowing people with beards and long hair, buying candy and ice cream and pistachio nuts and soda pop. Heads. And scornful speed freaks getting orange juice for their colds. And middle-aged ladies getting lox and chopped liver and painstakingly ignoring the hippie customers. We look at all the cans and tins and jars, bottles of nuts and dried fruit, rows of cheese wrapped in wax and foil. And laugh at each other in joy and amazement. Look in our wallets, make a quick calculation that the money I have left over from my last modeling job would buy enough food, even here, to keep us busy for days. So why don't we just be imaginative and get whatever comes to mind. We can feed some of it to Davy. Dozens of little packages, bright labels, individually wrapped in paper. We clutch our bundles and hurry to Davy's place. Past the candy store on the corner, crowds of people standing in the dusk and drizzle, grooving on each other and asking passers-by for change. Some cats smile and nobody bothers us, people hand us leaflets advertising rock concerts and be-ins, I hold one upside down as I walk and watch the street lights through it.

Arrive at Davy's, open the door. He is lying on the cot, looking really grey and strung-out.

"You guys are back, huh? Having a good time?"

Perhaps it's partly the acid, sometimes it does that, but he looks really bad. Maybe we just haven't been noticing how low he's getting.

"Wow, yeh, Davy, it's been really nice. We brought back some crazy food, maybe you'll have some with us."

"Maybe in a little while, O.K.? I'm just going to lie here for a while."

Jesse and I feel subdued and a bit depressed, decide to eat later. I make some hot tea with lemon to warm us. Sit by the window, drinking my sweet tea. Content now to sit alone, looking out into the twilight, blue-grey walls and shreds of laundry hanging. Watch rain dripping crystal down the window, laundry and garbage blowing in the harsh gusts of wind, the low keening city wind trapped between buildings. It has been a beautiful trip, but now is the long slow coming back, and an acute sense of isolation and helpless pity. Nothing to give, nothing to share, and Davy is lying on his cot, exhausted and probably getting sick; the buildings sink into dirt and darkness. I am closed around the picture I see; I enclose my own picture, as well, bent over and folded like a flower, contemplating loneliness. Many-petaled like a flower, containing infinite worlds within worlds, and each a picture of myself, bent in isolation, watching the wet laundry swaying in the wind and rain.

I shake my head, dizzy with descending images, drink some more hot tea, and turn from the window.

ANITA HOFFMAN
1942–

The Yippies were the first dope-smoking political party in American history. Their disruption of the New York Stock Exchange and the 1968 Democratic National Convention, and their involvement in anti-war rallies and smoke-ins, drew enormous media attention.

Anita Hoffman, former wife of Yippie cofounder and political activist Abbie Hoffman, wrote a memoir under the pseudonym Ann Fettaman. During the sixties, she participated in the Yippies' Halloween plot to send four thousand individual joints of marijuana to New York public officials and media figures. The author's narrative clearly reveals that marijuana laws are a big political issue, and that the media can be used effectively with humor and imagination.

From Trashing

One day early in October Crazy Fred came over to the house.

"Brother and Sister, I got a good project. I think you're both gonna love it."

"It's not founding another Free Store, I hope. I'm a little tired of that after three tries and three fires," Danny said.

"You kidding? This project's the easiest, sneakiest thing I've thought of since I started collecting welfare under three different names. All we need to pull it off is more bread."

"Oooh. Gee. That's unusual," I remarked.

"Wait'll you hear it. It's worth every cent we can steal. Here it is. For Halloween we send out twenty thousand joints in the mail. To judges, housewives, celebrities, the press, anybody we want. We send out regular envelopes with the joint of grass enclosed and a sheet of paper with instructions on how to smoke it and anything else we want to say."

"Whew. That'll spook them. I do like it. A lot."

"So do I. I think it'll be very easy and safe to do."

"It's a huge undertaking. Other people are already working on it. I won't even tell you how many. In fact, I'm not even sure. Nobody knows who else is involved."

"That's good, Fred. You know we don't like the limelight after the press screwed up our wedding."

"That's what I figured. There are two ways you can help. The first is, we need more grass, and I figured you'd be able to get some. The second is, we don't have money for postage. You hustle the grass and send out the joints. We'll supply the envelopes and letters, but your team will roll the joints and mail them."

Danny looked at me. "Want to go ahead?"

"Sure babes. I said I liked it."

*   *   *

As soon as I had the money next day, I went to see Cassandra about the dope. I was uptight about keeping that much grass in the house until Halloween, so I talked Cassandra into holding it for two weeks. This fit with Crazy Fred's plan. Halloween was on a Monday. Someone figured out that the "treats" would have to be mailed midnight on the preceding Friday to arrive in the Monday morning mail. So Friday, October 28th became D-Day.

Exactly a week before Halloween, with eight hundred dollars in my pocket I went to get my fortune told. Red came along and we lugged back two huge shopping bags filled with grass. I had never held so much at once. We dumped the contents on the kitchen table. Six foil-wrapped bricks of grass.

"How did you get so much?" Danny asked.

"So much? For eight hundred bucks she should have given us twenty keys instead of six," I growled.

"What? You got a terrific deal. Six into eight is what? About a hundred thirty-three bucks."

"Right."

"So what's wrong?" said Danny. "That's cheap. Last year a key went for about one eighty. You paid less than that, and they're napalming grass fields in Mexico. God knows what the price is now with Operation Intercept. Felix told me they're getting three hundred."

"I thought she might give it to us free. As her way of supporting community action."

"That fucking Nazi Kleindienst in the Justice Department," said Danny. "You know I saw a picture of him in the paper the other day burning fifty tons of good Mexican shit. He was grinning as though it was books or something."

Danny looked so serious as he stood at the table unwrapping the tin foil. I couldn't resist putting my arms around his waist. If Red hadn't been there I would have reached down to fondle his cock. I loved to pat and hold it beneath the corduroy of his trousers.

"Come on babes. This is serious business. We got work to do." He reached over and pinched the side of my waist. "We gotta spend the rest of this money. I want to get more stamps and some rolling machines so we can start making joints tonight."

"You and Red go buy the stuff," I said. "I'll stay here and wait for the Crawfords."

"They coming?" he asked.

"I told you. Samson has to sell some paintings, so Valerie's coming with him. It's sort of a celebration because Jasmine and Zeno finally left. They're going to Tibet or something."

That evening Red came over with Georgia and the six of us sat down at the table in the livingroom and began rolling the first batch. We figured out a way of using a window screen as a sieve. By two in the morning we had only used up about two and a half keys. We got about seven hundred joints a key. We were all unaccustomed to cleaning such large amounts, and the room became covered with a fine dust of pot. My joy at having so much extra grass around was cooled out by fear of a police invasion. The livingroom had been turned into one of the first authentic grass factories. What a waste. At one point Red passed around a cigar with about an ounce of grass in it. Just one puff of white smoke was enough to knock you out.

Late next morning, while Valerie lingered over her coffee, I set a bowl of grass on the kitchen table and started rolling. Samson left the house early to see his art dealer and Danny went to visit the Cannibals, a local commune of Street warriors.

Hours later Samson burst into the room. "My paintings went for three thousand!"

Valerie jumped up, tears in her eyes. "We have enough to make it through the winter."

"And we can finish the film series," Samson added.

He sat down and started rolling. Danny came home and told us that the Cannibals and other tribes were engaged in activities similar to ours. So the four of us worked like little elves until Red and Georgia brought over some Chinese food.

By the eleven o'clock news we had rolled all the grass into large piles of neatly stacked joints. Mayor Lindsay, the announcer said, was asking Albany for higher penalties for marijuana and LSD.

"Poor bastard," said Red. "He'll do anything, including jail his own kids, to get re-elected."

"Last year he spoke at Hofstra and called for repeal. I guess that wasn't an election year," I echoed.

"You should see what happens in Woodstock when they're up for re-election. The state police set up road blocks so that no long-hair driving a car is safe. If the pot geiger-counter doesn't detect anything in the car, they'll get you on some trumped up license or muffler infraction," said Samson.

"They invented that pot geiger-counter at the Hudson Institute, you know. Probably came up with the idea while they were stoned," I added.

"That's O.K.," remarked Danny. "Fuck 'em. We got our own scientists figuring out ways of hiding the stuff. Cassandra told me next year we'll have a definite method for putting acid in the reservoirs. The problem until now has been a dissolving agent that could distribute it evenly, but they've been working on it for a year now."

Wednesday morning the Crawfords headed back to Woodstock while we embarked on the second stage of Operation Halloween. Crazy Fred came over with more postage stamps, envelopes and thou-sands of leaflets. The envelopes had been addressed by a typewriter that was then destroyed. In the lower left hand corner they bore that popular hard-sell teaser "FREE GIFT INSIDE!" The orange and black letter read as follows:

High there fellow American!

Once again it's Halloween and the friendly spirits here at DRUG MENACE have decided to bring you a FREE SAMPLE!

It's called pot
maryjane
grass
weed or boo

Best of all

It's a Halloween treat for you!

Here's how to get the most out of the enclosed hand-rolled, hand-packed, deluxe imported joint:

1. Sit down.
2. Relax.
3. Light joint and inhale as you would a tobacco cigarette (if you could forget it was cancer-inducing).
4. Keep inhaling until you no longer can.
5. Let your breath out.
6. Repeat until you are feeling really good.

If you have enjoyed our product, look for us in your local kindergartens, elementary schools, high schools, colleges, and wherever young people gather.

Remember: if it's not a MENACING drug, it's diet pills, tranquilizers or booze. So stick with DRUG MENACE and let the magic of nature's own grass relax your body and expand your mind.

Help make Halloween a High Holiday
Sincerely yours,

The DRUG MENACE crowd.

P.S. Don't fink to the cops. Just being near this FREE SAMPLE can get you a year in jail.

Danny and I spent all day Thursday stuffing the remaining envelopes. By Friday we had four neatly packed cartons sitting by the livingroom windows.

Friday evening we caught the eight o'clock show at the Fillmore. We didn't go there very often, but The Creedence Clearwater Revival was playing that night and our friend Brad was scheduled to work the door, so we knew we could get in free. We had gone to the concert stoned, but Creedence was so good we emerged from the theater still totally out of our heads. The good feeling was further heightened by the prospect of our remaining task and the most exciting part of the Halloween operation—mailing the joints. It was eleven o'clock. After a quick egg cream at the Gem Spa, we picked up the cartons at our apartment and made our way to the subway.

The uptown train came along in about five minutes and was quite empty. We entered the car and sat in the middle of the bench. I put one carton on the seat next to me and one on the floor. Danny put down his packages and as the train jerked forward, shouted to me, "Eighty-sixth Street?" I nodded.

We sat quietly, reading the ads on the walls. I thought how silly I was to feel paranoid. It was so easy. Hardly anyone on the train, and no way for anyone to guess that we were carrying four thousand joints of grass between us. Mailing them uptown was probably unnecessary, but we were determined to mislead the narcs in every way possible.

Danny got up as we pulled into Grand Central. I shook my head "no," but he had his packages and was already heading out the door. He pointed to the Express train across the platform. "Come on babes, quick."

I've always hated switching to Express trains because they are invariably crowded. And getting off the Express at 86th Street meant climbing two long flights of stairs. I started to ask Danny why we couldn't stay on the Local, but before I could finish the doors began to close. Danny held the door and yelled for me to come, so I just grabbed my cartons and ran out.

We jumped on the Express train just as the doors slammed shut. Danny quickly disappeared in the throng. I tried to follow him but couldn't with the bulky cartons. I was trying to push my way into the aisle when I felt a hand fondle my left breast.

My left hand jerked up instinctively, still grasping the carton, and I swung around. It was a slight swarthy teen-aged boy. He started to giggle. I gave the kid what I thought was a stern look and turned to move on. But I heard a tough, threatening female voice in back of me say "You have some nerve," and I turned to see who she was talking to. Incredibly, it was me.

"Who d'ya think you are? Who d'ya think you are, girlie?" asked a short stock middle-aged woman with bouffant hair the color of orange caramel. "I bet you think you can just walk all over people, huh? Huh?"

I tried not to flinch at the whiskey fumes. "Oh, I'm sorry. Excuse me," I said softly when I realized I had bumped her with a carton. I was about to turn away.

"You people. I'd like to know who ya think you are? Filth. No respect for others." Her voice was getting louder and everyone at our end of the car was watching.

"I said I was sorry," I repeated and started moving toward the other end of the car. I was sure someone would call a cop and I could just see us trying to explain four thousand joints. I tried to move away.

But she was just warming up. "Think you own the world, you brats. Well, I got news for you. We could teach you some manners all right. If ya don't like it here, why don't ya leave? Instead of spreading your filth."

I spotted Danny ahead of me.

"It's all ya see on television these days. Your kind. I tell ya, it's disgusting. It's all ya see. I wish I was a cop, I'd show you what for. I'd show you what for all right. Yccch. . . . Disgusting. . . . Yccch. . . . Yccch. Just tell me who ya think ya are? Dressed like that? With that hair. Yccch. I bet ya got lice. Ya wanna know who ya are? I'll tell ya: Trash. That's what. Trash. T-R-A-S-H. Nothing but trash!"

"Why don't you lay off lady," I smiled demurely.

The crowd in the subway car seemed to agree. I knew Danny loved these kind of confrontations, but I suggested we move to another car.

I went first and nudged open the door. As

Danny stepped through with his cartons, he couldn't resist yelling back, "Get a haircut, lady!"

The next car was equally crowded, but relatively peaceful. We moved to a spot near the door and put our cartons on the floor. We were only there half a minute when a cop came in and pushed his way over. He was a young guy, but very big.

He looked at Danny for a few seconds before he spoke. "I don't know what you're up to. But you better not give me any trouble." He looked me up and down, looked at the cartons. A few seconds elapsed. He made a sour expression. "I'm keeping my eyes on you, so watch it."

Both of us remained silent. After a few more seconds he left. We decided to get off at the next stop. It wasn't until we got off that we realized the next stop was 86th Street. What a relief!

Park Avenue was deserted. We hiked down to 68th Street, using every mailbox along the way. By the time we had gotten rid of our last letter we felt high again. Somehow just the act of mailing all that grass was intoxicating.

There was no way of knowing how many people got high on Halloween, but we knew it was the busiest night in the history of the Narcotics Division. The story first broke in the afternoon papers and radio. The information was scanty but there were shocked reports that thousands of city-dwellers had received "a marijuana cigarette with a strange letter." By the evening formal procedures had been established for dealing with this crisis. It was announced at regular intervals on all the evening news programs. We heard it first on WCRT-TV.

IF YOU HAVE RECEIVED WHAT APPEARS TO BE A MARIJUANA REEFER, AS IT IS CALLED, ACCOMPANIED BY A LETTER BEGINNING "High there fellow American" DO NOT BE ALARMED. I REPEAT: DO NOT BE ALARMED. CALL YOUR LOCAL POLICE PRECINCT AND ASK FOR THE NARCOTICS DIVISION. THEY WILL SEND AN OFFICER TO PICK UP THE ITEM IN QUESTION AS SOON AS POSSIBLE. THE POLICE DEPARTMENT CAUTIONS YOU NOT TO BE UNEASY IF A PATROLMAN DOES NOT REACH YOUR HOME IMMEDIATELY. THEY ASK YOU TO BE PATIENT AND UNDERSTANDING IN THIS EMERGENCY SITUATION.

I was hysterical. "Holy shit, did you hear that? 'Emergency situation.'"

"The city's been invaded by a plant!"

"Yeah," I giggled. "We could've planned a bank robbery tonight if we'd known most of the force would be tied up. It's like something the Joker would have dreamed up to foil Batman."

RASA GUSTAITIS
1934–

While gathering material for a story on the human potential movement, investigative reporter Rasa Gustaitis visited Esalen Institute in Big Sur, where consciousness-raising is regarded as a course in higher education. While on the Coast, her first LSD trip was also on the agenda. Gustaitis describes the emotionally heightened interactions that occur between her and the others in her group, none of whom she knows well, after the LSD takes effect. Because of the length of her piece, only the first half is reprinted here.

Rasa Gustaitis. "'Is this what we've been looking for then?' I asked the doctor. . . . 'Is it all in this small pill?'"

From Turning On

Esalen Institute has strict rules against drugs on the premises but Big Sur is head country. I intended to take LSD sometime during my stay on the Coast, if the right opportunity arose, but did not plan to do it so soon. I am reluctant to add anything still more intense to my experience of watching [Fritz] Perls. Still, the trip being planned for this weekend is the sort of opportunity I have hoped to find. A man who has done a lot of work with LSD is visiting Big Sur and is to be in charge of a group trip that will include some local residents and a few people from Perls' seminar. We are to go to a house several miles from the Hot Springs on Friday night. As Perls has scheduled no seminar sessions until Sunday night, I have the time. I decide to take part.

On Friday I awake scared. I dreamed of a barren hillside with hawks circling above trenches and bomb shelters. Not a single blade of grass grew on the hill. Not a single human soul had been present. Was this some sign from my innermost mind that I should change plans? Will the dream come along on the trip? Does it mean that I'm at odds with myself and the world and will be one of those trippers who end up in mental hospitals?

By dinnertime I am completely calm and at ease. After all, if the worst happens and I go crazy on LSD, what better place could I find for that than Esalen? Surely there are enough people here who could help me regain my mental balance.

I eat a light dinner, as instructed. Then I dress for the trip. A sea-green velour blouse and orange pants should be comfortable, and I like the colors. I'm really looking forward to those kaleidoscopes. The death dream is forgotten.

After dinner, I leave in a car with a middle-aged couple from Perls' group. The man is a doctor, seemingly calm and kindly of disposition. The woman is very handsome and voluptuous and tends toward hysteria, I think. They are from one of the most prosperous suburbs of San Francisco and have taken many LSD trips together.

"So you're an acid virgin?" she says. "You'll be fun." She puts me off a little. Am I to be some kind of spectacle?

We drive south on the highway and turn right to descend a dirt road toward a small frame house that stands six feet from the edge of the cliff. A pale, somewhat sickly-looking girl with long blond hair and dark eyes opens the door: Mella, the hostess. (The names of the trippers are fictitious.) We enter a comfortable room with a fireplace, candlelight, Navajo tapestries on the walls, couches and soft chairs. Glass doors lead from the living room to the garden. Manos Hadjidakis' "Lilacs from a Dead Land" is playing softly on the stereo. I'm delighted by the warmth of this launching pad.

Several trippers have already arrived and spread mattresses, blankets and pillows on the rug. The guru looks up to greet us. He is building a fire. He is a tall, slim man in his late thirties with a quick smile and strangely bright eyes—bright but not deep, almost glassy. I watch him gather together logs and kindling and light them. The cut crystal on his necklace catches the reflections of the flames. Do I trust him? His movements are quick and assured. Yes, thank God, I do. It would be terrible if I did not.

Within a few minutes, the rest of the group arrives. We are twelve in all, counting Mella and the guru. But only ten of us are "going up," as it's put. The guru asks us to sit in a circle and stops the record player. This is a structured trip, he says. That means that there are certain rules, which he will explain, that we are to abide by. But first he wants to know if anyone here objects to anyone else's presence. We look at each other. Most of those here are strangers to me. There are two hip gypsies: a young man with gentle eyes, long blond hair and a red beard and, beside him, a nineteen-year-old girl who works at Esalen part-time. I noticed her in the dining room one evening because of her unusual facial expression. It was simultaneously ecstatic and vacant. Her features were somehow dissolved.

There's the doctor and his wife; a young psychologist and his wife, who are both friendly and attractive; a college professor who reminds me, for some reason, of a dancing bear; his very fat but sultry wife, and a tiny green-eyed girl in a long green dress whom I remember from that inter-racial weekend at Esalen. I disliked her then. She struck me as a total phony. Inside a fragile doll with a tinkly voice and sweet smile I sensed suppressed rage. When a man made her angry during one of the sessions she had suddenly risen from her chair, stalked across the room and slapped him. Physical violence was forbidden but how could anyone object to the tiny creature's attack? Beware of the Sugarplum Fairy! Yes, I feel venomous toward her and would have preferred not to see her here, but I don't really mind. There are no objections.

The guru now explains the structure. There are four rules. First, we are not to harm ourselves or anyone else either now or later. Second, if we want to leave the house alone and go beyond the road, we are to ask permission. Third, there is to be no intercourse without permission. Fourth, if he comes up to anyone and says "This is structure," he is to be obeyed. We are not to get upset if we hear people crying. And we are not to resent anyone who might push us away as we approach. For we might go off on very different trips and should all allow the others to choose their own direction. If anyone should want to come down at any time, the proper drug is available. However, in the many trips he has led, this has never proved necessary, our guru says.

He deals out the acid, different quantities to each of us. The professor, who is an old head, takes 400 micrograms. The Sugarplum Fairy wants just a little and is given 75. I get one and a half tablets, 250 micrograms, which is a medium dose. I hold them in my hand and look at them closely. A white tablet with a brown core and half of another. The passport, the ticket—to where? I swallow them and sit down on the couch opposite the fireplace to wait. The guru said it would be fifteen to thirty minutes before we would feel the effect.

I look at the bowl of fruit on the coffee table before me and at the candle beside it. Beyond the fruit and candle is the fire. People are settling down on the mattresses, the other couch and the chairs. "Lilacs from a Dead Land" is again playing.

The guru bends over me. "If you see anything frightening, walk toward it and it will disappear," he tells me. Then he holds his hand, palm down, over my midriff and moves it in a circle, without touching me. I feel a pronounced tingling and look up at him, surprised. He laughs. "A chakra message," he says.

Slowly, something is happening to my head. It begins to feel heavy and balloon-like at the same time and seems to sit loose on my neck, as if the muscles had suddenly gone slack. From the head and the neck, a torpor seeps down my arms, loosening muscle fibers; down to my wrists and to my fingertips. It is a pleasurable sensation.

Now the candle flame before me expands into a halo. The torpor seeps down through my body, down through my belly into my pelvis. I loosen and expand. On the mattress below me, Martin, the psychologist, and his wife, Eloise, are holding up the guru's necklace with the cut-crystal pendant. I noticed that Martin has on a handsome blue silk shirt hand-painted with golden patterns of leaves and peacocks. The two of them are swinging the guru's pendant high up between them and laughing in delight. But what is happening to Martin's shirt? It begins to glow. The leaves and the peacocks are moving. I think and shake my head. Yes the design is changing.

"Martin!"

"What?"

"Your shirt, look at your shirt. It's moving!" My voice is not quite my voice. It's a little out of control.

Martin looks down at his shirt, then unbuttons it, takes it off and puts it down on the floor. "Yes, you're right," he says "It is." The shirt turns into a jungle of plants and birds. I can let them move or I can make them stop. They are beautiful but almost—they are almost turning into serpents and monsters. I stop that and they become beautiful birds and leaves, growing a third dimension, glowing in gold and blue. "That's some shirt, Martin," I say, laughing. "Look, there's a valley in this jungle." My voice is unfamiliar. Gradually the flowing shirt loses its shirtishness completely. The blue-gold rises up like water sucked up by a vacuum into a cone that turns to gas when it touches the air. I sink to the floor and go into the jungle with Martin. He is an Oriental potentate. His wife, who comes to sit beside us, is a harem queen with a thick braid of black hair falling over her right shoulder. The guru's necklace around her neck shoots rainbows. But at the same time I also know that the three of us are sitting on the floor holding on to a Chinese shirt.

My watch is too tight. I take it off, and also my

ring, and lay them in the fruit bowl on the coffee table. Looking around, I see that others have also changed. The fat girl, the professor's wife, has turned into a presence, magic and mysterious. She is a cat woman glowering wickedly as she sits cross-legged under the grand piano, with unearthly jewels in her black velvet hair and elegant snake-eyebrows arching. The Sugarplum Fairy steps past me, unreal but so pretty, also with jewels by her ears.

Someone is doing something on my belly, I feel a pleasurable scratching around my navel but am not interested. It has nothing to do with me. It's the guru and Martin, they're doing something. The music is growing—a Bach cantata. Everything merges now, there is no more jungle, no more sultan, no more separation between sight and sound and touch, me and the music, the vast music. I am holding the doctor's hands and looking into his face. It has a new clarity. His eyes look at me and we meet in unlimited space. I put my arms around his shoulders. "So much space," says a voice I never heard but know to be mine. "It can be filled," he says, sadly. No, that's not what I meant, the space fills us. "I like the space," I say and touch his cheek with my fingers. The Bach chorale and he and I are one, rising and falling within vast cathedral spaces in great depths of sound. This is God, love, life—joyful pain, painful joy. Is this true? "Is this what we've been looking for then?" I ask the doctor. He is wiser, he must know. "Is it all in this small pill? Just a pill?"

"I know what you're asking," he says, "I have been here before." The words go so deep into me—though he has not answered me—that I fall around his neck and begin to cry. He is a prophet with those deep eyes and the beautiful clear craggy face. He speaks out of centuries of Jewish wisdom. I kiss his neck and stroke his face. I sense he wants gentleness.

Suddenly he says, "Carlotta!" and looks around for his wife. In a flash I see the room, where we were sitting on the mattress and other people are sitting and walking about. Where is the guru? I must know what is real. He is by the fireplace. Somehow, I get to him.

"Is it all in the pill?"

"The pill only opens the door," he says. "It's here and in you."

His voice is a gift. He is holding me up for I'm on my knees just barely rising from the swirling of unlimited multicolored space. Yes, yes.

"But all those books, all those centuries and prophets—they looked so hard and all the time it was so simple. It was in this pill." It's cruel and wrong. And now, will it vanish?

"Tomorrow, will it look the same as yesterday?"

"No, you will see, it won't be the same."

"Is this it then?"

"What?"

"What I've been trying so long to find out." The flowing is taking me away from him. But not yet. "I want to bring it back to those who aren't here."

"It's here for everyone." He knows, I love him. He has been here.

"But tomorrow I'll only have the same clichés to put on paper. I won't know how."

"This is *now*. This is *now*."

Yes. He has gone. And now I know that life is a constant flowing and we are part of each other. I have read it, thought it, but now I know and am overwhelmed with gratitude. If I can't write it down, it's all right. Someone else will go farther. Wherever I fail, someone else will rise. I feel a rush of liberation.

UNDERGROUND COMICS

Underground comics, which flourished in the sixties, often were satires of drug life-styles. There were more prominent women cartoonists active than at any other time. In 1973 Trina Robbins, Terry Balaweider Richards, Sharon Rudahl, and Diane Noomin contributed their psychedelic reminiscences to a comic book, *El Perfecto Comics*, honoring imprisoned psychologist Timothy Leary.

"If everyone dropped just one little tab . . . ," by Terre Balaweider Richards

"Michael from Mountains," by Trina Robbins

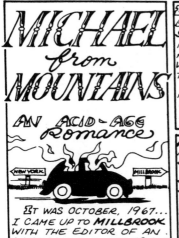

MICHAEL *from* **MOUNTAINS**

AN ACID-AGE *Romance*

NEW YORK   MILLBROOK

IT WAS OCTOBER, 1967... I CAME UP TO **MILLBROOK** WITH THE EDITOR OF AN UNDERGROUND NEWSPAPER AND HIS INDIAN GUIDE...

I WAS IMPRESSED BY THE **GENTLE SMILES** ON THE FACES OF THE PEOPLE AS THEY WANDERED ABOUT, THE OLD MANSION WAS PACKED WITH VISITORS...

AS I LAY ON THE ROOF IN THE SUN, SOMEONE PASSED ME SOME **ACID**. I SWALLOWED IT. NEVER BEFORE HAD I ACCEPTED ACID FROM A **TOTAL STRANGER.**

WE LEFT THE HOUSE AND WANDERED THROUGH AN ORCHARD. HIS NAME WAS **MICHAEL.** NATURALLY, HE CAME FROM **SAN FRANCISCO.** HE WAS BEAUTIFUL. WE WATCHED AN INCHWORM FOR AN **HOUR.**

BACK AT THE HOUSE WE RAN INTO **TIMOTHY LEARY.** I WANTED TO THANK HIM FOR ALL THIS LOVE AND BEAUTY BUT ALL WE COULD DO WAS STAND HAND IN HAND AND **SMILE** AT HIM.

HE CAUGHT A RIDE BACK TO THE CITY THAT EVENING. I SPENT THE NIGHT WITH SOME BIG TIME ACIDHEAD FROM THE **ORACLE**...

HE SHOWED UP AGAIN A WEEK LATER AT MY PLACE IN NEW YORK, WITH LOTS MORE ACID. HE TOOK ME TO A MACROBIOTIC RESTAURANT AND WE BALLED... THEN HE WENT BACK TO SAN FRANCISCO.

OM...

EEK!

OH, IT'S OKAY, HE'S MY GURU!

©1973 TRINA

MICHAEL FROM MOUNTAINS, GO WHERE YOU WILL GO TO; KNOW THAT I WILL KNOW YOU...

"The Happy Couple Take Acid," by Diane Noomin

"Acid Revolution," by Sharon Rudahl

Harvesting marijuana in California

CHOOSERS
& ABUSERS

The seventies did not have a single group of underground drug users on the scale of junkies or hippies. The period compared more to the twenties, when alcohol prohibition was ignored by drinkers who broke the law in countless speakeasies and homes. The favored consciousness-expanders of the sixties—particularly marijuana—were available everywhere, and cocaine soon joined them, especially in affluent circles. By the end of the seventies, even heroin sniffing and chipping was in vogue in some middle-class circles.

Drugs that permit escape, increase pleasure, enhance creativity and work routines, or provide a feeling of transcendence have proven difficult to suppress. The seventies began with an official declaration of "war on drugs"—a battle cry heard in each previous decade since the Harrison Narcotics Act of 1914. President Nixon was photographed with a wrapped brick of marijuana seized at the Texas border during the well-publicized and financed Operation Intercept. Later in the decade Latin American pot fields were poisoned or burned from the air, even as personal use of cannabis was beginning to be decriminalized in this country.

Still, only a fraction of the marijuana and hashish smuggled in from abroad was seized, and domestic cultivation increased, both in isolated rural areas and in city apartments under "grow lights." Many women, especially in the Sunbelt, grew it. (One of the popular home growers' manuals was Mountain Girl's *Primo Plant*, 1979.) LSD was widely produced in underground labs. Psilocybin mushroom-growing kits made home cultivation possible. Cocaine and Quaalude, a pharmaceutical hypnotic, were the social drug sensations. After playing a significant role in the Vietnam War, heroin from Southeast Asia flooded urban ghettos. Pharmaceuticals such as "reds" (the sedative Seconal) and "angel dust" (the anesthetic PCP) joined speed and smack as the official drugs of menace. Drug paraphernalia alone was a multi-million-dollar business.

To satisfy this gigantic, illicit-drug-consuming market, dealers became more numerous. Almost always men were at the top, but women were more extensively involved in smuggling and dealing operations than before. In instances of cocaine smuggling, they sometimes played the role of "mules," carriers of drugs across borders. Women had, of course, done this in the twenties and thirties but not college students and middle-class tourists. Accounts of women being arrested in foreign lands and detained in squalid prisons (the Antioch Seven in Turkey, the Lecumberri women's prison in Mexico, the Loretta Dooley case, and so on) appeared in newspapers and television newscasts. In her account of an ill-fated hashish-smuggling scam in Mexico, Susan Nadler conveys the intrigue, paranoia, and finally despair of being imprisoned in a foreign land.

The power of psychedelics to evoke evolutionary archetypes awakened many women to the goddess within. The use of LSD, peyote, and magic mushrooms influenced some women to become astrologers and tarot readers, midwives and psychic healers. The feminist movement received part of its energy and inspiration from women who gained insight and personal power from their experiments with mind-changing drugs. The holistic health movement of the 1970's was strongly affected by the psychedelic consciousness of such contemporary shaman women as Adelle Davis, Laura Huxley, Constance A. Newland, Jean Houston, Marcia Moore, and others, who used insights gained from tripping to develop breakthroughs in diet, self-analytical and transactional therapy, telepathic healing, and past-life influences. Psychedelic therapy with the dying, first suggested by Valentina Wasson and dramatically tested by Laura and Aldous Huxley, became a major research area. Joan Halifax *(The Human Encounter with Death,* 1979, in collaboration with Stan Grof) and others showed that by inducing ego-death and evolutionary perspectives, psychedelic drugs can counteract the fear of death. Elisabeth Kübler-Ross brought new recognition to Brompton's Cocktail, a potent eliminator of pain and anxiety composed of morphine and cocaine in an aromatic elixir.

While living with Peruvian and Mexican Indians, anthropologists Marlene Dobkin de Rios and Barbara Myerhoff ingested the local psychoactive substances (yagé and peyote) in ritual fashion to more fully understand the religious cosmology and behavioral patterns of an alien culture.

In "Fast Speaking Woman" Anne Waldman conveyed to poetry audiences the state of mind of the North American shaman woman. In "Billy Work Peyote" she took the shaman role in a psychedelic healing rite. Poet Patti Smith tapped the ceremonial power of a rock music performance. She performed on stage in Dionysian style, sometimes communicating like an oracle consumed by drug-induced visions.

Drugs and sexuality is a theme explored by several writers in this period. Sara Davidson's heroine in *Loose Change* (1977) chooses to take MDA, a psychedelic that enhances emotional receptivity, at a time of crisis in her deteriorating relationship with a longtime lover. Pat Carr's middle-aged college faculty wife in "Mermaid's Singing" (1977) asks her son's roommate to turn her on to marijuana, desiring to test its rumored

sexual uses. Lisa Alther's protagonist in *Kinflicks* (1975) terrifies her LSD guru and seducer by becoming aware of her goddess nature.

Drugs penetrated every level of society. Margaret Trudeau, wife of Canada's prime minister, and Betty Ford, the United States' First Lady confessed to drug use in their published memoirs. Hollywood was rocked by a number of pot and cocaine scandals involving actresses, none so politically explosive as the drug-overdose suicide of Jean Seberg in 1980.

As more and more people used drugs recreationally, the stigma attached to some illicit substances diminished. Penalties were generally less severe; marijuana was decriminalized in a significant number of states. But as the eighties neared, signs of a backlash against widespread recreational drug use were equally evident.

The concept of "drug of choice" gained in importance. It became necessary for drug consumers to know what they were putting into their bodies, and how drugs worked in combination. Some women of this period used psychoactive substances in conjunction with yogic and psychic disciplines to control and enhance the energies released. Educated and discriminating use of mind-altering drugs is evident in the pieces by Susan Sontag, Marcia Moore, and Jeannine Parvati.

The perspective of the drug-wise shaman gradually emerged in the seventies as an alternative to that form of mindless consumption known as "getting wasted." Clearly, the beneficial effects of drugs required an extraordinary ability to make intelligent choices regarding one's use of these abused substances. Drugs were, after all, going to remain an alluring feature of a world that was rapidly becoming a hallucination stranger than the effects of many of them.

ANNE WALDMAN
1945–

One of the most electrifying poetry events of the seventies was Anne Waldman's stage readings of her poem, "Fast Speaking Woman," a free adaptation of the Mazatec shaman María Sabina's sacred mushroom chant. Harnessing psychedelic energies through language is the shaman's art. To some in her audiences, poet woman became shaman woman.

In "Billy Work Peyote," Waldman performs a psychedelic healing ritual similar to the shaman's *velada*.

"13 Tanka" conveys the giddy philosophical humor of cannabis-altered consciousness.

From "Fast Speaking Woman"

I'm the mushroom woman
I'm the phantom woman
I'm the moaning woman
I'm the river woman
I'm the singing river woman
I'm the clear-water woman
I'm the cleansing woman
I'm the clay woman
I'm the glazed woman
I'm the glass-eyed woman

I'm the stone woman
I'm the stone tooth woman
I'm the woman with bones
I'm the fossil woman
I'm the soft flesh woman
I'm the doe-eyed woman

   that's how it looks when you go to heaven
   they say it's like softness there
   they say it's like land

   they say it's like day
   they say it's like dew

      *   *   *

I'm the night woman
I'm the black night woman
I'm the night without a moon
I'm the angel woman
I'm the white devil woman
I'm the green skin woman
I'm the green goddess woman
I'm the woman with arms
I'm the woman with wings
I'm the woman with sprouts
I'm the woman with leaves
I'm the branch woman
I'm the masked woman
I'm the deep-trance woman

Anne Waldman. "& for your sake we lie down/ in a bundle of cloud & for you we eat this medicine"

Billy Work Peyote

*a piece of sympathetic magic for
the life of William Burroughs, Jr.
sick in hospital Denver 1977.*

Keep it moving Billy. there's some motion. we're doing the clog dance for ya embattled or exalted—what?
Motions of fronds. these support systems   these rivers falling in & through you   you way back
deep deep legroom not enough to sit down & whisper in yr ear Billy   no nova Billy   More
nourishment Billy   we send you these stars dotted on the dotted swiss a most delicious grey for the
senses here, Billy, take them Billy   take these stars Billy
        Here, Billy, take the woodsmoke
    (moving Billy moving billy moving keep it moving)

We send you these scents & the pleasure of making a tent
    a tent for wanderers, for a wandering soul   lost yr shadow
here's a body to come back to Billy
                        & for your sake we lie down
in a bundle of cloud & for you we eat this medicine to
cure & puke it up again   I vomited for you Billy
                    churn it around
    (moving Billy moving billy moving keep it moving)

We three—me, Steven, Reed in still night I can't sit still
jumping up for you Billy   (moving keep it moving)
corn liquor to get the magic down
                        demodulation Billy
                        demon hypodermic Billy
                        corrigible Billy
                        Solomon's seal Billy
                        it's wobbling Billy
stock still
            indelible
    hyacinth blood Billy
    cards on the table Billy
    high drama & we're missing you Billy
            where ya been billy boy billy boy

    looking for you Billy
    studying your shank Billy
            universality Billy

            let it go

                passing it around

moving keep it moving billy moving keep it moving billy
    moving keep it moving billy moving keep it moving
        billy moving keep it moving billy moving
            keep it billy

13 Tanka

In Praise of Smoking Dope
For Ron Padgett's birthday, June 17, 1969

1.

Rather than worry
without result
one should put out
a joint of bad grass

2.

In calling it hemp
that splendid hemp
of long ago—how right they were!

3.

What the Seven Sages
craved long ago
was grass above all

4.

Rather than be wise
churning out the words
better smoke the dope
& weep happy tears

5.

How to speak of it
I know not
yet the thing
I prize most
is pot

6.

Sooner than be a man
I'd be an El Pino cigarette paper
holding the dope

7.

O what an ugly sight
the man who thinks he's wise
& never smokes the dope
Give him a good look—Look!
what a dope!

8.

Even a priceless jewel
how can it excel
a toke of good grass?

9.

Even jewels that flash at night
are they like the breath of grass
freeing the mind?

10.

Of the way to play
in this world of ours
the one that cheers the heart
is laughing dope tears

11.

If I revel
in this present life—O Marijuana
I may well be a bird
I may well be a flea

12.

All creatures that live
in the end shall die
well, then, while I live
it's pleasure for me

13.

Calm & knowing ways
these are not for me
I'd rather freak-out
with dope-sodden glee!

MARLENE DOBKIN DE RIOS
1939–

Marlene Dobkin de Rios. "I noticed as I drank that Antonio, to be sure that the 'gringa' got her share of visions, gave me a cup brim-full of the not so pleasant-smelling liquid."

To trip or not to trip? As an anthropologist, Marlene Dobkin de Rios was expected to maintain professional objectivity. As the lone *gringa* in a small village in the Peruvian Amazon, she was isolated from her culture and whatever support it could lend if the potent jungle brew proved too much for her psyche.

After five months of gathering data on the ritual use of ayahuasca (yagé) and after an "aesthetically rewarding" LSD trip, de Rios drank a brimful cup of the bitter hallucinogenic beverage.

Her account is the first published by a woman on the ayahuasca experience and is the culmination of her book, *Visionary Vine* (1971).

From Visionary Vine: Psychedelic Healing in the Peruvian Amazon

When I spent three months in 1967 studying mescaline healing on the Peruvian coast, I observed several ritual sessions where I was invited to drink the hallucinogenic potion. Yet, although it was readily available to me, I must admit that I was frightened, in fact horrified to imagine all the terrible things that self-knowledge might bring me. Sure as I was that I was harboring all sorts of incurable neuroses within, I hesitated and decided not to try the San Pedro brew. Many rationalizations sprung to mind—time was short and I might have bad side-effects. What would I do if the aftereffects were so severe that I couldn't continue my work? I felt alone, and what would happen if my self-protective shield was knocked over? And so, despite the kindly offers of my informants and the healers I visited, I resolved not to try the mescaline cactus.

When I returned home and wrote up my field experiences about San Pedro use, it seemed as though I had somehow missed the point. In October 1967, I was invited to participate in a conference sponsored by the R. Bucke Society in Montreal, Canada. Bucke was a Canadian psychiatrist who coined the term cosmic consciousness. The society which bore his name was concerned with religious and mystical states in which Bucke showed much interest, despite the general disdain and scorn such matters still hold for many serious scientists. At the meeting, after listening to various participants discuss some aspect of the question, "Do Psychedelic Drugs have Religious Significance?" I realized that the reality I reported on was quite a different one than that of people who used such substances for mystical or religious purposes. By the time I returned to Peru in June of 1968 to begin my ayahuasca study, I sensed that if I were ever to go beyond the detachment that I had so carefully cultivated, I would have to take ayahuasca myself.

Yet, as the months passed and opportunities presented themselves to try ayahuasca, I still managed to avoid the experience. Finally, the time approached for me to leave Iquitos to participate in a symposium on "Hallucinogens and Shamanism," which was to be held at the American Anthropological Association's annual meeting in Seattle, Washington. I knew that I would be addressing a large group of my colleagues about a substance which, in truth, I had to admit I knew very little. Although I had been collecting data for almost five months on ayahuasca, it was really just hearsay evidence. I often had the smug feeling that I was the only sane person in an insane world. Resolved then finally to take the plunge, I decided first to take advantage of the availability of a small dose of 100 micrograms of LSD, which my colleague and I originally planned to give to the healers we worked with at the end of our study. Unfortunately, this plan did not materialize, as legal production of such substances was terminated. Nonetheless, I was able to take the LSD at home under medical supervision, albeit in the comfort of my Iquitos house, surrounded by the music I liked, with a friend as company and in the presence of paintings, folk art, and flowers. Two weeks later I took an unknown dose of ayahuasca mixed with *chacruna* (probably containing DMT) under the supervision of don Antonio. My experience with LSD was simply one of the most aesthetically rewarding experiences I have ever had in my life. Accompanied by eighteenth century harp music which seemed endless in its reception, I could not really describe the aesthetic dimensions of the fast-moving kaleidoscopic visions, although many medieval images probably invoked by the quality of the music filled my vision. As the height of these pseudo-illusions lessened, I found myself discussing who I was, what I was doing, what I wanted from life, what life meant to me, and a series of questions that I hadn't been concerned with since I was a teenager. I might point out that at the beginning of the session, upon the advice of a friend, I decided to *ponerme en blanco*—or simply, to flow with the force of the experience. From my readings about drug experiments, I knew that a common feature of the "bad trip" was the resistance that a person might offer in attempting to hold back or try to control the drug's effects.

When I took ayahuasca, the previous LSD experience stood me in good stead in that my book-learned expectations had been replaced by the real thing. It was with enthusiastic expectation that I met don Antonio one Monday night, along with my colleague, to take the ayahuasca brew that had been prepared for me.

That evening in Belén, Antonio was even busier than usual, attending to the many patients who came to him to be exorcised or treated for assorted ailments. I sat patiently for over an hour, chatting with my colleague, Dr. Rios, who had just returned from a brief trip to Lima. He was full of details about the people we knew. Finally, Antonio led us through a maze of houses to a distant reach of Venecia, where a friend of his allowed him to use his floating balsa house for our session. Two other people were present, but I paid very little attention to them in my nervousness.

We got comfortably seated on the floor of the house, and Antonio passed the potion around. I noticed as I drank that Antonio, to be sure that the "gringa" got her full share of visions, gave me a cup brim-full of the not so pleasant-smelling liquid. Others who drank that night, in retrospect, seemed to have been given a much smaller amount.

The following is an account of what happened.

About ten minutes later, feelings of strangeness came over my body and I had difficulty in coordinating extremities. Quick-arriving visual forms and movements flit before my eyes some twenty minutes after taking the drink, and a certain amount of anxiety that was not difficult to handle was felt, especially when Halloween-type demons in primary reds, greens and blues loomed large and then receded before me. Very fast-moving imagery almost like Bosch's paintings appeared, which at times were difficult to focus upon. At one point after I touched the arm of my friend for reassurance, the primary colors changed to flaming yellows and pinks, as a cornucopia full of warmth filled the visions before my eyes and gave me a sort of peripheral vision extending toward the person I had touched. Then in harmony with the healer's *schacapa*, a series of leaf-faced visions appeared, while my eyes remained open. They were followed by a full-length colored vision of a Peruvian woman, unknown to me but sneering in my direction, which appeared before me. Then more visions arrived, followed by heavy vomiting and diarrhea which lasted for about three hours.

In New York, where I grew up, vomiting was hardly anything to celebrate, and I remember my concern at the terrible noises I made with the "dry heaves" that afflicted me. Yet, later on, when chatting with others, I realized that in the rain forest, people periodically induced vomiting in their children so as to purge them of the various parasitical illnesses which are rampant in the region. My colleague told me later on that don Antonio in his subsequent healing sessions would often refer to the gringa who had vomited heavily with ayahuasca and the terrible noises she made. He even imitated me to the great amusement of his audience.

Throughout the experience, any light was painful to my eyes. Time was experienced as very slow-moving. After-effects included physical weakness for a day or two, but a general sense of well-being and looseness in dealing with others.

At this point, it might be interesting to examine some of my experiences under ayahuasca, since my own lack of a cultural expectation toward the use of such a substance gave me differing responses than those reported by the informants with whom I worked, despite the fact that I had been collecting data on informants' visions. No jungle creatures filled my vision, nor did I experience the often-reported floating sensation. The visions I had contained symbols of my own culture. The unknown woman who appeared to me in my vision was dressed very much like the urban poor among whom I worked, but she somehow looked more opulent and well-off than many of the near-starving friends I had made in Belén. I remember my curiosity at her apparent dislike of me and that she should behave in that manner, but I didn't pay much attention to the vision nor did it change my mood at all. Later on, when telling of my experiences to friends in Belén, some ventured that this woman who appeared to me may have been responsible for a parasitic illness I developed during the course of my work. I could see how people appearing before a sick person might easily be linked to malice regardless of whether or not they are known to the patient. Had I grown up in this society and received continual conditioning toward a belief in a magical source of sickness, it is quite probable that I would have interpreted this vision as a revelation of who it was that caused me to become ill.

When I took ayahuasca, I was unaware of the unwritten rule about not touching another person. I was later told by the healer who guided my ayahuasca session that I had received a double dose of the potion by touching another person and magically had the experience of two doses. The vomiting and diarrhea that afflicted me, thus, were my own fault for not following precepts that were unknown to me.

✳   ✳   ✳

The feelings of well-being that dogged my steps for several months after the ayahuasca experience were one area, however, that did overlap with my informants' reports. Many people agree that the ayahuasca experience stays with them for a long time, relaxing them and making their dealings with others somewhat more easy and fruitful.

BARBARA MYERHOFF
1935–

The peyote hunt is the sacred journey of the Huichol Indians, and the core of their religion. Barbara Myerhoff and Peter Furst were the first anthropologists to accompany the Huichols on their arduous pilgrimage across the Mexican desert.

To prepare for this, Myerhoff eats a dozen peyote buttons under the guidance of Ramón Medina Silva, the tribal *mara'akame*, or shaman. She experiences a "Steppenwolf-like magical theater" of hallucinations that shows her the limitations of her "Western rationality." She is ready for the peyote hunt.

From Peyote Hunt: The Sacred Journey of the Huichol Indians

I returned to Guadalajara and continued working with Ramón and Lupe the following summer. We took up where we had left off, with daily taping sessions and holding lengthy planned interviews and unplanned conversations and observation.

At the end of a formal session one afternoon, I attempted to resume a conversation begun earlier inside the hut about *ti peyote*, "Our peyote," or *hikuri*, as Ramón called it affectionately, the hallucinogenic plant which plays such a central role in the religion. "Ramón," I asked, "what would I see if I were to eat peyote?" "Do you want to?" he replied unexpectedly. "Yes, very much." "Then come tomorrow, very early and eat nothing tonight or tomorrow. Only drink a little warm water when you get up in the morning." The Huichols, unlike the neighboring Cora and Tarahumara Indians, have no fear of peyote. Ordinary men, women, and children take it frequently with no sickness or frighten-

Barbara Myerhoff. "I asked it the question, *the one that had not been out of my mind for months. 'What do the myths* mean?'"

ing visions, as long as the peyote they use has been gathered properly during an authentic peyote hunt. Ramón assured me that the experience in store for me would be beautiful and important and I trusted him and his knowledge completely by this time.

The next morning he led me into the little hut and began feeding me the small green "buttons" or segments, one after another, perhaps a dozen or more in all. He cut each segment away from the large piece he held and prepared it in no way that I could see, for the small pieces I was given retained all their skin, dirt, and root. The tiny fuzzy white-gray hairs that top each segment were intact and only the small bottommost portion of the root had been pared off. The buttons were very chewy and tough, and unspeakably bitter-sour. My mouth flooded with saliva and shriveled from the revolting flavor, but no nausea came. "Chew well," Ramón urged me. "It is good, like a tortilla, isn't it?" But I was no longer able to answer.

After giving me what he felt was the proper dosage, Ramón indicated that he was going to wait outside and directed me to lie down quietly and close my eyes. For a long time I heard him singing and playing his little violin and then there were new sounds of comings and goings and soft laughter. "They've all come to stare at me and laugh," I thought. "Come on," I imagined them saying to each other. "Peek inside, we've got a *gringa* in there and we've given her a weed. You can get those anthropologists to eat anything if you tell them it's sacred. She thinks she's going to have a vision!"

But these thoughts were more amusing than ominous, for I really did not believe that Ramón would deceive me. After an inestimable period of time I began to be aware of a growing euphoria; I was flooded with feelings of goodwill. With great delight I began to notice sounds, especially the noises of the trucks passing on the highway outside. Although I discovered that I couldn't move, I was able to remain calm when it occurred to me that this was of no consequence because there was no other place that I wanted to be. My body assumed the rhythm of the passing trucks, gently wafting up and down like a scarf in a breeze. Time and space evaporated as I floated about in the darkness

and vague images began to develop. I realized that I could keep track of what was happening to me and remember it if I thought of it not as a movie-like flow of time but as a discrete series of events like beads on a string. I could go from one to the next and though the first was perhaps out of sight, it had not disappeared as do events in ordinary chronology. It was like a carnival with booths spread about to which I could always return to regain an experience, a Steppenwolf-like magical theater. The problem of retaining my experience was thus solved. There remained only the hazard of getting lost. But Ramón had prepared me for this; though he was outside the hut, I felt that as my guide and craftsman, he had left me a thread by means of which I could trace and retrace my peregrinations through the labyrinth and thus return safely from any far-flung destination. Assured by this notion, I started out.

The first "booth" found me impaled on an enormous tree with its roots buried far below the earth and its branches rising beyond sight, toward the sky. This was the Tree of Life, the *axis mundi* or world pole which penetrates the layers of the cosmos, connecting earth with underworld and heaven, on which shamans ascend in their magical flights. The image was exactly the same as a Mayan glyph which I was to come across for the first time several years after this vision occurred.

In the next sequence, I beheld a tiny speck of brilliant red flitting about a forest darkness. The speck grew as it neared. It was a vibrant bird who, with an insouciant flicker, landed on a rock. It was Ramón as psychopomp, as Papageno—half-man, magic bird, bubbling with excitement. He led me to the next episode which presented an oracular, gnomelike creature of macabre viscosity. I asked it *the question*, the one that had not been out of my mind for months, "What do the myths *mean?*" He offered his reply in mucid tones, melting with a deadly portentousness that mocked my seriousness. "The myths signify—nothing. They mean *themselves.*" Of course! They *were* themselves, nothing equivalent, nothing translated, nothing taken from another more familiar place to distort them. They had to be accepted in their own terms. I was embarrassed that as an aspirant anthropologist I had to be told this basic axiom of the discipline, but I was amused and relieved for in a vague way I had known it all along.

My journey ended many booths later, as I sat concentrating on a mythical little animal, aware that the entire experience was drawing to a close. The little fellow and I had entered a yarn painting and he sat precisely in the middle of the composition. I watched him fade and finally disappear into a hole and I made an extra effort to concentrate on him, convinced that a final lesson—a grand conclusion—was about to occur. Just as he vanished, an image flicked into the corner of my vision. In the upper righthand quadrant of the painting, another being had just jumped out of sight. I had missed him and *he* was the message. There it was! I had lost my lesson by looking for it too directly, with dead-center tight focus, with will and impatience. It was a practice which I knew was fatal to understanding anything truly unique. It was my Western rationality, honed by formal study, eager to simplify, clarify, dissect, define, categorize, and analyze. These techniques, exercised prematurely, are antithetical to good ethnographic work and this I was to learn and learn and forget and relearn. The message could emerge anywhere on the canvas; one had to be alert, patient, receptive to whatever might occur, at any moment, in whatever ambiguous, unpredictable form it assumed, reserving interpretation for a later time. In the years to come, the vision was to serve as my mnemonic for this principle and help me keep it in the foreground of my consciousness for all that was ahead.

SARA DAVIDSON
1943–

The following vignette from Sara Davidson's social history of the sixties perceptively describes the way a drug experience can provide an indi-

vidual with insight into her behavior patterns. The protagonist's MDA experience enables her to liberate herself from a repressive relationship. A body psychedelic popularly known as "the love drug," MDA often enhances emotional receptivity. Easily transcending her anxiety and resentment, a "stunned, amazed and euphoric" Sara realizes that her lover "had his own path to follow and that was perfect."

From Loose Change: Three Women of the Sixties

There was a lull in the seas on Twenty-third Street as 1972 began. Michael sent me roses on my twenty-ninth birthday. In his dreams he saw us soaring in a helium balloon, laughing and waving at the cheering throngs below. We made love with more ease and spontaneity than we had in several years. We decided to stop using birth control. We decided to take a psychedelic—MDA—it would be the first trip for both of us. Michael's openness, the fact that he was willing to explore a new realm with me, made me hopeful for our future.

During our winter vacation in Palm Springs, we lapsed into easy ritual. In the morning, he would awaken first, drive to the Spa and on his return, come and sit on my bed, bringing me a glass of fresh-squeezed orange juice and a plate of chocolate cake. We would play tennis, sun-bathe nude on the patio, then walk to the pool where he would gather me in his arms in the water and carry me around and around the shallow end.

"I'm dizzy," I laughed.

"No you're not, just relax." He put his face close to mine, then sang to me softly, "It was a very good year."

From the cold pool we went to the jacuzzi. "The pool is wonderful. Everything is perfect," Michael said. "Oh, Sara, this is what I want in life—to live in this beautiful desert."

By 11 P.M. he was in bed, holding his radio on his chest as the radio sputtered the news and the

Sara Davidson. "For the next six hours I lay on my back, stunned, amazed and euphoric."

next day's weather. "Saaaa-ra," he would call. "Come in here." I would turn out the lights and slip into his arms.

We planned to take the MDA on our second-to-last day. We had been assured by a friend who had taken the drug many times that, unlike acid, "it never produces a bad trip." As the day approached, though, Michael grew jumpy. "I'll be thrown into an institution. I'll never be able to think straight again." Dr. Pearl, he said, had warned him the drug would trigger an irreversible psychotic break-down.

"For God's sake, you weren't going to tell Dr. Pearl. You knew what he would say, he's hysterical on this subject."

Michael shrugged. "I told him."

So I took the drug, and Michael sat with me for a while but then he wanted to swim and lie in the sun and I told him to go ahead.

For the next six hours I lay on my back, stunned, amazed and euphoric. I could see my body from above and across the room. My mind spun and whirled, there was no holding on, the pictures and sounds flickered by as if someone were punching remote-control buttons. I heard singers and choruses in my head: James Taylor, "Love has brought me around," the Incredible String Band, "All will be one."

In the middle of the day Michael walked inside dripping with water in his black bathing suit. I saw him as a child, his limbs were transparent and his eyes incandescent with joy. He made love to me and although my nerves were disconnected, I felt us uniting at the roots. I stared at his face with complete accepting love. He had his own path to follow and that was perfect. All his tricks, his flamboyance, his playing and double dealing were his dance. It had begun long ago before I knew him and would continue regardless of what I thought or felt.

I saw, also, that I had never let myself blow up at him. So I whittled away, a little each day.

"Ho hum," I heard inside my head. It was a long buzzing sound, Hooooo hummmmmm, like the signals that humpback whales send out when cruising the deep.

I laughed. Michael laughed back. He was the sun. I was the moon. My voyage was darker. Hooooo hum.

He was loving and playful as he passed in and out of the room. He said he wasn't frightened anymore and wanted to take a trip with me soon. But I learned, months later, that he had reported just the opposite to Dr. Pearl: the drug had made me crazed and, worse, I had wasted a spectacular day of sun.

SUSAN NADLER
1947–

This excerpt of Susan Nadler's personal account, which was written while she was doing time in a Mexican prison, captures the moment when the smuggler's paranoia is strongest. Nadler's intuition is more developed than her lover Andrew's and their friend's, but their attempt to smuggle 250 kilos of Moroccan hashish in an armoire in the hope of each making four thousand dollars results in the arrests of all three.

Money sent by family and friends in the States enabled the author to buy her freedom after she served two years of a much longer sentence.

From **The Butterfly Convention**

Anyhow, the three of us conspirators—me doubling over in pain and tired from the debilitating heroin I had snorted last night, Andrew, trying to be cool—cool fool sitting on a hill, and Ted, wondering if his goddam ass is covered—we call Aero Cargo and discover that the package was indeed there, but we need 700 pesos or $56 to cover the taxes. For a minute I feel a huge, uncontrollable wave of paranoia overtake me and I want out—out of this bullshit riff of waiting and never knowing if we're being watched—and you know the ol' story—if you get busted overseas, you're in for the hassle of your life—and Mexico, for all intents and purposes, is definitely overseas. And I want to run away and forget my $4,000, and my arms with tracks marks all over them, and the man I supposedly loved, who lived in a world of pipe dreams. But only for a minute because I knew I was in too far. So Ted scrapes together about 300 pesos and some French francs from Morocco and we all pile into the Safari and head for town to cash a check and I get the eeriest feeling that someone is watching me—but Andrew assures me that it's only paranoia creeping up—and to keep my disease to myself because paranoia is a disease—a communicable one—you have it and to get rid of it you pass it on, brother. And on the way into town Ted explains that the so-called package is, in reality, 250 kilos of hash built into an armoire. And it should weigh 500 pounds altogether, he was a few pounds short—and he sent it out himself and there is glass in the doors and intricate carvings all over. Well—we three ain't dummies—and we know we can't haul the armoire in a Safari jeep, so we hurriedly head for José Cortezar father's mattress factory. There we find José passed out and green, nodded out under a tree. "Hey brother" (brother my ass), "we need you for a leetle while." And Andrew and Teddy explain to José that a package has come in—they don't need to explain what it is—he nods—and a smile slips on his face—he too gets turned on by the idea of smuggling—sure, man— he will get a truck and four of his father's workers to help us unload it. Smuggling is like a drug in itself. The excitement and the fear get you as stoned, if not more so, as any drug. I always had the Mata Hari complex. Suddenly, I just don't want to be around. I want to go to the beach and swim and lie in the sun—but Ted insists that I go—just to keep it in the family . . . again, paranoia, please brother—ol' misery sure 'nough loves its company. So we meet José at the casa—me in a tiny top and cut-offs, Andrew in his hat and Ted in his pants and shirt—we make tracks for the office of Aero Cargo in José's truck. I really didn't want to be there, and I pray to whoever may be there listening to get me out of this. At Aero Cargo there is an overabundance of workers and *hombres* but we walk with our heads held high—no pun intended—I mean we were on top of the world—temporarily, man, so temporarily. Everyone is staring so hard at us—and I know that Ted is trying to avoid being noticed—he keeps to the paneling of the office wall, leaving Andrew to pick up the package, which is in his name. Andrew pays the taxes—he is sweating so much now—and I take his hand, because I know that he is weak, and trying so hard not to show it. And Ted is very businesslike as José and his four helpers lift up the extraordinarily heavy package and put it on the truck. Suddenly Ted panics and whispers to me, "Susan, it's a goddam new crate it's in—I packed the armoire and it wasn't in that crate—it's brand new, I never saw it before," as if I can come up with the answers. This debonair businessman, this big-time con artist turns absolutely beige and really, I mean this is no joke, I wish that I had a picture—his hair stands up and he really looks like a goddam chicken with his beaked nose. I say, "Hey man, let's pass on this deal and leave the friggin' dope here until we can figure it out." But greed triumphs as usual as Ted decides, well, maybe the Mexicans broke the crate and had to make a new one. Because he assures me, sweat on the backs of his hands, the package never went through the U.S. Customs, but directly from Tangier to Mexico and after all, what can we do now? Andrew is too busy helping José to notice the newness of the crate and Ted neglects to tell him. I mean, after all, who is Andrew except the flunky who will bear all the responsibility if anything happens, because the package is in his name? And we

wave good-by to all the people at the Aero Cargo office, not realizing that about one-quarter of them are police. The drive back to the apartment is very quiet—except for José who chatters all the way, stoned and ignorant of the situation. I guess ignorance might be bliss after all.

Once we return to the apartment, all the workers and José and Andrew have the unenviable task of uncrating the armoire and bringing it up the steps. Ted and I run ahead—throw out all the grass in the apartment but two joints, which I hide in my make-up case along with two mandrax. We stash the cocaine and household heroin in silver foil high in the closet, where I imagine it still is. Then I make fruit salad for lunch and snort the cocaine we left out. The armoire finally comes into the apartment. Four tired Mexican peons, one now definitely exhausted José Cortezar, one pooped-out Andrew, and the metadirector Ted deposit one of the most beautiful pieces of furniture I have ever seen in our living room. I give tall glasses of lemonade to all the workers and thank José, who is leaving for Ensenada in two hours. He flies out the door, and finally Andrew and I collapse in the middle of the floor with Ted pacing up and down, looking suspiciously out the window.

The armoire is a fine example of the lost art of woodcarving. It's about nine feet tall and five feet wide and the front of it is carved delicately with small figures, deer and goats. And I say to Ted, "Where the hell is the hash?" And he smiles to himself and walks over to the armoire looking more calm and less like a scared rabbit, because he is back in his role of he-man-adventurer smuggler. We stand on a chair and I see that the whole top and bottom of the armoire are false, full of hidden shit—so to speak. Suddenly, Ted turns green again, his hair stands up like little blades of dried-out grass and he whispers, "Someone goddam opened this, I can tell—it's not the finished color of the armoire. Now it all fits, the unfamiliar crating and the smiling Mexicans and I'm getting the fuck out of here." Filled with fear, he thinks only of himself—and gentle Andrew poor soul, he is cool, man, and not to be daunted in his hour of triumph, he says, "Hey man, relax, we both know that the package never went through U.S. Customs, and if they had wanted to bust us we would never have received the package." And me, free me, I have to pee fast and remember the day, two years long gone, when Ivan and I were met by the F.B.I. and I cry because as I try to put everything in context and remember, I have the electrifying realization that soon I will only remember. I stay in the bathroom a long time, feeling myself marooned. It's June, and I feel another lousy riff coming on. And as I walk back into the other room I hear Ted droning on, ". . . and man I've seen too many TV shows and I know the trip—get hip—if they want us, we are right now surrounded—they're only waiting for us to open up the panels and remove the hash. So let's get out of this place—maybe they'll forget our faces. Also, remember, Andrew and Susan, they can't get us for something that we didn't do, for all we know the package was a gift to Andrew from a friend in Morocco—and we're cool (cool fool sitting on a hill) since we have no idea what's in the armoire." And the chicken putters into the other room and says he wants to make reservations to leave that night—and I have the disease (paranoia) bad—I say to Andrew, "Honey I'm scared that they have us. Let's go to town and make reservations to leave (why the fuck aren't I at the beach?) and stay away until we feel that the vibes are O.K." And Andrew chuckles and languorously stretches out without a single doubt, like he's home free, and says to me, "Baby, you and your paranoid buddy Ted (my buddy?), you two fly out of here tonight and I'll stay here for a few days to make sure that everything is fine—go and get your passport and visa and open tickets—we'll drive to town, make reservations, and you'll be safe in L.A. tonight." I start to think, something here stinks, why wouldn't he let me go yesterday. But at this point, ladies and gents, I went to collect my papers, follow my instincts, and split. I was so nervous I never even put shoes on—I took one mandrax to cool myself down—pulled my hair back, and in cut-offs and a little top (as usual) headed for the car with Andrew and Ted. The mandrax was just starting to take its effect and the three of us walked to the jeep. Ted—almost visibly shaking, got in the back, Andrew got in the driver's seat, and (did I remember to lock the door?) I was just climbing into my seat when I looked up and saw a huge

Mexican, about six-two, with a mustache, a sombrero, and a machine gun—and I looked at Andrew and he looked at me and I looked at him and he looked at me and I said out loud, "Do you believe this?" And suddenly there were thirty Mexican police. It was hard to tell exactly how many since all of them were *Federales* not dressed in uniforms; and thirty machine guns and pistols and the heat, and I'm getting thrown against a car and being frisked (a little stoned by now, yelling "Hey man, what the fuck do you think do you think you're doing?"), but no one understood English and handcuffs on *Señor* Andrew—the package was in his name and someone in God's name help me—keep it cool on the outside Susan—I mean really, what is going on? And an older man, maybe forty-five or so with a mustache and a .38 revolver asks me (Jesus—it seemed like everyone in town had gathered around our apartment building and was watching—screaming) for the key—and I don't want to go into my purse because I have grass there—keep cool—God help me to hold onto my purse—and it was like a goddam movie—the police acted like we were Bonnie and Clyde. And they break down the door—and all this Spanish talk and pandemonium and four of the big *Federales* push Ted (who has totally blown it and is hysterical by now and whispers to me "Don't tell them a thing, cry, act innocent—ask them why are they here?"), and I remember the joints in my purse, however, at this point I'm stoned on my downer and belligerent as hell—and two of the *hombres* identify themselves as American F.B.I. men and casually say to me, "Congratulations, girlie—you are part of the first hash bust ever in the Baja—and you're in for the longest and hottest summer of yer life." Andrew is handcuffed and crying, "Honey, I'm sorry, I know you've seen this movie before." I can't cry, but as I watch the four *Federales* take hatchets and break into the armoire on the top and the bottom looking for the dope I maneuver my hand into my purse, unzip my make-up case—keeping my eyes on as many of the cops as I can—slip out the two joints and mandrax and stash the joints behind the pillows of the sofa. At least they can't grab me for possession—so I thought! And no one sees me—only Andrew and he winks at me. The sweat is pouring off his face now, and since he is handcuffed and unable to wipe it off he asks me to. As I do, the older gentleman asks me if I know what is coming out of the armoire in kilo bags (only the best hash he'll ever see) and I say no—and another man—this one older, less fluent in English, and definitely more belligerent-looking, is checking out Ted's arms for needle marks. Ted never had the guts to shoot a B-B gun, let alone dope—and I wonder if this is it for me, with enough track marks on my arms to sponsor a roller derby, but he sees only deep tan and some rather large black-and-blue marks—and a man who identifies himself, amid all the noise of hatchets and yelling, as the district prosecutor of Baja—he looks at me rather softly and says, "Susan (how the hell does he know my name unless they have been watching me?), Susan, do you know how serious this is?" And I hostilely spit out, "I don't know what's going on here, what is this all about?" (He's now going through my clothes—at least the house is clean of drugs.) "I demand my rights." And he asks me why I don't cry and I answer that I have nothing to fear, I am innocent. Meanwhile, the two American F.B.I. motherfuckers are telling me that I have to give them the name of someone to call in the States for me because I won't be able to get near a phone, and anyway the lines are never working—and I say no—I don't need help—I'm protected, my good karma will get me out—and one says to Andrew, "O.K., Buster, who should we call for her?" and Andrew gives them my parents' phone number and for the first time I feel fears well up because they can't possibly go through this again. The apartment is now in a shambles—the drawers are on the floor—the clothes are everywhere—the music and books all over—I can't bear the pain. The district prosecutor tells us to go to the car now—we are being taken to jail. So we are marched down the stairs and they try to handcuff me and (still hostile from my downer) I kick out—and they laugh—I see one of many *policía* pocket my locket, given to me by my father on my sixth birthday and inscribed "To Susan Beth," and I scream out at this thief, but no one cares. I am just another prisoner without rights and there are hundreds of Mexicans looking for action gathered outside our house. I see Mr. Cortezar in the corner, shaking his head. Oh, the

gossip now, and I wonder where José is, but my thoughts are interrupted by the friggin' F.B.I. man telling me that in Mexico you are guilty until proven innocent. Andrew, Ted, and I are shown into a yellow VW, I can't believe they put us together. Ted says, "Baby, keep your mouth tight. We'll get you out of here—you just don't know a thing." Andrew tells me not to worry, the brothers will get us out—and we do have such good karma. This reality crashed down so quickly—good-by you dreamers, good-by—the realities sure do change. There is a great disparity between the dream and the fact.

The drive to the jail is short; everything is very close in La Paz. The jail, or Edificio M. Sobarzo, is an old hospital with thick walls and a lot of police hanging around outside. They take us out of the car at gunpoint, it is around four o'clock now, and I scream for Andrew to come with me. He is dragged away and the district prosecutor takes my purse and finally looks through—stops and takes out my make-up case, now empty of drugs. He then looks over my diary and I get weak in the knees—all my notes about methedrine madness and heroin. He confiscates it and I am led to a cell isolated from the rest of the jail. There are at least thirty male eyes following me—the cell they lead me to looks very small—perhaps it is a single cell for me alone. I start to panic as they open up the huge barred door and push me into a dark hole—good-by sunlight, good-by dark-eyed girl, you were so free so free, and the door swings shut with me wondering what in the fuck is going on.

LISA ALTHER
1944–

In Lisa Alther's first novel, *Kinflicks* (1975), the heroine's guide and would-be lover, suddenly envious of her transcendent state, terminates her first LSD trip with a shot of the tranquilizer Thorazine while she is blissfully peaking. The following is her recounting of the experience.

From Kinflicks

In several staggered flashes of insight, like flashbulbs popping around a celebrity, I understood the Cartesian mind/body split. I also understood Beauty and Truth and Ultimate Reality. Unfortunately, I lacked the words to explain it all to poor Hawk, who sat huddled in woeful ignorance beside me. In fact, I concluded that there was nothing that I *didn't* now understand. My thoughts raced and swirled like darting birds, linking up in ever more intricate patterns and tying all existence into one neat bundle of interchangeable subatomic particles, all activated into the appearance of a cosmos by . . . *me!* In short, I was God. I could create and destroy this world by nothing more taxing than a simple act of will. I laughed munificently, as befits a resident deity.

Then I stopped laughing. Yes, it was true: I had transcended even laughter. With serene clarity, I surveyed all that I had created, and I found it good. Never mind trivia like wars and poverty and injustice. They were merely chimera. Bishop Berkeley in Philosophy 108 had been right all along. I had conjured up the entire world for my private entertainment. Rape and murder were merely my divine stag films. Only I existed. Neat and marvelous me! Oblivious to piddling human emotions, able to regard the multiple miseries of existence with detached amusement, I had clearly arrived at the pinnacle of spiritual evolution, and was in imminent danger of becoming the world's leading citizen.

After several centuries, spent basking in the glow of my moral perfection, I happened to glance up and see Mr. Army Deserter himself, hiding his shame behind his bushy beard, swaying above me and holding a gleaming syringe the size of a Nike missile. He reached down and unzipped my jeans. I shrieked with laughter at the idea that he thought he could screw God. He had had his chance when I was a mere mortal, and he had turned me down. Now that I had become a deity it was out of the question. I pushed his hands away.

"I'm going to inject this in your hip to bring you down," he thundered, jabbing me through my jeans.

Down it did bring me. Down and down and down. Spiraling down from heaven and into the murky twilight depths of hell. A fashion show was in progress, featuring the Seven Deadly Sins—Miss Malice, Miss Greed. They were all actually me.

PAT CARR
1932–

In "Mermaids Singing," a marijuana cigarette is a "sort of deus ex marijuana" for a middle-aged woman attempting to bridge the generation gap with a young man her son's age. She wants to demystify her husband's affair with a younger woman. The conscious hedonism of sixties' marijuana smokers is compared to the sex-and-alcohol syndrome of "mudfast fifties' morality."

Pat Carr. ". . . it was her one chance to see what it was all about, all the things Alec constantly raved over, the new awakening, the new consciousness, freedom, everything . . ."

The light comedy of the heroine rolling and smoking her first joint gradually turns to psychological drama.

The story appeared in Pat Carr's prize-winning collection, *The Women in the Mirror* (1977).

"Mermaids Singing"

"It's pretty strong stuff, Mrs. Estes." He looked at her dubiously, holding a fat brown cigarette in each palm.

"There's some heroin mixed with the shi—er, a—the grass," he said floundering for a word.

"That's all right, Philip." She lifted it from his hand, careful to keep the ends rolled. It resembled a plump dried tropical fish.

"Okay. If you say so, Mrs. Estes." Then, "Have you got any records? We could use a beat with this."

"There's some stuff Reed left. Over there."

He knelt down and dealt the record jackets out like cards, found one that he carefully arranged on the console. He glanced back at her. "Here," he said coming back quickly. "You hold it like this."

"Are you sure this will smoke?"

"Oh, yes, ma'am."

He brought out a gold Dunhill that seemed so incongruous with the self-rolled dark papered cigarettes that she had to smile.

"Like this?" she said to cover the smile, not to hurt his feelings.

He nodded, intent on steadying the flame against the twisted paper point.

"Cup your hands around it and draw in like you were breathing in steam, or something," he said, briskly lighting his own.

She sucked her breath and the already thick smoke from the dry burning leaves grated the lining of her throat and made her eyes water. She swallowed, reswallowed, trying not to cough.

He sat opposite her, hunched over his own cigarette, inhaling ritually, with his eyes shut.

She'd never learned how to inhale ordinary fil-

ter cigarettes, and the new harshness searing her throat was unpleasant. But it was her one chance to try it. She knew she could never call and ask him to come again and it was her one chance to see what it was all about, all the things Alec constantly raved over, the new awakening, the new consciousness, freedom, everything Alec said their generation, and particularly she, had missed with their mudfast fifties' morality, her one chance, and she was determined to go through with it.

She drew in hard and held the smoke trapped in her chest.

Philip was leaning back, still inhaling with his eyes shut, cupping the plump dry cigarette with practiced hands. It was amazing how much he resembled her son Reed there in that fireplace chair. It was amazing how much they all looked alike with their hair long to their shoulders like that. She couldn't remember boys in her college days all fading into such a sameness even though they all had short hair, but perhaps it was because these kids were so commonly healthy and all had such straight teeth.

"Feel anything yet?" He was looking at her.

"Not yet."

"How about if we move over to the couch, Mrs. Estes, and I can see up close how you're doing it? You should begin to feel something pretty soon if you're doing it right."

"My name's Laura, Philip." She stood up, aware that she'd almost called him Reed.

"Yes, ma—, uh, Laura."

They sat down on the crushed velvet, close, and he put his own cigarette in the ashtray, placed his hands around hers as he guided the rolled damp paper toward her mouth.

His hands completely covered hers and she looked at them as they came closer to her face. The fingers were long and the nails square, gleaming. It had been a long time since anyone had held her hands, and she felt a vibrating, pulsating in her elbows, temples.

She inhaled obediently, swallowing the smoke.

"Good girl."

He kept his hands on hers for one more drag, then picked up his own. "Just relax and don't think about it. Let it happen."

They smoked silently for what seemed a long time, but when she looked at the cigarette in her fingers, the ash was hardly longer than when she'd sat down.

"Why did you want to do this, Mrs., uh, Laura? Does Mr. E. know?"

"Alec won't be back from his trip until late tonight."

"But why did you want to . . . you know?"

She looked at him, his blue eyes slightly glazed, but serious, intent on her face, and it didn't seem to matter if she told him the truth, it didn't seem to matter how much or what she said.

"He's having an affair with a younger woman."

He nodded.

"His partner's wife. Young, very much . . ." She couldn't think of the word. ". . . very much attuned," she said finally, "to expression, communication, the idea that sex is just another way of relating to people. She and Alec see each other a couple of times a week and he tells me about their relationship. She's apparently very honest and open, and Alec says that it's only the conventions that are getting in the way of my understanding and enjoyment. He wants me to . . . They smoke, and . . . well, you know," she finished lamely and took another harsh pull on the cigarette.

He was nodding.

It was the first time she'd said anything to anyone, and it was more difficult than she'd thought. It was hard putting it in words, thick lumped words as heavy as modelling clay, and as she was saying them, she realized she didn't understand at all.

He looked lazily down at his cigarette. "It'd be better if we had a roach clip to get the rest of this, but I guess that's probably enough. It's pretty strong and we don't want to get too much." He seemed to be speaking very softly and slowly. "Too much of anything is too much."

She hadn't noticed before, but looking down she saw the cigarette was short, hot on her fingers. She nodded at him and carefully put the stub in the ashtray, her hand floating free, uncoordinated.

"Okay?"

She nodded and leaned back.

His arm was over the back of the sofa and he touched her hair.

"Alec says they're merely good friends."

"M-m-m-m-m-m."

"He talks about it quite as if it's the most natural thing in the world. But I can't seem to understand. Sex isn't like shaking hands in the street, is it?"

He leaned over her slowly and put his mouth over hers even as she had it open to add another word.

His lips and tongue were moist, surprisingly experienced.

"I—"

"Sh-h-h."

She felt light under him, that he was buoyant above her, their bodies touching and yet not touching as though they were covered by transparent casing, glass sheaths bridging the space between them, her mind filled with swirling reds, oranges, sunflower bursts of magenta. The long hair was strange, awkward, tangling in her hands, womanish, out of place around the male chest that pressed down, away, down, and yet hardly touching her breasts.

Then, what seemed a long time later, she opened her eyes.

The room was still yellow with afternoon sun and his young body lay sleeping across her. Her legs were paralyzed with his weight and she wasn't sure she was breathing.

She saw a long slender strand of dust trailing down from the fireplace mirror.

"Philip." She touched his bare shoulder warm under her palm.

"M-m-m-m-m-m?"

"I can't move."

He opened his eyes and smiled at her.

It had been an equally long time since anyone had opened his eyes and smiled at her.

"I can't move. I'm not sure I can breathe."

"Oh," he said and slid off on his knees to the rug. He leaned back on his heels. "That was good."

She didn't say anything and sat up carefully.

He was watching her. "You still have a nice figure, Laura."

"Thanks a lot."

He grinned. "That was a dumb thing to say."

"That was a dumb thing to say." But she smiled at him.

"I meant it as a compliment."

"I know." She touched his long hair.

"That was great. In waves like the sea. I could almost hear mermaids," he said happily.

A line from Eliot came to her with startling clarity. "I do not think that they will sing to me."

"What?"

"Just something I thought of."

She was suddenly exhausted, drained, inert, tired as she'd never been in her life.

She forced another smile and started picking up the clothes she could reach from where she sat on the couch. He handed her the sweater near him and sat watching her dress.

"You okay?"

"I'm just so tired."

"It does that sometimes the first time."

He stood up and started to tug on his own clothes.

"I'm tired of everything, I think." She pulled the sweater over her head and smoothed her hair. "Of the whole thing. You know, everything."

He nodded. "It sometimes does that, too." He looked down at her. "You focus on things different, see, and you can't really go back to the way things were before."

"Sort of a deus ex marijuana, hm-m?"

"What?"

"Nothing."

He fastened the wide belt and settled it on his hips. His T-shirt had the faded print of a huge violet and orange butterfly. "Laura, would you like to go get a hamburger?"

"Thank you, Philip." She stood up beside him and put her hands on his shoulders, kissed him lightly beside the mouth. "But I don't think so this time."

"I—certainly . . ."

"Sh-h-h."

He nodded, stood uncertainly for a second, and then, "See you around, I guess."

"Um-m-m-m-m."

He looked back at her from the archway to the hall. "So long."

"Good-bye, Philip."

The front door closed and she leaned against the mantel.

Then she took a deep breath that filled her lungs in two separate syllables and went into the bedroom.

She opened the bureau drawers and laid the stacks of shirts out on the bed. Then the socks, underwear, handkerchiefs, the box of cuff links, tietacks he never used, the miscellany that filled his top drawer. From the closet she took out the neat hangers of jackets, slacks, suits, the entire shoe rack, the row of ties, belts.

He was so neat and orderly, so careful that everything matched. His clothes covered the entire king-sized bed. What she couldn't get in his suitcases she'd stuff in cartons from the garage.

"It's twenty years too late, Alec," she said silently, not really needing to say it, already having decided, having reached a conclusion she seemed to have known for months without actually being aware of it, voicing it. "For them it may be real, but for you it isn't, and I've had enough," she said inside her head, moving her lips.

She stood looking down at the bed of suits and shirts and polished shoes. She could hear Philip's young voice saying, "Too much of anything's too much," and she smiled tiredly. She'd have to clear off the bed and put the things on the doorstep before she could lie down.

"It's time for them to sing to me, Alec," she said aloud.

LORNA DEE CERVANTES
1954–

Lorna Dee Cervantes is a northern California poet. The following poem, written in 1978, is from her book *Emplumada* (1981).

Lorna Dee Cervantes

Meeting Mescalito at Oak Hill Ceremony

Sixteen years old and crooked
with drug, time warped blissfully
as I sat alone on Oak Hill.

The cemetery stones were neither erect
nor stonelike, but looked soft and harmless;
thousands of them rippling in the meadows
like overgrown daisies.

I picked apricots from the trees below,
where the great peacocks roosted and nagged
loose the feathers from their tails.
I knelt to a lizard with my hands
on the earth, lifted him and held him
in my palm—Mescalito
was a true god.

Coming home that evening
nothing had changed. I covered Mama on the
    sofa

with a quilt I sewed myself, locked my bedroom
door against the step-father, and gathered
the feathers I'd found that morning, each
green eye in a heaven of blue, a fistfull
of understanding;

and late that night I tasted
the last of the sweet fruit, sucked the rich pit
and thought nothing of death.

MARCIA MOORE
1928–79

Ketamine hydrochloride (Ketalar) is an anesthetic drug with psychedelic potential. Extensive accounts of its effects are found in John Lilly's *The Scientist* (1977) and Marcia Moore's *Journeys Into the Bright World* (1978), cowritten with her husband, Dr. Howard Sunny Alltounian.

Prior to her ketamine experiments, Moore, an author of popular books on yoga and astrology, had taken LSD once in the 1960's with positive results. But like most traditionally educated occultists, she viewed psychedelics as an inferior form of enlightenment. Ketamine changed her view.

During a carefully arranged session in Big Sur, the author felt her ego dissolve minutes after the injection. She experienced states of consciousness of which she had read in the "writings of Eastern philosophers and Western mystics." Ketamine led Moore to develop a system of reincarnation psychotherapy called "hypersentience." Her work was cut short by her tragic and mysterious death in 1979.

Marcia Moore. "The loss of personality does not bring extinction."

From Journeys Into the Bright World

Toward the end of the afternoon the three of us drove to Big Sur's world-famed Esalen Institute where we luxuriated in the outdoor mineral baths while watching the sun sink over the sea and the stars come out. As the darkness deepened Jane lit candles and incense and I was reminded of the purificatory bathing rituals said to have been practiced in the legendary temples of Greece, Egypt, and Atlantis where sleep therapy was commonly practiced. Gazing at that candle flame against the sky I hoped that if my long-time dream of helping to launch a holistic healing center ever came true the work would be carried on in a place with natural hot springs.

Returning to the house we met Jane's spiritual "little brother," a slender young man with long hair who had adopted the East Indian name Rama. Although Rama lived reclusively back in the hills he made occasional trips to Mexico where he was able to obtain a supply of ketamine. Although he did not bother to explain the nature of his mission to the authorities, presumably he was breaking no law since no steps had been taken to ban this particular medicine.

Somehow, in an understated way, it was conveyed to us that Rama would share his precious elixir with us if we so desired. Isabel, who is fortunate enough to be naturally clairvoyant and able to tune in on cosmic verities without a chemical booster, declined, but I gratefully accepted the offer. From start to finish the issue of payment was never raised. I knew that Jane, who worked hard for a living, was not affluent. Certainly Rama was not making a fortune as a drug runner. The purity of their intentions was incontrovertible.

As the evening wore on Jane, with a minimum apparent effort, produced an exquisite dinner for four. The menu consisted of fresh baby artichokes which, to our amazement, had no chokes, salad, soup, fruit, nuts, and a discreet glass of wine. No one seemed to be in any hurry to do anything. Around ten o'clock Isabel excused herself to retire to a small side bedroom and I made my place for the night on one of the livingroom mats.

As I relaxed, Rama explained that he would be the one to administer the injection. The sterilized needle would be inserted not into a vein but directly into the muscle tissue. I was simply to let go and enjoy the experience. It was clear that Rama was an expert with the hypodermic which he thrust into my arm smoothly and painlessly. I noticed that the fluid was as clear as water and took only a couple of seconds to leave the syringe. In less than two minutes, far sooner than expected, the rush began.

SESSION 1
April 1976   *Big Sur, California*   *50 mg*

It started with a slight giddiness and a noise like the chirping of crickets. The cricket chorus rapidly swelled to a smooth purring roar similar to that produced by the motor of a well-tuned racing car. This was not one solid sound but rather a propeller-like staccato whirr which seemed to come from an external source. I felt effulgently happy and at ease, even though the traceries of dark beams against the white ceiling were now dancing back and forth and dissolving into a kaleidoscopic reverie of geometrical designs. The sensation was reminiscent of the times I had inhaled nitrous oxide at the dentist's office. But that had been like standing at a door. This time I was going in. It also felt like going home. My voice thickened; speech was impossible, and then I was spinning round and round like tumbleweed and the sense of familiarity was becoming greater and greater. . . .

In the next half hour, during which the drug was operating at maximum potency, I never lost consciousness, even though ordinary body awareness was totally gone. To an observer I would have appeared completely insensible, deeply anesthetized. Yet, even though the memory of that state remains it can only be called "indescribable." To speak of a thunderous silence, or a multidimensional sphere turning upon itself, or of identification with undifferentiated vibratory energy is probably as close as words can come to portraying a truly ineffa-

ble condition of existence. This inner realm, full of sound, color, and sensation was itself entirely formless. Here there could be no distinctions between subject and object, this and that, I and thou. Only the vast nameless faceless process remained, churning on and on and on. Somehow it seemed evident that it would continue to roll around that way forever like a ponderous wheel upon which the chariots of the gods might ride on to eternity.

It came to me that this was also a millwheel by whose grinding action my small personal concerns were being entirely rubbed out. The last husks of "I-ness" were wrested from my grasp, pulverized, and shucked off like chaff reduced to dust. Yet the light of awareness shone on undiminished. That is, the ego was gone—yet the Self was exactly as it always had been.

For a discipline-prone individual like myself who had always made a staunch effort to remain on top of every situation this necessity to relinquish every last vestige of control was an amazing state of affairs. But now there was no choice but to drop all sense of separate identity, all plans, purposes, thoughts, feelings, and desires, and simply urge onward upon this sonorous revolving circuit of primal power. There was nothing, absolutely nothing that could be done except to submit and let it be. In all this I did not feel that I was being elevated to a higher level of existence. Rather, the substance of my earth-bound psyche was being inexorably reduced to its own common denominator, like molecules and atoms dissolving into some infrangible substratum of electricity.

To summarize that instant—and insistent—transformation I would say that the lesson this and subsequent ketamine trips taught me was that one can discard all traces of ego awareness and individual volition and still be more than one was before. The loss of personality does not bring extinction. It seems to me, therefore, that any thoughtful person who tries the same experiment and achieves similar results must be disposed to accept the fact of immortality. How else can it be possible to drop the body, emotions, and mind and still exist as a self-aware entity in a realm of infinite and animate potential? How else can one suffer the loss of every known form of sensory perception, pass through that roaring void of hyperkinetic numinosity, and then return intact to the human condition? Even though we sink down through the bottomless abyss, falling all the way to its nethermost depths, there is something in us that endures and rises again into the light of a new day.

For years I had read of such states of being in the writings of Eastern philosophers and Western mystics, but most of what they had said had of necessity remained book knowledge. In general, their world pictures related about as closely to my ketamine experiences as the blueprint of a house relates to the daily exigencies of functioning within that structure. We are indeed fortunate that blueprints are provided and they are indisputably useful. On the other hand, such line drawings can convey only the barest impression of how it actually feels to live, move, and grow up within that home situation.

Unquestionably the most interesting part of this first ketamine trip was the gradual process of spacing back into the body. As it dawned on me that I still possessed a physical form and would have to repossess it my first thought was, "Oh dear, I have completely blown my mind. Now my friends will have to deal with a zombie. What a bummer for them!" At that point it didn't seem remotely possible that I could ever return to the phenomenal world of things and doings in which I had formerly functioned.

Vaguely it entered my head that I was on a lecture tour and was supposed to be speaking about something called "hypersentience." The word had a somewhat familiar ring but I couldn't recall what it signified. What was it? "So now I'll have to cancel the tour. Will Isabel go on alone? Well, life continues even if this small self is out of the running."

The music in the background was ethereally beautiful. Jane had put on a record of Hindu chants and I had never heard such superlative sounds. Listening was sheerest ecstasy. "Rama, Rama . . ." the voices flowed on and I was melting into that iridescent current of divine love. "Everything is perfect, absolutely perfect!" I exclaimed to myself in wonder. How could Jane have known that this music

would be so soul-satisfying just at this time!

As I began to look out of my eyes once more I became aware that Jane was sitting silently beside me. It seemed so terribly important that she should be there, and that we should be sharing this sacred interval together. I fancied that we were fellow priestesses in ancient Egypt, that I had been lying in a stone sarcophagus in a death-like trance, and that she was my hierophant who would usher me back to the world of the living. Images of colonnaded temples, sphinxes, pyramids, and winged figures floated behind her. I loved her enormously and felt that we had been through something like this before in one of the mystery schools of legendary eras. Surely we would remain soul sisters forever. "You are my initiator," I whispered, certain that she would understand.

For some reason I also wanted to convey to her that I thought that ketamine was a gift from Venus. Not just that it was a Venusian substance in the astrological sense but that I felt as though it had actually been brought, or manifested, from another, higher planet as a gift of grace to help relieve the present human plight. But the idea was too complex and I gave up trying to speak of it.

When once again I was able to look at my watch I realized that the entire experience had lasted less than an hour. My mind felt pure, peaceful, and refreshed though when I tried to move I discovered that I was still dizzy. I knew that I would sleep well that night—as indeed I did.

The following morning I felt as though the conduits of my consciousness had been thoroughly cleansed. Stepping outside was like witnessing the dawn of creation. Every leaf and flower was polished to a brilliant sheen, the sea sparkled and the air was dewy fresh. I knew that there would be many impressions to ponder on the way north. Seemingly, some element of my former personality had died, but some other part that was far more vital had been reborn. Whatever it was that wanted to come to life was important, but I didn't yet know how or why. Perhaps it would be enough simply to wait patiently and without pushing or prodding see what might emerge from a new season of growth.

SUSAN SONTAG
1933–

Susan Sontag, one of America's leading women of letters, discussed writers and their drugs in a March 1978 interview in *High Times* conducted by Victor Bockris.

From a High Times Interview

High Times: Do you do any of your writing on grass?

Sontag: I've tried, but I find it too relaxing. I use speed to write, which is the opposite of grass. Sometimes when I'm really stuck I will take a very mild form of speed to get going again.

High Times: What does it do?

Sontag: It eliminates the need to eat, sleep or pee or talk to other people. And one can really sit 20 hours in a room and not feel lonely or tired or bored. It gives you terrific powers of concentration. It also makes you loquacious. So if I do any writing on speed, I try to limit it.

First of all, I take very little at a time, and then I try to actually limit it as far as the amount of time that I'll be working on a given thing on that kind of drug. So that most of the time my mind will be clear, and I can edit down what has perhaps been too easily forthcoming. It makes you a little uncritical and a little too easily satisfied with what you're doing. But sometimes when you're stuck it's very helpful.

I think more writers have worked on speed than have worked on grass. Sartre, for instance, has been on speed all his life, and it really shows. Those endlessly long books are obviously written on speed, a book like *Saint Genet*. He was asked by Gallimard to write a preface to the collected works of Genet. They decided to bring it out in a series of uniform volumes, and they asked him to write a 50-page preface. He wrote an 800-page book. It's obviously speed writing. Malraux used to write on speed. You have to be careful. I think one of the interesting things about the nineteenth century is it seems like they had natural speed. Somebody like Balzac . . . or a Dickens.

High Times: They must have had something. Perhaps it was alcohol.

Sontag: Well, you know in the nineteenth century a lot of people took opium, which was available in practically any pharmacy as a painkiller.

High Times: Would opium be good to write on?

Sontag: I don't know, but an awful lot of nineteenth-century writers were addicted to opiates of one kind or another.

High Times: Is that an interesting concept, the relationship between writers and drugs?

Sontag: I don't think so. I don't think anything comes out that you haven't gotten already.

High Times: Then why is there this long history of writers and stimulants?

Sontag: I think it's because it's not natural for people to be alone. I think that there is something basically unnatural about writing in a room by yourself, and that it's quite natural that writers and also painters need something to get through all those hours and hours and hours of being by yourself, digging inside your own intestines. I think it's probably a defense against anxiety that so many writers have been involved in drugs. It's true that they have, and whole generations of writers have been alcoholics.

JEANNINE PARVATI
1949–

The following excerpts are from the chapter, Herbs for the Mind, in *Hygieia: A Woman's Herbal* (1978). The author is in the forefront of the contemporary renaissance in lay midwifery and herbal therapy.

Jeannine Parvati. "The utter sensuality of this plant was overwhelming."

From Hygieia:
A Woman's Herbal

LSD

In *Lunaception*, and reported again in *Moon, Moon*, the estrogenic effects of psychedelic agents such as LSD reportedly induce ovulation. We personally know a few sisters who did conceive during a trip (altered state of consciousness) though believing themselves infertile, way outside the expected time of ovulation. Since I believe that accidental pregnancies come from unacknowledged desires for a baby, it seems congruent with psycholytic theory that LSD can catalyze a pregnancy. However, personally I'd never take a psychoactive drug when pregnant, about to conceive, or still in the birthing space. Though, there are many pregnant botanists, midwives and herbalists who would, and do. Again, listen to your brain-heart, and the movements within, your feelings. If you feel comfortable making the decision to trip with your baby (baby getting a magnified dose due to her tinier body weight or mass), then make an informed decision. Refer to science, your own experience, and information coming from any channel. LSD is magnificent and for a fetus, it must be ultra-magnificent—but is it dangerous?

PEYOTE

I know of some women, not Indians, who wear a peyote button nestled high in their vaginas like a cervical cap. A peyote suppository, perhaps? Once I felt their presence, the alive and vibrating plant, in my astrology teacher's room. The peyote blended into the scene gracefully so it took awhile to locate the source of this heavy pulling I was feeling. When at last my eyes caught the peyote, the utter sensuality of this plant was overwhelming. I was floored. Just imagining wearing peyote in my vagina is almost too much! The women who tell me about this say that this is an exquisite way to "suspend" ordinary consciousness. And peyote have always looked like cervixes, which look somewhat like sea anemones anyway. The earth and the water—the succulent peyote.

With all mind-altering herbs, the normal "set" of consciousness is broken for a time/space you are prepared for and invite. Taking these herbs can give parents an opportunity to feel their world as their children. An eye-opener, always. The first times I took LSD or marijuana, my awareness of the world was akin to an infant's. Since then I have grown up from this primal space. Yet this quality of feeling fresh, one within the baby space, is still here in transcendent moments.

PSILOCYBIN MUSHROOMS

Why get high? Why expand psychic awareness? What's to "alter" about consciousness anyway? And just what is a soulful guarantee? I bring these questions to *Teo-Nanacatl*, and the goddesses visit me. From this experimentation with herbs for the mind, I realize nothing, have no questions answered, penetrate no further the mysteries. Attention focuses instead on the wound that doesn't mend and a healing does occur. It is for this "reason" that I include the psychedelic and psycho-active herbs.

Though LSD is not an herb, it is a widespread and well-known psycho-active agent. It is of our generation of test-tube babies and instant gratification, all well symbolized by the chemist's blotter paper; an invisible nectar.

"Everything that is essential is invisible to the eye"—*The Little Prince*. And so we finally come to what is essential, what matters. I first began searching for God with LSD as the introduction into the realm of the invisible and have come to celebrating with mushrooms the presence of all the Gods and Goddesses. Gods and Goddesses are my name for forces that move me, through me, and are not exclusive of monotheism at all. There are just many faces to the Supreme Spirit.

Teo-Nanacatl was yesterday's visitor, and having entered this abode of soul called Jeannine Parvati, is now written as first in my heart on the list of plant allies for healing. Again, please do not infer a prescription here. One woman's mushrooms may be another's . . . Your own friends will find you.

ABOUT THE AUTHORS

Cynthia Palmer and Michael Horowitz are directors
of the Fitz Hugh Ludlow Memorial Library
in San Francisco, the only library in the world exclusively
devoted to the literature of mind-altering drugs.
They were co-editors of Aldous Huxley's
Moksha: Writings on Psychedelics and the Visionary Experience.

Mr. Horowitz was coauthor of *The High Times
Encyclopedia of Recreational Drugs* and the editor of
History of Coca. He has also been a professional rare-book
cataloguer for the past twenty years.

They live with their four children in Sonoma County
in northern California.